CRASH!

Aviation Disasters and the Cultural Debris Fields

Randy Malamud

BLOOMSBURY ACADEMIC
NEW YORK • LONDON • OXFORD • NEW DELHI • SYDNEY

BLOOMSBURY ACADEMIC
Bloomsbury Publishing Inc
1385 Broadway, New York, NY 10018, USA
50 Bedford Square, London, WC1B 3DP, UK
29 Earlsfort Terrace, Dublin 2, Ireland

BLOOMSBURY, BLOOMSBURY ACADEMIC and the Diana logo are trademarks of Bloomsbury Publishing Plc

First published in the United States of America 2025

Cover design by Eleanor Rose
Cover image © lineartestpilot / iStock / Getty Images

Library of Congress Cataloging-in-Publication Data

Names: Malamud, Randy, 1962– author.
Title: Crash! : aviation disasters and the cultural debris fields / Randy Malamud.
Description: New York : Bloomsbury Academic, 2025. | Includes bibliographical references and index.
Identifiers: LCCN 2024014188 (print) | LCCN 2024014189 (ebook) | ISBN 9781501394775 (paperback) | ISBN 9781501394782 (hardback) | ISBN 9781501394799 (ebook) | ISBN 9781501394805 (pdf)
Subjects: LCSH: Aircraft accidents in popular culture. | Aircraft accidents—Social aspects.
Classification: LCC NX180.A37 M35 2025 (print) | LCC NX180.A37 (ebook) | DDC 700/.4556—dc23/eng/20240624
LC record available at https://lccn.loc.gov/2024014188
LC ebook record available at https://lccn.loc.gov/2024014189

ISBN: HB: 978-1-5013-9478-2
PB: 978-1-5013-9477-5
ePDF: 978-1-5013-9480-5
eBook: 978-1-5013-9479-9

Typeset by RefineCatch Ltd, Bungay, Suffolk
Printed and bound in Great Britain

To find out more about our authors and books, visit www.bloomsbury.com and sign up for our newsletters.

CRASH!

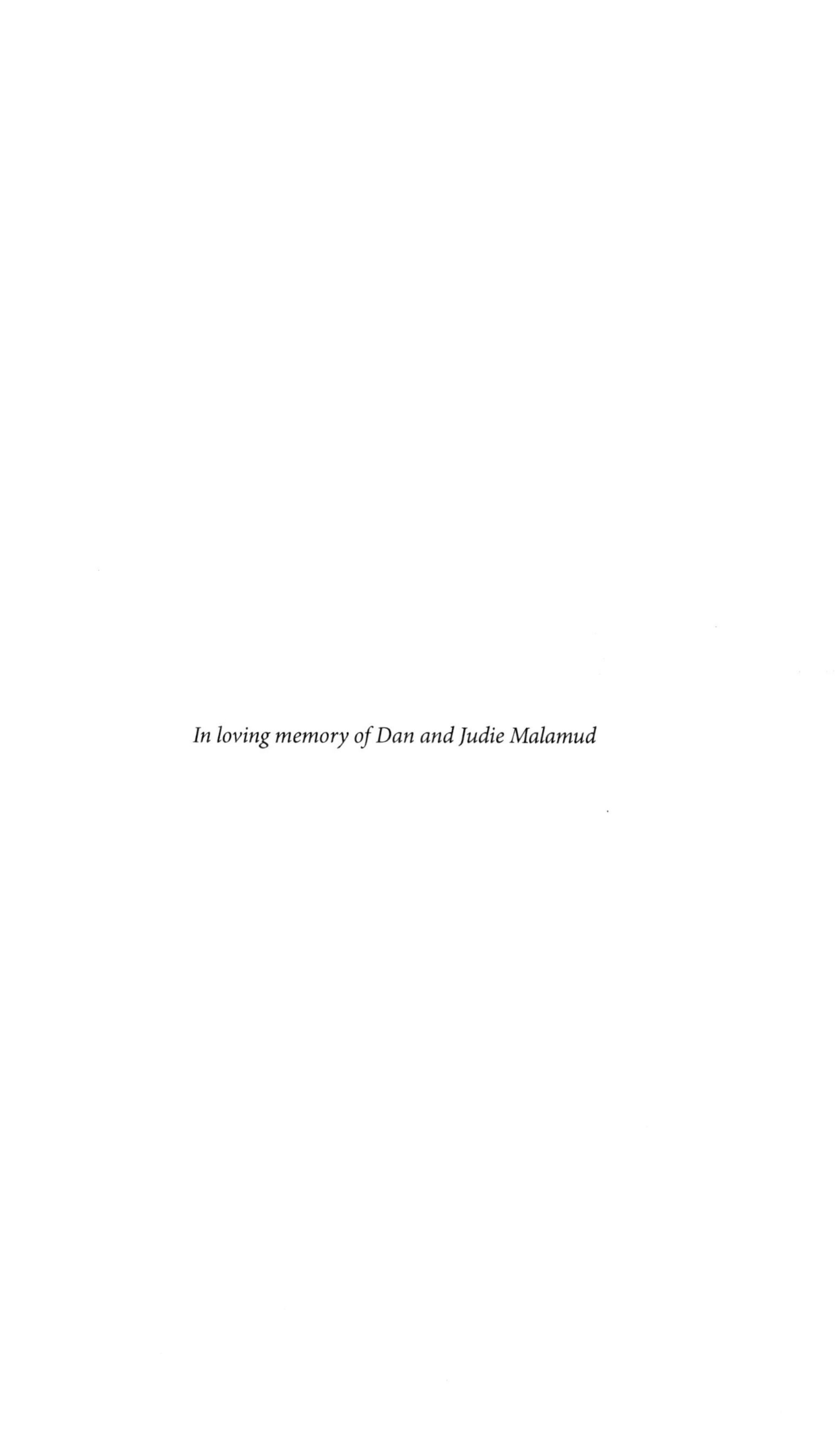

In loving memory of Dan and Judie Malamud

Contents

Illustrations

1

Aviation and Its Discontents

Every time that a new technology has been invented, a new energy harnessed . . . one also invents a new negativity, a new accident.[1]

Paul Virilio

✈ Uh-oh

The first fatal airplane crash was piloted by Orville Wright (of all people!) in his eponymous Wright Model A. The co-founder of aviation survived but his passenger, Signal Corps Lieutenant Thomas Selfridge, did not.

Demonstrating a military prototype of the Model A, Wright's flight on September 17, 1908 carried a heavier load than ever before: the men's combined weight was 320 pounds. Four minutes into the flight, as they circled Fort Myer—adjacent to Arlington National Cemetery, where Selfridge would be interred a few days later—one of the wooden propellers broke off. A new elongated design, it had never (until now) been tested.

The propeller dislodged a wire bracing the rear vertical rudder, sending the plane into a dive from its altitude of 100 feet. It crashed nose-first into the ground, throwing both men forward into the tangle of wires connecting the biplane's top and bottom wings.[2] Biographer Fred Howard describes the original debris field:

> The skids [undercarriage] collapsed, the wings turned up, the motor tore loose and struck the ground with a thud like a small earthquake. For a second or two the Flyer and its occupants were entirely concealed in a boiling cloud of dust. . . . Gradually the extent of the damage became visible. The Flyer's wings were knocked out of shape, its skids smashed to kindling. The left propeller was intact but both ends of the right propeller were broken off. One of the broken pieces dangled by a shred of its fabric covering. Orville and Selfridge were pinned beneath the upper wing, their faces buried in the dust.[3]

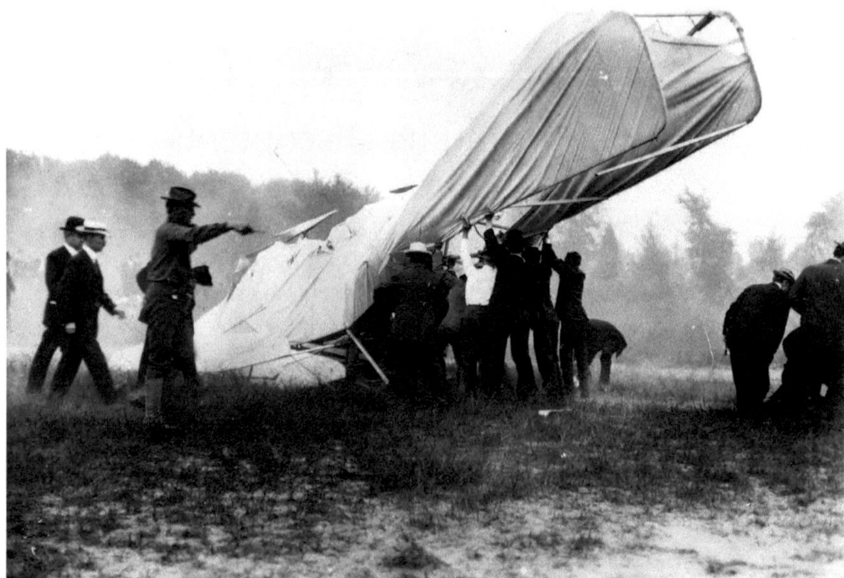

Figure 1.1 After the first fatal crash ever, bystanders extricate Thomas Selfridge from the wreckage; at right, people attend to Orville Wright, on the ground just out of frame.

Wright was hospitalized for weeks: a fractured leg, broken ribs, and damaged hip caused him pain for the rest of his life. Although he continued flying after the crash, it was always physically uncomfortable.

Selfridge—like the Wright brothers, an airplane designer—hit one of the framework's wooden uprights, fracturing his skull. He underwent surgery but died without regaining consciousness. He was not wearing protective headgear; had he been, he might have survived. It's common protocol to identify and rectify safety lapses after a crash, to ensure the same problem doesn't recur, a practice aviators adopted from the very start. When the US Army began flying planes in 1909, soon after Selfridge's death—the accident happened on a flight trial during the Wrights' bid for the contract—pilots and passengers wore heavy head protectors resembling football helmets.[4] The Wrights also modified the defective propeller after the crash: "The blades were redesigned and made heavier at that point and canvas was added down their concave sides," writes Richard Stimson. "The tubes supporting the propeller axles were braced so that any vibration would not cause the propellers to reach the wires bracing the vertical rudder in the tail."[5]

But if such trial-and-error safety fixes were on point in that crash, one aspect was well below par: the victim's final words. According to Wright, Selfridge's last utterance was "Uh-oh"[6]—an extremely understated ejaculation, perhaps reflecting the absence of a tradition in this trope. Today, final words have become a florid and fetishized feature of plane crashes, but Selfridge could not have known that he was supposed to expire on a more dramatic note, something along the lines of "That's it, I'm dead" (the pilot's last words on Surinam Airways flight 764, which ran out of gas, hit a tree and crashed during a foggy third landing attempt in 1989, killing 176 out of the 187 people aboard), or "United 173, Mayday! The engines are flaming out—We're going down!" (the aircraft ran out of fuel while the crew was distracted with landing gear problems in 1978, causing ten fatalities out of the 189 on board), or "Brace yourself. Ma, I love you!" (Pacific Southwest Airlines flight 182 collided in midair with a small Cessna in 1978, killing all 135 on that flight as well as both people in the other plane and seven more on the ground).[7] Then again, as the Model A had only 100 feet to fall, perhaps there just wasn't enough time for a grandiloquent farewell.

Media coverage of that ur-crash anticipated what would become the template for reporting on such disasters. The lead story in the next day's *New York Times* began by describing the moments before the tragedy:

> **Selfridge Enjoyed It Keenly**
>
> As the aeroplane dashed off the rising track Lieut. Selfridge waved his hand gayly to a group of army officers and newspaper men and threw back some laughing remarks that were drowned in the whir of the propellers. As he swept around Selfridge evidently was enjoying himself thoroughly. When the machine sailed above the heads of the crowd at the head of the field it could be seen plainly that he and Wright were holding an animated conversation. Selfridge interrupted this for a moment to wave a greeting to his friends.

Irony, which is frequently the central premise of plane-crash journalism, flourishes in the genre's inaugural example. Selfridge was having a "gayly" animated time up in the air—until he wasn't.

At the moment of impact, the *Times* recounted, witnesses reacted (as they still do) with chaotic turmoil, dread and confusion. People simply didn't know (they still don't) what to do, how to process what they had seen. "From the largest crowd that has yet witnessed a flight" (how ironic!),

> there arose a cry that was neither a scream nor a groan. For a moment there was not a movement, and then the people surged across the field. Col. Hatfield, in

> command at the army post, issued some quick, sharp orders and the cavalry guard dashed forward. The crowd was frenzied and the cavalrymen were compelled to use actual force in many instances in controlling it. To cries of "Stand back, there," the press paid not the slightest attention. Many were friends of Wright or Selfridge, and these insisted upon drawing close.
>
> "If they won't stand back, ride them down," was the order issued. And the troopers obeyed to the letter. None was seriously hurt in the crush of men and horses, but this was due only to a miracle. The scene around the wreck of the aeroplane was one of wild confusion. Through the heavy, dun cloud of dust men galloped. Officers were shouting orders that in the excitement were not heard, or if heard were not understood. Automobiles honked through the confusion, their owners proffering them to convey the injured to the hospital, and women called out questions hysterically.

Selfridge's expertise with the precise mechanism that failed—another poignant irony—was an angle that current crash stories, too, would undoubtedly highlight:

> It is a singular thing that Selfridge designed the propeller of the Baldwin airship [a dirigible produced that same year], which was considered a marvel for efficiency, and yet met his death by the breaking of a propeller.[8]

"And yet": the ironic reversal, the last thing in the world we would've expected. On some level (ground level!), every plane-crash narrative is written in the key of "and yet." How interesting—but also, how inevitable—that the first news story about the first fatal plane crash presented all the tropes and tones, bits and bobs, that would comprise so many other crash narratives to come. It was breaking news: it's not as if the writers and editors could have met to strategize about the genre's rhetorical components. No, the idea of how to write plane-crash stories had been formulated long before it was necessary to write plane-crash stories—and not just years before, but centuries: see Chapter 2, "Plane Crashes Before Planes."

The *Times* included a photograph of the aircraft before it crashed. Still today such a picture, if available, will accompany the story to accentuate the dramatic irony all the more sharply: the "before and after" aspect of the plane, and of the passengers' fates. The *Times* did not publish the "after" image, Figure 1.1 above, taken by prominent early aviation photographer C. H. Claudy. Perhaps they didn't have access to it, or perhaps the editors considered it too morbid. (My guess is the former: if they'd had it, I think it would have run.) Claudy had been photographing the dozens of test flights that month, spectacles that attracted hordes of spectators: 5,000 were at Fort Myer the day Wright crashed.

Mary Winter, who was there "when that horrible accident occurred to Mr. Wright's aeroplane & poor Mr. Selfridge was killed," wrote to her friend Eleanor Bliss: "I saw it & I can't get the picture of it & the horror of it out of my mind. The machine moved with the freedom & ease of a bird & I had seen it so often that I had gotten no feeling that there was any danger in it—so much so that I was really crazy to go up in it myself."[9] The letter captures her dramatic astonishment, and empathy, and shock, and the persisting trauma of witnessing the crash—alongside, strikingly interwoven, the flight's beauty, its aura of natural grace. Winter conveys her sense of the miracle these aviators experienced in their newfangled mobility, and her dismay at how in an instant, before her eyes, their transcendent performance failed. Her churning emotions eloquently set the stage for the angst that would be written, spoken, filmed, sung, painted, tweeted over the coming generations, as aviation got better and better, more expansive, serving ever greater numbers of travelers with ever greater convenience, while airplanes continued to crash again and again.

Probably the Fort Myer crowd had not come to see a fatal crash, at least not consciously. But even though there had never been one before, the possibility must have entered their minds. Then as now, airshow audiences would of course hope an accident wouldn't happen, but if it did, that sure would be something to see.

Orville Wright described the tragedy in a letter to his brother Wilbur, which I'll call the first-ever plane-crash investigation report:

> On the fourth round, everything seemingly working much better and smoother than any former flight, I started on a larger circuit with less abrupt turns. It was on the very first slow turn that the trouble began.... A hurried glance behind revealed nothing wrong, but I decided to shut off the power and descend as soon as the machine could be faced in a direction where a landing could be made. This decision was hardly reached, in fact, I suppose it was not over two or three seconds from the time the first taps were heard, until two big thumps, which gave the machine a terrible shaking, showed that something had broken.... The machine suddenly turned to the right and I immediately shut off the power. Quick as a flash, the machine turned down in front and started straight for the ground. Our course for 50 feet was within a very few degrees of the perpendicular. Lt. Selfridge up to this time had not uttered a word, though he took a hasty glance behind when the propeller broke and turned once or twice to look into my face, evidently to see what I thought of the situation. But when the machine turned head first for the ground, he exclaimed "Oh! Oh!" in an almost inaudible voice.[10]

(The *OED* lists "Oh! Oh!" as a variant of "uh-oh.")

Orville and his assistants later examined the wreckage, which was recovered from the debris field for analysis, confirming their initial impression that after a propeller broke from extreme vibration, it clipped a wire that supported the tail; as the tail collapsed, the Flyer went into a deadly dive.[11] They also constructed a replica of the plane, upon which they performed tests as part of their investigation.

Some believe President Theodore Roosevelt was supposed to be on this flight instead of Selfridge, though the evidence is historically skimpy: it may be true, or it may be merely truthy, one of those close-shave anecdotes that crashes regularly precipitate. Roosevelt purportedly expressed a desire to accompany Orville on a test flight; Wright supposedly said he thought it too risky for the president to take such chances. Roosevelt did finally fly, without incident, in 1910, becoming the first US president (though out of office by then) to take to the air. His pilot, Archibald Hoxsey, crashed two months after that flight, plummeting from 7,000 feet while attempting a new altitude record. The Wrights paid for his funeral.[12]

"When you invent the plane, you also invent the plane crash,"[13] writes cultural theorist Paul Virilio. Theoretically this is a logical, if unsettling, assumption. But just because things are theoretical doesn't mean they won't actually happen, as Orville Wright and Thomas Selfridge demonstrated all too literally. Uh-oh.

✈ But what's going on?

A slew of aviation mishaps lie on my flight plan ahead, but my interests extend beyond merely the precise incidences of the crashes themselves. I want to explore their larger contexts: what leads up to them, and what lingers on in their aftermaths. How do people respond—how do we process and understand them? How do we clean up after a crash, literally and imaginatively? What stories do people tell about plane crashes, and what kinds of lessons do we learn? How do we console ourselves afterwards—how do we memorialize the trauma? And how, with such grisly images and thoughts rattling around in our minds, do people ever manage to get back on an airplane again? How do we convince ourselves that the next crash won't happen to us? (If that's not such a difficult proposition statistically, it can be more challenging psychologically.)

What does a crash *mean*?

I imagine myself as a freelance consultant attached to an air-crash investigation agency, heading up its cultural studies division—never mind that this branch is nonexistent and nobody in the history of aviation ever requested a humanist's help investigating crashes. If I had to explain how I see my assignment, I'd say, "I suppose I'm building the plane as I fly it": a cliché expressing the common wisdom about how *not* to build or fly a plane, as well as how not to do whatever the metaphor is describing.

Even so: with the methodical deliberation of a forensic accident analyst I will sift through a widely-scattered range of cultural data, accumulating and sorting ideas, attitudes, and perspectives in the stories that emerge from the wreckage, along with those suppressed because they are too traumatic or too incoherent. I will examine a fleet of discourses: poetry, fiction, music, memoir; history and art; film, television, newspapers, websites, and other media; politics, war, commerce and capitalism, globalism, militarism, patriarchy, myth, humor, philosophy, religion; aviation and regulatory jargon. And I will report back with insights that are, to be sure, often disturbing, but also, in good measure, powerfully complex, poignantly compelling, and even unexpectedly existential.

Over the years I have worked on this project and the decades before that in which I nurtured a merely amateur obsession, I have become a Sartre of the skies, a Dostoevsky of the debris field. Plane crashes have led me to ponder the purpose of life, which we navigate between the Scylla and Charybdis of choice and destiny; order and chaos; confidence in the glorious modern world and anxiety about how we move through this world, and high above it—possibly, like Icarus, *too* high?

We fly prolifically—for business and pleasure, weddings and funerals, package tours and voyages of personal exploration. Certainly we fly too much, as Greta Thunberg and anyone else concerned about climate crisis insists. Swedes coined the word *flygskam*—flight shame—to prompt us to start winding down our aeromanias sooner rather than later.

I am myself a Delta million-miler, and might conceivably make it to two million if the *flygskam* and the thread-cutting fates do not intervene. Like all the hundreds of thousands of passengers traveling six miles above the Earth at any hour of the day, I implicitly consent to trust the elaborate storehouse of technologies and mechanics, theories and practices, undergirding our wanderlust. But a crash throws a colossal monkey-wrench into all this—the things we believe in and rely upon, the sense of power and adventure and invulnerability and infinitude we take as our birthright. A crash compels us to revisit fundamental unexamined presuppositions: What made us think this was a good idea?

Most basically, how do we even ask these kinds of questions about aviation and its discontents? In what language, and with what vocabulary, will this investigation unfold?

A routine, safe, successful passenger flight says something like "Doing what we do best!" (American) or "Fly the friendly skies" (United) or "Delta is ready when you are!" Delta's slogan used to be "We love to fly and it shows." As an English professor, I'm partial to Southwest's marketing campaign circa 1970, in pentameter no less: "How do we love you? Let us count the ways." TWA's tagline was very good, eloquent in its simplicity: "Up up and away" (spondee, anapest). India's Jet Airways celebrates "The Joy of Flying." KLM's slogan is, well, Dutch—"The reliable airline"—and Lufthansa's betrays a tinge of Germanic exceptionalism: "There's no better way to fly." Alaska Airlines: "We Care A Lot." None of these are very detailed expressions, or very meaningful, but they offer a starting point.

A flight's default text recirculates the discourse of corporate promotion that is so ubiquitous in its signage, its advertisements and branding, its jingles, its recordings played on loops while customers wait on hold, and all the other ways a pithy logo(s) is driven into our consciousness. The braggadocio is fastidiously superlative. Focus-group-tested platitudes are copiously visible and audible on each flight, both spoken and set to music, sometimes prerecorded and sometimes intoned live by flight and cabin crews. These compact buzzwords are what a normal flight says, and they are meant to seem as carefully calibrated as how a normal flight flies: the language succinctly summarizes, and symbolizes, the smooth, predictable, business of aviation that everyone else is taking care of, ready when I am, friendly, joyful, reliable, doing what they do best, up up and away.

A crash, on the other hand, says: Fuck! Not infrequently, "fuck" is precisely what the pilots say: their final word, as captured on audiotape, politely redacted in official accident reports but not in *mine*. In one impending crash (Air California flight 336, February 1981, no fatalities), a pilot descending into John Wayne Airport saw another plane that had delayed its takeoff roll too long sitting on the runway he was headed for, and said—according to the printed transcript—"Ah #." "In accident reports, # is defined as a 'nonpertinent word,'" Charles Perrow writes, "though it certainly seems pertinent at this point in the event."[14]

Richard Hugo's poem "Where We Crashed," a long thin vertical screed, typographically evokes the nose-dive leading to the titular debris field. The word-column captures the challenge of finding appropriate language in the throes of an imminent disaster. At first, the angst is relatively temperate:

should
have found
more sky
you end
here
boom
now
boom
gone
no more
gone
good-bye
bye bye

But as the ground gets closer, the poem becomes a florid discharge of fuck-like final words:

aluminum
hole open
out
sweet
cheese-eating
jesus
out
clumsy
nothing
fuckass
nothing
shithead
nothing
moldy
cunteyed
bastard[15]

Many crash poems manage to find a less vulgar, maniacal timbre, and are able, as Hugo's is not, to cohere into a stable amalgam of stanzas and rhymes instead of frenzied f-bombs. Kamikaze pilots composed astonishingly gentle Zen poetry before their final flights, investigated in Chapter 9. Myriad voices and lexicons comprise the textualities of the debris field.

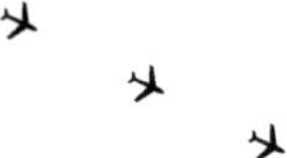

Examining cultural vestiges of crashes feels like trying to find a (figurative) black box lurking somewhere in the "terrain" of the text or image at hand. If and when the National Transportation Safety Board (NTSB) does open a humanist investigation branch, I've prepared a spiel about how my lit-crit skills make me an expert at "reading" and analyzing a panoply of wide-ranging artifacts. I would deploy my interpretive insights to unravel and elucidate the complexities of crash narratives: nuances, ironies (galore!), subplots, red herrings, ambiguities, ruptures, and so forth, not to mention the basic question of what happened (i.e., plot). If this crash narrative is not precisely the crash itself, it is closely related: it parallels the crash—as my silver-tongued colleagues might say, it limns the crash—providing a perspective that will help illuminate what happened. My students often discover with delight that such critical textual analysis may answer questions we didn't even know to ask. A narrative specialist like me can help the extant ranks of investigators educe and examine richer narratives, and also, examine these narratives more richly. That's not redundant: both the stories themselves, and the ways we engage with these stories, will be enhanced.

Black boxes generate a primary narrative, a seminal text. Most commercial airplanes carry two, whose exteriors are actually a sharp orange, easier to detect in a debris field. "Black" is a metaphor: see, it's already useful having an English prof on the job! A black box connotes mystery: it is "a device which performs intricate functions but whose internal mechanism may not readily be inspected or understood."[16] Coined in the 1930s, the term predates by a decade the invention of these devices (during the Second World War) for aviational forensics.

Because airplanes often crash nose first, black boxes are usually in the rear of the hull.[17] The CVR, or cockpit voice recorder, captures the final minutes of conversation (warts and all: usually just dully repetitive checklist scripts, until the *fucks* fly freely as the plane plummets and the prospect of tragedy accelerates) along with mechanical flight deck sounds. The recording overwrites itself every half-hour in older models; newer ones capture two hours. The other black box is the FDR, flight data recorder, which preserves dozens of data inputs such as altitude, airspeed, heading, flap position, smoke alarm status, and auto-pilot activation. On the first flight in 1903, the Wrights' airplane included a crude anticipation of an FDR that tracked engine revolutions, distance traveled, and duration.[18]

Usually these vital stores of information are easily found—the boxes emit pings for weeks—though sometimes they are more elusive. Occasionally, though rarely, they are damaged too extensively for the data to be retrieved, or they cannot be found.

The crash of Air France flight 447 over the Atlantic, en route from Rio to Paris, necessitated one of the most expensive and extensive recovery operations ever. The plane crashed in June 2009, but the black boxes were not found until 2011. When France's Bureau d'Enquêtes et d'Analyses pour la Sécurité de l'Aviation Civile finally located them, investigators were rewarded with conclusive answers to questions that had lingered unresolved for two years. Their report found the crash arose from, as often happens, a deadly confluence of circumstances and mistakes. When ice crystals formed in the (imperfectly designed, and subsequently modified) pitot tubes, which calculate airspeed, the autopilot disengaged. The malfunction was not inherently catastrophic, but Air France had failed to provide sufficient training on how to react. There was a large dollop of human error: senior pilot Marc Dubois, found to be deficient in flight deck management and communication skills, had had only one hour of sleep the previous night. He reminds me of the aristocratic aviator from Jean Renoir's 1937 masterpiece, *La Grande Illusion*: mannerly but limited, Captain de Boëldieu describes himself as "superfluous." Renoir's pilot, though, with better luck (and/or better skill) than Dubois, survived his crash. Renoir, himself a WWI aviator, also survived a crash landing. Assessing real pilots in light of cinematic archetypes typifies what humanists can contribute to crash investigations. (And yes, I submit, *La Grande Illusion* absolutely offers a useful springboard for investigating Air France's non-illusory crash—watch it and see.)

Black boxes recovered from debris fields "are visually fascinating," writes aviation photographer Jeffrey Milstein. "In addition, they are emotionally charged: some crushed, some burnt, they tell stories of the tragedies that occurred. It is hard not to look at some of them without being reminded of our vulnerability."[19] The most interesting revelation (to me) from flight 447's black boxes was first officer Pierre-Cédric Bonin's final words—"Mais qu'est-ce qui se passe!!?" (But what's going on!!?)[20]—which are what propelled me to engage existentialism as I traverse my debris fields. *Au contraire*, Bonin's co-pilot, first officer David Robert, declined to employ philosophical *argot* as the end loomed. His last words: "Putain, on est mort!" Fuck, we're dead.[21]

Sometimes a cultural black box is just what we need to resolve the mystery and close the case: Rosebud. Shantih. It was all a dream. The butler did it.

Even when located, black boxes may or may not be able to provide the data, the clues and contexts, to resolve the investigation. The equipment could be damaged by the force of impact, or spoiled by languishing underwater for too long. Sometimes it just doesn't record the necessary information. But usually, it furnishes fairly precise answers to the terrible mysteries that follow in the wake of a crash. If Søren Kierkegaard had been able to discover the philosophical equivalent of a black box—if he could have exposed and analyzed the repressions he called "hidden inwardness"—he might have been less depressed and befuddled. The idea of a black box as a metaphor provides a compelling quest-object for those of us whose *métier* is to figure everything out.

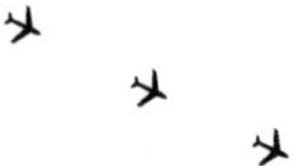

"But what's going on?" Black boxes inform that there is, unsurprisingly, *a lot going on* in aviation. And there's much more going on beyond the basic data these devices capture: rules, training, protocols; sociological and anthropological constructions of science, work, and identity; all the components of business and industry underpinning commercial flight; resonances of military culture that significantly inflect aeronautical development and flight crew ethos.

The field of mobility studies fleshes out all these integrated, overlapping discourses, which are vital even though the phenomenon under investigation here might seem to be not mobility per se, but rather, its antithetical frenemy, immobility. The "mobilities turn"—a phrase signifying the high profile of mobility studies lately—foregrounds sociocultural dimensions of travel and transportation infrastructures. "It sometimes seems as if all the world is on the move," writes John Urry in his landmark book *Mobilities*. Students, soldiers, terrorists, tourists, refugees, businesspeople, are all in motion, he notes, as he describes the networks that facilitate their activities. Urry's "mobilities paradigm" theorizes global society as "a wide array of economic, social, and political practices, infrastructures and ideologies that all involve, entail or curtail various kinds of movements of people, or ideas, or information or objects" culminating in "a movement-driven social science."[22] This emergent interdisciplinary field examines "the dynamic relationships between the combined movement of bodies, objects, and ideas,"[23] a triad of intersecting mobilities that categorically underlies every jot and tittle of my own investigations.

Urry's macrocosmic conception of mobility includes everything from bicycles, buses, cars, ships, trains, and of course airplanes, to walking, climbing, dancing, wheelchairing. It's a kinetic way of looking at *what's going on*: where we go, and why, and how: how fast, how often, how high, how far. How safely. Urry's "aeromobility" chapter mentions crashes briefly, as a system disruption: a digression from mobility, an obstacle. I argue that mobility studies must confront aviation disasters much more centrally; they are not just an aside.

Immobility inflects and informs mobility. Crashing is on the minds of a significant percentage of the passengers and probably the crew, airline executives, and the media, whether or not they would admit it. When crashes occur, they're surprising, and traumatic, but also expected—even inevitable. There are protocols aplenty because they have happened before and will happen again. However sporadically, ironically, dysfunctionally, crashes are constituent elements of aviation, and thus of mobility.

Urry concentrates on how systematized mobility has become. A systemic failure, I suggest, is a constituent element of that system; if it isn't perceived as such, it should be. The nodes and spaces of aeromobility, Urry writes, include terminals, aircraft cabins, hubs, the terrain overflown. I insist upon including the debris fields (i.e., the terrain not overflown, but rather, unexpectedly impacted) as one more airspace, and a keenly important one: a macabre archive of failure whose contours and resonances comprise the crux of my exegetical energies. To be sure, the fewer debris fields there are, the better. But we must integrate these divergences, the worst-case scenarios, into our models of mobility. Though they embody the cessation of movement, we must somehow move through them, and beyond them.

A plane that *is crashing* is not—not yet, and not necessarily—a plane that *has crashed*. But what's going on? Desperately, heroically, calmly and methodically, even if a crash seems inevitable, the pilots still attempt to maintain everything that should be going on to ensure continued flight, while simultaneously trying to suspend (obviate, remediate, reverse) the things that are going on in a crash. "The test of a first-rate intelligence is the ability to hold two opposed ideas in the mind at the same time, and still retain the ability to function," F. Scott Fitzgerald wrote in "The Crack-Up."[24] Despite these opposed ideas—the plane is flying, the plane is crashing—pilots, who we hope have first-rate intelligence, must *still retain the ability to function.*

Indeed, not infrequently, pilots recover from seemingly-calamitous emergencies and return to standard operating procedures, always receiving a profuse ovation at touchdown from a plane-full of passengers pretty sure they had bought the farm.

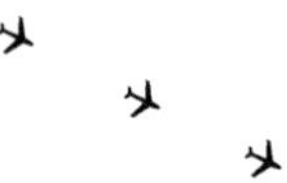

A brief diversion to investigate cultural black boxes in action. There are a few suppositions about how the phrase "bought the farm" entered mid-twentieth-century aviation idiom. The *OED* suggests military origins: "*to buy the farm* (also *ranch, plot,* etc.) perhaps with allusion to the notion that a farmer whose farm is damaged by a military plane crash would be owed restitution by the government."[25] Snopes fact-checkers offer a variant interpretation: "The death benefits paid to the beneficiaries of soldiers who died in battle were often enough to pay off the mortgage on the family home or farm, hence the deceased was said to have 'bought the farm.'"[26] So it's either the dead pilot's own farm the government buys and bequeaths to his survivors, or else the farm that his plane damaged by crashing into. It seems unlikely that crashing into a farm would cause expensive damage, unless the plane hit the farmhouse or silo directly, but how often would that happen? Especially over friendly territory? Presumably if a P-51 Mustang crashed into a Bavarian farm during a WWII sortie, the US Air Force would *not* have bought it.

Farmer's Almanac fleshes out Snopes's connotation: the phrase

> comes from a 1950s-era Air Force term meaning "to crash" or "to be killed in action," and refers to the desire of many wartime pilots to stop flying, return home, buy a farm, and live peaceably ever after. When they died as a result of a collision or were shot down, their buddies would shake their heads and mutter, "Well, I guess he bought the farm."[27]

It reminds me of how parents might tell children their dead dog went off to live at a nice ranch in the country; although untrue, it's a more comforting thought. The phrase morphed over time to include non-military air crashes, and death in general, as *OED* usage citations indicate: "The police dispatcher says a plane just bought the farm"; "If the clot is in a coronary artery, you've bought the farm."

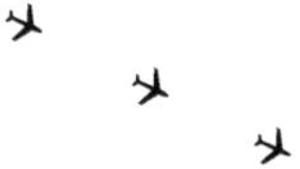

Sometimes passengers think they've bought the farm, only to survive. And sometimes, they crash.

A crash reads as an interruption: the tragic abeyance of what had been, just moments earlier, *a lot going on*. As the smoke clears, mechanical cessation mirrors mortal cessation, which is harder to see in the debris field—because the scale of aeronautical wreckage dwarfs that of bodily wreckage, and corpses are more likely than metal to be consumed in a fiery explosion—but infinitely more tragic.

Mobility has apparently become immobility, although many interim (or supplementary, or alternate) mobilities can be detected: survivors running or crawling away from the plane if they can; medics and firefighters, news reporters and corporate handlers, possibly some search-planes, and even johnny-on-the-spot investigators, all moving toward the debris field. In its functional condition aloft, the airplane had been a means to an end (LAX, JNB, PEK) in its mobility network. Now, for the specialists who manage mobility disruptions, the plane, or what's left of it, is itself the destination: no longer manifesting mobility, it now *attracts* mobilities, plural, as if to compensate for its own deficiency of movement.

The airplane's normal mobility reads as calm and repetitive: the pilot's pleasantly dull welcome, a few boilerplate-impromptu words augmenting the corporate slogans. Stow carry-ons, safety announcements, arm doors and cross check, number three for takeoff, the usual sounds and vibrations signaling rotation, the energy of lift-off pushing passengers gently back into seats, landing gear retracted, a soft ping indicating that the aircraft has reached 10,000 feet, recline seats, activate wifi.

But when aeromobility begins to wane, these patterns, sounds, and feelings all change, giving way to a panoply of other ad hoc mobilities that are uncomfortable because they are unfamiliar. A smooth flight becomes wobbly, unstable. Airspeed and altitude drop toward zero, a pretty keen nihilistic metaphor. Nothing to be done, as Samuel Beckett puts it in the opening line of *Waiting for Godot*. Life's but a walking shadow, a poor player that struts and frets his hour upon the stage and is heard no more, the Scottish Play laments. Cormac

McCarthy: The point is there ain't no point. See how literature helps illuminate what's going on, even when—*especially* when—it might seem as if there's nothing going on.

The supplementary text for a plane that *is crashing* is an emergency checklist, tailored to the specific situation at hand: engine failure, smoke in the cabin, birdstrike, computer breakdown. The simple protocol will (ideally) answer the $64,000 question—*but what's going on*?—and suggest the remedy. My book, too, presents a detailed cultural checklist of what's going on, in the debris field and beyond, as humanist methods and perspectives augment conventional investigations. If the praxis of aviation has failed, someone else has to pick up the baton and run with it: that's me. Compensatory imaginative, metaphorical, metaphysical mobilities will have to suffice when traditional avigation dissipates.

A plane crash renders aeronautics insufficient to the point of vanishing because it fundamentally undoes (erases, subverts, destroys) the scientific premise of flight: lift, thrust, drag, weight. There's more than that going on to keep the plane airborne, but how wonderfully compact and concise the basic formula is, like an Imagist poem. (Aha, QED!) At the fracture point, when *crashing* becomes *crashed*, aviational praxes become mostly irrelevant. As an aircraft lies strewn in failure, the postmodern theorist will observe, the laws of physics become most strikingly present in their absence. We must now displace and ultimately abandon the primacy of aeronautics—which is why I am especially well qualified, as a humanist, to continue this journey beyond the point where aviators have lost their lexicon, their author/ity.

We can still draw upon aeronautics to help determine what actually happened, as opposed to what was supposed to happen, in a crash. But we can also turn to T. S. Eliot: "Between the idea / And the reality . . . Falls the Shadow. Between the conception / And the creation . . . Between the essence / And the descent / Falls the Shadow."[28] *The descent!* It's as if Eliot anticipated that I would someday come along to apply his poetry to plane-crash investigations. Isn't "the Shadow" a resonant, provocative formulation of the gap between idea/reality, and between flying/crashing? If aeronautical discourse is still valuable in crash investigations—perhaps even superior to modernist poetry, many would maintain—it may also seem maladapted; at least it does to me. The function of plain-speaking plane-speaking (diametrically opposed to poetry-speaking) is keeping planes aloft, and nobody enjoys using it to figure out why a plane isn't.

One of the commonplaces of flight training is the idea (growing out of Bernoulli's principle and Newton's laws of motion) that "the plane *wants* to fly."

This tenet, which is almost uniformly true, assuages me with its comforting physics and reassuring conviction on a flight that feels as if it is becoming suboptimal, though sometimes the Rolling Stones chime in with a resisting voice—you can't always get what you want—which undercuts that soothing mantra.

Humanist plane-crash investigations will generate such dynamic (instead of aerodynamic) textual (instead of structural) tensions (instead of equilibrium). The stability, predictability, and uniformity of practical aviation will give way, in *impractical* aviation (i.e., crashes) to countervailing strains of irony and symbolism; polyvalence and its multiple possible truths; indeterminacy, subjective relativism, aporia.

Why didn't the plane want to fly any more?

That question would have been considered a pathetic fallacy in an earlier era, but today new materialist ontologies incline us to grant agency to airplanes. And we will launch a multitude of other arrows from our fecund theoretical quivers: the humanist air crash investigator will invite reader-response—what does this crash mean *to you*? An always-already progress narrative, a teleological positivism of flight, demands to be deconstructed, queered. The aviation industry's overwhelmingly white male power structure, from engineers to CEOs to pilots, invites decentering by feminist and critical race theories. Monolithic hegemonic absolutism plummets in tandem with the aircraft. The striking contrast between the phenomena (and the narratives) of crashes in wealthy Western and Northern countries, compared with those in the poorer global South and East, suggests Marxist and postcolonial interventions.

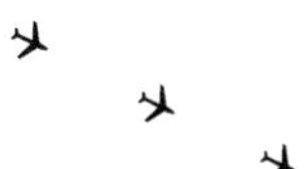

Studying plane crashes makes every other travel glitch seem completely inconsequential. Crying babies? Lost suitcase? Plane delayed a few hours? Let me tell you, it could be so much worse! Aviators have a limited, zero-sum level of attention, focus, bandwidth. I'd prefer they spend the lion's share of that (I suggest over 97 percent) on keeping the airplanes aloft. *Up up and away. There's no better way to fly.* If they get me onto my connecting flight, so much the better, but as long as they don't crash I'm not getting bothered if they forget to serve drinks and nuts.

Though it goes without saying, I will say it anyway: most planes make it from point A to point B (or, in a diversion, point B-prime, and then on to B). Nearly every flight, on every type of craft, every airline, every day, from every airport, arrives safely. It's just a very, very small proportion that don't—practically negligible, hardly even worth thinking about. And yet: as Rilo Kiley sings in "Wires and Waves": "Sometimes, planes, they crash up in the sky."[29] (And elsewhere.)

If, disregarding the best practices of aviation, an airplane ends up impacting terrain or water, or catches on fire, or collides with another plane, or runs out of gas, or its flight instrument panels go out, or a fuselage rupture depressurizes the hull and the plane implodes, or the vertical stabilizer snaps off, or lightning strikes, or air traffic control gives erroneous or confusing guidance, or pilots (who are, after all, as human as their passengers) miscalculate or lose situational awareness or experience hypoxia or simply forget which buttons to push, which switches to flip, in which order, or which checklists to follow to restore stability after a faulty maneuver ... well, in any such case, as diligently as the crew in command tries to sustain lift-thrust-drag-weight, that elegant formula is on the cusp of becoming palaver.

And again, even in the most dire situations—engines out, flying blind, coming in on a wing and a prayer—an enormously troubled flight still might, quite possibly, *not* crash. Knowledge is power. Capt. Chesley Sullenberger's 2009 "Miracle on the Hudson" is one of the most amazing recoveries in the history of crashes. The forces of flight, however attenuated they seemed, did indeed endure. The crew's aeronautic training allowed them to drift down onto the river without power (but *not* without knowledge—Sully was a certified glider pilot), saving the lives of all 155 souls on board. US Airways flight 1549 definitely did want to fly. A dose of luck, or perhaps merely expert training and operational brilliance, saved the day. "If you can walk away from a landing, it's a good landing," explains test pilot Chuck Yeager. "If you use the airplane the next day, it's an outstanding landing."[30]

But at the farthest extreme, an exceptionally small percentage of flights no longer adhere to the laws of physics in their final moments—or, more accurately, these flights *are indeed* adhering to physics, but in a very different pitch than pilots intended and passengers hoped. A plane crash is a self-consuming artifact: the flight is no longer a flight; the plane, fundamentally, becomes no longer a plane. A crash demands an array of tools and methods and vocabularies and praxes to allow its investigators to assess the situation, the horror, the debris. While there are already a plethora of such practices, my intention to add a few more cannot hurt (and might even help).

✈ Am I going down?

Air travel has never been safer. Fatalities have declined remarkably over the last half-century. In the 1970s there were four to six accidents per million commercial flights, globally; now, that number ranges between 0.15–0.25 most years. "Am I going down?"—an app that calculates the odds of crashing on my next flight (ATL-BOS on an Airbus A320) as 1 in 4,512,032—informs that I'd have to fly the route every day for 12,361 years before the answer would be "yes." A more erudite source, the scholarly journal *Aviation*, estimates "the value of likelihood of having one flight without the death of a given passenger each year" increased from 99.9991 percent in 1972 to nearly 99.9999 percent in 2000, and "in 2008 the probability of taking a flight during which a given passenger suffers death is equal to 0.0000005."[31] In 2021, the lifetime odds of dying as an aircraft passenger in the US were too small to calculate.[32]

Nevertheless it *is* a non-zero possibility. If some are still afraid of flying (40 percent of the general public experience some level of fear associated with flight, and 2.5 percent, including me,[33] have a clinical phobia[34]), that's because we are bad at interpreting risk. "Our fear of flying may not be rational, in the sense of proportionate," Sophie McBain writes. "But is there any experience that better encapsulates so many modern anxieties than to be hurtling through space at miraculous speeds, suspended thousands of feet above solid ground by forces most of us can't really understand, and at the mercy of two pilots who might not truly understand the tech they are using either?"[35]

If worrying about crashing is not precisely logical, neither is it precisely illogical. The band moe. speaks for me, or sings for me, in their 1998 song "Plane Crash":

> I'm not afraid to fly, I'm not afraid.
> Yeah, I guess I'm afraid.
> Fear is a good thing, it teaches us humility,
> And it can keep us sane.
> So I'll fly high if I have to.
> If I could, I'd take the train.[36]

Be that as it may, this book is not about *Flugangst*, the incomparably expressive German word for neurotic aviation anxieties. Whether or not we are afraid of crashing, crashes happen—not all that often statistically, but not all that infrequently numerically. I take crashes as a given, obviously hoping there will be as few of them as possible, and heartened that the feedback loop of ever-increasing knowledge makes this statistically-safe enterprise even statistically-safer every year.

At least broadly, most plane crashes share a fairly consistent set of patterns and narratives in terms of how they are processed, before they fade away (pretty quickly) in the public consciousness—until the next one happens. In this sense they are roughly comparable to school shootings, destructive weather events, terrorist attacks, infrastructure failures: one hurricane is not exactly the same as another, and a bridge collapse is not an engine explosion, but all these disturbing, high-profile, unexpected mass-casualty events share overlapping facets.

The news stories, the images, the follow-ups, the water-cooler banter, all generate a common discourse, shaped by what Arjun Appadurai calls mediascapes and ideoscapes. Mediascapes (a portmanteau connoting vast worldwide *landscapes* of *media*) describe how technologies impact the flow of news across cultures and borders in a globalized era. What used to take weeks or months, with today's turbocharged telecommunications, becomes immediate and boundless. Ideoscapes, the landscapes of ideas, are cognate phenomena: people's views and perspectives have practically infinite potential audiences.

Appadurai features prominently in mobility studies because his scapes are themselves mobile and far-reaching, and also because they inspire mobile citizens to move, physically and literally, in tandem with these global scapes that comprise more abstractly metaphysical iterations of mobility. Three other scapes—ethnoscapes ("moving groups and persons" such as tourists, immigrants, exiles, "who constitute the shifting world in which we live"), finanscapes (rapid dispositions of global capital), and technoscapes (technology moving "at high speeds across various kinds of previously impervious boundaries")—similarly accelerate the proclivities of mobility, hence of flying, and hence of crashing.[37]

A vibrant circulation infuses all these scapes—and circulation is certainly a mode of mobility—which Appadurai also describes as a flow, adapting Mihaly Csikszentmihalyi's formulation of that term. Safe flights circulate (ATL-BOS-ATL), and safe flights flow, in the mode of Csikszentmihalyi's "flow state,"[38] another familiar concept in mobility studies. A flow state is characterized by complete concentration on the task (I sure hope the flight crew is completely concentrating); a feeling of control over the task (again, it is devoutly to be hoped that the aviators are in control); clarity of goals (take off, fly, peanuts, land); transformation of time, speeding up and slowing down (flying from Dubai to Chicago seems almost instantaneous in some sense, and also interminable);

effortlessness and ease. The effortlessness, and all these other safe happy feelings, resonate in the slogans which seem crafted precisely to celebrate a flow state: "Being there is everything" (Air New Zealand); "Catch the Spirit!" (Spirit); "Life is a journey, travel it well" (United); "Something special in the air" (American). I wonder if Csikszentmihalyi moonlighted as a jingle-writer?

If the concepts of scapes, flow, and circulation are so important in flight, how do they manifest in crashes? Obviously, when an airplane goes down, it stops flowing and stops circulating, abandoning the traverse of scapes (landscapes, seascapes, airscapes, ideoscapes). But a crash has its own circulatory flow independent of the ruined hull. The crash (figuratively) detaches itself from the wreckage. Just as the plane *wants* to fly, so too does the flow want to flow and the scapes want to scape. And being theoretical, unencumbered by the need for such material technicalities as engines and flaps and all that, the concepts continue on their (theoretical, metaphysical) flightpaths, unimpeded by the tragic actuality of the debris field below.

Ideoscapes comprise what Ole Jensen calls "imagined mobilities, or the mobilities of ideas and representations."[39] Thus, the ideoscape may stay aloft after a crash, powered (symbolically) by the mediascape, and indeed that ideoscape becomes all the more energized when the aircraft abandons the air—becoming more of an idea than an airplane. As long as the mediascapes are working, which they always are, a crash will become a fertile, horrible, fascinating, haunting ideoscape: people will be keenly attentive, with a vast range of intellectual responses (anxious, fearful, traumatic, therapeutic, empathetic, restorative, statistical, logical, illogical, existential, forensical, profane, resigned, obsessional, schadenfreudian, *creative*), ideas which they will exchange with others—and that's my cue.

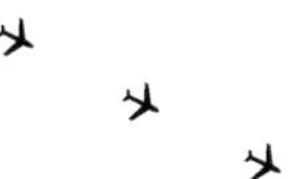

Moving from theoretical to practical applications of Appadurai's scapes, there are variations in terms of rhetorical and conceptual patterns of different crash narratives, but even those variations are predictable. The amount of attention paid to a particular plane crash, and the type of attention, correlate with a fairly simple rubric: how many died? How striking are the debris field images? What airline was it? Western audiences think—not without some reason, though also not without some xenophobic prejudice—that less-developed countries have inferior aircraft, sloppier maintenance, and less competent flight crews. The crash of a Boeing or Airbus widebody, compared to that of a Tupolev flown by Bashkirian Airlines, hits closer to home. (No pun intended—although if not intended, also not avoided. I must caution that macabre humor pervades crash discourse: perhaps to deflect the literal horror, detaching from the chaos by making it something to snicker at, however inappropriately. How often do airplanes crash? Just once. "Jokes and lightheartedness tend to be fairly common" at crash sites, investigator Dennis Shanahan explains, intended to foster a "very superficial involvement" with the traumatic event, which helps mollify painful emotions.[40])

Uzbekistan Airways retired their Soviet-era Tupolev-154s in 2010, as did Aeroflot, though not before eight of their fleet had crashed. Bashkirian, a now-defunct Russian regional airline, suffered a Tu-154 crash, a midair collision with a DHL cargo carrier over Germany in 2002, that killed all seventy-one aboard both planes. In 1996, Vnukovo Airlines—named for its hub at Vnukovo, the oldest of Moscow's four airports, and also now defunct—lost a Tu-154 attempting to land in Svalbard, Norway, the world's northernmost airport. It crashed after misflying an offset approach (which is to say, it tried to land where the runway wasn't), killing all 141 aboard: not the Tupolev's fault, but still, bad for the brand.

Air Koryo, North Korea's state carrier, is the last commercial airline, at the time of this writing, still flying Tu-154s. Western accounts of North Korean crashes serve as obvious metaphors for the regime's failings (and by implication, because the aircraft were Soviet-made, *their* collapse as well). A 2015 crash, according to South Korean assessments, was part of an air force tournament—where Kim Jong Un was the guest of honor—commemorating North Korea's Victory Day.[41] That's what comes of their excessive nationalist pageantry, the mediascape implied. A 2010 crash of another North Korean military jet just inside China's border was, according to reports, flown by a pilot trying to defect.[42] I wonder if North Korean media blame Western airplane crashes on craven capitalist corruption; I expect they do.

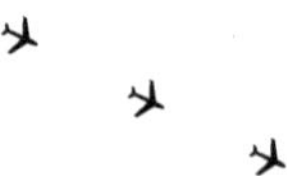

Besides body counts and geocultural prejudices, what differentiates higher-profile crashes from the rest? A "regular" crash might be the consequence of an engine fire, weather hazards, instrument failure, pilot error: these are all common causes, and often it's several such garden-variety sandtraps happening at once. A more unusual crash receives more elaborate media attention: a military downing of civilian aircraft, for example. Russian separatists shot down Malaysia Airlines flight 17 over Ukraine in 2014. Soviet missiles destroyed Korean Air flight 7, mistakenly identified as a spy plane when it accidentally drifted into their airspace in 1983. A negligent US Navy attack brought down Iran Air flight 655 over the Strait of Hormuz in 1988, and in 2020 Iranians destroyed Ukraine International Airlines flight 752, mistaking it for a cruise missile, just after takeoff from Tehran. A missile strike, possibly by the Italian military, was believed responsible for the 1980 crash of Aerolinee Itavia flight 870 from Bologna headed to Palermo but downed over the Tyrrhenian Sea, near the island of Ustica. Italian media called it *Strage di Ustica,* the Ustica Massacre. There is compelling evidence that a misfired missile from a French Army training exercise brought down Air France flight 1611 over the Mediterranean in 1968, but a half-century later the jury is still out on that one.

"Suicide by pilot" crashes receive lurid coverage: on Germanwings flight 9525 in 2015, LAM Mozambique flight 470 in 2013, and EgyptAir flight 990 in 1999, after one of the two cabin crew had temporarily left the flight deck to answer a call of nature, the suicidal pilots locked them out and went into a nosedive. (Albert Camus, from *The Myth of Sisyphus*, on existential absurdism: "There is but one truly serious philosophical problem, and that is suicide."[43]) Certainly plane crashes always leave victims' families, and the public at large, feeling aggrieved, but incidents like these evoke significantly heightened outrage. Plane crashes are always ironic, but suicide-piloting is *way too* ironic: pilots are supposed to keep the planes flying, full stop. There are expectations—which strengthen with each suicide crash—that airlines should do a much better job assessing and maintaining pilots' mental health, just as we expect them to ensure that their fleets' pneumatic systems and navigation computers are continually in tiptop shape.

Unusual passenger rosters generate more interest. A sports team crash guarantees front-page news coverage. Eight Manchester United players and three club staff died when their BEA Airspeed Ambassador crashed on takeoff from Munich in 1958. Fourteen Wichita State football players and their coach crashed en route to a 1970 Utah State game, and later that same year thirty-seven Marshall University football players and nine staff died in a crash on final approach, returning from a game against East Carolina. Speaking of gruesome humor: Man United's opponents sometimes taunt them with an obnoxious appropriation of a line from Monty Python's song in *The Life of Brian*, "Always look on the bright side of life," rendered as "Always look on the runway for ice."[44] (Obviously this didn't begin until the film was released two decades after the tragedy—apparently it's never too late for morbid crash wisecracks.) That Munich crash happened as a sheet of slush accumulated, and British European Airways flight 609, attempting liftoff after two aborted attempts, skidded through a fence at the end of the runway, impacting a fully fueled truck, which exploded.

It doesn't have to be a whole team—a single athlete or celebrity on board increases media play: Jim Croce, Kobe Bryant, Aaliyah, Dag Hammarskjöld, Patsy Cline, Jenni Rivera, Roberto Clemente, Otis Redding, Ricky Nelson, Knute Rockne, Stevie Ray Vaughan, Rocky Marciano, Will Rogers. Rockne's 1931 crash led to the retirement of wooden airplanes: the Fokker F-10A's wing became structurally fragile when moisture weakened the glue.[45] The "subsequent outpouring of national attention changed the crash investigation process forever," George Bibel writes. What had been an erratic behind-the-scenes operation became more regimented and transparent. National grief and massive news coverage of the Notre Dame football coach's death made secrecy about aviation safety unacceptable; "full disclosure would become a way of life."[46]

Why so many sports and entertainment figures? They have "aeromobile lifestyles," Veronika Zuskáčová writes, marked by the frequency with which they fly and a sense of "being above average, being a part of the global elite that moves in high-speed" and "enjoys the luxury of privileged spaces."[47] Traveling from gig to gig or game to game, they are statistically more likely than the average person to experience a crash. Because they fly so often, celebrities may embrace attitudes of insouciance or inevitability about the risks. Reba McEntire lost eight bandmates when a twin-engine Hawker Siddeley jet crashed just after takeoff in 1991, en route from a San Diego show to their next concert in Ft. Wayne, Indiana. McEntire, recovering from bronchitis, skipped the flight, intending to travel the following day instead. After the crash, she vowed, "I'll keep on flying. I'm not going to quit because there are too many opportunities that I have open to me. Staying busy is the best thing for all of us, and knowing that the families want us to go on because they know their family members in the band would want us to."[48]

After what turned out to be Patsy Cline's final concert in 1963, inclement weather blanketed Kansas City. Singer Dottie West suggested Cline join her for the eight-hour drive to their next show in Nashville, but Cline demurred, fatalistically: "Don't worry about me, Hoss. When it's my time to go, it's my time."

It was. With country singers Cowboy Copas and Hawkshaw Hawkins, she boarded a Piper Comanche, flown by a pilot later determined to have minimal experience, which crashed in a Tennessee forest.[49]

Crashes involving prominent passengers garner considerably more resources in recovery and investigation efforts.[50] Is it somehow worse when Glenn Miller dies in a crash than when a random, unfamous citizen perishes? Of course not . . . but also, the evidence suggests, perhaps so. If celebrities are piloting themselves—JFK Jr., John Denver, Antoine de Saint-Exupéry—the stories seem all the more ironic, and tragic.

More celebrity crashes: Carole Lombard returned home after a 1942 War Bond tour of Indiana, impatient to see her husband Clark Gable. The final leg, TWA flight 3, a DC-3 from Las Vegas to Burbank, crashed into a cliff on Potosi Mountain shortly after takeoff, killing all onboard. "Though she had been strongly urged to return to Hollywood by rail, she found herself unable to face three days on the 'choo-choo train,'" her obituary said. "Her plane was not a sleeper but she didn't mind sitting up. 'When I get home,' said Miss Lombard, 'I'll flop in bed and sleep for twelve hours.'"[51]

Another Hollywood power couple, Vivien Leigh and Laurence Olivier, experienced (and survived) two plane crashes together: shortly after their 1940 marriage, flying from Lisbon to Bristol, their plane's flight deck burst into flames, eerily echoing a dream Olivier had had. Six years later, flying from New York to London, their Pan Am Clipper developed engine trouble and tried to return to LaGuardia Airfield when an engine caught fire and fell off. The plane made a crash-landing with wheels up, a "belly landing," at an emergency field in Connecticut.[52]

Performance artist Laurie Anderson survived a plane crash in the 1970s:

> I got very phobic about that for a while. But then I got over it. You know, what happens when you're in a crash is you join a crash club, and you talk endlessly about your crash because you don't want to bore your friends with it. And they've heard about the crash so many times. And so you also protect yourself in other ways. I mean, after that crash, in which some people died, and it was very traumatic to drop through the air. And I—as we were doing it, I thought I'm in a plane crash. I'm dropping through the air, and then we crashed. I walked away with nothing. Other people lost their lives. What happened with me on that was—I was—I flew the next day because I knew [otherwise] I'd never fly again. So with that however, I would fall asleep as soon as I got on the plane for, like, three years. I would fall into—almost a deep trance. I actually had to, like, pin a little note to my shirt saying I'm not in a coma. . . . My mind protected me from

> being there anymore. And words protected me in this, you know, the crash club where you talk about the story until it sounds very uninteresting, until you're beyond bored with it.[53]

Her coping process resembles therapeutic exercises (that I have done for decades) of reframing and refocusing traumatic thoughts to make them banal, stripping them of their power to frighten.

Finally, in the annals of celebrity crashes, there's the one that didn't happen. Singer Paula Abdul has spoken often about her 1992 experience:

> During the end of my world tour, the *Spellbound* tour, when I was traveling from one city to the next, in a small seven-seater plane, one of the engines blew up and the right wing caught on fire, and we crash-landed. I didn't have my seatbelt on and I hit my head on the top of the plane. I withstood 15 cervical spinal surgeries and I had to take seven years off.

Her story has been profusely debunked: there is no contemporary news reporting of the incident, nor any NTSB investigation (which absolutely would have occurred). Different accounts give conflicting details: she said she crashed in an Iowa cornfield (channeling Buddy Holly?) heading from St. Louis to Denver, but such a flightpath would have missed Iowa by 200 miles. Abdul claimed there was no media coverage because she squelched the story: "'That's something I quietly made go away—no paparazzi or tabloid stuff. I took care of that. I didn't want people to feel sorry for me or to count me out.'" But in another interview: "Well, it did get some attention, but I didn't want to make a—I worked it out publicity-wise." Yet another retelling incorporated this "trauma" into her narrative of perseverance: "I was knocked out unconscious. And when I came to, all seven of us were holding hands. Everyone was saying prayers. But all I could think about was, 'This isn't right. It's not my time to go.'"[54] Clearly not.

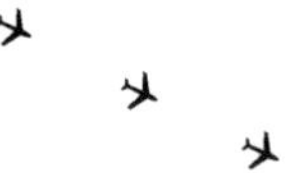

Crashes in strange circumstances increase mediascape attention. Air New Zealand flight 901 crashed into Mount Erebus on Ross Island, Antarctica, in 1979, killing all 237 passengers and twenty crew. It was a sightseeing flight, a.k.a. "flightseeing"—which is a bit odd (though I'd do it), flying ten hours from Auckland to Auckland just to see cool views out the window. In a sense they weren't going anywhere, making the irony/tragedy more poignant. It was a

CFIT—controlled flight into terrain, a term reeking of irony—meaning that the pilots never lost aeronautical control, but rather, lost situational awareness during a "sector whiteout." When a layer of clouds blended with snow on the mountain ahead, pilots couldn't detect the contrast between sky and land (which strikes me as an existential void).

Malaysia Airlines flight 370 disappeared in 2014—demonstrably confirmed as a crash only years later when airplane debris began to wash up on land. Possibly a pilot suicide, it remains officially unexplained, adding to its enduring fascination. Anything could have happened: maybe the plane landed secretly on some isolated Indian Ocean island (the US Diego Garcia military base was a popular guess) or the Philippine Sulu archipelago, and the entire manifest of passengers and crew are living happily in tropical isolation. And they broke off a few parts of the 777, setting them adrift to throw people off the trail? Or perhaps it was shot down (by a joint US-Thai training team?), or hit by a meteor, or hijacked by aliens. If these "theories" seem unimaginably ludicrous, that explains precisely why people are still so interested in that crash a decade later. People like ludicrous: ludicrous sells. "Man stands face to face with the irrational,"[55] Camus explains.

Another strange crash: A Learjet flying from Orlando to Dallas in 1999, climbing to its assigned altitude on autopilot, lost cabin pressure, incapacitating all six people onboard due to hypoxia—a lack of oxygen. Missing a westward turn, the plane continued on a northwestern course for four hours, 1,500 miles, still on autopilot, until it ran out of fuel and crashed into a field near Aberdeen, SD. Added to these unusual circumstances—imagine a plane flying itself for hours with unconscious or dead passengers *(it wants to fly!)*—one victim was a famous golfer, Payne Stewart, supercharging the algorithms that make some plane crashes more newsworthy than others, more interesting than others.

The 2010 Smolensk air disaster (on a Polish Air Force Tu-154, that antiquated Soviet workhorse) had highly unusual circumstances, aeronautical and historical, political and cultural, that combined for an especially salient story. Passengers included Poland's President Lech Kaczyński and his wife Maria, many senior military officers, and eighteen parliament members. They flew from Warsaw for the seventieth anniversary of the Katyn massacre, a trauma that remains, even generations later, a flashpoint of Polish anger toward the USSR/Russia, which accepted responsibility for the killings but failed to acknowledge them as war crimes. Mass executions killed 20,000, many of whom were officers and intelligentsia (not unlike the 2010 flight's passengers). Stalin's secret police targeted victims to demoralize Poles by murdering the cream of their society.

The Polish delegation traveled to Smolensk to commemorate the massacre jointly with Russian leaders, which was (or *would have been*) a significant rapprochement in this longstanding discord. When the plane crashed, ironies and conspiracy theories were pervasive amid the cultural debris. Some Poles thought Russians had somehow caused the crash, victimizing them yet again. Perhaps they had planted a bomb on board, or artificially produced the dense fog around Smolensk's airport.[56]

In fact, extremely bad weather was compounded by what pilots call "get-there-itis," a fervent determination to continue a flight (rather than divert on a safer route, to an alternate airport with better conditions) beyond the logic and checklists of flight safety. As an occupational mark of pride, pilots confront and surmount aviation challenges; taking the easy way out might make them seem less skillful, less heroic. Amplifying this particular instance of get-there-itis, Polish Air Force Commander-in-Chief Andrzej Błasik entered the flight deck during the dangerous approach, increasing the pilots' stress level and confusion about their predicament. Błasik apparently bullied the pilots into continuing a perilous descent so they wouldn't be late for this momentous ceremony. Final words (in translation) from the flight crew: "Fucking hell! . . . Fuckkkkkkkkkkk." The airplane was talking too: its last automated words (in English, the universal language of aviation) were, "PULL UP, PULL UP."[57] It wanted to fly.

Ironies heaped on ironies. Crashes usually feature overlapping ironies, things that shouldn't have happened but did, and not just one—which might have been managed—but several: a perfect storm, a cascade of dominoes, a chain of mistakes. (The antithesis of a perfect storm is what aviators call the "Swiss cheese model": layers of built-in safety redundancies, ensuring that if a problem slips through a hole in one layer, it will be caught by another.) "Modern airplane disasters usually result from a series of improbable, almost random events," writes Bibel. "It is somewhat reassuring to realize how many things have to go wrong for the typical crash to occur."[58] A good story, too, can be anatomized as ironies laid over ironies. She cut and sold her locks of hair to buy him a fancy watch chain, but he had traded his watch to buy her a pretty comb. Trying to create life, the mad scientist sparks rampant death. He thinks she is dead and cannot live without her, so he kills himself, prompting her (she was *not* dead!) to kill herself. Investigating how irony impacts narratives turns out to be perfect preparation for investigating how irony impacts aviation.

✈ ✈ ✈

Culturally memorializing a crash is a narrative coda. Memorials may take the form of art or poetry or film, but the most obvious method (and *not* the most effective, in my opinion) is a monument. Smolensk victims were commemorated by a harsh, ominous, and frankly dreadful sculpture erected in Warsaw in 2018. One might argue that its bleakness is appropriate to the event, but I will not. Jerzy Kalina's black granite block "refers to an airplane gangway, plane stabilizer and catafalque" and features a two-meter deep underground section symbolizing the pits where thousands of Poles were buried after the Katyn massacre. The ninety-six crash victims' names are inscribed on the sculpture,[59] whose aesthetic strikes me as ironically, inappropriately, "Soviet."

Compare this to a makeshift memorial that emerged near the crash site immediately after the disaster. The construction is as pretty and human as Kalina's is cold and off-putting, as moving as the granite is stultifying. The impromptu tableau makes me think about the tragedy, and the people—victims along with mourners; it poignantly foregrounds what happened, and where it happened. The Warsaw monolith makes me think of monoliths, and really nothing more. The idea that it evokes a gangway is curious and dopey: step right up! And representing a stabilizer—an aerodynamic surface like fins at an airplane's tail, providing pitch and yaw control—is even more bizarrely incoherent: as if a clunky mock-up of a crucial aeronautical component could somehow, even symbolically, redress the disaster after the fact?

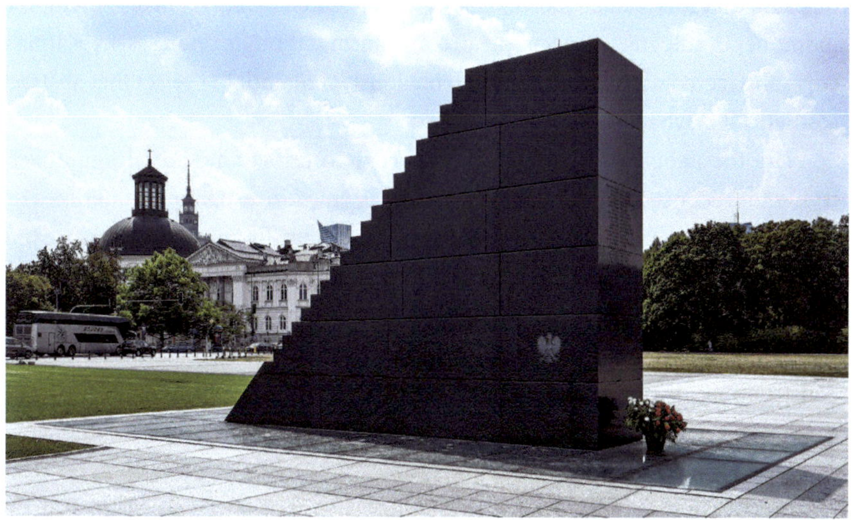

Figure 1.2 Monument to Smolensk crash victims in Warsaw's Piłsudski Square.

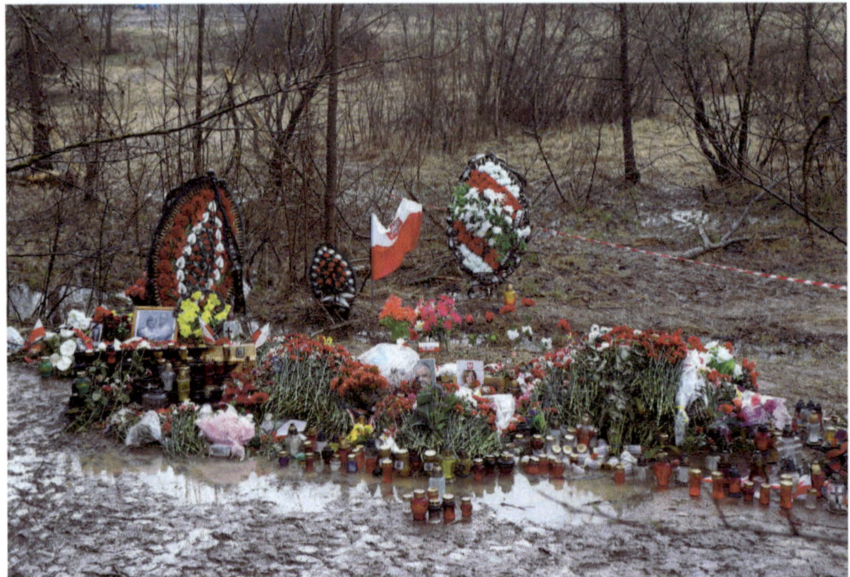

Figure 1.3 An improvised memorial to the Smolensk victims, near where the plane crashed.

The better monument is made from memorial candle lamps (covered, against the wet weather) and flowers, along with photographs of victims, and a few religious and nationalistic details: a cross, a Polish flag with eagle crest. Is it macabre that it is shaped like a plane? Possibly. In fact, many "official" memorial monuments integrate aspects of airplane forms, though often, as in Kalina's, coyly abstracted so as not to seem too obviously referential. (I reject that abstract aesthetic: it is what it is.)

Were the people who created the improvised on-site memorial figuratively trying to "reconstruct" the plane somehow, as crash investigators sometimes do (because putting the puzzle pieces back together may illuminate how they came apart)? The inclement weather that doomed the Polish aircraft is evident in the mud in which this "plane" rests. How does this plane relate to the real one? Is it a symbolic plane to heaven? A way of denying (or softening) the reality? This construction, like the actual shattered hull, manifests some disarray—several candles have fallen over; branches are down at the margins of this spontaneous display. I cannot be sure, but the branches could possibly have broken off trees the Tu-154 clipped coming in too low. If so, what a morbid yet powerful element of this memorial spectacle they are.

✈ Ruins are the beginning

Growing up in mid-century postwar rubble, Anselm Kiefer drew inspiration from Germany's bombed-out wreckage, creating in his paintings and sculpture an aesthetics of debris: "Ruins, for me, are the beginning. With the debris, you can construct new ideas."[60] His country's ubiquitous destruction "was not a devastating experience. For me, it was fantastic," he said. "I had all the bricks, all the debris. I could do what I wanted as a little boy. So, I liked it."[61]

Kiefer's canvases comprise a debris field of the art studio: in addition to paint they include straw, clay, wood, ash, lead, scraps of fabric, chunks of concrete. These materials sometimes shed when the art is displayed. Curators "have fastidiously collected the fallen debris and returned it to him, presumably in the expectation that he might want to repair the damage." But Kiefer "is not, it turns out, a preservationist. He's keener on ruins."[62]

In investigating what comes out of a crash—what it leaves us with, and how we confront the disturbing breakage in its wake—I start with the most obvious patch of material afterbirth (afterdeath?), the debris field. Like Kiefer, I am drawn to the ruins, mesmerized by their potential to generate new and creative expressions. Paint itself, the quintessential ingredient of visual art, may be perceived as a ground-down, repurposed resource composed of such ecological *debris* as colored rocks and minerals, copper and ore, bones, plants, sand, soil. Such assorted substances found in the landscape—in a *field* of some sort—become the components of a kind of expression (for instance, a painting of a landscape) very different from the original objects. Still the art grows out of—and, we can say, somehow reiterates—those elements upcycled from the "debris."

So too with the detritus from plane crashes. Considerably ground-down as it lies strewn across debris fields, the wreckage evokes an object—an airplane—that once was whole, and now lies tragically, but also fascinatingly, separated into its constituent parts: unfurled, deconstructed.

Another type of debris-art is the Japanese tradition of *kintsugi*, a centuries-old process of mending shattered pottery by gluing together its fragments and then, rather than trying to hide the seams that highlight the breakage, dusting them with gold or silver, accentuating the value of restoring broken artifacts. Philosophically, *kintsugi* signifies "bad things can happen that might shatter us," Emily Esfahani Smith writes. "But we don't have to stay broken or hide our wounds. We can put ourselves back together, and the scars we wear at the broken places become a reminder of the tragedies we've endured and how we overcame them—a mark of beauty in an imperfect life."[63]

During crash investigations, shattered airplanes are sometimes reconstructed to facilitate forensic examination. Though their seams are not gold-laced, there is a comparable sense that a broken plane nonetheless retains some aviational value, just as a broken plate can still have aesthetic value. TWA flight 800, JFK-CDG, crashed off Long Island shortly after takeoff on July 17, 1996, killing all 230 aboard. Initial assessments of the cause were uncertain and conflicting: some eyewitnesses thought they saw a missile hit the plane. The NTSB salvaged wreckage from the ocean floor, recovering 95 percent of the plane, but analysts felt the loose debris provided insufficient evidence for a definitive report. Hoping they could make a better determination if they reassembled the pieces, thirty workers spent months reconstructing the 93-foot-long 65,000-pound fuselage in a warehouse. This reassembly allowed investigators to conclude confidently that the crash cause was not a bomb or missile, but an electrical failure that ignited a fuel tank, which exploded.[64] The Transportation Department subsequently mandated that airplanes with center fuel tanks install a device to prevent such explosions by replacing highly volatile oxygen with inert nitrogen as they empty.[65]

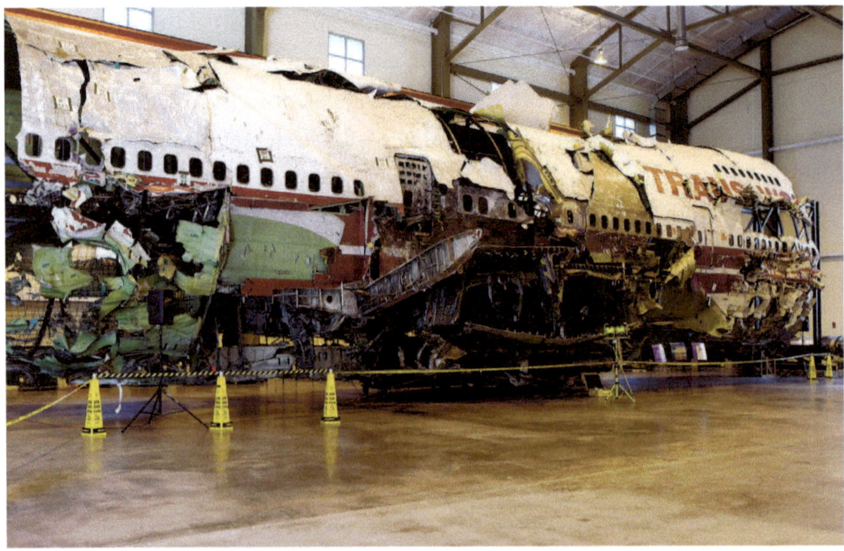

Figure 1.4 Debris from TWA 800, reassembled at the National Transportation Safety Board Training Academy, evokes the art of *kintsugi*.

When the investigation concluded in 2000, the NTSB used the rebuilt airplane to train other investigators, and also made it accessible to those whose lost friends and families on flight 800. The broken-but-intact plane provided a degree of comfort: mourners sometimes left flowers or mementoes on the seats where their loved ones spent their last moments alive. In 2022, more than twenty-five years after the crash, the NTSB decided (after conferring with families) it was finally time to dismantle the site. "Heidi Snow Cinader, whose fiancé, Michel Breistroff, died in the crash, acknowledged that losing the reconstruction might be hard for families who visited regularly," a news story reported. "'It's been a very important resource for all of us who went through it,' she said. 'And I feel like it served a very valuable purpose.'"[66]

Inspired by Kiefer and *kintsugi*, I see debris fields, sites of destructive disaster, as being also—if you look at them a certain way—palettes of raw materials with which something can be (re)constructed. Debris fields initiate and enable some kind of art, or story, or memorial. Extrapolating imaginative projections of what comes after debris fields—what grows out of them, what people may make of them—we find strikingly inspired creations. Airplane becomes debris, debris field becomes ... what? Memorial site, and/or museum (New York's 9/11 Memorial Museum, Bologna's Museum for the Memory of Ustica); locus of reflection (Lockerbie's memorial garden, Shanksville's memorial plaza); inspiration for music (Don McLean's "American Pie," Woody Guthrie's "Deportee"), literature (*The Little Prince*, *Lord of the Flies*, "An Irish Airman Foresees His Death"), art (Paul Nash's *Totes Meer*, Roy Lichtenstein's *Whaam!*), film (*Rain Man*, *Sully*, *United 93*, *The Horror at 37,000 Feet*), television (*Breaking Bad* episodes 20–4) trauma life-writing (Laurie Anderson, Roald Dahl, Ernest Hemingway). Debris fields speak to us. Randall Jarrell's noirish-surreal WWII poem "Losses" offers a peculiarly uncanny iteration of such expression:

> It was not dying: everybody died.
> It was not dying: we had died before
> In the routine crashes—and our fields
> Called up the papers, wrote home to our folks.[67]

For Jarrell—a celestial navigation tower operator, "a job title he considered the most poetic in the Air Force"[68]—the crash sites are "*our* fields," in the dead speaker's first-person voice, because *we* crashed into them: we died there, and pieces of us remain there. Imagining those fields actually speaking, notifying survivors and mediascapes of what happened, Jarrell affirms my fundamental point that one way or another, debris fields have a great deal to tell us about crashes.

We may look at debris fields and see just debris: broken, static ruin. The debris is not doing anything—it is simply there, and that very there-ness (instead of what should be *up*-there-ness), its motionlessness (when it should be moving faster than anything else), its fragmentation (when it should be sleekly riveted into one unified mechanical assemblage) reads as existentially paralyzing frustration, meaninglessness. But the etymological analysis that the humanist crash investigator brings to the operation reveals that lurking behind (or within) this tepid debris, this sad inert noun, is a verb! "Debris," from the Old French "*debrisier*," means to break down in pieces, to crush. The cognate Middle English dēbrīsen, also a verb, means to shatter, or even to kill by shattering. So "to debris"—to make debris—is dynamic. What initially seems like a bleakly hapless signifier of dull rubble is actually, anciently, infused with action, movement, agency. It's a keenly tantalizing word once we realize what it means: it piques our interest, it raises the stakes, it draws us in. Yes, it's dangerous, but as every reader knows, danger is compelling. Perceiving and understanding danger better prepares us to grapple with it.

Debris, then, is both product and process: debris is also about how it came to be debris. When we see it on Kiefer's canvases, or in a field after a crash, we are also seeing (or, we *should* see) how it arrived in this condition, at this place. Plane-crash victims, the people in the debris field, have been killed by shattering—just as the etymological backstory foretold, never mind that airplanes were centuries off in the future. The debris invites us—especially literary critics, humanist investigators—to read, examine, understand, decode, interpret: to reveal the narratives (or poems, songs, screenplays, paintings, dreams) that germinate in debris fields and emerge into the world.

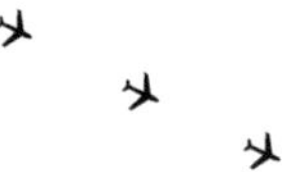

Like T. S. Eliot's still point of the turning world in *Four Quartets*, the debris field is an amalgam of motionlessness and movement. I will explore this terrain both literally and metaphorically. It marks a flight's end (thus, *still*), as well as the beginning of what comes after (*turning* into something else)—and something always does come after. In the narrative of an aviation disaster, a crash is the climax, not the conclusion. The debris field is an especially potent access-point

(*point!*) that connects the phenomenon of a crash with its consequences, its reverberations in the *world*.

A debris field is a zone of land or water strewn with gaseous detritus, metal, plastic, and fiberglass composites, and an overwhelming array of fragments, large and small, mechanical and corporeal. The relative intactness vs. brokenness of the debris varies according to the airplane's size, speed, and angle of impact, and the extent of fire and explosion during and after the crash. The debris field represents a definitive, inarguable depiction of an airplane's failure. That failure is quite possibly also a pilot's failure, and/or an engineering team's failure, possibly facilitated by a network of failed traffic control and navigation systems, and perhaps failed maintenance protocols, or failure to properly negotiate the weather, or to avoid a flock of birds who had the misfortune to get sucked into an engine as their own flightpath crossed coordinates with the airplane's at the wrong place and time.

(Birdstrikes happen 10,000 times a year at US airports, usually below 3,000 feet. Mourning doves are the most common victims, but ducks and geese, especially Canadian geese, wreak the most damage.[69] Canadian geese were what brought down Sully's plane over the Hudson River. In the first recorded birdstrike, on September 7, 1905 over Dayton, Ohio, the pilot, Orville Wright, had been chasing flocks of birds and eventually hit one.[70] The debris dead birds leave on airplanes is called "snarge," an amalgam of feathers, guts, and blood that crash investigators analyze to identify what species of bird was struck, in the interest of minimizing subsequent avian-aviator collisions.)

It is not hyperbolic to characterize debris fields as hellscapes, representing the horrific pain of those who crashed as well as those who survive them. But this wreckage may be also, paradoxically, a sacred site, where families imagine their loved ones taking their last breaths and now interred beneath, or amid, the debris. Of course the bodies are recovered and removed, to the greatest possible extent, but it's improbable that no atom of human remains *remains* in debris fields. One might almost imagine something serene here: a metaphysical tranquility where terror ceased, releasing victims from the torment they must have experienced hurtling downward.

I am fascinated by this wreckage that survives, or somewhat survives, a disaster's furiously destructive forces. I posit that the debris has an ironic power—channeling the action lurking in the word's ancestral verb-energy—to initiate some kind of restoration not only in the mechanical realm of aviation (ensuring that whatever caused this crash doesn't cause another) but also in the human realm of emotional recovery. I will look keenly, again and again—I hope it will not seem as if I am gawking—at these nightmarish fields. And while there are many reasons to look at debris fields, I acknowledge also that one may very reasonably choose to look away: Craig Greenlee writes about the 1970 Southern Airways crash of Marshall University's football team, many of whom he had known as a former player. All seventy-five onboard died when the plane clipped the treetops on approach to the airport. As Greenlee flew out a few days later en route to his best friend's funeral, "I never looked for any visual signs of the disaster. Clean-up of the crash scene had not been completed. On takeoff from Tri-State airport and again on the return trip, I made a conscious effort *to not look out* the passenger window. I simply didn't want to visualize what it must have been like for the people on that plane in the moments before their demise."[71]

Debris discovered by so-called souvenir hunters sometimes turns up for sale on eBay: a fuel injector from a 2011 crash of a military Hawk T1 on England's south coast;[72] fragments of a 1966 XB-70 Valkyrie mid-air collision (captured on film during a photoshoot for the military plane's manufacturer) that came down near Barstow, California.[73] Usually if such listings are publicized, they are quickly taken down: profiting from a crash is considered appallingly profane. But some such sales take place nevertheless, unnoticed by the public or media. I do not in any way endorse this—I find it indecent. But it indicates, if grotesquely, at least one way to calculate the "value" inherent in these broken fragments of crashed planes.

There are many more humane ways to account the value of debris fields. I think of Eliot again, this time from *The Waste Land*: "These fragments I have shored against my ruins."[74] That poem, like much modern art and literature, is enamored of debris: Eliot's Unreal City is "notoriously a place that stacks up broken and resonantly jumbled material stuff," writes Leo Mellor, typifying "how swathes of first-wave modernism had a yearning for locating in the urban landscape violently disordered debris—and then for attempting the extraction of meaning from it."[75] The debris of the modern era may be unpleasant, disorienting, and simply ugly, but in the wake of tragedy (whether a specific one like a plane crash, or, more generally, the miasma of wars and genocides, pandemics, totalitarianism, economic crises, nuclear annihilation), debris may be all we have, all that remains. For Eliot, broken fragments may be repurposed to stave off even worse breakdowns. Mellor's formulation of the modernist praxis nicely encompasses my own mission here: *attempting the extraction of meaning* from the violently disordered debris that marks the site where aviation has failed.

✈ Impact

Plane-crash investigators like to say that all accidents are preventable. I'm not sure I fully believe this, though I'd like to. If it's not unilaterally true, I think it mostly is. Still, crashes happen fairly regularly, which does not negate their statistical rarity: a very small percentage of a very large number is still a significant phenomenon. We discuss them with friends and colleagues, even if there isn't all that much to say in the immediate moment: Did you see the news? Just awful. Can you imagine? They exert a fierce grip on the cultural consciousness, yet after an initial keen shock, they dissipate and we go on with our lives, until the next one happens. Horrific and deadly, they challenge our idealized confidence that modern life generally functions smoothly. Although we mostly stop talking about them once the dust has settled, still, there's more to be said, more that stays with us.

My interest in crashes began as part of cognitive-behavioral therapy, treatment I underwent—three times—to help manage my fear of flying. (Xanax helped, too.) The cure involved going to the airport to watch planes take off over and over—from airside lounges before 9/11, afterwards from parking lots—and not crash. Eventually I came to accept that, despite my morbid presentiments, planes basically don't crash. But some do! (I never saw any.) Taking my therapy deeper into the anxious crevices and crannies of my overactive psyche, I began researching aviation disasters.

The methodically plodding prose of official crash investigations I read counterpointed the sense of anarchic chaos that triggered panic attacks for me every time planes twitched or fluttered. I still wondered what it would be like if my flight crashed, but displacing the habitual florid terror, I thought instead about NTSB narratives: metallurgical testing reports, treatises on jet fuel vapor chemistry, decade-long compilations of maintenance records.

There are, perversely, aspects of crashes that I find sublime. I like that whatever failure caused the problem—human and/or mechanical—is almost always discovered and fixed so it likely won't recur: remember how the first fatal crash inspired propeller design modifications and helmets for flyers. Object lesson: The best way to prevent plane crashes is by having plane crashes. Call it shameless narcissism, but a plane that crashes today diminishes the risk that a plane (that I could be on) doesn't crash next year—and it's not just *one* plane that won't crash, but probably a great many.

The de Havilland Comet, the first commercial jet, debuted in 1952; in 1953 and 1954, three Comets crashed shortly after takeoff, killing all passengers on all flights. It turns out that the plane's distinctive square windows were deadly design bungles: pressure from inside the aircraft created excessive stress around the window corners, making the fuselage more susceptible to fatigue, cracks, and ultimately disintegration.[76] Have you flown in a square-windowed plane recently? Problem solved—and tens of thousands of planes built since the 1950s did not crash because of what was learned from the Comet's flaw.

Today air crash investigators do not dawdle (three crashes!) before a problem is recognized, investigated, and addressed. Boeing was lambasted for its 2018–19 Max 8 debacle because it took *two* deadly incidents before they began to look seriously at flight-control system problems. The planes, flown by Ethiopian Airlines and Indonesia's Lion Air, illustrate how crashes involving certain countries' airlines are regarded differently from crashes in other fleets. Although the flight-control software mistake was the US manufacturer's fault, investigators initially assumed that the African and Asian airlines made mistakes that Western pilots wouldn't have; Boeing was later fined $2.7 billion for colluding in this narrative, which delayed the safety interventions that were at first considered unnecessary for smarter American pilots. (Chapter 7 investigates the racism of debris fields.)

Another fix, the ground proximity warning system, has saved untold thousands of lives. In the 1960s, safety engineer Don Bateman started working on a device that warns pilots "with colorful screen displays and dire audible alerts like 'Caution Terrain!' and 'Pull Up!' when they are in danger of crashing into mountains, buildings or water," and continued to refine it during his fifty-year career at Honeywell. The most common cause of airplane deaths had been crashing into land or water because of poor visibility and bad weather. Boeing data about commercial jets worldwide found "just six such accidents from 2011 to 2020, killing 229 people onboard, compared with 17 accidents from 2001 to 2010, which left 1,007 people dead, and 27 accidents from 1991 to 2000, killing 2,237."[77] Bateman's career offers a personal example of how crashes may enthrall us, and how they lead to safer aviation. His interest in airline safety began when he was nine: "one of his friends looked outside their classroom window in Saskatoon and saw debris and what appeared to be people falling from the sky. Two military planes, with 10 men aboard, had collided in midair. Don and his friend sneaked out of school early and rushed to the crash site," and the rest is history.

I'm fascinated by the breaking news and the morbid rituals—waiting for developing details, watching the rescue mission, then the recovery mission, experiencing pathos vicariously, following speculations on what might have caused the crash. Early conjectures are sometimes accurate, especially if there are obvious factors like storms, but often they are premature and erroneous. Still, there's a website, PPRUNE.org (Professional Pilots Rumour Network) where aviators anonymously share instantaneous hunches—even though they know hasty guesses run counter to the spirit of aviation safety—about what happened.

People can get irrationally spooked by plane crashes, though that tends to dispel after a few days as they realize, more sensibly, that *they* didn't crash, and probably won't. The airline that suffered a disaster keeps the route on the schedule—a different airplane (obviously), but the same type and model; a new flight number is an easy change to alleviate anxieties for jittery flyers. The plane is dead, long live the plane: putting aside the tragedy of flight 432, flight 567 is ready for takeoff. (I'm not superstitious, Michael Scott says on *The Office*, but I'm a little stitious.)

The crash cycle ends with the slow but persistent process of figuring out what went wrong, and why, and how to fix it. That part of the story, the investigation and findings, gets less news coverage than the crash. It's a follow-up story, rarely front-page. So long after the disaster, months or even years, people don't usually remember it well. Fuzzy memories of a few details stick in people's minds, but cultural reactions to a crash recapitulate the dynamics of the crash itself: an unexpected, stunning, overwhelming, explosive first impact, followed by an eventual calming after the flames burn out, the dust settles, and the debris gets inspected and carted away. The impact (literal and figurative), all-consuming at the beginning, dissipates soon precisely because the story, like the airplane, seems all-consumed.

But I take comfort in how the massive, methodical postmortem analysis seems to supplant the incident's initial chaos. Horror and confusion are transformed by investigators' steady, deliberate work. They recover a sort of control—not over the specific tragic flight, but of other users of a given aircraft type, or runway, or airport, or flightpath, or ATC protocol. The crash's explosive convulsions become quietened. Mistakes that caused the accident generate progress, contributing to the library of knowledge and experience that is precisely what makes aviation safer.

I have never lost anyone I love, or even anyone I know, in a plane crash. To those who have, my project here might well seem contrived, perhaps even morally offensive. I can only plead human nature. People gawk at disasters: traffic jams extend for miles on the *other* side of the highway from a terrible accident as drivers slow down to see what happened ("rubbernecking"), how bad it was, what condition the vehicles are in, what the emergency rescue teams are doing, whether they can glimpse the victims. Probably the experience of gawking involves gratitude that we did not crash ourselves, as close as we are to the scene. We may resolve to do whatever we can to avoid being in something like this in the future, to learn something from this tragedy: drive at a reasonable speed, pay closer attention to the road, put away our devices.

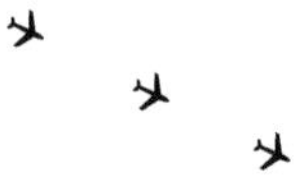

Speaking of cars: Mikita Brottman's *Car Crash Culture* explores automobile crashes similarly to how I investigate plane crashes. Some find it "disturbing" and "ghoulish" to focus the lens of cultural criticism on such terrible calamities, she writes, but she aims, as do I, "to confront some very deep-seated fears and anxieties. . . . If nothing else, the need to give the accident some kind of order" is "a superstitious need to assert (or to feign) control over the uncontrollable." She felt "an unusually heightened sense of consciousness and a powerful feeling of vitality and well-being" when she herself experienced a car crash. "And let's face it: we all feel a slight thrill at the thought of any serious accident." Brottman intriguingly suggests "an accident is something more than an accident. . . . When the automobile suddenly becomes a coffin, how befitting is it to see a cryptic revelation reflected in the shattered windshield. Are wrecked cars"—and, I'll add, wrecked planes—"hieroglyphs, transitional objects that forge a link between the sensible world of knowledge and the unknowable realm of the occult?"[78]

In Don DeLillo's 1985 novel *White Noise*, Prof. Murray Siskind, whose field of expertise is car crashes, finds them anything but tragic. "I tell my students not to look for apocalypse in such places. I see these car crashes as part of a long tradition of American optimism. They are positive events, full of the old 'can-do' spirit." As depicted in movies and on television, "Each car crash is meant to be better than the last. There is a constant upgrading of tools and skills, a meeting of challenges. A director says, 'I need this flatbed truck to do a midair double somersault that produces an orange ball of fire with a thirty-six foot diameter, which the cinematographer will use to light the scene.'" If students find these crashes appalling, wasteful, gory, Siskind refocuses them: "I tell them it's not decay they are seeing but innocence." A movie car crash is not a violent act, but "a celebration. A reaffirmation of traditional values and beliefs." A crash is "a high-spirited moment," staged by people "able to capture a light-heartedness, a carefree enjoyment," he explains: "a wonderful brimming spirit of innocence and fun."[79]

Siskind's characterization of car crashes is troublingly perverse. *White Noise* is a perverse book—is mine, too?—presenting (like me) offbeat ways of thinking about crashes. A thread of continuity links Brottman's paradoxical description of the "vitality and well-being" that emanates from a car crash; DeLillo's paradoxical assertion of optimism, innocence and fun; and my own paradoxical acknowledgment of the unlikely appeal of plane crashes that I've uncovered in my investigations. Many of the crash narratives I've investigated, while lamenting aviation disasters, also somehow celebrate them. Crashes can terrify or (and) thrill us. They can send us into depths of existential paralysis, but/and, they can also attune us to the cutting edge of modernity's miraculous mobilities.

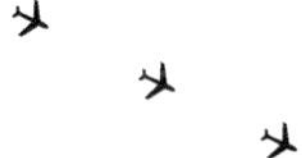

"We live in the fantasy that we are in control," writes contemporary painter Tom Judd. "But we like the excitement of things being out of control."[80] Judd's *Arrival*, Figure 1.5, shocks viewers with what seems like a macabre disjunction between title and image. Yes, in a sense, this *does* depict an arrival, but certainly not the kind passengers would have preferred. Judd's dark irony illustrates my point about how the discourse of mobilities must be versatile enough to embrace immobility as well. There are many variants of arrivals, some of which deconstruct the mobilities template pretty starkly, yet they are still part of the paradigm: nosedives are indeed one way planes can arrive.

Arrival is part of a series, "Deconstructed," including similarly brutal depictions of a car crash, a flood, a hurricane, a bridge collapse. Do we really, as Judd claims, *like the excitement* of thinking about such loss of control? Do we enjoy creating/experiencing art that highlights, and even celebrates, that disorder? Edgar Allan Poe's Imp of the Perverse may be at play here, but beyond that, artists *do* aspire to discover and share new things, which may include insights about aviation that are not as pleasant and self-congratulatory as the aspects that are usually celebrated. Knowledge is not always pretty, but painful information is still valuable, making us better able to understand the world and function in the world.

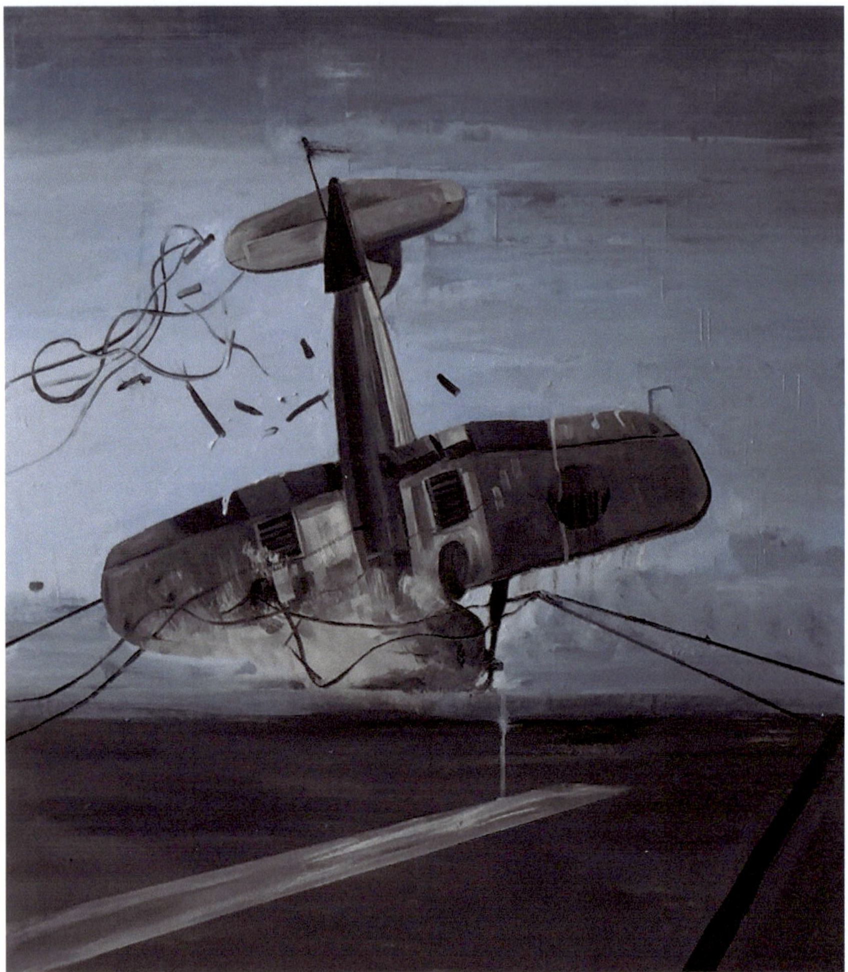

Figure 1.5 Tom Judd, *Arrival* (2017).

Judd's paintings depict "those moments where that illusion of being in control is disrupted and we are left in a state of surprise and perhaps wonderment."[81] Like Brottman's "slight thrill" of experiencing a car crash, her "powerful feeling of vitality and well-being," Judd's uncomfortably frank explanation of his attraction to the macabre, *surprise and perhaps wonderment*, parallels my own fascination with plane crashes and whatever insights we can recover from the debris. *Arrival* inspires my fleurons—the typographical glyphs I use to separate sections, as at the end of this paragraph—which may strike some as distasteful. I mean to remind my readers (just as Judd reminds his viewers) that, to put it as simply as possible, this happens: this is what we are investigating here.

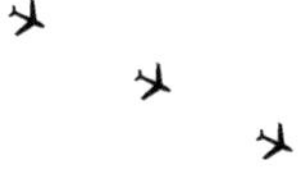

Plane crashes (along with car crashes, bridge collapses, and many other types of spectacular and random tragedy) illuminate a realm that most of us, most of the time, keep sublimated. I'm not sure I'd call it, as Brottman does, a "realm of the occult," but I agree that crashes, oxymoronically, *transport* us to some point of view, or state of mind, jolting us beyond the straight and narrow guardrails that mostly conscribe our safe, predictable journeys (both physical and metaphysical) through the world. Conceptualizing the spectacle of aviation tragedy includes some kind of frisson. *"YOU . . . are there,"* the announcer intoned with slow, bold gravitas introducing Walter Cronkite's historical-reenactment show from the 1950s titled, appropriately enough, "You Are There." Yes, I am there. I cannot help but imagine what it would have been like to be present at the moment—to have seen a crash as a spectator, or even more intensely morbid, to have been on a flight that crashed. Does your life flash before your eyes? Would it almost be worth crashing to experience that? Not really, not quite, but . . .

Investigator Dennis Shanahan, who has interviewed hundreds of crash survivors, explains how they describe what it feels like as the plane is going down. "I've come to the general conclusion that they don't have a whole lot of awareness that they've been severely traumatized. I find them very detached. They're aware of a lot of things going on, but they give you this kind of ethereal response—'I knew what was going on, but I didn't really know what was going on. I didn't particularly feel like I was a part of it.'"[82] Perhaps experiencing a plane crash would be anticlimactic: *what was all the fuss about?!*

Do we ever understand a plane crash? I think the people who analyze them and write the reports would say yes, as would the pilots who return to their flight decks after a crash.

The more I think about plane crashes, the more I feel inclined to say, no. The more I learn, the more eludes my comprehension. Plane crashes resist being known. They are large, conflagrational, unexpected, uncanny mysteries: the mechanical and aerodynamic failures they embody tend to leech also into interpretive failures, at least as I read them here. I understand the positivist discourse that other investigators bring to their crash reports, and I feel strongly persuaded, when I read these documents, that the safety teams have done their work meticulously and they know what they are talking about, and yet: there remains an aporia, a gap, a trace of uncertainty that humanists cannot let drop. As vigorously as I try to find and present an authoritative "textuality of the crash" that we can read and grasp, a persistent, pervasive ineffability endures. The closer I get to understanding what happened, the more I realize I cannot get all the way there. (Some accuse humanists of rejecting narrative certainty because if we discovered it, we'd be out of a job.) We are flying into fierce, protracted headwinds.

"But what's going on"? If I were writing a film treatment—a reasonable strand of a humanist crash investigation—I'd follow up first officer Pierre-Cédric Bonin's question in the seconds before the Air France disaster with a flashback. Scene: A couple of hours earlier, Bonin spends his off-duty rotation relaxing in the rest-area cubby. From his travel bag he pulls a rumpled paperback copy of Camus's 1942 tract *The Myth of Sisyphus*. Voiceover: an erudite French-accented speaker describes the absurdity of trying to find meaning in an incomprehensible universe, and the tension between our desire for order and happiness versus an indifferent natural universe that refuses to provide this. "A man who has become conscious of the absurd is forever bound to it." We keep advancing questions about the meaning of life and the grotesque incoherence of death—"*but what's going on*?"—only to find our exigeses, like Sisyphus's boulder, tumbling back down the mountain. "Never has the absurd been so well illustrated or at such length,"[83] Camus writes, an apothegm that would serve well as an epigraph for every aviation accident report.

But putting aside existential dread, I will get to work discovering and analyzing allusions, subplots, analogies, intertexts, palimpsests, rhythms, patterns, forms, and of course ironies. I have invented—I hope not too perversely or unwisely—this idea of a cultural debris field, which fascinates me, but which it is now my burden to describe and interpret, and I am starting to worry that I may have set myself a task that lies beyond my capabilities.

"Ah, but a man's reach should exceed his grasp."

One could certainly imagine Wilbur or Orville Wright saying this, but it was actually Robert Browning: the pentameter gives it away. Browning's next line—"Or what's a heaven for?"[84]—could *so easily* have come from the Wrights, couldn't it? Heaven is for aviation! Had they read "Andrea del Sarto," Browning's 1855 dramatic monologue? Perhaps that thought, or something from its zeitgeist, was in their minds as they tinkered around in their Dayton workshop; I like to think so.

Sisyphus again: "Is an absurd work of art possible?"[85] To transpose that query into my Camusian crash critique: can we find order, pattern, beauty, inspiration, in a place as unlikely—as absurd!—as a debris field? Camus induces us to lower our expectations: "Individuals seek order, harmony and even perfection, yet can find no evidence that such things exist," philosopher Jack Reynolds explains. "In *The Myth of Sisyphus*, Camus seeks to rectify this, basically by encouraging individuals to give up their desire for a reasonable and coherent order to the world."[86] But I will try to resist Camus's cynicism and aspire to find, in the broken pathos of the debris field, the art (the reason, the coherence) of the absurdity splayed out in this unpromising landscape.

✈ Ground death

Flying out of Boston or Newark always makes me recall 9/11, as does walking around lower Manhattan. As rare as it is to be involved in a crash, being *in situ* makes it seem more likely, more imaginable. Near where I once lived in Brooklyn's Prospect Heights, there was a street corner (Sterling Place at Seventh Avenue) marked by a small, obscure sign informing that United Airlines flight 826, a McDonnell Douglas DC-8, had fallen to the ground at exactly that spot in 1960, killing six Brooklynites in addition to all eighty-four on board. The sign left it at that, but of course I've followed up with my own investigations. Ten brownstones were destroyed, along with a delicatessen, a laundry, a funeral home (!), and a church: the Pillar of Fire Church (!!!). A witness said the crash site resembled "the bombed and burning villages of the Korean War."[87] One eleven-year-old boy who fell from the plane, Stephen Baltz, traveling alone, was miraculously found alive in the snow, though he died the next day from extensive burns. He was conscious when he arrived at Methodist Hospital, telling doctors: "I remember looking out the plane window at the snow below covering the city. It looked like a picture out of a fairy book. Then all of a sudden there was an explosion. The plane started to fall and people started to scream. I held on to my seat and then the plane crashed."[88] Embedded in a memorial plaque at the hospital—odd, but memorable and moving—are the four dimes and five nickels he had in his pocket.[89]

I've found photographs of that debris field, and though it was twenty-five years before I arrived there, still, I could vividly imagine myself—*imagination* being the humanist's stock-in-trade—on the day, in the place, suffering the random calamity of dying on the ground as an airplane crashed down into me. Or I could have been a few blocks away, seeing the impact from a safe distance. I feel pretty sure I would never fly again if I saw a crash in person, however logical or illogical that may be. On a related note, I am always astonished when, after plane crashes, tragedy-beset airlines fly tragedy-beset families to somewhere near the site of the accident, or to a memorial service. Really? How can people get on a plane to fly to where their children or parents crashed (on the same airline!) the day before? I can't imagine I could.

The Brooklyn crash was a mid-air collision: a rare occurrence, and even rarer now thanks to vastly expanded air traffic radar and the TCAS—traffic collision avoidance system—that alerts pilots if a potential collision with another aircraft is imminent, automatically adjusting the flightpath to avoid it. The DC-8, approaching Idlewild airport (now JFK), collided in midair with TWA flight 266, a Lockheed L-1049 Super Constellation descending into LaGuardia. The accident's probable cause was that the United flight was several miles off course. (*Probable*: sometimes—not often, and less so now than in the past—crash investigations cannot pinpoint a definitive cause. If they're not completely certain, they'll say so.)

The Lockheed crashed near Miller Field, a Staten Island army base ten miles from where the DC-8 fell to earth, and some TWA debris ended up in New York Harbor. All forty-four aboard died, though nobody on the ground. Witnesses said the blood-drenched snow and bodies made them think of a battlefield,[90] similar to how people described the scene in Brooklyn; it's interesting to reflect on how debris fields resemble battlefields. The total death toll of 134 (including those Brooklyn bystanders) made the crash the world's most deadly aviation accident at the time. That record stood until 1969, when Viasa flight 742 from Caracas to Miami crashed after takeoff, killing all eighty-four on board as well as seventy-one on the ground, which was also, at the time, the highest incidence of ground fatalities.

But there have been higher tolls of ground deaths since then: any "worst crash" of whatever kind carries that designation only until an even worse one comes along, which it always does. At least 225 people died on the ground in 1996, perhaps 100 more than that, when an Air Africa Antonov An-32B overran the runway and plowed into a street market abutting the airport after a failed takeoff from Kinshasa, Zaire (now the Democratic Republic of the Congo). That country is regularly ranked as one of the most dangerous places to fly due to dilapidated airport infrastructure, traffic navigation and surveillance equipment;

weak safety regulations; aged aircraft; poorly trained flight crews and maintenance workers; and heavy storms during rainy seasons.[91]

Ground fatalities from the 9/11 terrorist hijackings were enormous: an estimated 2,606 people died who were not on the planes when American flight 11 and United flight 175 hit the World Trade Center; 125 on the ground died when American flight 77 crashed into the Pentagon. There were no ground deaths when United flight 93 went down in Shanksville, PA, into an empty field.

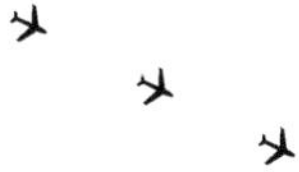

Airshows cause significant numbers of deaths, both in the air and on the ground. The Blue Angels, a US Navy aircraft team, stages aerobatic performances for public relations and recruitment, but also just to do cool stuff: loops and rolls, tight turns, opposing passes (two planes flying toward each other in what appears to be a collision course) and mirror formations (back-to-back, belly-to-belly, or wingtip-to-wingtip with one jet flying inverted). They are quintessential daredevils, and sometimes when people dare devils, the devils prevail. Their swagger has a high mortality rate: twenty-seven Blue Angels pilots (about 10 percent of those who have flown in the squadron's history) have died in airshow or training crashes.[92]

There are dozens of other national air display teams—South Korea's Black Angels, Thailand's Blue Phoenix, the Greek Zeus team, the Hawks of Romania, and many more. And unsurprisingly, there have been numerous airshow crashes. As at auto speedway races, audiences hope for safe performances but cannot be completely surprised (maybe even a bit thrilled, as Brottman suggests) if mishaps arise. Damien Jurado channels this macabre irony in his 2002 song "Air Show Disaster," which repeats, over and over, with an oddly sedate vibe: "It's another nice day for an air show disaster, just another nice day for an air show disaster."[93]

Since planes fly directly overhead, an airshow debris field is often coterminous with its viewing stands. Seventy died—three pilots, sixty-seven spectators—in the Flugtag 1988 show at Germany's US Air Force Ramstein Base. Italian Air Force pilots from the *Frecce Tricolori* (Tricolor Arrows) troupe collided while performing when one flew off course, crashed to the ground in a fireball, and "cartwheeled straight into the middle of an area of concession stands and picnickers alongside the runway, spewing fire and airplane parts over tents, cars, barbecue grills—and people." They were performing their "arrow through the heart" routine, where nine planes split into two formations and fly loops forming a heart while trailing red, white and green smoke. The tenth, meant to arch down in a solo loop through the bottom of the heart as the two formations pass beneath him, arrived too low and a second early.[94]

Ramstein's was the deadliest airshow ever until the 2002 Sknyliv airshow disaster, where a Ukrainian Air Force Sukhoi Su-27 crashed during an aerobatics presentation near Lviv, killing seventy-seven spectators. After two pilots ejected (and survived) during a misflown rolling maneuver, their plane hit the ground and skidded toward some stationary aircraft which exploded on impact. The blame was placed mainly on the pilots, who were imprisoned after being found guilty of attempting maneuvers they were not competent to perform. A Google search for "Sknyliv airshow disaster" returns several extremely graphic, disturbing, stunning videos.

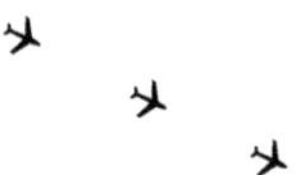

All forty-nine aboard died in the 2009 crash of a Colgan Air Bombardier Dash-8 on approach to Buffalo, which also caused a single ground death. The pilots on flight 3407, young and tired, had been flirting with each other, the CVR transcript informs. The younger one had little piloting experience and had commuted (with minimal sleep) on two connecting flights, a trip that took close to an entire day, from her home in Seattle to Newark, where the flight departed. The other pilot had previously failed several flight checks. They were not at the top of their game, and when their plane went into a stall they made a rookie mistake, pulling its nose up. Everyone knows you have to fly *down* into a stall to recover: it feels counterintuitive, but the most immediate need is to build up speed so you can then pull up.

One of several contributing factors to the crash was Colgan's inadequate procedures for managing approaches in icing conditions. In the CVR transcript, five minutes before impact, First Officer Rebecca Shaw says, "I've never seen icing conditions. I've never deiced. I've never seen any—I've never experienced any of that. I don't want to have to experience that and make those kinds of calls. You know I'd've freaked out. I'd've seen this much ice and thought oh my gosh we were going to crash."[95]

Besides the crew and passengers, Douglas Wielinski died when the plane hit his Clarence Center home, five miles from the airport, bursting into flames as its fuel tanks ruptured on impact; the rest of his family escaped with minor injuries. Is there no limit to the amazingly horrible things that can befall you at any moment?

His wife, Karen Wielinski, wrote a book about the tragedy called *One on the Ground*. The day after the crash,

> I sat in a hotel suite and watched a news crawl race across the bottom of the television screen—The crash of Continental flight 3407 resulted in the loss of everyone aboard the plane and one on the ground. That "one on the ground" was my husband Doug. Although I knew it was not intentional, that phrase always made me feel like Doug was an afterthought.[96]

Doug and Karen had been watching television with their daughter, Jill. He left to go upstairs to bed, which is where he died.

> We had been watching a video of *American Idol*. Around ten, Doug left the family room. A few minutes later he returned and sat on the couch. I asked if he wanted to keep watching the video. Would Doug have survived if he had stayed in the family room? But he didn't stay. He asked how much longer *American Idol* would last. "About an hour," I said. Then he made me laugh with teasing so typical of him. "I don't have time for that!" he said as he hopped off the couch. That was the last thing he said to me and the last time I saw him.

Noting that the Colgan crash occurred less than a month after Sully's Miracle on the Hudson, in which everyone survived thanks to the pilots' outstanding training and experience, Karen writes, "I wondered what if more experienced pilots had been at the controls of flight 3407. From all indications, the 3407 pilots panicked and improperly responded to 'stick shaker' and 'stick pusher' warnings."[97]

Wielinski describes what it's like when a debris field is your house: she had to get new birth certificates and credit cards; the community—individuals and businesses—provided copious donations to replace the physical items she had lost: food, clothes, toothpaste, cellphones, car; the basketball coach gathered a box of memorabilia commemorating her daughter's star season to replace items that were destroyed; she didn't have photos of her husband to display at his funeral. The NTSB retrieved 40,000 personal artifacts from the debris field, an unusually high number, due to the presence of so many things from the Wielinski household.

A friend transformed the recovered scraps and fragments—the debris—of Doug's sports T-shirts and baseball uniforms into a quilt. Karen became friends with Gerri Pomponio, whose house in Queens was destroyed when American Airlines flight 587 crashed into it in 2001, just after takeoff from JFK, killing five on the ground (along with 260 on the plane) including her husband, Franco. On the one-year crash anniversary, Karen watched "a large contingent of 3407's passengers' family and friends" walk the five miles from their house to the Buffalo-Niagara International airport, "such a symbolic gesture—completing the journey of those lost that night." But she didn't join the procession: "For us, there was no journey to complete. Doug was home."[98]

It was "just" one person, less tragic (quantitatively) than many other crashes with more ground casualties, but still, the crash narrative makes Wielinski's death seem especially appalling: the stupid, distracting pilot banter; the exhausting cross-country commute that left the 24-year-old first officer unfocused; the stall from which they could have recovered easily if they had followed basic flight training guidance. So many highly improbable, ridiculous circumstances: Wielinski just shouldn't have died. As random as it is to be a passenger in a plane crash, being a victim on the ground is profoundly more ironic, more incomprehensible, more existentially absurd.

2

Plane Crashes Before Planes

This, however, cannot be properly termed flying, but only an easier and slower method of falling.

Francesco Milizia

✈ 'Melancholy Exits'

Thinking about unlikely, unlucky plane-crash victims who weren't even on a plane, like Doug Wielinski and his kindred spirits in Brooklyn, Kinshasa, Caracas, lower Manhattan: as unimaginable as it would have been to die in a plane crash while walking through an urban street market, or in New York City's tallest skyscrapers, or lying in your own bed, imagine experiencing such a calamity lying in your own bed in 1785. In the Irish village of Tullamore, County Offaly, the agent of this disaster was (obviously) not an airplane, but a hot-air balloon, believed to be unpiloted, that ignited when it snagged a building just as the county surgeon—a fecking Englishman!—was launching it. A letter in *Hibernian Magazine* two days later offers a vivid eyewitness accident report:

> A most dreadful fire took place on the fair day, by which nearly a hundred houses and offices were totally consumed. The melancholy accident was occasioned by the liberation of a fire-balloon, which two gentlemen encouraged an English adventurer to prepare for the amusement of their friends. Having been launched from Dr. Bleakley's yard, it took its direction with a smart wind towards the barrack, where its progress was interrupted by the chimney; and having, on the shock, taken fire it communicated to Christopher Beck's house, and raged with ungovernable fury, notwithstanding the efforts and the assistance of a number of people collected by the circumstance of the fair, till every house front and rear in Barrack Street (except one thatched and four slated houses) was entirely destroyed. The utmost distress has been experienced by the miserable inhabitants, [to] whom the remaining houses are scarcely sufficient to afford

> shelter; and several of the wealthier residents have suffered losses nearly to their total ruin.[1]

If there were fatalities, which would seem inevitable, they were not recorded.

Plane crashes as a trope, a cultural touchstone, emanate from spectacles that significantly predate aviation's Kitty Hawk origin story. There's nothing new under the sun: people have always died dramatically, ironically, gruesomely, in large numbers, caught in the binary paradoxes of progress/failure, control/chaos, intended/unlucky outcomes, leaving behind troubled and confused citizens, families, survivors. Poking around through that antecedent wreckage reveals what palimpsests underlie plane-crash debris fields.

The first successful human flight was Jean-François Pilâtre de Rozier's 1783 trip in a Montgolfier *globe aérostatique*, a hot-air balloon made of silk and paper. A couple months earlier, the same vessel had flown with three nonhuman passengers—a sheep, a duck, and a rooster—to check whether it would be safe for people: there were concerns about how high altitudes would affect living creatures. The sheep's physiology was thought to be similar to a human's, while the duck, at home in the sky and unlikely to suffer harm, was used as a control. It's unclear why the rooster was on board.

After the farm animals survived their adventure, de Rozier and co-pilot François Laurent, Marquis d'Arlandes, flew 900 meters above Paris (where Benjamin Franklin was among the spectators), from the Bois de Boulogne on the city's western edge to Butte-aux-Cailles across town, traveling nine kilometers in twenty-five minutes.[2] Though they had enough fuel to fly farther, they set down because burning embers from the fire (that produced the "hot air") were beginning to scorch the balloon's fabric.

In 1785, the first aeronaut became the first air crash fatality (asterisking the Irish balloon blaze earlier that year, where information about deaths was not preserved for history). De Rozier and his friend Pierre Romain ascended in a different model than the one he first used: his own invention, which he called a Rozière. Launching from a seaside town, Bologne-sur-Mer, they hoped to fly across the English Channel: favorable winds carried them in a westward drift at an altitude of several thousand meters, but shifting currents brought them back near where they started and onlookers watched the balloon deflate. Some thought it caught fire: the Rozière's experimental fuel contained highly flammable hydrogen. The balloon plunged to the ground, killing the balloonists in Wimereux, five kilometers from where they started.

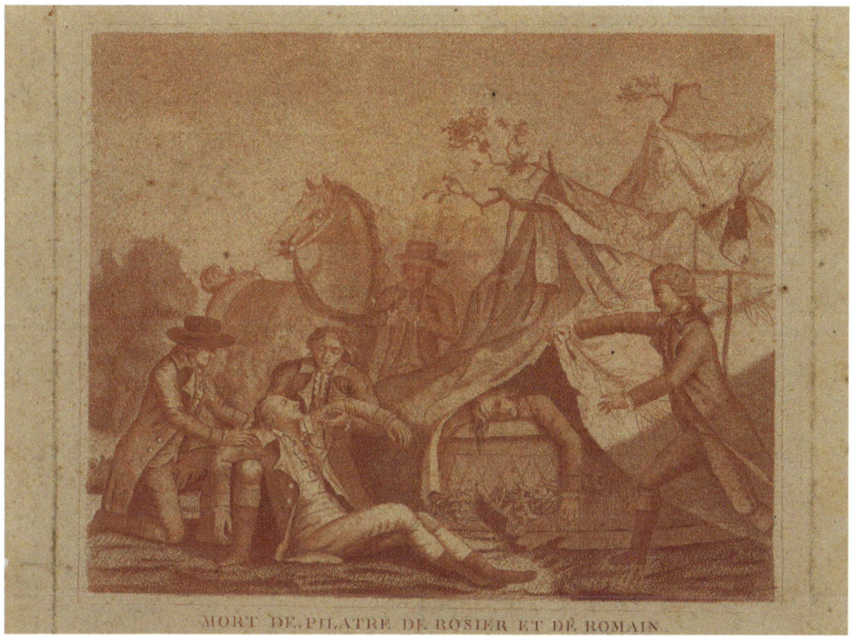

Figure 2.1 "Death of Pilatre de Rozier and de Romain. As they were found after their fall." Below: "Victims constant in their utter strength. The path of honor drives them to death."

For the sake of argument, if you'll indulge me, let's think of this as a plane crash—albeit long before airplanes existed. The 1785 Irish and French balloon crashes anticipated the danger and misfortune subsequent aviators faced on airplane flights that might end in spectacular death, destruction, and debris. Balloon tragedies began to teach people how to imagine something unimaginable: the thrill of victory and the agony of defeat are two sides of the same coin. The classical tableau in Figure 2.1 is emotionally striking, if also rather stiffly staged. It depicts nature (trees, horse, field, skies) and the drama of life and death, heroic adventure and tragic failure, that takes place within this landscape, beneath the heavens that the adventurers had briefly broached. The balloon debris—the "envelope," it's called—presents striking close-up visual testimony of the crash. Torn, unkempt fabric ironically unravels its original geometric precision, the beauty of its lines, curves, hatchings, and ornamentally embroidered designs. (Today too, one defining feature of the debris field is the airliner's sleek, elegant livery—its graphic appearance, its colors and design—mangled and askew: see Figure 2.8.)

A rich pathos colors this crash scene depiction, invoking the brave virtue we are meant to feel in these aeronauts' noble deaths. The balloon basket semiotically suggests de Rozier's sarcophagus; the torn fabric, his funeral shroud. Romain, supported by two men on the ground beside the balloon, reportedly did not succumb immediately but was conscious enough to ask for water before he expired.[3]

The eighteenth-century finery of the outfits, buttons, cravats, hats and wigs (on both victims and rescuers), and remnants of the ornate balloon design, contrast starkly with the crash site's disheveled mess. The man standing center-image seems already to be delivering a eulogy, while another, holding up the

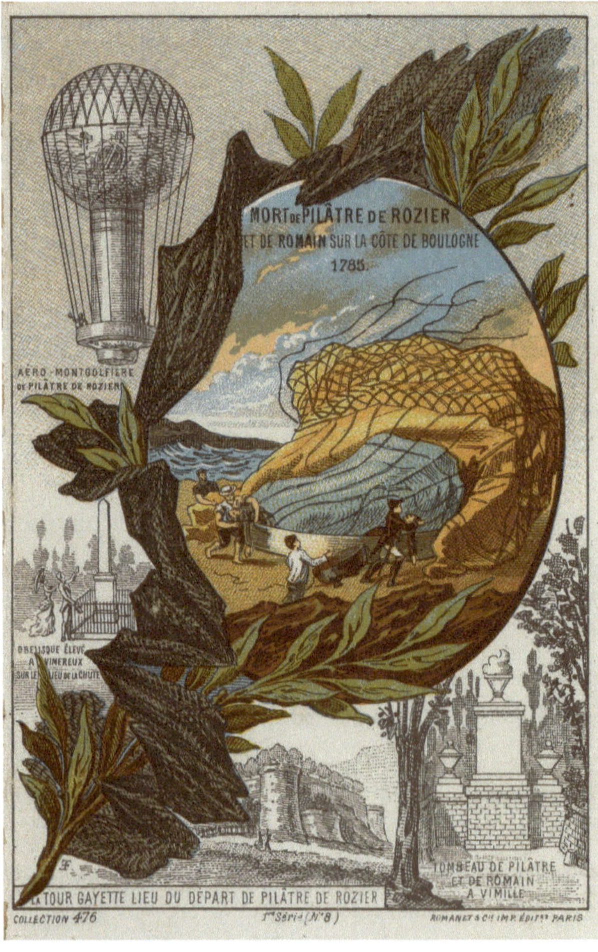

Figure 2.2 Deaths of Pilâtre de Rozier and de Romain.

panels of canvas (the "gore"), ceremoniously draws attention to the wreckage. The fabric, the most striking element of this debris, caught and broke branches off a tree in the fall. As today, part of the debris field's striking aesthetic involves how mechanical fragments mix eerily with the nature into which the machine crashed—trees, hills, muddy ground. Nature's upheaval mirrors the greater tragedy of the vehicle, and people, whose disaster caused this ruin.

A nineteenth-century depiction of the same crash appears on a collectors' card from a series about the history of ballooning. While the classical print in Figure 2.1 offers a single composed moment that encapsulates the entire catastrophe, Figure 2.2, a more middlebrow account, presents a busier infographic with several discrete elements. The background scenes, rendered in monochrome, encircle the central element, the moment of the crash, highlighted in color. The subordinate images depict de Rozier's and Romain's tomb; the site of their launch; a balloon in flight in happier times (not the ill-fated Rozière but the successful 1783 Montgolfier); and an obelisk erected at the crash site. The card presents a narrative model like the kinds of stories we reconstruct today surrounding the climactic moment of a plane crash, just as these images graphically surround the balloon's crash.

There is more action in Figure 2.2 compared to the formally arranged Figure 2.1 People on the collectors' card, less fancily dressed, attend to the victims with more alacrity, less theatricality. First responders try to revive the victims, but their arms hanging limply out of the basket suggest nothing can be done. As in the more staid version, the collectors' card highlights the envelope canvas as the main feature of the debris—large and colorful, streaming messily, not (as it would have been just a few moments earlier) neat, symmetrical, aerodynamically proper. Today plane-crash narratives often include, as this card does, a file photo of an undamaged aircraft juxtaposed with a vista of chunks and pieces littering the debris field.

Some of the webbing ("load tapes") in Figure 2.2 is relatively intact—the card's other, un-crashed balloon shows how it's supposed to look. But some of the ropes have gone awry: severed, twisted, useless. The canvas is blowing in the breeze—a sublimated and ironic inscription of that force, wind, which is so important to balloon flights. There is still wind, those flapping ropes show, but the balloon can't navigate it. It is like the engines that stand out in plane-crash debris-field images: concentrated irony. If they worked—if the cowlings and blades, compressors and turbines, weren't destroyed—this wouldn't have happened. It's an engine but not an engine: a pile of debris that formerly

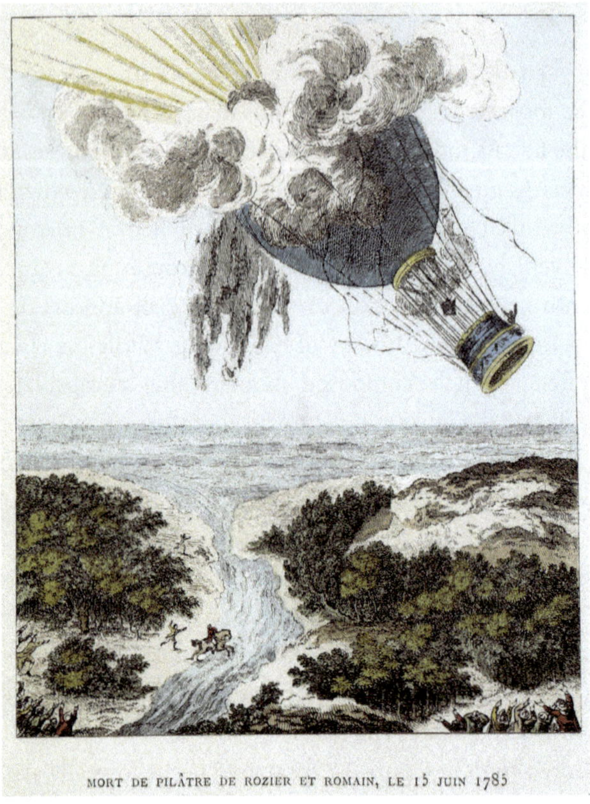

Figure 2.3 The precise moment of the Rozière's failure, in gory dramatic splendor.

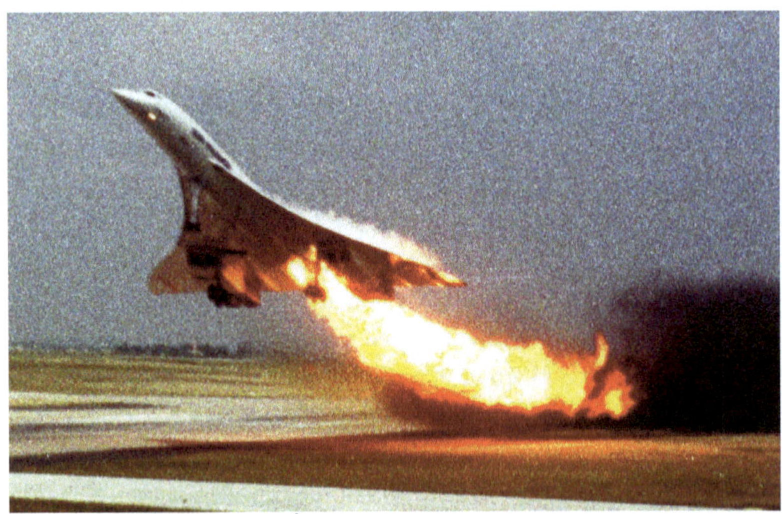

Figure 2.4 Air France 4590 aflame as it takes off from Charles de Gaulle Airport, its fuel tanks punctured.

functioned as a mechanism. The collectors' card's ropes and fluttering canvas serve the same visual purpose, de-ballooning the balloon.

Ubiquitous surveillance cameras make it possible, sometimes, to capture the moment of a plane crash: the combustion, the break-up. Figure 2.3 shows how early mediascapes created their own renditions of such horrible but unignorably compelling scenes. Although this balloon explosion was drawn a century after the event, it still presents itself as an eyewitness perspective, a *YOU . . . are there* moment. All these visual representations of the 1785 disaster—multiple versions, in multiple forms and aesthetics—indicate how ravenously the public sought to engage with the experience of this ur-crash. As we'd say today, it went viral.

Compare the perspective in Figure 2.3 with Toshihiko Sato's remarkable photograph, Figure 2.4, of the moment Air France flight 4590—the Concorde—lifted off from Charles de Gaulle airport on July 25, 2000. It was doomed before it left the ground: during the takeoff roll, it ran over a strip of metal that fell off the plane ahead, puncturing a tire. Tire debris hit the Concorde's engine, rupturing three fuel tanks and damaging the wing. The plane struggled to stay airborne—*Il voulait voler!*—but within two minutes it crashed into a hotel, killing all 109 aboard and four on the ground. The pilots were trying to limp to Le Bourget, once Paris's main airport (where Charles Lindbergh's *Spirit of St. Louis* landed in 1927), ten miles away.

The Concorde, like the Rozière, was sleek, cutting-edge technology: simply amazing in so many ways, aeronautically and culturally. I have asked before, and will ask again, how we can ascertain that any given crash is somehow worse than another one. That is probably the wrong word, the wrong way to appraise crashes comparatively—and yet, I think, we do often read crashes that way, judgmentally, on a subjective continuum in which some are deemed to be more tragic, more horrific, more ironic, implying that others are less so. Some crashes, like these two from 1785 and 2000, represent the scary, horrible failures of inventions that embodied their culture's brilliance and power. Both aircraft symbolically manifested their ingenuity, their potential to go new places, farther, faster, higher. The Rozière and the Concorde, like the *Titanic*, the Apollo spacecrafts, the transcontinental railway, the Model T, and the Michaux Velocipede, represented forms of transportation (and commerce and discovery and independence and imaginative boundlessness) that included a hefty metaphorical dynamism along with their already impressive literal capabilities of mobility. When such vehicles crash, killing people who were supposed to be able to move more spectacularly than anyone else, it takes a toll on our identity. Perhaps we aren't as smart as we thought, nor as invulnerable to the limits of the human condition. Disasters like these—especially exacerbated by the proliferation of raw, disturbing, continually re-traumatizing depictions of the moment of explosion, the moment of failure—may deeply diminish our cultural pride and confidence.

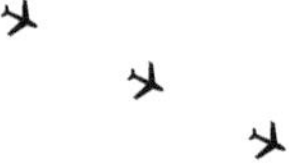

Some people would never get into a hot-air balloon again after seeing images of its destruction—or onto a Concorde after its crash, or a spacecraft after the Apollo 1 and Challenger disasters, or a dirigible after the Hindenburg explosion, or a steamship after the *Titanic* sank, or a submersible after the *Titan*, checking in on the *Titanic* debris field, imploded to create its own supplementary debris field.

But many do. Nobody forgets these events, but most are able to accept the crashes as a possible/acceptable risk associated with the otherwise-magnificent experiences that technologies of mobility enable. Soldiers who see comrades killed generally keep fighting with a sense of the mission still to be completed; so too crashes may dissuade some, but many are willing to get right back on that horse (or balloon or supersonic transport) as engineers fine-tune how to get it right—how to achieve what the pioneers of these mobilities set out to do, which was never going to happen without some setbacks. At the 1954 investigation into de Havilland Comet crashes, the UK Air Registration Board's head "lectured his inquisitors before they could even get to the first technical question," writes Sam Howe Verhovek. "You know, and I know, the cause of this accident," said Lord Brabazon. "It is due to the adventurous, pioneering spirit of our race. It has been like that in the past, it is like that in the present, and I hope it will be in the future.'"[4] It comes with the territory.

Drifting back to eighteenth-century France: alongside myriad images of the Rozière's tragic spectacle, there were also copious written accounts. England's *Derby Post* published this report from a correspondent on the scene the day after the crash:

> Poor Pilatre de Rozier and a Mons. Romain ascended in the grand Balloon, at seven this Morning, and made a fine Appearance in the Ascent, bidding fair for a prosperous Voyage to England, but in half an Hour, when they were at a great Height, and about three Miles from the Town, the Balloon caught Fire, and of course fell to the Ground. The two Intrepid Adventurers were dashed to Pieces. I was with the Bodies in half an Hour and never saw any Thing so shocking.

> I examined the Bodies, but do not find any Thing broke above the Middle, so that they must have come down perpendicularly, but their Legs and Thighs are broke in many Places. I shook Hands with Rozier almost the last Person in his Life Time; he was a fine young Fellow, and thought for several Days past had a Presentiment of his untimely End in his Countenance; he has been Indefatigable for this Week in preparing his accursed Machine—I hope to never hear of another being attempted in this or any other Country. . . .
>
> The late celebrated Mr Pilatre de Rozier was the *first* hardy Adventurer, who ascended attached to a Fire Balloon at Paris on the 15th October 1783, about ten Months after Mr. Montgolfier had invented that singular Machine. On his return from the Sky, he received the Compliments due to his Courage and Activity, having shown to the World, the Accomplishment of what had been for ages desired and attempted in Vain.
>
> It is thought the melancholy Exits of M. Pilatre de Rozier and his no less unfortunate Companion, will in some Measure check the too-soaring Ideas of the many Candidates for aerial Fame, who are now in our Metropolis, who had pledged themselves to the Public shortly to encounter, at the Peril of their Existence, the Dangers of an Element as fickle as it is unknown.
>
> M. Rozier was to have been married immediately on his Arrival in England, to a Miss Dyer, a beautiful young Lady of great Fortune in Yorkshire.[5]

The grisly level of detail would not be out of place in a modern crash narrative, especially the richly described scene of corporeal trauma in the debris field: today's accounts might (or might not) be a touch less gory, but would describe the same thing in basically the same way. The writer's chiding tone is interesting: overstepping the bounds of safety, the adventurers suffered the consequence of hubris, their "too-soaring Ideas." It's a brilliantly cruel rhetorical flourish: if only their physical contraption could have *soared* as high as their fancies. Still today, mediascapes sometimes construct crash narratives as karmic retribution for those who have undertaken flights that the media eye/I finds somehow unworthy. Today's journalists, though, probably wouldn't editorialize quite as flagrantly as the *Derby Post* correspondent who sneers, "the Balloon caught Fire, and of course fell to the Ground." *Of course.*

The eighteenth-century account resembles modern crash stories in its heavy irony—the aeronauts "made a fine Appearance in the Ascent, bidding fair for a prosperous Voyage to England, but . . . " Yes, there's always the *but*: that's when things start to get interesting. The correspondent's meeting with the victim is a classically poignant if-only-we-had-known: "I shook Hands with Rozier almost the last Person in his Life Time." *Accursed Machine! . . . at the Peril of their*

Existence . . . the Dangers of an Element as fickle as it is unknown. The dramatic Derby documentarian is not pulling any punches: WATCH OUT! Don't try this at home. Don't lust after fame.

The penultimate paragraph summarizes this whole tragic, frenzied scene in an arresting phrase: *melancholy Exits.* What a resonant expression, dripping with lugubrious pathos, which could equally well suit so many more recent stories in my investigations. The explosive 1783 Irish balloon crash, too, was described as a "melancholy accident," a phrase commonly used in newspapers of the day reporting especially ironic, unexpected, bizarre misfortunes. Perhaps it was a melancholy century; the advent of deadly aeronautical mishaps might well have accelerated this sensibility.

For a less melancholy coda, I take a moment to remember the first *survivor* of an aviation accident. Iordache Cuparencu, a Romanian circus-master who became a pioneer of ballooning, landed safely after his 1806 flight over Warsaw burst into flames. Then again in 1808, also in Warsaw, strong winds buffeted and ruptured his balloon, which fell from the sky and ignited as it neared the ground; two onlookers helped him safely out of the basket.[6] Cuparencu stands at the front ranks of some crash victims who had better luck than others.

The fall of Icarus

Continuing back in time, well before Messrs de Rozier's and de Romain's aeronautical misadventures, we find a string of crash victims—a tradition, a lineage—predating not only airplanes but also balloons and pretty much any other type of aeromobility infrastructure. These folks just flew, whether or not (not!) they had any mechanical support system to abet their aspirations. Without a vehicle, the crashing object will be simply the "pilot" himself (always *him*: I think we can guess why). Piloting what? The man is both the pilot and the piloted.

Consider the melancholy exit of Icarus, a premonition *avant la lettre* of what would become a plane crash. His fall left in its wake both tragedy and, for others who might contemplate similar adventures, a pretty clear baseline of auto-aeronautical best (and worst) practices. Ambitious young men who fancy themselves indestructible, wearing bespoke feathered "wings" held together with wax, would do well not to fly too close to the sun. The aerodynamics will fail at some point—today's aviators call that ceiling "maximum certified altitude"—leading to an inevitable death plunge. Like some pilots who crash today, Icarus was dazzled by the appeal of what he thought he *could* do in flight, but inattentive to what he *couldn't* do.

The myth of Icarus has recirculated across the ages in such forms as Pieter Bruegel the Elder's Flemish Renaissance painting, and modern poems by W. H. Auden and William Carlos Williams. All warn of hubris and overweening ambition, cautioning against the obstinate adventurer who sublimates the considerable chance of danger, underestimating its likelihood and overestimating his own resilience. Fly straight, not high, they all warn. If and when the wings fail and the grandstander crashes into the sea, nobody is going to be very surprised—onlookers won't go out of their way to rescue him. Busy leading their own lives, they're unlikely to risk anything (not even the loss of a few minutes' work) to save a rash adventurer who thinks he can soar to the sun.

The spectators' response these writers and artists imagine is the diametric opposite of my own fanatically obsessive attention to plane crashes. I would *not* turn away from the disaster. If there was any way I could help, I would, and plowing my field (as a figure in Bruegel's painting is doing) would have to wait. But Auden's ethos arises from his cultural context. When he wrote "Musée des Beaux Arts" in 1938, anyone lucky enough to escape Europe's "labyrinth"—Daedalus and Icarus were fleeing imprisonment in King Minos's Cretan maze—would have done well to fly a true track, straight and steady, without indulging in superfluous aeronautical frivolity.

Crashes happen when pilots push the envelope. Some consider standard guidelines overly restrictive, valid for other (less adept, less ambitious) pilots but not themselves. Their particular talents, instincts, and training, and especially their *desire* to transcend timid rules and limits, somehow justify flying faster or higher, or in some other way contravening the (Daedalian) procedures and checklists carefully established to keep the flying object, whether plane or person, inside the safety zone. Hotshots seem oblivious to the tautology that exceeding safety boundaries means the flight is no longer safe.

Perhaps the myth of Icarus—albeit dubiously interpreted, I'd have to say—inspired so many other instances across the ages of failed one-man-no-vehicle "flights," reiterating the mythical boy's hapless plunge. "There is an art to flying, or rather, a knack," Douglas Adams wrote in *The Hitchhiker's Guide to the Galaxy*. "The knack lies in learning how to throw yourself at the ground and miss."[7] Even if the ancient legions of fanboy Icarian adventurers had somehow been able to hear Adams's twentieth-century advice, would they have had the self-awareness to implement its simple wisdom?

Icarus stands—or, more accurately, Icarus *falls*—at the beginning of a tradition of mythical flyers (and almost always crashers), a corps whose battalions include angels, the unique auto-aviational figures who *don't* crash. The ur-figures of smooth unmechanized flight, invulnerable to fate, physics, or folly, angels are the exception who prove the rule that artisanal wings, however cunningly crafted, are a bad bet.

Angels' wings flourished in visual representations from the Middle Ages on, though they appeared in written texts long before that: the Book of Isaiah describes winged seraphim (*six* wings apiece!) in heaven. Similar figures appear in Christian and Islamic sacred works. In Japanese Buddhism, *Tennin* ("heavenly people"), spiritual creatures whose feathery kimonos facilitate flight, resemble Western angels. Many ancient cultures have myths about flying deities. The gods of ancient Egypt, Minoa, and Mesopotamia were often portrayed with magnificent wings, and the Persian god Ahura Mazda, the highest Zoroastrian deity (literally), is depicted as extensively bewinged.

Like airplanes, angels fly up to the heavens. If there are few aeronautical congruities between angel wings and airplane wings, still, both embody a powerful sense of mysterious and compelling splendor. Spectacular, mystical, and exotic, angels' wings "serve as symbols of God's power and loving care for people," writes Whitney Hopler, citing Psalm 91:4—God "shall cover thee with his feathers, and under his wings shalt thou trust: his truth shall be thy shield and buckler." Wings show "how wonderfully God created angels, giving them the ability to travel from one dimension to another (which human beings may best understand as flying) and to do their work equally well in heaven and on Earth."[8]

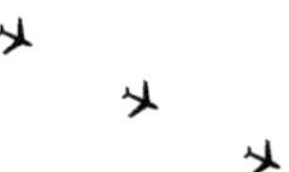

Angelic wings always work—in stark contrast to the strange and silly contraptions of humans who muddled around for centuries with half-baked ersatz-wings. People (both real and mythical) who crafted these devices inspired by angels, or by our flying feathered friends, hoped their inventions were indeed angel- and avian-adjacent, but unfortunately both cherubim and chickadees turn out to be poor analogues for human flight.

Bladud, featured in Geoffrey of Monmouth's twelfth-century *History of the Kings of Britain*, was imagined to have lived two millennia earlier. Famous for his

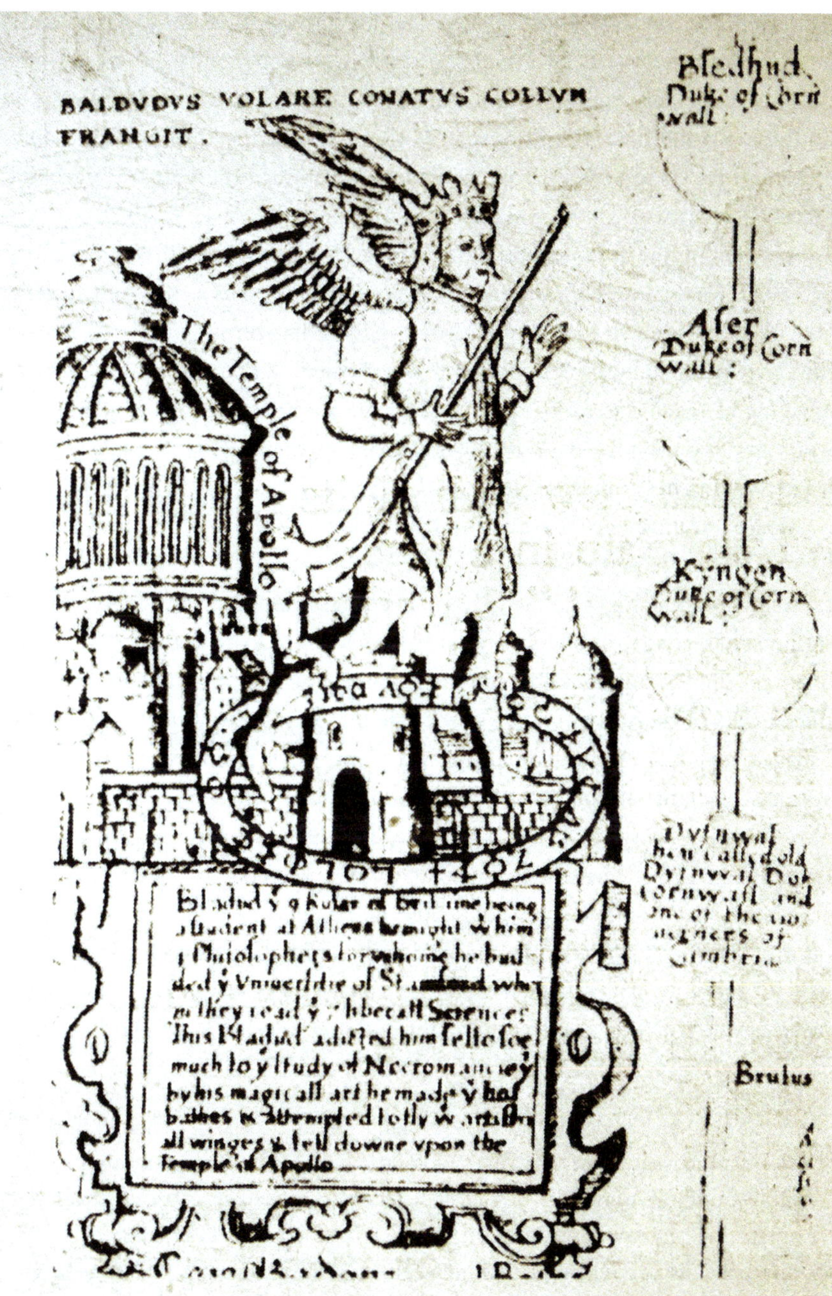

Figure 2.5 King Bladud tried to fly over London with artificial wings.

son, King Leir (Lear, to Shakespeare), and for his commitment to necromancy, he communicated with spirits of the dead, who apparently gathered a great distance away. Airplanes not yet having been invented, he constructed wings to fly there. Bladud died, Geoffrey writes, when he "attempted to fly to the upper region of the air" and "fell upon the Temple of Apollo where he was dashed to pieces."[9]

Another mythical would-be flying monarch was Persia's fifteenth-century-BCE Shah Kai Kawas, who wanted to rule over the heavens as he did over earth. He attached eagles to the corners of a wooden wing-frame, who tried to catch raw goat meat hanging out of reach above them. At first the birds flew up, grasping to reach this food, but eventually they got tired and plunged into the wilds of China. Badly bruised but not killed in the crash, the Shah returned home, vowing never to fly again.

Kibaga, an imaginary Ugandan warrior-chieftain, mounted into the air under his own power (or perhaps with the aid of a magical cloak) flying invisibly over his enemies, dropping rocks on them. His fatal crash came about when his adversaries simply shot their arrows blindly skyward; one happened to hit its mark.[10] Like many other ancient legends about human flight, this seems to be a cautionary tale about the dangers of mortals aspiring to penetrate the heavens. Also like many legends, Kibaga's story still resonates: the fact that airplanes now exist does not diminish the appeal of such mythomobility as Kibaga's. Sophia Nahli Allison's 2019 documentary film, *Dreaming Gave us Wings*, explores legends of flying Africans "passed down from generation to generation since slavery—a secret, suppressed gift of our ancestors" that inspired enslaved people to imagine new freedoms, including returning to Africa. These stories "became both a truth that enabled survival and an oral archive of resistance. Flight became a secret language for runaway slaves, and it continues to represent black mobility toward liberation."[11] In her children's book *The People Could Fly: American Black Folktales*, Virginia Hamilton imagines

> the story of enslaved Africans who remembered and reclaimed their ability to fly, escaping their imprisoned lives. Hamilton believed that "come fly away" and similar phrases were part of the coded language used by African slaves in organizing runaway attempts. In her story, one by one, they embrace their spiritual truth and return to their native form, weightless bodies ascending from the plantation field: "They say the people could fly. Say that long ago in Africa, some of the people knew magic. And they would walk up on the air like climbin up on a gate. And they flew like blackbirds over the fields. Black, shiny wings flappin against the blue up there."[12]

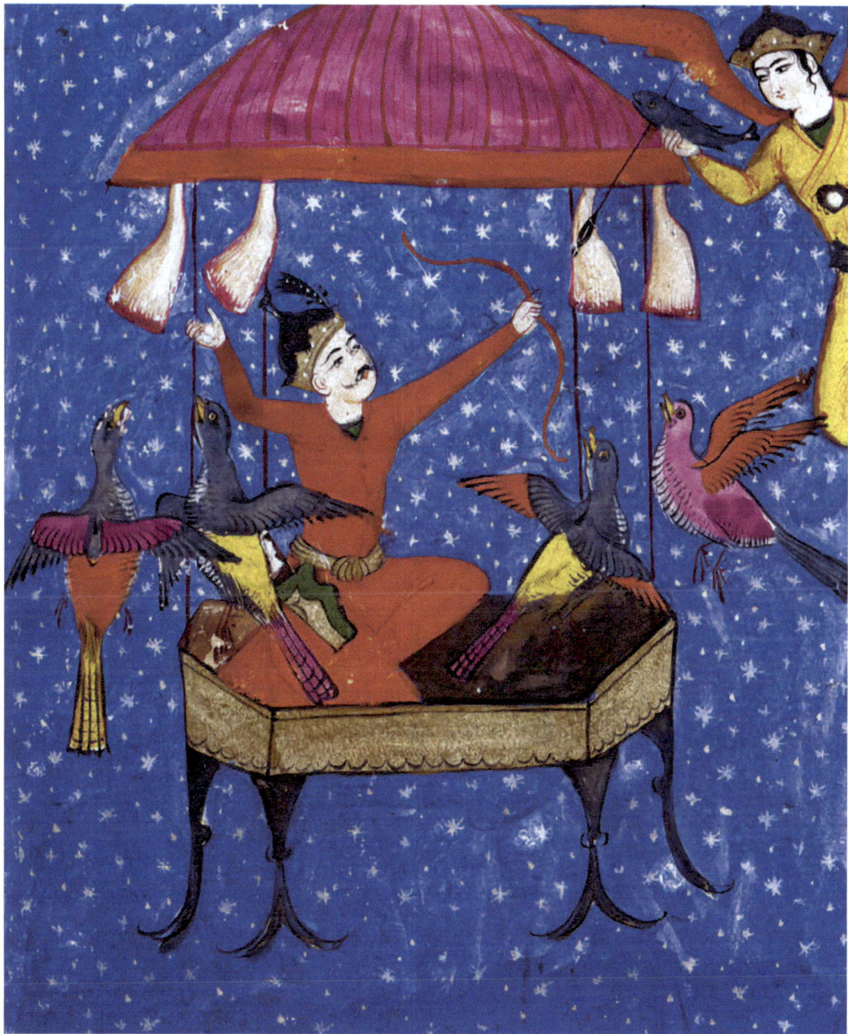

Figure 2.6 Shah Kai Kawas on his flying throne.

What initially reads like aerodynamic failure in ancient crashes may be reimagined as a creatively empowering narrative, waiting for its time to achieve an eventual cultural ascendency. If crash investigators had been around to write up a report on Kibaga's flight, they would have given low marks for aviation and situational awareness. A humanist on the team would award ten points out of ten for future metaphorical applicability, though.

Philippe d'Alcripe wrote sixteenth-century moral tales (a.k.a. tall tales) in *La Nouvelle Fabrique des excellents traits de vérité*. One depicts a French laborer who, after drinking too much curdled milk, decided (as you do) to have a bit of fun by crafting a flying apparatus.

> Without notifying his wife, who most likely would've scolded and slapped him into his senses, the worker cut a winnowing basket, used to separate corn kernels from husks, in half, fashioning them to his back. After failing to lift himself off the ground, the man got a brilliant idea: he needed to find a tail in order to look and act more like a bird. Being a laborer, the man had a nearby shovel, which he placed between his legs and secured with his belt. Climbing to the top of a nearby pear tree, he jumped off, soared through the air for a split second and then fell headfirst to the ground, where he broke his shoulder. The shoulder never healed properly, preventing him from making any more drunken, misguided attempts.[13]

The problem with bird-copycatting (copybirding?) is fallacious aeronautical adaptation of avian mobilities. People's recurring attempts to fly like birds are predicated upon a simple syllogism: I wish to fly, birds fly, I will make myself birdlike. Their anthem might be the Steve Miller Band's "Fly Like an Eagle," whose singer wants to fly like an eagle to the sea, let my spirit carry me.

Still today, pilots refer to their aircraft as "the bird flying us to Tampa today." Plane names have long appropriated bird names: Cessna Skylark, F-16 Fighting Falcon, Lockheed Blackbird, de Havilland Dove. The Přikryl-Blecha PB-5 Racek was a sleek 1930s Czech two-seater: "*racek*" means seagull. The earliest airplanes featured an especially large number of bird names: the Gloster Grebe (1932), the Fairey Flycatcher (1922), the Curtiss Oriole biplane (1919). It makes sense that the spirit of biomimicry—engineering designs based on biological life-forms—was ubiquitous at the dawn of aviation, a time when the tradition of flight was almost completely monopolized by birds, while airplanes were merely a scraggly flock on the horizon.

Are there such things as bird crashes? Why don't we see dead birds everywhere? Occasionally, as Capt. Sullenberger knows, they crash into airplanes. Alice Oswald's "Swan," about a dead bird whose spirit ascends from the detritus of her corpse, opens with a debris field as its central metaphor:

> A rotted swan
> is hurrying away from the plane-crash mess of her wings
>   one here
>   one there

getting panicky up out of her clothes and mid-splash
  looking down again at what a horrible plastic
mould of herself split-second
climbing out of her own cockpit[14]

Oswald's swan has not *had* a plane crash, but *is herself*, metaphorically, a plane crash. Such surreal, novel ways to regard crashes are what humanist air crash investigators add to the process: thinking outside of the (black) box. Even if it's literally imprecise, it may be more imaginatively resonant.

In an interview, Oswald elaborates upon her symbolism of flight: "The swan is a beautiful thing when it flies. But as it rots, that is a form of flight, too. It's kind of leaving its body and leaving the earth. I was just thinking about those two paradoxical forms of flight."[15] She construes death as a kind of metaphysical flight after the termination of a live bird's physical flight. In plane crashes, too, we might think of death as where the passengers *go*—what's going on—after working airplanes stop working. The crash doesn't have to be the end of the journey: it can be a place to make a connection onward to the next leg. Mobilities, even if fantastic or supernatural, continue on beyond immobility. Some people believe in an afterlife and some don't; I wonder if crash investigation reports might offer a postscript, for those ticketed onward to heaven (or hell—see Chapter 9), concerning the ultimate destination for all the souls on board.

We rarely see dead-bird debris fields because natural decomposition occurs quickly, in just a couple of days, and scavengers—rats, foxes, and carrion-eating birds—often consume birds' bodies even sooner. If we may be oblivious to bird crashes, especially in the absence of investigative reports, Matthew 10:29 asserts that Someone is indeed keeping tabs on avian aviation mishaps, averring that not a single sparrow shall fall to the ground without God's knowledge and consent.

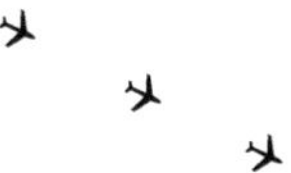

It wasn't just fictional characters who tried to fly before flying machines existed. Italian alchemist/engineer Giovanni Damiano de Falcucci was one of numerous medieval human beings who embraced the fashion of designing wearable aviation accessories and plunging directly to a painful, if not fatal, splat. In sixteenth-century Scotland, John Damian (as he was known there) gathered eagle feathers to manufacture a set of personal wings. The breed used for such a contraption is significant: it makes sense to collect feathers from strong, high-flying breeds (as Steve Miller suggests) if you hope to fly high yourself. Damian alit from the walls of a royal court, twenty meters high: "Frantically flapping the makeshift wings with as much energy as he could exert, Damian soared away from the side of Stirling Castle. Nevertheless, he only traveled as far as he could jump, and after that short trip, he was violently pulled down to the hard earth by the unsympathetic force of gravity." His first (and last) "flight" terminated in a trash heap, which at least broke his fall.[16]

Damian's crash narrative traveled the mediascape of his age in the form of William Dunbar's long mocking poem, "Ane Ballat of the Fenyeit Frier of Tungland, How He Fell in the Myre Fleand to Turkiland" ("A Ballad of The False Friar of Tongland, How He Fell in the Mire Flying to Turkey.") The best bit:

For feir uncunnandly he cawkit,
Quhill all his pennis war drownd and drawkit,
He maid a hundreth nolt all hawkit
Beneth him with a spout.[17]

which means,

Fearfully, uncunningly, he shat,
all his feathers were drenched and soaked,
he made a hundred cattle all streaked
beneath him with his discharge.

(Dunbar's imagery, beyond compare, certainly ranks among the Greatest Hits of Debris Fields, special recognition for bodily fluids.) There is no evidence the would-be aviator was headed for Turkey. Presumably the poet felt free to imagine (poetic license!) where the uncunning figure lying crumpled, mired, at the foot of the castle wall might have gone if he'd had a more reliable flight plan.

Other Italian plummeters included Giovanni Battista Danti and Paolo Guidotti. Danti was a contemporary of Leonardo da Vinci, who famously designed his own flying machines—"ornithopters," which used flapping wings (again, biomimicry) to generate lift and propulsion. Leonardo's wings were never actually constructed: give him credit for combining brilliantly inventive imagination with good common sense, knowing his limitations. Danti, on the other hand, "glued feathers to his arms and moved them rapidly up and down, hoping the feathers had some physical property that aided the mechanics of flight. Unfortunately, trial flights by Lake Trasimeno ended up in violent crashes on the roof of Saint Mary's Church."[18] A century later, Guidotti made wings out of whalebone covered in feathers, climbed to a high point in Lucca, and "flew" 350 meters before falling through a roof, breaking his leg.

Eighteenth-century Italian architect Francesco Milizia describes other intrepid flappers:

> Oliver of Malmesbury, an English Benedictine, and good mechanic, in 1060, Bacville, a Jesuit of Padua, a Theatine of Paris, and a number of others, have all been thus desirous of soaring into the regions of air, and have all been equally successful. This, however, cannot be properly termed flying, but only an easier and slower method of falling.[19]

"Bacville"—the Marquis de Bacqueville—tried to fly across the River Seine in 1742. "With large wings resembling paddles attached to both his hands and feet, the Marquis jumped from a terrace on his mansion and proceeded to float toward the gardens. For a moment the Marquis appeared to have control, but after a short while he began to waver, and he eventually fell, slamming onto the deck of a barge and breaking his leg."[20] The Eastern Airlines slogan, "The Wings of Man," would have been *les mots justes* for Bacqueville, Danti, Guidotti, et al. Or, alternatively, Air France 447 pilot David Robert's "Fuck."

João Torto jumped from a Portuguese cathedral tower in 1540 with cloth-covered wings attached to his arms and an eagle-shaped helmet; he fell a short distance to the roof of a nearby chapel, but because his helmet had slipped over his face, obscuring his view, he kept falling to the ground, fatally wounded.[21] You get the point: there were lots of crashes before plane crashes. Some of the biomimicry was inspired by Giovanni Alfonso Borelli's *De Motu Animalum* ("Movement of Animals"), which included a description—erroneous, unfortunately—of the mechanics of bird flight.

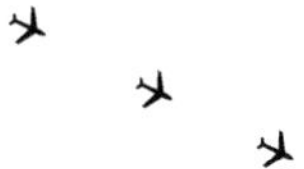

I recall plummeters of yore when I watch BASE jumping today: the recreational sport features people jumping from fixed objects using a parachute (bravo!) to coast safely to the ground. The acronym BASE describes where they dive from—buildings, antennae (i.e., radio masts), spans (bridges), and earth (cliffs). A subspeciality, Wingsuit BASE jumping, is more evocative of those dim daredevils from days gone by. A "wingsuit" (exactly what it sounds like: think flying squirrels) enables some degree of aeronautical control over lift and drag, so jumpers can glide a bit, and modify their speed and fall rates. While BASE jumpers still sometimes plummet to their deaths, their fatality rate is lower than that of their ancient predecessors. An online memorial, BASE Fatality List, pays tribute to 431

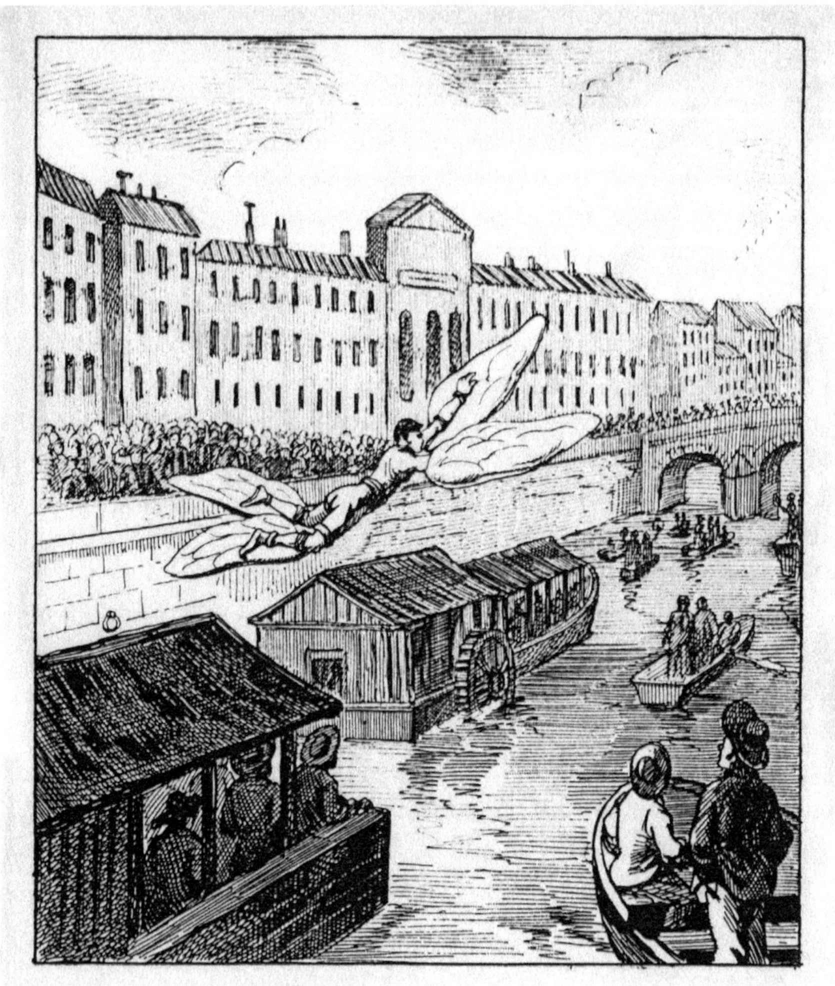

Figure 2.7 The Marquis de Bacqueville tries to cross the Seine the hard way.

jumpers who died between 1981 and 2000, from such causes as drowning, "object strike," "bridle entanglement," and most commonly, "impact in terminal freefall."[22]

Shipwrecks etc.

Can shipwrecks be read as early avatars of plane crashes? We can agree to disagree, but I'm going to say yes. Individual airplanes are often named, and these names commonly honor nautical predecessors in the traditions of mobility, the seagoing vessels that traversed the world before airplanes had been invented. Pan Am 103, which crashed in 1988 at Lockerbie, was named Clipper Maid of the Seas. Painted in demure blue script on the plane's nose just beneath the flight deck windows, that phrase appears prominently in photographs of the wreck (minus the word "Clipper," which was on a piece that broke off from the fuselage), one of the most striking and commonly reprinted images from the Scottish debris field. Other Pan Am 747s were named Clipper Ocean Spray, Clipper Crest of the Wave, Clipper Sovereign of the Seas; the Clipper Mayflower flew the airline's first transatlantic route. Early Pan Am Clippers, Flying Boats, landed on their fuselages in harbors because they were too large for airfields.[23] Such names, alluding to the nineteenth-century multi-mast sailing schooners designed for speed, connect airplanes to ships semiotically, thus at least loosely linking plane crashes and shipwrecks.

Ancient myths described flying ships, which Clive Hart calls "early manifestations of UFOs." Their locomotion was enabled, according to legend, because they were lighter than air. A ninth-century Lyons bishop described a place called Magonia where ships sail into the clouds and crews would somehow

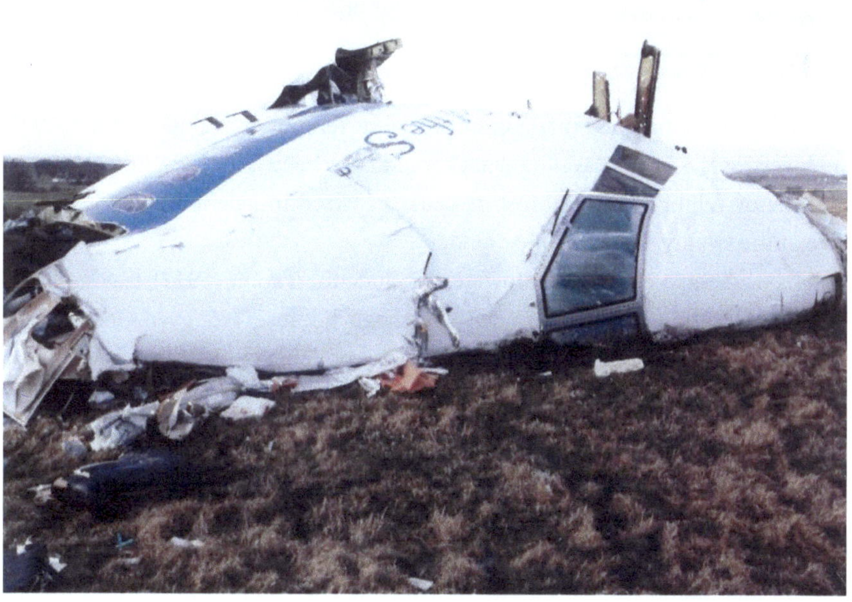

Figure 2.8 The 747's ruptured nose, a focal point in Pan Am 103's debris field.

pillage villagers' crops. In 1755, Father Joseph Galien proposed that a flying ship—ten times as heavy as Noah's Ark and larger than the city of Avignon—could navigate the skies, leveraging the difference in densities between the layers of air. Nicole Oresme's fourteenth-century work *Le livre du ciel et du monde* ("The Book of Heaven and Earth") proposed that a ship could float on the calm upper air: "A boat would remain up there as naturally as a boat floating at rest in the water. If the receptacle were perpetual, it would remain there eternally."[24] So yes, let us entertain the premise that a ship is a plane and a plane is a ship.

The term "aircraft" has nautical roots: the word "craft," describing a vessel, was originally applied to boats and other nautical conveyances. "Aircraft" in the mid-nineteenth century denoted hot-air balloons and also "airships" (dirigibles), another nautical-to-aeronautical word-link. "Aircraft" became primarily referential to airplanes rather than balloons around 1910.[25] For airplanes, as for ships, forward and aft denote front and rear; aviators sometimes refer to a plane's port or starboard sides. Airplanes, like ships, comprise a fleet. The casing surrounding plane engines is called a nacelle, a word that originally meant a small boat.

Aero*nautics* is a significant linguistic connection between ships and planes: seafaring, but in the sky. And "navigate" works for both: to steer or control a vessel's course. Originally the vessels were ships, *nāvis* in Latin, but later air vessels, too, navigated. Some airplanes begin and end their voyages in the water like ships—seaplanes, floatplanes and flying boats exemplify overlaps between seacraft and aircraft. Flying hovercrafts, too—neither fish nor fowl—are amphibious vehicles that cruise in water and also fly, though just a few feet up. There has been only one major commercial hovercraft crash: on March 4, 1972, a Hovertravel SR.N6, traveling what should have been a nine-minute ride from the Isle of Wight to the Hampshire coast, capsized in gale force winds, killing five of the twenty-seven people on board.[26]

History's most notorious shipwrecks include the *Titanic* (1912), leaving 1,517 dead due to an insufficient number of lifeboats because "Not even God himself could sink this ship"; the *Sultana* (1865), after a boiler exploded while it sailed the Mississippi River, killing 1,168 Union prisoners being repatriated from Confederate prisons just after the Civil War; HMS *Victory* (1744) sank in a storm in the English Channel, leaving 1,150 sailors dead; *Mary Rose* (1545), Henry VIII's favorite warship, left 500 dead when it sank near the Isle of Wight, possibly because of faulty design. These incidents manifest all the basic contexts and tragic ironies that attend plane crashes; centuries later, explorers still return to watery debris fields to observe and salvage the perpetually fascinating wreckage.

Casting our craft a little further, might we consider volcanic explosions, earthquakes, tsunamis and the like as being proleptic iterations of plane crashes? These are natural, as opposed to mechanical, disasters, yet many aspects of these events resemble the sounds, images, and feelings accompanying plane crashes—power, terror, devastation, shock and bewilderment; debris left in their haunting aftermaths. An eruption's terrifying flames, the overwhelming breaking apart of everything in an earthquake, are not far-fetched comparisons with the chaos that marks aviation disasters. Orville Wright's 1908 plane crash "struck the ground with a thud like a small earthquake."[27] Juliane Koepcke, who survived a 1971 plane crash, describes the sensation as her plane plummeted down: "The physical laws have been suspended. It's like an earthquake."[28] At least figuratively—good enough for humanist investigators!—these data affirm that plane crashes are earthquakes. Hurricanes, typhoons, cyclones: the extreme physical forces of destruction, whipped up seemingly out of nowhere, resemble plane crashes, and both plane crashes and natural disasters *do* come from somewhere—they have causes even though they seem random. Plane crashes often incorporate a vector of unfortunate coincidences, a "perfect storm": that metaphor suggests a parallel between plane crashes and weather-related disasters.

An asteroid hit! A large object plummets out of the sky, leaving a crater that could be roughly the size of a plane-crash debris field, though it could also be over 100 kilometers in diameter. If the physics of an asteroid impact somewhat resemble those of a plane crash, they are immensely more destructive (having fallen to Earth from *much* higher in space). The 2013 Chelyabinsk meteor was estimated to be about twenty meters in diameter, comparable to an airplane, but its 500-kiloton explosion was thirty times more powerful than the atomic bomb dropped on Hiroshima. The impact caused 1,200 injuries, but no reported fatalities.[29]

Asteroids, tsunamis, volcanoes, et al. anticipate plane crashes: they give a point of reference concerning unexpected and incomprehensible devastation. Avalanches, like plane crashes, involve the physics of gravity. If the plane's debris field may vanish in flames or water, an avalanche's vanishes in snow: the opposite of fire, but still deadly.

Industrial accidents? Mining collapses? The Triangle Shirtwaist Factory fire? Boston's Great Molasses Flood of 1919, when a storage tank exploded and two million gallons of syrup coursed through the streets, leaving twenty-one dead and 150 injured? Were those plane crashes?

Before the Wright brothers made airplanes, they made bicycles. Is a bicycle crash, then, a logical precursor to a plane crash? Today, about 1,000 die annually in US bicycle crashes (mostly involving car collisions).[30] In the nineteenth century, a large, unwieldy front wheel precipitated frequent crashes of penny farthing bicycles. Figure 2.9 depicts the *YOU . . . are there* moment of a bicycle crash—the scene crash spectators crave despite themselves (ourselves), whether it involves a train, an airplane, a dirigible, or any other agent of mobility gone awry; the bottom inset indicates a respectable debris field. At the top, a strip of similar incidents reminds viewers that a bicycle crash is not a one-off mishap: like plane crashes, balloon crashes, shipwrecks, and "winged" human splats, they happen again and again, which means that they register as a general phenomenon, both mechanically and culturally. That little old man leaning precariously on his cane toddling along in the last bicycle-crash doodle—not even riding a bicycle, though about to suffer a bicycle crash nonetheless!—recalls ground fatality Douglas Wielinski, minding his own business one evening when Colgan flight 3407 crashed into his bedroom.

When plane crashes started happening, cultural experiences of earlier cognate disasters must have inflected people's understanding of these tragedies. Archetypes of historical disasters and destruction reiterate each other, molding our behavior in terms of how we process them. Communities mourn, anger is processed, blame apportioned, memorials are built. Changes are made to lessen the likelihood of similar future catastrophes. After the Great Molasses Flood, investigators found that faulty riveting and other tank-design flaws were partly responsible, along with such procedural sloppiness as failing to fill tanks first with water to check for leaks.[31] There has never been another fatal molasses explosion.

The rest of this book will focus, as advertised, on plane crashes—tossing in an occasional helicopter or spaceship (again: *ship*!)—but I wanted to sketch out a wider context first, gathering together as many data points and debris fields as possible to supplement these investigations.

Like avalanches or meteor impacts, plane crashes become part of permanent cultural and historical records: lists are kept, comparisons are drawn. The television series *Breaking Bad* grimly parodies this tragedy-accounting. It annoys chemistry teacher Walter White when a plane crash sends his school community into what he considers an overly depressed funk. He is touchy about it because the midair collision that (literally) hit his community was indirectly his own fault, through a far-fetched chain of circumstances—a perfect storm—involving the overdose death of an air traffic controller's daughter amid turf wars sparked by White's side-hustle meth lab. He could have saved the woman when he found

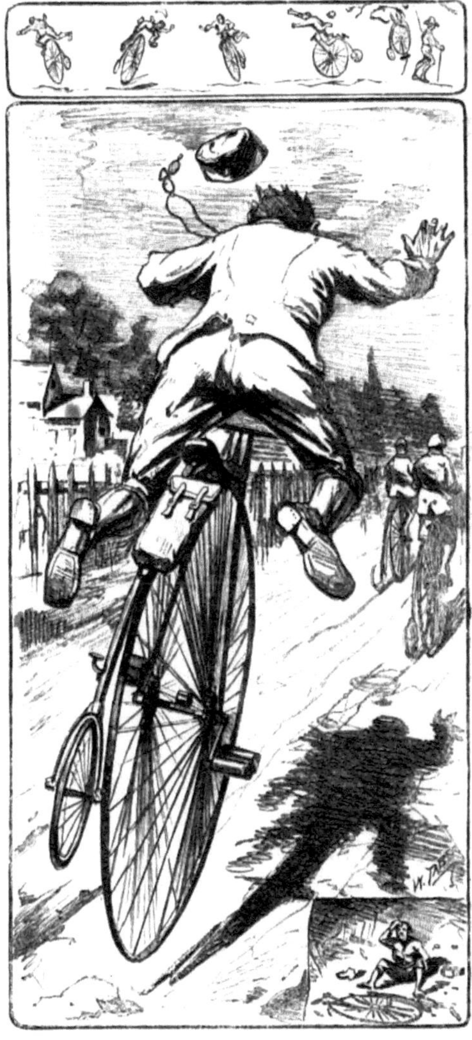

Figure 2.9 Unpaved roads and awkwardly large tires present crash hazards for nineteenth-century bicycle racers.

her suffocating in her own vomit, but he declined to aspirate her. When her father returned to work, still grief-stricken and poorly focused, two planes collided over Albuquerque because he failed to direct one out of the other's path. The crash resembles a 1986 midair crash near Los Angeles: ninety died when Aeromexico flight 498 hit a small private Piper Archer, and the air traffic controller's distraction was a contributing factor. (His name: Walter White!)

At a pep rally to help the community heal, Mr. White suggests students "look on the bright side." Trying to minimize the accident, he says: "What you're left with, casualty-wise, is just the 50th worst air disaster. Actually, *tied* for 50th. There are, in truth, 53 crashes throughout history that are just as bad or worse. Tenerife? Has anyone heard of Tenerife?" he scoffs.[32] (We will get to Tenerife, the deadliest plane crash ever . . . at this writing.) Again the question recurs: what makes one crash worse than another or, as Mr. White explains, *better* than another, or 53 others?

Diversion

Aircraft Accident Report NTSB/AAR-88/09

After every US plane crash, as well as crashes elsewhere involving US carriers or US-built planes, the National Transportation Safety Board dispatches a go-team, a group of specialists in operations (focusing on the accident flight's history and crew performance), structures (documenting airframe wreckage and the accident scene), powerplants (examining engines/propellers), systems (investigating hydraulic, electrical, pneumatic and flight control mechanisms), air traffic control, weather, human performance, and survival factors.[33] Other countries have their own similar agencies and processes. The UN's International Civil Aviation Organization coordinates and connects the world's crash investigation teams: the Nigerian Safety Investigation Bureau, the Center for Investigation of Accidents in Transport of the Republic of Serbia, Armenia's Airworthiness Department in the General Department of Civil Aviation, and scores more.

NTSB investigators compile crash reports that little resemble my own *CRASH!* report. When I began researching these seminal documents, I found them long and tedious, overloaded with minutia, largely impenetrable. But gradually they began to engage my interest and I became acclimated to their jargon, acronyms, and codes, their rhetorical structures, their ethos. I learned to sniff out the good parts, details and insights that emerged despite the stultifying texture of the prose and data, the regulations and manuals, meteorological and engineering documents, airport maps, black box recording transcripts. It wasn't the most compelling way to read about plane crashes, but I wanted to familiarize myself with this canon so I could be clear about what I wanted to improve for my own humanist accident investigative reports. I came to appreciate that the prose was intentionally languid and listless: it resisted the frenzied energy of all the plane-crash narratives I've compiled precisely because, finally, these reports don't really want to *be* plane-crash narratives: their function is averting crashes rather than embracing them, so it would be rhetorically inappropriate, countereffective, to indulge even the smallest whiff of titillation.

Having solved the riddle of the crash report, I adapted to its off-putting ennui and began to get enough into them (and to get enough out of them) that I could transmogrify the crux of these texts into my own livelier, wittier approach, salvaging and reconfiguring something of their focal point: plane and pilot seemed safe and ready for a good flight, but something unexpected happened.

Archived at ntsb.gov, an extensive database of Aircraft Incident Reports is searchable by date or specific aircraft. Arbitrarily, I decided to revisit the investigation of Continental flight 1713, which crashed on November 15, 1987, killing twenty-eight of eighty-two occupants. Departing in a snowstorm from Denver's Stapleton Airport en route to Boise's Gowen Field, the plane crashed almost immediately after takeoff. The document was completed ten months later, on September 27, 1988. Doused in the vernacular of administrative bureaucracy, Report No. NTSB/AAR-88/09 is listed on its technical report documentation page as Government Accession No. PB88-910411, Accident No. DCA88MA004, Work Unit No. 4772A.[34]

Weighing in at ninety-three pages, a typical length for an investigation of this sort of crash, the report presents four chapters broken down into thirty-five subsections, eighteen sub-subsections, and five sub-sub-subsections along with six appendices. Some of these headings are: Factual Information, History of the Flight, Injuries to Persons, Damage to Airplane, Personnel Information, The Captain, The First Officer, Flight Recorders, Fire, Crash/Fire/Rescue Activities, Engine Teardowns, Preflight Activities of the Crew, Continental DC-9 Training, Airport Snow Removal, Airplane Deicing and Subsequent Contamination, Airplane Maintenance and Certification, The First Officer's Actions During Rotation, Findings, Probable Causes … among many more. These headings themselves suggest a sketchy sense of what happened to flight 1713. Snow, fire. "Rotation" is the moment the airplane lifts off the runway, rotating around its lateral axis. "Rotation speed"—VR in pilot callout—is an enormously important data point (especially in this particular mishap), meticulously calculated based on the airplane's model and weight, the runway's altitude, wind conditions, temperature, and other criteria. VR comes just a few seconds after "decision speed," V1, when the plane is moving too fast to abort takeoff and so must proceed to rotation even if something has gone wrong: if there's a problem after V1, pilots say, we'll fix it in the air.

NTSB/AAR-88/09's executive summary outlines what happened on that snowy runway:

> On November 15, 1987, Continental Airlines, Inc., flight 1713, a McDonnell Douglas DC-9-14, N626TX, was operating as a regularly scheduled passenger-carrying flight between Denver, Colorado, and Boise, Idaho. The airplane was cleared to take off following a delay of approximately 27 minutes after deicing. The takeoff roll was uneventful, but following a rapid rotation, the airplane crashed off the right side of runway 35 left. Both pilots, 1 flight attendant, and 25 passengers sustained fatal injuries. Two flight attendants and 52 passengers survived.
>
> The National Transportation Safety Board determines that the probable cause of this accident was the captain's failure to have the airplane deiced a second time after a delay before takeoff that led to upper wing surface contamination and a loss of control during rapid takeoff rotation by the first officer. Contributing to the accident were the absence of regulatory or management controls governing operations by newly qualified flightcrew members and the confusion that existed between the flightcrew and air traffic controllers that led to the delay in departure.[35]

The ensuing pages recount, in gruelingly granular detail, every imaginable aspect of flight 1713. I quote a few extracts to convey a sense of style and method:

> The operator of a deicing truck that assisted in the deicing of flight 1713 stated that the trucks had been ordered to spray the tail surfaces of every airplane going through the deice pad. He characterized some accumulations of snow on airplanes as 1 inch, but he did not specifically remember the upper surface accumulation on flight 1713. He recalled an ice/slush buildup on the nose gear of the airplane, which he removed....
>
> At 1351:12 the crew of flight 1713 contacted clearance delivery for the second time with the radio call "taxi from the ice pad." The clearance delivery controller later stated that when he received this transmission he thought flight 1713 was still at its gate and was asking for clearance *to* the deicing pad. He did not notice that the captain had used the word "from" in his radio transmission....
>
> At 1414:31, flight 1713 was cleared for takeoff. The winds were reported to be from 360° at 14 knots with a runway visual range (RVR) of 2,000 feet. The captain was making the cockpit callouts and was conducting the duties of the nonflying pilot; the first officer was in charge of takeoff. At 1414:51, increasing engine sounds were recorded on the CVR. At 1415:06.7, the captain recorded that the power was set at 95 and 93 (N2 engine compressor revolutions per minute in percent). At 1415:17.1 he announced 100 knots. He called "V1" at 1415:28.5, "rotate" at 1415:30.9, and "positive rate (of climb)" at 1415:36.5. Less than a second later, the sounds of nosewheel rotation stopped. At 1415:39.5, the

sound of a compressor surge was heard, followed by an exclamation by a crewmember and three more engine compression surges. The sound of initial impact with the ground was recorded at 1415:43.8. . . .

A fuel-fed flash fire ignited somewhere in the left wing area shortly after the wing began to contact the ground during the impact sequence. A "fireball" associated with the flash fire was momentarily noticed inside the cabin by several passengers. After the wreckage came to rest, several small residual fires that caused minor damage to airframe components were quickly extinguished by the first fire department units to arrive on scene.[36]

Here's a compelling plot point: the report informs that the first officer was fired from a previous job at a small commuter airline, where training records described him as "weak on memory items on V1 cut." (Weak on V1: that's a smoking gun!) He lied on his Continental employment application, stating he left that job of his own accord. He failed a flight check in his previous job after "habitual difficulties in single-engine procedures and directional control," and he "made little progress in training because he repeated the same mistakes." He had "a chronic problem of stepping on the wrong rudder and becoming disoriented." His flight check instructor called him "tense and unable to cope with deviations from routine." As for the captain, the report faults him because he "should have realized that he was exposing the airplane to airfoil contamination [snow accumulating on the wing] for too long a period and should have returned to the pad for another deicing before takeoff." He also showed poor judgment allowing an inexperienced first officer to attempt a takeoff in difficult weather conditions.[37]

The report reproduces airport maps highlighting wind sensor locations, and a description of Stapleton's deicing procedure:

The deicing fluid mix tank holds 9,000 gallons and was heated to between 170° and 180° F, with 150° being the minimum acceptable temperature. The tank was refilled when the fluid level reached about 1/3 full. The mix ratio was capable of being computer controlled; however, on the day of the accident, the assistant supervisor of maintenance manually controlled the mix of the deice solution to achieve about a 20° spread between ambient air temperature and the freezing temperature of the mix.[38]

A relatively brief discussion (six out of ninety-three pages) of the rescue effort strikes me as underplaying the most interesting aspect, especially given the significant number of survivors. Within minutes, crash/fire/rescue (CFR) teams arrived at the crash site, which was virtually adjacent to the runway. Impact damage and debris delayed initial evacuation by ten minutes. Two and a half hours after the crash, rescuers extricated the last six passengers.

If the human-interest narrative is soggy, though, a data graphic grabbed my attention: an "injury-distribution diagram." The DC-9's seating chart is embellished with a visual key indicating the fate of every passenger in every seat: minor injury, serious injury, fatal (blunt trauma), and fatal (mechanical asphyxia). There were more deaths among passengers seated closer to the front, fewer among those farther back. Passengers included two babes in arms (the wonderfully baroque designation still used to denote an infant without a seat assignment): one, in seat 5C, died of blunt trauma, and the other, in seat 24E, had no injury—the only person in that category. The person holding that six-week-old baby girl had a minor injury, and the adult in 5C suffered serious injury. One baby survived, perfectly fine, one didn't: that's an example of the kind of information that's lurking, buried deeply, in these reports, that rises to the surface for me. I suppose I can understand why they didn't lead with that, but . . . I would: that's where my investigation would begin.

Near the report's end, a small detail struck me as the kind of thing a filmmaker might seize on in a touching close-up to capture the atmosphere of that difficult, dangerous rescue effort. "The triage tags used to indicate injury severity could not be used because of the cold weather. The strings used to attach the tags to injured people became entangled and frozen together, rendering the tags unusable. Consequently, only five or six injured people received triage tags. Also, the pens used to write on the tags malfunctioned due to the frozen ink."[39] That sticks in my mind, helping me to visualize the debris field in the throes of chaotic danger. It's just one tiny piece of the whole operation, but all the more comprehensible, for me, precisely because it *is* tiny.

Like the rescue effort, the debris field is discussed briefly and undramatically: scientifically, not humanistically. There are two grainy photographs, each featuring a large chunk of wreckage. The images, adequate but unimaginative ways of capturing the crash site's intense drama, provide little of the productively inspiring stimulation I have found at every debris field I investigate—a fascination that is by turns dramatic, traumatic, aesthetic, existential, meditative. If some pictures are worth a thousand words, these aren't. A detailed "Wreckage Diagram" identifies and orients the locations where the horizontal stabilizer motor came to rest, along with the overwing exit door, the left elevator balance weight, the empennage and tailcone, the fuselage, and a lone cabin window frame that detached from the fuselage. The flight manual was found sitting loose in the debris field: that must have been an eerie find for the investigators (but if it was, they don't mention it). Some areas of the debris field are identified as burned, fuel-soaked, or Skydrol-soaked (Skydrol is hydraulic fluid).

The report describes the crashscape, detailing the texture of physical impact and destruction:

> Three major ground scars were found at the accident site. The first ground scar began 8.244 feet down and 114 feet to the right of the runway 35L centerline. The 214-foot scar angled away from the runway approximately 20° and then turned slightly back toward the runway.... Left wing debris was found in a line between this area and the second ground scar, a crater 11 feet by 11 feet by 9 inches. Examination of the dirt in the crater revealed pieces of glass identified as the outer glass panel of the left cockpit "eyebrow" window. A third major ground scar contained green glass lens material. Other debris in the area of the third crater consisted of various airplane components, including pieces of cabin interior, overhead compartment fragments, and passenger luggage.

I'm not sure where the green glass came from—one of the plane's exterior lights?—though the report's intended readers would probably know.

The report is, finally, dull as dishwater, turgid; but among the numbing prose and dryly minute analysis, glimmers of drama and pathos occasionally break through. The report encompasses the raw material of a crash, which my book will expand and enrich with the brio of humanism. It's not that what they do is unimportant, but rather that what I do, which is related to but also different from what they do, is also important—and in some ways, more compelling. I focus on things they overlook, things that, I firmly believe, belong somewhere in these crash investigation archives. (I am *fine* if they want to stick all my findings in appendices.)

The NTSB is interested in what can be learned about precisely why this plane crashed into this spot at this moment. I think crashes are more fluid, more interactive, so my *CRASH!* report will generalize and theorize more widely. Loosely adapting T. S. Eliot's opening lines from *Four Quartets*: crash present and crash past are both perhaps present in crash future, and crash future contained in crash past.

3

Existential Aviation and Poetic Premonitions of Death

Here's a phrase that apparently the airlines simply made up: near miss. They say that if two planes almost collide it's a near miss. Bullshit, my friend. It's a near hit! A collision is a near miss. "Look, they nearly missed!" "Yes, but not quite."[1]

George Carlin

✈ But again, what's going on?

A crash would seem to be an ineluctable empirical reality—*here* is where the airplane began to lose altitude, *these* are the pilot's final words, *here* is the debris field, *there* is where the cowl door detached, puncturing a fuel pipe. The immediate moment of disaster bewilders, but as crash investigations proceed toward discovery, they transform the confusion into clarity.

But what if the cause is not ascertained? What if no scintilla of debris is found? Hervé Le Tellier's 2020 novel *The Anomaly* hypercharges the elusiveness of a definitive resolution as he revels in the existential uncertainty of a crash (but is it even a crash?) that happens (and also, perhaps, does not happen … or, conceivably, happens twice, the second one canceling out the first?) on a CDG-JFK Air France flight that lands normally as scheduled in March, and then, four months later, lands again … less normally … the same airplane, with the same people on board as in March (confirmed by DNA testing of "both" cohorts of passengers), the same ketchup stains in the same places on the Boeing 787's carpet.

A team of physicists, mathematicians, philosophers, spiritual leaders, military strategists, and Nobel Laureates convenes in an Air Force hangar to solve the intolerable mystery. Did the plane fly through a wormhole (as happens regularly in science fiction stories like *Dune* and *Star Trek*)? Did some advanced civilization devise an extravagant biocopy of the first plane? Or is the whole episode—and beyond that, perhaps, even life as we know it—an ornate digital simulation? ("Like in *The Matrix*?" the President asks. No, in that film, real people lived in a virtual world, a logician explains. "In our hypothesis it's the other way around: we're not real living beings; we believe we are humans when we're actually just programs.")

If this speculative fabulation explains little about actual crashes, it demonstrates with harrowing intensity how necessary it is to arrive at some solid degree of factual, observable certainty about them. That insight arises by negative exemplum as Le Tellier depicts a profoundly ambiguous, implausible version of an aviation tragedy, a surreal enigma which unsettles our rational intellect in a way that parallels the novel's viscerally terrifying scenes of turbulence over Nova Scotia. The atmospheric unsettlement stands in for the actual depiction of a crash: the flight's turbulent disruption signifies, and/or displaces, a disastrous aporia, an aporia of disaster. The plane

> has no air to support it, and it starts to plummet. Despite the soundproofing on the door to the cabin, [the pilots] are sure they hear the passengers scream. The plane spends ten interminable seconds in freefall before diving into the cumulonimbus in the worst possible place, to the southwest of the column, at an alarming slant, a thirty-degree angle adopted by the autopilot that has taken over from manual controls. The Boeing is instantly churned in spiraling currents of cloud, and just as instantly the cockpit lights up because it's dark as night, soot black, and there's a horrendous racket: hundreds of enormous hailstones pelt the windows, occasionally leaving impact marks on the reinforced glass. Those few seconds feel like an eternity, and then despite the tornado's gusts, the plane finds a warm, rising current and a semblance of support, producing that intense crushing trough-of-a-roller-coaster sensation.[2]

When the plane lands again in June (stepping in the same airstream twice, Heraclitus might say), Le Tellier provides no concrete language to understand what happened. Was it flying for four months? That seems inconceivable. Did it crash and resurrect in space? In time? In a virtual schema outside of conventional space and time? Le Tellier never characterizes the incident as a crash—it's called an "anomaly," or sometimes a divergence (as every person becomes two people, coded, e.g., "André March" and "André June"). Whatever happened, such surrealistic aviation is extremely undesirable. In the rigorously planned process of flight, the ideal is consistency, predictability. Anomalies are inconsistent;

divergences are unpredictable. So what the novel describes is the antithesis of rational, acceptable aviation. In the real world, crash investigations—methodical examinations of aviation tragedies—serve to tamp down any whiff of unruly existential uncertainty.

Certainly a crash *is* an anomaly. And what happens in *The Anomaly* is an anomaly. So through the logic of syllogism, is this novel a crash narrative? Not necessarily, but possibly? It's a gray area between crash and non-crash, raising the (existential!) prospect of non-binary ways of thinking about crashes. George Carlin, I think, would approve: his famous comic routine interrogates the linguistic accuracy of a miss/near-miss and hit/near-hit. Carlin's brain-twisting freeplay prompts us to consider any crash/non-crash not as a mutually exclusive opposition, but as a puzzle of some sort—and not really an aviational puzzle but a logical puzzle, wrapped up in a narrative coating.

It's something like the puzzle of Schrödinger's cat—let's call it Schrödinger's crash. Any flight (on which one is not actually traveling) may be considered, or imagined, as simultaneously crashed or not crashed, depending on some random event that may or may not occur. Eventually, we are almost always able to determine whether the flight arrived safely or crashed . . . but not always. Amelia Earhart? Malaysia flight 370? A small number of planes have disappeared with no trace. Probably they crashed. Possibly they landed, and the passengers and crew stayed put and formed a new society? (See my investigation of *Lord of the Flies* and other "robinsonades" in Chapter 8.) Flying Tiger flight 739, with 107 people aboard, vanished en route from Guam to the Philippines over the Mariana Trench in 1962: no distress calls, massive search effort, no sign of survivors. When an Indian Air Force Antonov An-32 disappeared with twenty-nine on board flying over the Bay of Bengal in 2016, India's largest-ever search and rescue effort turned up no trace. All these people are most likely dead, though it's possible to imagine a course of events in which they're not. Crash/not-crash?

After most of Le Tellier's novel equivocates about what happened aeronautically, the final paragraph resolves (somewhat) the narrative uncertainty, providing a bona fide crash in all its incontestably explosive reality. When a third iteration of this same Air France flight appears over the North Atlantic heading for New York, the US President decides the world can't handle any more existential chicanery; the consequences of the 243 March/June passenger and crew "doubles" have been extremely disconcerting. So he simply orders his Air Force to shoot it down. No French existential mystery here: that's a good, decisive, American crash! And then, in the postmodern narratological spirit that infuses *The Anomaly*, it seems that the plane crash somehow triggers the entire world to crash. Certainly the novel itself does, in a dithyramb, as the words, like the airplane, break into hapless fragments: aviationally/linguistically useless, no longer able to sustain the flight/the story.

> It's difficult to describe what happens, there's no word in the language to define accurately the slow vibration through the planet, the infinitesimal pulsing that is felt at the same time all over the world

Thus begins the final paragraph, which proceeds to crumble into its final, tragic literary evocation of debris—perhaps the best form-follows-function depiction of a plane crash I've encountered throughout my investigations:

f c ffe wi h its I y bra d g i tor Mi el' h d a d i th b l
on An' t gue No e c d a c ly sa h w ti e gr
ua ly sp d un l t re w. a u
re l, b r l y pe c pt
le w h i t e n
o i s e
d st
e

n
d[3]

✈ ✈ ✈

Like Hervé Le Tellier and George Carlin, Don DeLillo too explores the linguistic, narratological, and philosophical resonances of the crash/not-crash. In *White Noise*, as protagonist Jack Gladney waits at the airport to collect his daughter, passengers coming off another flight—which obviously arrived safely—describe what they were certain, in the moment, was an impending crash:

> The plane had lost all power in three engines, dropped from thirty-four thousand feet to twelve thousand feet. Something like four miles. When the steep glide began, people rose, fell, collided, swam in their seats. Then the serious screaming and moaning began. Almost immediately a voice from the flight deck was heard on the intercom: "We're falling out of the sky! We're going down! We're a silver

> gleaming death machine!" This outburst struck the passengers as an all but total breakdown of authority, competence and command presence and it brought on a round of fresh and desperate wailing.

Of course the passengers' terror spikes drastically when they hear the flight crew freaking out. This hysterical panic (*silver gleaming death machine?!*) is simply not something any pilot would ever conceivably express—they always err toward the opposite extreme. In my research, I have listened to many recordings of conversations between pilots in crisis and air traffic controllers. It sometimes seems ridiculous, inhuman, how calmly aviators (and controllers too) sustain their cool in the face of imminent catastrophe, keeping their heads when all about them are losing theirs. The discourse DeLillo renders is completely fictive, absurd. And even when real-life pilots do go off-script and give voice to their existential fears, it is only off-mic (that is, into the CVR, but not, as DeLillo's pilot ejaculates, into the public address system) and only in the flight's very last moment when it doesn't matter any longer because it has become ineluctably futile to preserve the hopeful pretense of control and survivability. Pilots say "FUCK!" instead of "We're falling out of the sky! We're going down! We're a silver gleaming death machine!" because the monosyllabic profanity is more efficient: they are willing in the final second before the crash, but not the final fifteen seconds—a time long enough that survival could still be snatched out of the jaws of disaster—to call out a word that is not on the emergency checklist, a non-regulation personal commentary.

In DeLillo's cabin, the terror continues:

> Objects were rolling out of the galley, the aisles were full of drinking glasses, utensils, coats and blankets. A stewardess pinned to the bulkhead by the sharp angle of descent was trying to find the relevant passage in a handbook titled "Manual of Disasters." Then there was a second male voice from the flight deck, this one remarkably calm and precise, making the passengers believe there was someone in charge after all, an element of hope.

But DeLillo's trademark existential tragicomedy hasn't yet run its course.

> "This is American two-one-three to the cockpit voice recorder. Now we know what it's like. It is worse than we'd ever imagined. They didn't prepare us for this at the death simulator in Denver. Our fear is pure, so totally stripped of distractions and pressures as to be a form of transcendental meditation. In less than three minutes we will touch down, so to speak. They will find our bodies in some smoking field, strewn about in the grisly attitude of death."

Dramatic irony—the deplaned passengers are telling this story—reminds us that this disaster will not actually happen. But the Sturm und Drang here is somehow better, I'd say—more real, more convincing, more definitive—than in any actual crash that I have investigated. The imagined crash site in *White Noise*, even though it will not manifest, is the Platonic ideal of a debris field: *bodies in some smoking field, strewn about in the grisly attitude of death.*

DeLillo's account of a near-miss (*near-hit!*) displays quibbling sophistic wordplay like Carlin's:

> Aboard the gliding craft, a stewardess crawled down the aisle, over bodies and debris, telling people in each row to remove their shoes, remove sharp objects from their pockets, assume a fetal position. At the other end of the plane, someone was wrestling with a floatation device. Certain elements in the crew had decided to pretend that it was not a crash but a crash landing that was seconds away. After all, the difference between the two is only one word. Didn't this suggest that the two forms of flight termination were more or less interchangeable? How much could one word matter? ... The basic difference between a crash and a crash landing seemed to be that you could sensibly prepare for a crash landing, which is exactly what they were trying to do. The news spread through the plane, the term was repeated in row after row. "Crash landing, crash landing." They saw how easy it was, by adding one word, to maintain a grip on the future, to extend it in consciousness if not in actual fact.

In the immortal words of crooner Vera Lynn, wishing makes it so: "the term 'crash landing' spread through the plane, with a pronounced emphasis on the second word," and then, suddenly,

> the engines restarted. Just like that. Power, stability, control. The passengers, prepared for impact, were slow to adjust to this new wave of information. New sounds, a different flight path, a sense of being encased in solid tubing and not some polyurethane wrap. The smoking sign went on [*sic*, 1985], an international hand with a cigarette. Stewardesses appeared with scented towelettes for cleaning blood and vomit. People slowly came out of their fetal positions, sat back limply. Four miles of prime-time terror. No one knew what to say. Being alive was a richness of sensation.... The first officer walked down the aisle, smiling and chatting in an empty pleasant corporate way. His face had the rosy and confident polish that is familiar in handlers of large passenger aircraft. They looked at him and wondered why they'd been afraid.[4]

(Really? I know why.)

✈ This tumult in the clouds

Just sixteen years after Orville Wright's transformative milestone—on December 17, 1903, he lay flat on his stomach for the Wright Flyer's twelve-second, 120-foot flight above the beach at Kitty Hawk, North Carolina—and eleven years after the first fatal plane crash (also piloted by Orville, who survived it, though his passenger didn't), W. B. Yeats published "An Irish Airman Foresees His Death."

If aviation was still fairly rickety in its early decades, Yeats's poem, by contrast, is eloquently sleek: deftly crafted, deeply resonant. It is, as far as I can determine, the very first poem about a plane crash, and also, in my opinion, the very best. The learning curve for pioneering pilots was slow and choppy, but poets took off and soared high from the start.

The titular Airman is Major Robert Gregory, though his name does not appear in the poem. Ireland's most famous pilot at the time, his mother was Yeats's patron and dear friend Lady Augusta Gregory. He crashed while flying with his squadron on the Italian front in early 1918. The day after Lady Gregory learned he died, she wrote to Yeats: "The long dreaded telegram has come—Robert has been killed in action. . . . It is very hard to bear. . . . If you feel like it some time, write something down that we may keep. You understood him better than many."[5]

Yeats *did* feel like it, and composed the poem Lady Gregory requested:

I know that I shall meet my fate
Somewhere among the clouds above;
Those that I fight I do not hate
Those that I guard I do not love;
My country is Kiltartan Cross,
My countrymen Kiltartan's poor,
No likely end could bring them loss
Or leave them happier than before.
Nor law, nor duty bade me fight,
Nor public man, nor cheering crowds,
A lonely impulse of delight
Drove to this tumult in the clouds;
I balanced all, brought all to mind,
The years to come seemed waste of breath,
A waste of breath the years behind
In balance with this life, this death.[6]

Yeats's poetic control connotes aeronautic control, his mastery of words and images evoking a pilot's mastery of flight dynamics. It's almost as if he is Major Gregory's co-pilot (though only figuratively: there would have been no room for a poet, or anyone else, aboard the Royal Flying Corps' single-seat biplane). Yeats provided his bereaved friend with a lyrical reprieve, an antidote, for the anguish of her son's death. The poem's smooth, orderly flow—and smooth order is a poet's métier—resists, and maybe even overwrites, the rough chaos of the crash itself. It's as if Yeats depicts another of those crash/not-crash scenarios. Major Gregory's plane did crash in reality, but doesn't in the poem (even though the poem is about the crash).

While Gregory's name doesn't appear here, he is identified in another elegiac poem by Yeats, "In Memory of Major Robert Gregory." He appears, again unnamed, in two other Yeats poems, "Shepherd and Goatherd" and "Reprisals." The latter also invokes crashes briefly at the opening—Gregory's own, along with those of aircraft he destroyed in battle:

> Some nineteen German planes, they say,
> You had brought down before you died.
> We called it a good death.[7]

Stories of wartime crashes often express this duality: it's bad if my plane crashes, but good if yours (the enemy's) does. Generally, the two outcomes are mutually exclusive, although two planes, one from each side, could crash into each other, destroying both at once, or shoot each other down simultaneously in a dogfight. But "your" plane crashing makes it less likely that "my" plane will. And even when "my" plane crashes, it is statistically "a good death" if, as Yeats explains, that one fatality was the cost for nineteen enemy fatalities; war is, in the final analysis, a numbers game. Still, irony lurks in that sentence, "We *called* it a good death." Yeats doesn't necessarily believe that Major Gregory's actually *was* a good death, even as he writes that it was, but he puts on a brave face, invoking the larger picture: the necessary fight against German aggression, the Airman's valiant sacrifice. We must call it a good death even if it leaves us bereft. The phrase leaves an ambivalent residue, as I think was intended. Consolations proffered after a crash are not necessarily authentic; it's hard to know just what to say.

This binarism recalls an attitude about crashes discussed in Chapter 1: a random plane that crashes due to some mechanical defect makes *my* next flight safer, because someone will discover and fix whatever flaws caused it. Feeling good, or lucky, that another plane—not mine—has crashed reflects, partly, a sense of assurance in the always-improving aviational design, safety, and maintenance practices; and also, partly, superstition: it may seem as if there can be only so many crashes in a given week or year—which is of course ridiculous—so if yours goes down, that makes mine (feel) more immune to the whims of fate.

A talented artist, Gregory joined the RFC (which later became the RAF, Royal Air Force) primarily because he loved flying. When George Bernard Shaw, a family friend, met him on the Western front in 1917, according to a letter Shaw sent Lady Gregory after Robert's death, the Airman said "the six months he had been there had been the happiest of his life." Gregory thrived in the face of danger, Shaw thought, believing that "war had intensified his life as nothing else could."[8] He had been awarded a Military Cross and named a chevalier in the French Légion d'Honneur for "conspicuous gallantry." He had "engaged in one-to-one combat in March 1917 with Manfred von Richthofen—the Red Baron, Germany's WWI ace—and actually succeeded in bringing his plane down, the only occasion this happened in von Richthofen's career before he was killed by ground fire in 1918."[9] ("Peanuts" fans will recall that Snoopy downed the Red Baron, in a crash narrative that is, like Yeats's, a numbers game: ten, twenty, thirty, forty, fifty or more—that bloody Red Baron rolled up the score.)

Major Gregory was thirty-six when his Sopwith Camel, one of the best-known WWI fighter aircraft (and Snoopy's preferred ride), crashed on the Italian front as he flew a test exercise. At the time, people thought he could have been the victim of an Italian pilot's "friendly fire," or his airplane might have experienced mechanical malfunction. A century later, Geoffrey O'Byrne White, Irish Aviation Authority director (and Lady Gregory's great-grandnephew), said he believed Gregory became incapacitated at high altitude—possibly he fainted—because of an influenza inoculation he received earlier that day.[10] This indeterminacy means the crash investigation is still in some sense open, so it is not superfluous to add my own findings to the report.

A passage in Yeats's "occult diary" offers tantalizing insight into Major Gregory's own thoughts about plane crashes. Written two years before the Airman's demise, the entry "confirms that [Yeats's] trope of Gregory foreseeing his death was not simply a matter of poetic license," writes James Pethica. "Robert had indeed dreamed of a plane crash, and discussed that dream with Yeats shortly before signing up." Yeats memorialized that conversation:

> Robert Gregory told me of a dream he had of seeing a falling aeroplane. It fell beyond some trees which were behind a wall. Said he had told his cousin that he

> had had such a dream. She said she had had the same. He made her describe it before he told his. It was the same, the same wall & trees. Might have been symbolic as certain curious events followed, *foreseen* [emphasis mine] by these people he said or a deluded dream of actual events & told in symbolic dreams. On the other hand he is now in London trying to enter flying corp.[11]

These dreams Yeats reports are proleptic—anticipating something that has not yet happened—as is the memorial poem itself. Yeats narrrates the still-airborne part of Major Gregory's final flight in the gripping first-person voice of a dramatic monologue—specifically, an interior monologue: alone in his plane, the conceit is that the pilot *thinks* this hypnotically eloquent narrative to himself, while Yeats serves as the amanuensis, the transcriber, who preserves it for posterity. Indeed, the poet is like a Cockpit Voice Recorder—or more precisely, a Cockpit *Thought* Recorder—in a flash-forwarding black box.

The poem leverages both foresight and hindsight, the latter making it an example of dramatic irony. As Yeats composed the elegy in 1919, of course the poet knew the 1918 flight would end tragically (as does the reader, from the title), but Major Gregory himself doesn't know that in the moment of the poem—or does he? Its almost-mystical force reflects a sense that the pilot may have had a presentiment of his looming death (which would make the irony ironic: yes, *it is* a good poem).

"Writing beyond the ending," a concept from feminist literary criticism, implies that a text doesn't necessarily end with the last word.[12] In "An Irish Airman," the final line sketches out a brief flash, off in the distance, of an imagined crash, an expected crash. It's a cliffhanger: when the poem concludes, "In balance with this life, this death," we wonder, "*What* death?" Provoking such wondering is the simplest way writers provoke reading beyond the ending. Such foreshadowing is an eerie narrative device that appears in several other crash texts (and real-life crashes) as well. It is not unheard of for a person to board an airplane with a feeling that it is destined to go down, perhaps because of weather or warfare, a challenging flightpath, a ramshackle aircraft, or just some hunch, a pit in the stomach. Still, unless Major Gregory's crash was the result of pilot-suicide (it wasn't), and even with his keen attunement to premonitions, he couldn't have been as dead sure of death as he seems: he couldn't have known with as much certainty as Yeats implies that he was about to crash right then and there. If a pilot noticed his fuel gauge sputtering near empty, or saw flames leaping from where an enemy fighter pilot's artillery (or, alas, friendly fire) pierced his gas tank, then the fact of his impending death might have been as definitive as the poem indicates. But warning signs like those do not appear in this lyric: no mechanical emergencies or combat dangers, no suicidal ideation or pilot error. Instead, the mood is subdued, transcendent, philosophically contemplative. And the specific philosophical discourse is, as I proleptically suggested earlier, existentialism: the perfect mode in which to contextualize the physical (as well as metaphysical) phenomenon of aviation tragedies.

Is it a paradox that the best plane-crash poem does not explicitly depict or contain a plane crash? Or is it somehow rational and functional? As keenly as I'm drawn to crashes, they are of course terrible and traumatic. Perhaps Yeats's crash-poem-sans-crash is so powerful, so memorable, precisely because of this paradox, because of what's not here. I note also that wartime plane crashes sometimes disappear: the time and resources for investigation aren't always available. There may be too many crashes in too many places to allow recovery of every wreck, analysis of every debris field (many of which, like Major Gregory's, are aquatic, thus all the more difficult to examine). Poet Howard Nemerov, who served as a US WWII pilot, depicts the evanescence of physical death and debris in warplane crashes. "The War in the Air" begins:

For a saving grace, we didn't see our dead,
Who rarely bothered coming home to die
But simply stayed away out there
In the clean war, the war in the air.

Seldom the ghosts come back bearing their tales
Of hitting the earth, the incompressible sea,
But stayed up there in the relative wind,
Shades fading in the mind.[13]

Major Gregory didn't bother coming home to die—he simply stayed away out there. The idea of a "clean war" is delusory: the trauma is just as potent whether or not we see the spot where crash victims hit the earth or sea. But there does seem to be something oddly, aesthetically, existentially "clean" about the mood in Yeats's crashless poem—quiet, calm, measured, neat—which Nemerov's perspective illuminates.

✈ Existential aviation: freedom/finitude

There is every reason why existentialism should be so well suited to aviation narratives, whether safe or tragic. Will I live or die, land or crash? Some people—more than you might imagine—experience such obsessive anguish every time they fly. Does the flight's outcome depend upon factors that can be predicted and controlled, or unforeseen and unlucky events? Such uncertainties are woven into the fabric of existentialism.

Freedom is a fundamental touchstone in existential thought, as it is in the minds of aviators as well. The freedom to go anywhere, to defy gravity, sparkles effusively at the beginning of another famous poem involving a military Airman, John Gillespie Magee, Jr.'s "High Flight":

> Oh! I have slipped the surly bonds of Earth
> And danced the skies on laughter-silvered wings;
> Sunward I've climbed, and joined the tumbling mirth
> of sun-split clouds,—and done a hundred things
> You have not dreamed of.[14]

Charles Lindbergh describes the exhilaration of being aloft, unfettered: "What freedom lies in flying! What Godlike power it gives to men!"[15] His wife and co-pilot, Anne Morrow Lindbergh, expresses similar sentiments: "Flying was a very tangible freedom. In those days, it was beauty, adventure, discovery—the epitome of breaking into new worlds."[16] Pilot-author Richard Bach writes, "An airplane stands for freedom, for joy, for the power to understand, and to demonstrate that understanding,"[17] in his book *Nothing by Chance*. Bach later wrote a better-known novella, an existential parable that also celebrates the freedom of flying (for birds), *Jonathan Livingston Seagull*. Any number of inspirational posters and memes confirm the sentiment that aviation, at its best, promises boundlessness, or at least what feels like an infinite range: "Live Fast, Fly High, Be Free." Geographically, atmospherically, intellectually, emotionally, flying—at least ideally—means transcending restrictions and limitations.

In existentialism, freedom tends to be a sort of white whale, more often sought than found: highly desired but rarely and imperfectly actualized. Freedom is in perpetual dialectic tension with constraint and immobility. Both philosophers and pilots construe the antithesis of freedom as limitation, finitude. In an airplane, the finitude of the fuel tanks is a constant challenge to the freedom of flight: what goes up must come down. For passengers, cramped imprisonment in a stuffy flying tube diminishes what might otherwise feel like unfettered liberty. And death—well, there's the rub. It is always a possibility, amid and despite the freedom of flight, every time anyone steps onto an airplane: always has been, always will be.

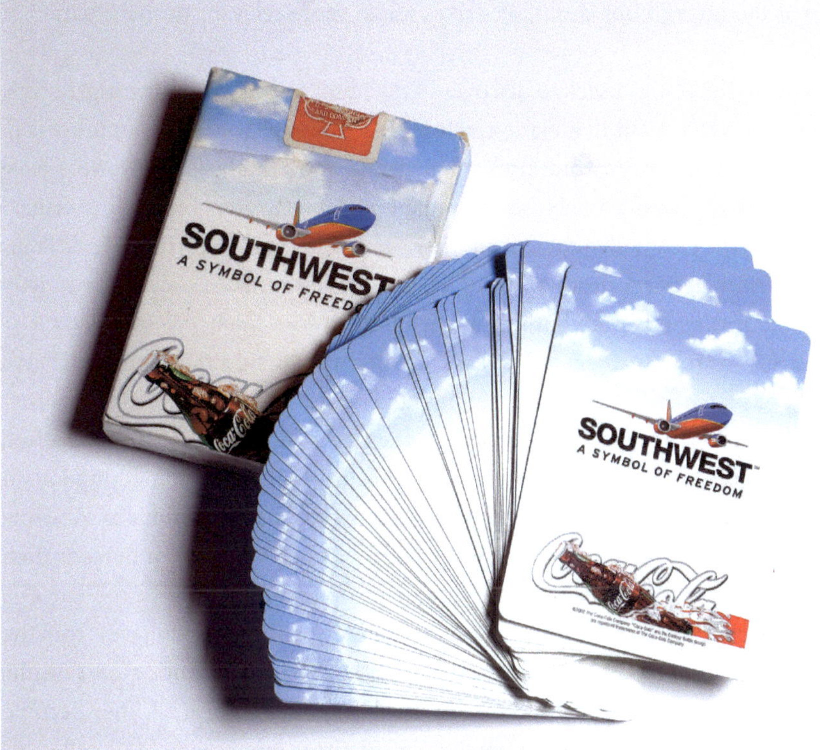

Figure 3.1 Flying makes you free.

Like a plane crash, existentialism is fundamentally morbid and depressing. As a paradigm, existentialism is more intuitive than rational, which seems contrary to the highly rational discourse of aviation. But if a crash represents precisely the failure of rationality, it makes sense that such an eventuality would precipitate a turn toward existentialism. Van Meter Ames calls existentialism "a philosophy of fear,"[18] making its applicability to an aviation disaster all the more salient. Some people, as they are going down, might say a Hail Mary, or the Jewish *Vidui*, a prayer recited in the face of approaching death: *Elohai v'Elohei avotai v'imotai* . . . . "Although I pray for life and health, I know that I am mortal. If my life must soon come to an end, let me die, I pray, at peace." My own plan (are you surprised I have one?) is to intone a passage by Kierkegaard as my life hangs in the balance, from *The Concept of Dread*: "Dread is an alien power, which lays hold of an individual, and yet one cannot fear oneself away. Dread then makes the individual impotent."[19] If this seems less apposite than "pray for us sinners now and at the hour of our death," it strikes me as more relevant to the situation at hand.

One of the things I seek to discover in my humanist air crash investigations is what a person's death in a plane crash means: how we (who survive) process it, how we remember someone else's tragic demise, how it affects our world. I have found myself mostly unable to formulate a definitive answer to this crucial question. The closest I've come is another Kierkegaard proverb, from *The Sickness Unto Death*: "The greatest hazard of all, losing one's self, can occur very quietly in the world, as if it were nothing at all. No other loss can occur so quietly; any other loss—an arm, a leg, five dollars, a wife, etc.—is sure to be noticed."[20] We think of plane-crash deaths happening noisily, not quietly. But paradoxically—and paradox is the pervasive mood of the debris field, as high becomes low, speed becomes stillness, whole becomes broken—there's also something muted and hushed about it. The screams inside the cabin would be inaudible to someone watching from the ground; the explosive impact, noisy for a few minutes, is then quiet for the rest of eternity. The vast majority of people who "experience" a plane crash are bystanders of some sort, far enough (in time and space) from the actual event that the loud disaster seems quiet, quietened. We notice these deaths so intensely that perhaps, paradoxically, we don't *notice* them at all. They become muted and impersonal lists, templates of victims, monuments and reflective parks, drily bureaucratic forensic reports. Even famous people who die in plane crashes, and certainly regular everyday folk, make a small quick blip in the mediascape and then putter out—briefly supplanted by the victims from the next crash, who soon follow them into quiet ephemerality, and on and on.

✈ Existential aviation: God

Speaking of prayer: Nietzsche, Kierkegaard, and Sartre grappled mightily with uncertainty about the presence of God, an ambivalence which resonates in the existentiality of plane crashes. Airplanes ascend to heaven, the realm that for ages was imagined as a place where God and angels meandered ubiquitously, but people don't—or didn't, before 1903. As aviation punctures a boundary between the human and spiritual spheres, that permeability provokes a consequent existential angst: will we find God up there? (And if so, would He be at 3,000 feet? 30,000?) Do angels cavort in cloud cover? Seraphim probably aren't kitted out with transponders and collision avoidance systems: could there be a midair airplane-angel crash? Does aeromobility invade a metaphysically sacred place where we have no business venturing, at least not until we have shuffled off our mortal coils? Is Charles Lindbergh's effusion about the ecstasy of flying—"What Godlike power it gives to men!"—sacrilegious? Are we encroaching on the empyrean? Is God specifically (and proleptically) forbidding us from flying up to look for Him—"Thou canst not see my face: for there shall no man see me, and live"—in Exodus 33:20?

Honest to God, Anglican Bishop John Robinson's 1963 bestseller, argued—with an existentialist tinge that traditional visual depictions of God were obsolete. A skyey God was too remote and detached from human problems here on earth, he wrote. A pithy newspaper headline described his theology: "Our Image of God Must Go." Another story about his book asked, "When did people stop thinking God lives on a cloud?"[21] I'd say it was around the time of Robinson's book: millions who began flying the friendly skies in the mid-twentieth century stopped imagining that God lived up above, I posit, simply because when they ascended themselves, they caught no glimpse of the Deity. What does it mean if

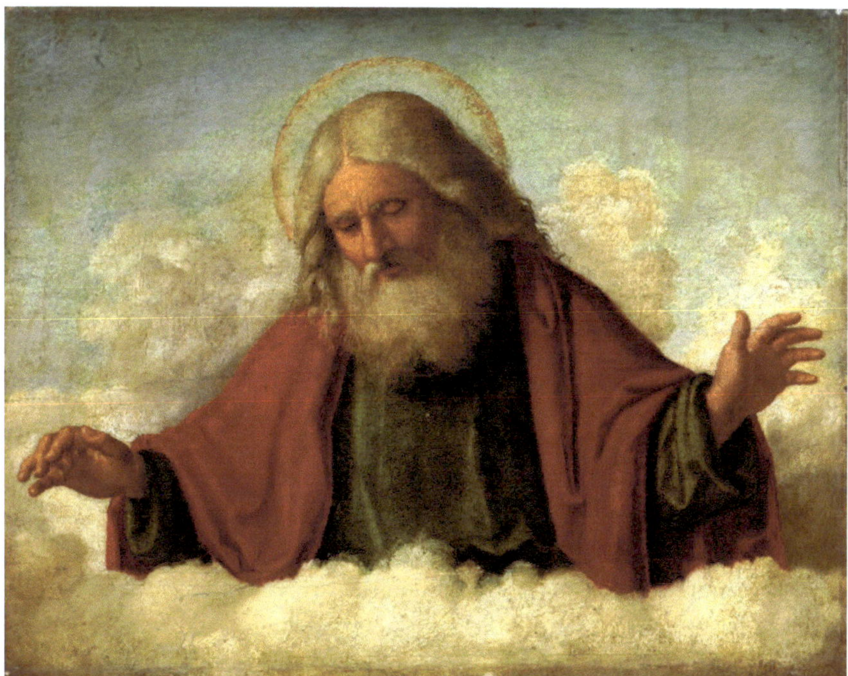

Figure 3.2 Giovanni Battista Cima da Conegliano, *God the Father* (*c*. 1510). If this image is accurate, God presents a flight hazard.

people pierce the heavens and discover there's nothing there (but clouds and air)? What if aviation's spiritual lesson is empirically proving that—as another existentialist of some renown said—God is dead?

Pilots' last words, sometimes profane and sometimes existential, are also, sometimes, devout: a final radio check-in (or sign-off) with the Almighty after air traffic control has proven ineffectual for salvation. In the 1996 crash of Saudi Arabian Airlines flight 763 and Kazakhstan Airlines flight 1907 near Delhi (killing all 349 on both planes, the world's deadliest midair collision), the Saudi Arabian cockpit voice recorder revealed that the pilots recited the Islamic prayer for those facing death: "Astaghfor Allah, Ashhau Unlaelaha Ella Allah" (I seek forgiveness from Allah, I witness no other deity but Allah).[22] The pilot's final words on Garuda Indonesia's 1997 crash into a mountain (following flight controllers' misdirections) was "Allah Akbar" (God is great).[23] When China Airlines flight 676 crashed in 1998 attempting to land in Taiwan in bad weather, the pilot's last words were "Oh my God! Oh my God!"[24]—which may or may not have been intended as a spiritual cry. In the same vein, "Christ!" was the final utterance from the flight deck before Colgan flight 3407 approaching Buffalo crashed into Douglas Wielinski's bedroom.[25] Gameel al-Batouti, the 1999 suicide-pilot of EgyptAir flight 990, repeated, eleven times, as he plunged his plane into the waters off Nantucket, "Tawakkalt ala Allah," (I rely on Allah).[26] The pilot's last words in the 2019 Houston crash of an Atlas Air cargo plane: "Lord, you have my soul."[27] Existentialism, though, undercuts such religious appeals—its key precept, Ames writes, "is dread of freedom, since man must make decisions ... without the help of God."[28] However devout these pilots sound as they call out to a supreme being, they must also realize in the moments before crashing that they are experiencing existentialist turbulence, without God's guidance.

Like any revolutionary innovation, aviation may be construed as a challenge against an omnipotent deity. For centuries, notwithstanding plummeters' fervent ambitions, human beings could not attain "Godly" altitudes; but then eventually, as aeronautical proficiencies increased, we could. Many religions posit an absolute separation between human and divine realms: excessive human accomplishment blasphemes God's power. If we were meant to fly, countless skeptics have opined, God would have given us wings. Adulation of aviation implies that "the faith in technological progress is stronger than the traditional belief that heaven is the abode of God or the gods," writes Christina Anders.[29] For devout believers, this antagonistic binary between God and Garuda, Jehovah and JetBlue, Allah and Alaska Airlines, creates anxious uncertainty that stokes the engines of existentialism.

The Tower of Babel exemplifies haughty human ambition that had to be squelched. God was angered when people aspired to build a structure tall enough to reach heaven, a parable easily applicable to the modern-day project of flight. God did not want humans cavorting around through His extraterrestrial stomping grounds. The consequent punishment is oddly prescient in its relevance to aviation: "let us go down, and there confound their language, that they may not understand one another's speech" (Genesis 11:7). God made all the Tower-builders speak different languages so they could no longer understand each other and never again join forces to plot such an assault on the troposphere.

The language of aviation today is English: the vast majority of pilots, especially on international routes, must learn what's known as "aviation English"—relatively simple, technical, precise, as free as possible of idiom—to communicate with each other and air traffic controllers. As in the time of Babel, people still need to be able to speak clearly with each other to achieve something transcendent, and God was right that linguistic confusion ("babbling") would make their enterprise impossible. Some pilots speak better English than others. Several crashes have been caused at least in part by miscommunication attributed to imperfect language skills. In the deadliest crash ever, the 1977 Tenerife runway collision of two 747s, misunderstandings between the control tower and KLM flight 4805's crew arose from confusing English diction. Their takeoff roll was premature—causing them to plow into Pan Am flight 1736 that was also on the runway—because they thought they were *cleared for takeoff* when ATC meant to instruct them merely to *stand by for clearance*. "The language pilots use can literally save lives," writes Thomas Devlin:

> The horrific accident in Tenerife spurred the aviation community into strictly defining airport terminology to be as clear and concise as possible.... Before 1977, pilot lingo was a largely unregulated mix of phrases from the military and NASA. While many of these base phrases remain, they could no longer be ambiguous or have double-meanings.[30]

But imperfect communication involving non-native English-speakers continues to cause crashes. The 1996 collision between Saudia flight 763 and Kazakhstan Airlines flight 1907 was blamed on "inadequate knowledge of English language of Kazak pilot, resulting in wrong interpretations of ATC instructions." Instructing the Kazak crew to fly at 15,000 feet, controllers warned of other traffic at 14,000 feet, but the flight crew misunderstood that as a directive that they themselves should fly at 14,000 feet.[31] As unlikely as it might seem, the Tower of Babel story inflects these crashes, and even in some sense explains these crashes. It doesn't rank as a causative factor in official accident investigation reports, but it does in mine.

✈ Existential aviation: the leap of faith

Aviation, like religion, requires a leap of faith, a concept Kierkegaard grappled with in *Fear and Trembling*. Early "leaps" by winged plummeters, insufficiently aviational, were also, one might say, insufficiently faithful to the doctrines of flight. The "faith" became more coherent, more dependable, as aviation progressed beyond birdsuits and began to integrate aeronautics. For early religious communities, too, faith became more sustainable as societies progressed beyond killing brothers, sacrificing sons, and worshiping idols, toward more functional, sophisticated theologies.

As faith in God waned amid the currents of existentialism, perhaps faith in aviation replaced that. The miraculous technologies, the devout conviction in the laws of physics, the fly-by-wire systems which today allow airplanes practically to fly themselves (as God was once believed to control everything—all-knowing, all-wired): do these suggest that belief in aviation, which uplifts humanity both literally and figuratively, may supplant the belief in God that was already foundering amid pervasive religious skepticism? It *is* possible to believe in both God and airplanes: Robert Florey's blockbuster *God is My Co-Pilot* ("The men who flew by faith and fury!"), based on Colonel Robert L. Scott Jr.'s memoir, pulls this off, as does Harold Adamson and Jimmie McHugh's patriotic WWII song "Comin' in on a Wing and a Prayer," though these are exceptions that prove the rule. Both are from the 1940s; I have not discovered more recent aviational devotion, or devotional aviation, of much note.

Are plane crashes, unleashing floods of existential doubt that course through debris fields, signs of God's irrelevance? People lament, after a crash: how could an all-powerful benevolent deity let such horrific things happen? Pilots (like clerics), dressed in immaculate vestments, are emblems of social rectitude and dignity with what they consider a sacred calling, protecting their flocks if danger threatens. Yet sometimes, despite all their devotional efforts and purity of character, people die, horribly, in large numbers. Where is God now, the existentialist wonders? Have our scientific feats angered the Almighty? Does rationalism fail to explain the mysterious ways in which God works?

Angst, despair and dread: the emotional and intellectual sensibilities of a plane crash are precisely the moods that infuse the writings of Heidegger, Kierkegaard, and Sartre. Existentialism is "a wilderness where each person is hemmed in by frustration and headed for death," as Ames characterizes it.[32] People on a plane that is about to crash are obviously *headed for death*, underlining the relevance of existentialism to their immediate crisis. And *wilderness* serves well to describe the site where the plane and its passengers, headed for death, will arrive: the debris field. Wilderness is the antithesis of civilization and socio-industrial order. Intact and aloft, an airplane represents the apex of civilization, so the site of its destruction is a metaphorical wilderness. Even more literally: airports, where planes are supposed to land, are almost always near cities, thus proximate to the heart of civilization. By contrast, debris fields, where planes end their journeys if they are having an existential crisis, are usually somewhere off in the actual wilderness: forests, prairies, mountain ranges, oceans. (Takeoffs and landings, though, the most dangerous phases of flights, account for a significant number of crashes that do occur in "civilized" spaces.)

Yeats's poem is a case study in existential aviation, a world turned upside down, governed by a sense of absurd but inevitable fate: the nonsense of an Airman fighting those he does not hate and protecting those he does not love, possibly (or possibly not) killed by friendly fire. It all seems illogical, if not unethical: why fly?

✈ "This life, this death": existential balance vs. existential chaos

A measured tone creates tension between form and content in "An Irish Airman": a plane-crash poem should be anxious and scary, but indications of tragedy here are surprisingly scarce. Except for the title's (and poem's) last word, this lyric is on an even keel, as meticulously navigated and stable as a safe flight would be. Its binaries and paradoxes, while provocative, do not seem fatal—although, in fact they will be, as the smooth, pleasant poem/flight transforms, at the very end (and beyond the ending), into an imminent crash. I have often wondered what it feels like for pilots in the sudden moment when they realize they will crash:

everything was on point, until it wasn't. This horrifying awareness may last for a few minutes, or may register for just seconds before the end. The abrupt finality of Yeats's elegy, with its last word's uncompromising thud, represents one way, a quick way, of aesthetically depicting that moment of resignation, understanding and even accepting what will happen. Yeats's last word isn't "fuck," as it is for many pilots, but maybe "death" is his genteel poetic approximation of Major Gregory's fleeting realization that his flight and his life are about to end.

Lady Gregory must have wondered what his final moments were like, as would any crash victim's relative. The answer is unknowable, but Yeats—uncannily, poetically—fills that blank space. He depicts the fighter pilot's last thoughts as quiet, delightful, lonely: such calm solitude would be especially agreeable during wartime. Yeats bestows this gift of imagined tranquility, his poetry having tempered (by poetically balancing aviational imbalance) the more likely reality of terror and shock. "An Irish Airman" illustrates one possibility (out of many) of what human creativity, creative humanity, can do with a plane crash: how we might remember and memorialize it—stylized, neutralized, condensed. Dependably patterned repetitions of sounds and rhythms are the literary techniques that help readers see, consciously or subliminally, that there is overarching order in the universe. If we enjoy poetry, we are grateful that poets detect and capture that macrocosmic orderly design in their poetry's design, in a way that enhances our sanity and pleasure in the world. When it becomes too painful to confront reality, writers and artists can create something else: a myth, a fantasy, a parable, a wish.

As Yeats presents the moment of calm before the storm, the normalcy before the tragedy, he depicts Major Gregory as perfectly balanced. The poem's words, its parts, present a delicate equipoise that evokes the aeronautical condition of equilibrium—especially vital for combat pilots, whose flights always vividly balance life and death. Pilots fly by the seats of their pants: as rational as they are, they are also intuitively attuned to the weather, the winds, the engines, the weight of their plane, and a hundred other inputs they are listening for, feeling, sensing, *balancing*, as they cruise through the sky. And pilots must sustain their own internal balance: vertigo, a spatial disorientation resulting from physical and neurological instability, is responsible for one in ten instances of pilot incapacitation.[33] In a poem, a body, or an airplane, the failure to sustain balance is existentially devastating.

Major Gregory's persona demonstrates his premonitions about his equilibrium via Yeats's poignantly understated awareness of "this tumult in the clouds," a keen way, mannerly and sober, of describing the tableau of what will—but has not quite yet—become an aviation catastrophe. (Tumult: agitation, disturbance; a proleptic intimation of more dire imbalance ahead.) It is an aestheticized gesture, a poetic grace note, mind over matter, with no trace of the fraught anxiety that most people—non-poets, non-pilots—would bring to a moment like this. Another striking phrase is the "lonely impulse of delight," a wonderfully incisive and compact depiction of flying, and strikingly ironic in a crash poem. Remember Mikita Brottman's assertion that there is something thrilling in a car crash; this thrill resonates in Major Gregory's impulse of delight just before he dies in his plane crash. Grimly counterintuitive, the delightful impulse becomes all the more fascinating, and illuminating. Words, words, words: short, regular, reassuring lines, rhythmically precise, interwoven with soothing rhymes, repetitions, and patterns, hold the title's promised tragedy (temporarily) at bay.

The proleptic sense of a crash is anticipatory, imagined—perhaps feared, or perhaps accepted, fatalistically, as something possible at any moment of flight. Antoine de Saint-Exupéry often embraced the fatalism of flying:

> I believe, and I am not the only one who does, that Aeropostale has lost a lot of its charm ever since we have had dependable engines and radios on board. We no longer experience that little pang of anguish that was so appealing: Will I make it? Won't I have a breakdown? Where am I? Those are the questions that we used to ask ourselves, before. Now, our engines are secured against any incident: there is no skill involved in finding our route because the direction finder displays it for us. Really, in these conditions, flying a plane has almost been reduced to a simple bureaucratic task. It's a life that is lacking in the unexpected. We like this one too, but the other one . . .[34]

Saint-Exupéry tempted fate by writing this. On July 31, 1944, did he experience "that little pang of anguish that was so appealing" as he flew his Lockheed P-38 on a reconnaissance mission for the Free French Air Force, monitoring German troop movements? Did he wonder, "Will I make it?" (He didn't make it.)

The mood of impending danger surfaces in numerous accounts of plane crashes, but none achieves the delicately ominous resonance of Yeats's: a quiet tragedy cloaked in a visionary apotheosis, even a kind of ecstasy, that typifies the best-case scenario of flight, despite the curse of peripeteia—the *reversal* that poets enjoy so greatly—which means it will conclude unhappily. This poem comprises a takeoff roll into a survey of aviation tragedies. It is an ode to a miraculous achievement that exemplifies enlightenment and omniscience, freedom and power . . . until it doesn't.

"An Irish Airman" is a compact document, sixteen lines of tightly rhymed tetrameter. Its balance is all the more obvious as the speaker makes a point of saying "I balanced all." The large ideas that animate this poem—life and death, hate vs. love, heroism vs. humility—are in balance with each other, as are its places (the European panorama of battle vs. the local terrain of Kiltartan, a small remote Galway crossroads) and spaces (firmament vs. land, clouds vs. crowds). The technique of chiasmus in lines 14–15 emphasizes this intricately patterned balance. The word literally means "crossing"; handbooks of poetic technique—frequently giving this very example as illustration—define chiasmus as a rhetorical figure in which grammatical constructions are mirrored or repeated in reverse order: "The years to come seemed waste of breath, / A waste of breath the years behind."

It is formally ironic that the poem is balanced so smoothly on its flightpath, while the upcoming events—withheld from the poem but resonating in the titular spoiler—embody the aeronautical imbalance fated to occur just beyond the ending. A keenly patterned poem is like a perfectly plotted flightpath: a smooth, predictable ride, where everything happens exactly as it should, no surprises, a testament to the deeply honed skills of the poet/pilot. The balance is emphasized via Yeats's conspicuous repetition: that is, the repeated elements are balanced against each other. Of the 105 words that comprise this poem, over half—fifty-five—appear more than once (and supplementing those, the sixteen rhymes, too, are repeated sounds). Several words are repeated as phrases: the chiasmus elements, "the years" and "waste of breath," along with "Those that I," "I do not." The word "balance," too, is balanced, repeated. The poetic balance ironically counterpoints what will happen as soon as the poem is over: an airplane in its death spiral is unbalanced, unstable, aeronautically agitated. It has no rhyme nor rhythm.

The poem's repeated words and phrases evoke the repetition of reading through an aviation checklist, and also of the radio call-and-response between pilot and base. An evocation of radio patter would not have been anachronistic when Major Gregory crashed. England's Marconi Company had invented radio transmitters and receivers for war planes in 1916, replacing wireless telegraph systems that sent ground-to-air and air-to-ground messages in Morse code. The balanced repetition of words between air and ground might be combat commands like "Fire," from commanders on the ground, which the pilot would confirm by repeating the word. A speaker might also repeat his words because they could be difficult to hear with the imperfect new technology: e.g., "I need five more minutes, I SAY AGAIN, five more minutes."[35] (Communication could travel only about ten miles, so wireless operators often had to work in ground stations behind enemy lines; many hundreds of them were killed in WWI.[36])

The poem's detached peace as Gregory flies above a continent that is violently self-destructing in war reflects a pointed political paradox. Ireland was ambivalent about participating in WWI. Irish nationalists resented how the war overshadowed their own social and political causes, while foregrounding England's. Lady Gregory publicly opposed conscripting Irish citizens for military duty "on the grounds that obliging Irishman to fight in a British war would 'destroy all hope of peace in Ireland and goodwill towards England in our life time.'" Her son, though, was less hostile to the British imperial cause.[37] Still, Ireland was an unlikely ally as it contended with its slow, difficult struggle for independence from the British Empire. Major Gregory considers his country to be Kiltartan, the village near his mother's estate, Coole Park (where Yeats frequently visited). But he was actually flying over Padua, not Ireland, when he crashed. Suppressing that actual setting, Yeats conspires to sustain the pilot's fantasy of focusing on his own little patch of Irish homeland.

But the scale of aviation, like the scale of this World War, is large: continental. It is delusory to imagine that the military establishment sponsored Major Gregory's aviation so he could fly contemplative sallies over Galway. No, the point of his flying was to kill Germans and destroy the enemy's world. The more one tries to tease out these thoughts about love and hate, and grapple with the question of how the poetically balanced, peaceful skies relate to the turmoil of battlefields and ruins that look so small and harmless far down beneath the Sopwith, the more one gets pulled into the contortions of existentialist confusion and distress. No one, not even Ireland's most accomplished pilot, can fly above the tumult of the Great War as if it were just a field of storm clouds on his flightpath. The ultimate failure of aviation to soar above human foibles—again, remember Icarus—reveals the inevitability of its existential streak: lift, thrust, drag, weight, angst.

✈ A Canadian Airman foresees his death

Like "An Irish Airman Foresees His Death," John Gillespie Magee Jr.'s "High Flight" is mostly about flying rather than crashing. Yeats's poem is indeed finally, if barely, a crash poem, as the airplane is destined to go down just beyond the end of the poem, the final word of which is "death." "High Flight" seems to have even less of death in it: in fact, none per se in the poem, though an ominous tumult lurks just offstage.

Oh! I have slipped the surly bonds of Earth
And danced the skies on laughter-silvered wings;
Sunward I've climbed, and joined the tumbling mirth
of sun-split clouds,—and done a hundred things
You have not dreamed of—wheeled and soared and swung
High in the sunlit silence. Hov'ring there,
I've chased the shouting wind along, and flung
My eager craft through footless halls of air. . . .

Up, up the long, delirious, burning blue
I've topped the wind-swept heights with easy grace
Where never lark nor ever eagle flew—
And, while with silent lifting mind I've trod
The high untrespassed sanctity of space,
Put out my hand, and touched the face of God.[38]

Magee, whose mother was English and father American, grew up mostly in China and the UK. At school in the US when WWII broke out, he joined the Royal Canadian Air Force because the US had not yet entered the war. I consider Magee a Canadian Airman rather than—as some others do—an American, or Anglo-American, pilot. The Canadians have embraced him devoutly as a national hero, and the feeling was reciprocated on his part: he was enormously grateful the RCAF allowed him to fly. (I am sure Yeats made the right decision calling Major Gregory "An Irish Airman" rather than "A British Airman"—despite Gregory's imperial vacillation, it's unquestionably what he would have wanted.)

Magee wrote "High Flight" just after flying a Spitfire Mk I up to 33,000 feet in August, 1941. This would not be an especially high flight today. Normal passenger cruising altitude ranges from about 30,000–39,000 feet; smaller private jets can cruise at 41,000–45,000 feet, and military jets often fly at 50,000 feet and higher. But in the mid-twentieth century, passenger jets flew at around 13,000 feet and fighter planes usually no higher than 20,000–25,000 feet.

Magee composed the poem on thin, airmail onion-skin paper when he returned to terra firma. "I am enclosing a verse I wrote the other day," he wrote to his parents in September. "It started at 30,000 feet, and was finished soon after I landed."[39]

Three months later, in December 1941, Magee died in a plane crash.

The conceit of Yeats's elegy was that Major Gregory didn't know his death was imminent, and yet . . . he sort of did: he had a hunch. And in Magee's case? I am inclined to make a similar inference here. There are numerous parallels between this poem and Yeats's, between Magee's situation and Gregory's. As air force pilots in a raging war, of course, both knew death could come at any moment, in so many different ways. It seems reasonable to see in "High Flight" something of the same presentiment Yeats ascribed to Gregory.

Both airmen were flying for countries that were not their own, and both crashes were "accidents": admittedly, a nebulous descriptor in military aviation. But if plane crashes are always ironic—they simply aren't supposed to happen—these were especially so: both men survived the most dangerous risks of wartime aviation, only to die in what seemed like less valiant circumstances. No enemy gunner shot them down, as Gregory had downed nineteen German planes. Many war fatalities are not precisely combat deaths; we chalk this up to the general danger of all the explosives and warplanes and tactical exercises that inundate the sites of hostilities.

Perhaps we elide these accidental deaths into the general body count of military actions. Perhaps we pretend they died in combat, and perhaps in a sense they actually did: anything soldiers do during wartime, even something as mundane as eating breakfast in a mess hall, could be considered at least indirectly part of the process of combat. But also, certainly, crashes like these rankle. Parents may resign themselves to the loss of their child in a battle defending the values of good against evil, but what about a training mishap, a seemingly unnecessary death?

Magee died when practicing combat maneuvers: his Spitfire VZ-H collided in midair with an Airspeed Oxford trainer, used to prepare pilots for military aviation, over Lincolnshire, UK, at low altitude. (The low altitude is just one more drop of irony for the author of "High Flight.") The Oxford pilot, Leading Aircraftman/Pilot-Under-Training Ernest Aubrey Griffin, was nineteen, as was Magee. An eyewitness account from a pilot flying alongside Magee, Sergeant Pilot Dwayne Linton, offers hauntingly resonant detail:

> We were stringing down in fours, line astern, from 20,000 feet. We were whip-cracking. I was flying in the number-four position, directly behind Magee, who was in the number-three position. It was difficult to hold in close since I was on the swing-out of each turn. We entered a hole in the cloudbase at about 2,000 feet and lined out just under the clouds at 1,500 feet doing 350 mph.

> It was hard to see any great distance due to the haze. I caught a glimpse of an Oxford twin-engine bomber-pilot trainer approaching just under the clouds to my right and directly at right angles in front of our section leader. I pushed my radio switch on and yelled to the leader to miss that airplane. He immediately pulled up into a steep climb with his number two right behind him. Number three was so close that there was no possibility of avoiding an air-to-air collision. Pilot Officer Magee crashed right into the middle of the bomber trainer's fuselage. There was a momentary explosion of fire, and flaming aircraft parts were everywhere. My evasive action was a screaming turn to the right and down. I pulled out into level flight at less than a hundred feet from the ground. I saw a stringing parachute near the vicinity of the crash. Magee had managed to get out of his aircraft but he was too low for his chute to open and he was killed instantly. The Oxford's crew was also killed.[40]

Another colleague in Magee's squadron, First Lieutenant R. I. A. Smith, recalled the scene in a letter to Magee's brother:

> Smith describes rushing to John's crash site along with the Squadron's Intelligence Officer, Hart Massey. They could not get close to the burning Spitfire wreckage as the heat and flames were cooking and exploding the 20-mm cannon and .303" machine gun rounds! Nearby they found a hole in the ground with the imprint of Magee's body at least a foot into the soft soil. He had struck the ground with his back. There was nothing that either one could do.[41]

Linton and Smith give a distinct sense of exactly what a crash looks to a pilot. Reading these evocative narratives feels almost like watching a film-reel version of the disaster. Compare Linton's and Smith's language to Yeats's: very different ways of describing the same thing.

After Magee's death, "High Flight" became instantly and enormously popular, at least partly because it seemed to somehow prophesize his crash—a moving achievement for a poem, if also a bit macabre. Sylvia Plath's late poetry has a similar force, as does that of many war poets like Wilfred Owen and Rupert Brooke who died shortly after their poems were written. Imagine the hair-raising resonance of a poem that begins, "If I should die, think only this of me ... "—written in 1914, and published in 1915, a month after Brooke's death. Such posthumous poetry—or, in the case of Plath and Magee, *nearly* posthumous—speaks to us from beyond the grave, as if these writers had the power to transcend death, which is compelling indeed. After a plane crash, it is common for victims' loved ones to wish or pretend or even believe that their loved ones are not eternally lost—that they can somehow still communicate. Magee's and Yeats's poems stoke this fantasy.

Magee crashed four days after Japan attacked Pearl Harbor. At a moment when people desperately needed to figure out something to say, something uplifting and impassioned, transcendent and sublime, "High Flight" perfectly fit the bill. In early 1942, the US Library of Congress included Magee's onion-skin manuscript in an exhibition called "Poems of Faith and Freedom." "High Flight" was displayed alongside two famous WWI poems, Brooke's "The Soldier" and John McCrae's "In Flanders Fields" (also published posthumously). Magee's, the only WWII poem in the exhibit, quickly became one of that war's best-known poems, thanks in part to the Library display.[42] Archibald MacLeish, Librarian of Congress, lauded Magee as the first WWII poet.[43]

Magee's parents wrote to the RCAF that when they received his poem, shortly before his death, "we felt then that it had a message for American youth but did not know how to get it before them. Now his death had emblazoned it across the entire country. We are thinking that this may have been a greater contribution than anything he may have done in the way of fighting."[44] His bereaved family captures the sense that the poem embodied some destiny—they say they recognized it even before their son's death—bolstering my contention that this poem, like "An Irish Airman," foresees a plane crash.

If Pilot Officer Magee was now with the angels, that would be a high flight indeed: it's as if his poem was preparing for this highest of flights, readers might have imagined in its posthumous circulation. In both this poem and the elegy for Major Gregory, readers could derive some comfort in the aftermath of tragedies if they feel, as the poems seem to suggest, that the pilots knew what was about to happen, or at least what might happen. They were prepared, and they met their violent deaths in a state of acceptance. The last thing they were doing, flying, was what both of them loved most, and that too mitigates our sadness. These poems, with their aviational exuberance and their vibrant sense of freedom and will, tamp down some of the darker emotion that crashes provoke, the feeling that it must have been so horribly scary at the end.

"High Flight" is a sonnet, in iambic pentameter—not all that different from Yeats's framework, sixteen lines of iambic tetrameter. Yeats had two more lines, two fewer syllables in each line, and a total of 105 words against Magee's 114. Sonnets often feature peripeteia, though it's usually within the poem, and here we need to read beyond the ending to get that enormous "but." Magee's speaker wheeled and soared and swung and chased and flung (*but* ... crashed not long after); he piloted a high flight (*but* ... life is full of ups and downs).

Magee's poem features moments that, especially in retrospect, suggest death: leaving earth, ascending through halls of air to a sanctified realm where one may touch the face of God. "The poet does not mention nor, strictly speaking, hint at the nearness of death," Charles Garton writes, "but with the antecedence of Yeats and with our own retrospective knowledge that the young Magee was so soon to lose his life, it does not seem an unwarrantable forcing to see death in the background."[45] Well versed in poetry, Magee was especially drawn to the WWI poets, so it seems certain that, as Garton suggests, he would have been familiar with how "An Irish Airman" subtly, implicitly, depicts Major Gregory's crash and death. Magee would know, from Yeats's precedent, that a poem can be about a plane crash even if a plane does not crash within the poem.

Thanatos, the death-drive, infuses this poem. Like Yeats's (intentional) elegy for Major Gregory, Magee's poem too serves as an elegy (albeit accidental, and/or prophetic) for himself. Is his "High Flight" *too* high? We remember the stories of Icarus and Babel: aspiring to rise too close to the heavens results in punishment, downfall.

Like Gregory, Magee had to know he could die every time he took off; did he foresee his own death in this poem, as strongly as Yeats believed Gregory foresaw his? He died from what amounts to friendly fire, as Gregory possibly did too. Both poems are situated in "the clouds above" (Yeats), "the sun-split clouds" (Magee). Both are first-person dramatic monologues, internal monologues, with an unabashed narratorial "I": that word appears seven times in "An Irish Airman Foresees His Death" and five times in "High Flight"; "my" appears twice in each poem (and Yeats adds an extra "me"). The interiorized self-reflexivity of this front-and-center "I" figure appears in both poems via the word "mind": Magee flew "with silent lifting mind," and Gregory "brought all to mind." Both poems encompass the pure sensory delight of flying, and also its mental/metaphysical/spiritual aspects.

Compare Magee's *tum*bling clouds with Yeats's *tum*ult in the sky. It's a small point of overlap, that *tum*, perhaps not an intentional echo of Yeats, but a coincidental indication that these two men's stories, and sensibilities, are eerily similar. Another incidental but provocative verbal parallel is Yeats's "balance" and Magee's "Hov'ring" (which is an aeronautic manifestation of balance).

Neither "An Irish Airman" nor "High Flight" leaves any explicit debris field, an observation that prompts us to realize that both these plane-crash poems not only lack crashes, but don't even really have planes in them. The aircraft are of course implied, and evanescently feathered in: there are "wings" and a "craft" in

Magee's poem, and an "Airman" and "clouds" in Yeats's; both poems depict experiences and perspectives that one could achieve only in an airplane. But mostly, literally, the planes are absent, which makes these crashes (also absent) even less distressing. The crashes do not happen within these poems but even if they did, they would leave no fragments of metal and wires strewn across the ground precisely because the airplanes are, let us say, ephemeral. (Poetic!)

In addition to softening the crash impacts, the absent airplanes make the poems seem all the more about pure flight—what the pilot sees and feels and imagines, untethered to the mechanics of aviation. In most flying (and crashing) poems, but not these, the airplane's physical presence mediates the interplay between the person and the animating energy of air/wind/clouds, lift/thrust/drag/weight. Especially if a poet foresees that a flight might end in a crash, it makes sense to remove the aeronautical equipment from the scene before the poem takes off.

✈ Redux

Both Airman poems have been widely recycled in other cultural forms and venues. The Waterboys recorded a musical version of Yeats's poem on their 2011 album *A Conversation with Mr. Yeats*, in a traditional precise, insistent Irish folk style: a bit folk-operatic, a bit electric-rock. It's a "now" version of the poem, but it pays homage more than adequately to the original. Shane MacGowan, frontman of Celtic punk band The Pogues, also did a cover version of the poem: a weird, forceful spoken-word delivery, voiced over (but not sung to) a loud, bouncy musical backdrop. He seems pedestrian, churning out Yeats's words as if conveying a kind of forced dreariness (a la Brecht), a non-performance. His unpretty delivery contrasts with the vibrant music—perhaps MacGowan means to evoke the speaker's attempted refusal, in Yeats's poem, to toe the line of imperial patriotism and European militarism.

Magee's poem has also been set to music. John Denver's 1983 song, "Flight (The Higher We Fly),"[46] adapts "High Flight." Denver died in a 1997 crash of the light, homebuilt Rutan Long-EZ he was piloting; listening to him sing the song feels proleptic, reiterating the premonition in Magee's poem itself.

Orson Welles broadcast an emotionally intense reading of Magee's poem in 1942, and received requests from airbases around the world to record it.[47] Welles helped make the poem—sometimes called "the pilot's creed"—a paean for aviators everywhere. Plaques bearing the poem were sent to every RCAF station.[48] John Gilling's 1957 film, *High Flight*, was loosely inspired by the poem. Russell Crowe, playing a Canadian WWII pilot, recites the poem movingly—slow, self-consciously dramatic—in the 1993 film *For the Moment*. NASA Astronaut Michael Collins typed the poem on an index card he carried on his Gemini 10 flight, and Apollo 15 Lunar Module Pilot James Irwin brought a copy of "High Flight" to the moon. The US Air Force made short films showing various planes in flight, accompanied by patriotic music and a voiceover of "High Flight," which television stations used as sign-offs at the end of each day's programming.

Some of these adaptations and reiterations take the melodramatic flowery strain which is already present in Magee's verse and run with it; arguably, they overrunneth. About Yeats's "Irish Airman," as subjective as this may seem, I can say definitively that it is a great poem. With "High Flight," we have to peck and sniff around a bit to appreciate its literary accomplishment. "It is striking that Magee's fame is based on that one poem, especially when one considers the poem's literary value,"[49] writes Christina Anders, who is not alone in her skepticism about its aesthetic quality.

Magee borrowed elements of his poem, in ways that we might regard today as "sampling" or postmodern, but which have also been called plagiarism. The last six words, "and touched the face of God," match the last words of Cuthbert Hicks's poem "The Blind Man Flies," published three years earlier in *Icarus, An Anthology of Aviators' Poetry*. Hicks's penultimate line, too—"For I have danced the streets in heaven"—anticipates the mood and images of "High Flight." That same anthology

> includes the (unfortunate) phrase "on laughter-silvered wings," which Magee stole for the second line of "High Flight." Moreover, the penultimate line of "High Flight"—"The high, untrespassed sanctity of space"—sounds an awful lot like a line from a poem in *Icarus* by someone known by the initials C. A. F. B., "Dominion over Air."[50]

The first and last lines of "High Flight" appear on Magee's gravestone, as well as those of many other aviators through the generations. President Ronald Reagan quoted from those lines in his televised address to the nation after the 1986 Space Shuttle Challenger explosion—one of his best-received speeches, and arguably one of the most powerful presidential addresses ever. Concluding his graceful elegy for the astronauts, he said,

> The crew of the space shuttle Challenger honored us by the manner in which they lived their lives. We will never forget them, nor the last time we saw them, this morning, as they prepared for the journey and waved goodbye and "slipped the surly bonds of earth" to "touch the face of God."[51]

Presidential speechwriter Peggy Noonan said Magee's poem "just came to me. I just remembered it from seventh grade."[52] The phrases Reagan excerpted convey a noble sense of dignity, serenity, that helped comfort a nation in shock after having watched the searing explosion live on television. That's how poetry soars on when aviation fails.

As a counterpoint to Reagan's Magee-inspired eloquence, though, writer Ben Lerner offers a dissenting perspective. He recalls "Reagan's official narrative processing of the national disaster" leaving him and his young friends needing to supplement that with "a kind of sinister transpersonal . . . shadow language." They told dark jokes, "our way of dealing with the remainder of the trauma" that the president's elegy "couldn't fully integrate into our lives."

I said earlier that dark, often offensive humor comprises part of the discourse of aviation tragedies. The jokes Lerner remembers are disturbing, and I am ambivalent about recirculating them here—but I do so because they help us understand the wide range of ways in which people think and talk about aviation disasters, and even, however crudely, come to terms with them via a multitude of rhetorical strategies. "Did you know that Christa McAuliffe was blue-eyed? One blew left and one blew right. What were Christa McAuliffe's last words to her husband? You feed the kids—I'll feed the fish. What does NASA stand for? Need Another Seven Astronauts. How do they know what shampoo Christa McAuliffe used? They found her head and shoulders." Jokes like these "seemed to come out of nowhere," Lerner writes, "or to come from everywhere at once. Folklorists who study what they call 'joke cycles' track how—particularly in times of collective anxiety—certain humorous templates get recycled, often among children."[53] McAuliffe, a New Hampshire school teacher who was planning to conduct experiments and teach classes from the Challenger, was the focus of attention before the explosion and even more so afterwards. The nation was so excited about her adventure as the first teacher in space, making her death seem especially terrible—all her students were watching—and heightening the public's stunned response. The anguished irony surrounding McAuliffe's death explains why Lerner's jokes are mostly about her.

✈ Plane-crash dreams

"An Irish Airman Foresees His Death" is a dreamy poem, and Yeats knew Major Gregory had had dreams about crashing. While there is wide disagreement about how to ascertain what dreams mean, lots of people have lots of dreams about plane crashes, so of course the Internet provides much "wisdom" about these. A grain of salt is advised, though some of these interpretations seem at least somewhat plausible. I agree with the Internet that plane crashes mean something, and more than just *this aircraft crashed into that spot killing these people, and we need to fix the wiring*. Crash dreams help illuminate the far-ranging and diffuse symbolism, the polyvalence, the cultural resonance, of these tragedies.

While these dreams are not real, they still affect us. Behavioral scientists explain how people grapple with this paradox: every morning, many people "fight the urge to change travel plans despite having foreseen their death in a fiery plane crash," write Carey Morewedge and Michael Norton. "The bitter thoughts and strong emotions that such experiences evoke attest to the potency of information 'revealed' in dreams."[54] "Revealed" is in scare quotes because the dreamt-of crashes didn't really happen, which excludes them from conventional NTSB accident investigations, but not from my humanist version. The "bitter thoughts and strong emotions" compel me to investigate these dream-crashes even though they are merely debris fields of the mind. Virginia Woolf captures the popular Freudian zeitgeist about the potency of imaginative nighttime experiences when she writes that it is "in our dreams, that the submerged truth sometimes comes to the top."[55] Nightmares are "a way for us to process our fears," writes psychotherapist Annie Armstrong Miyao, and "help us prepare for worst-case scenarios, solve problems, or better understand our existential fears."[56]

So, what might these dreams mean? The website Dreams.co.uk—hosted by a mattress company, so they should know!—explains that "Aeroplanes in dreams usually mean that you're heading towards success but if something went wrong in your dreams then you may be starting to drift away from the right path." Crash dreams "are symbolic of your emotions during your waking life. If you dream about a plane crash it's likely to represent some form of inner turmoil . . . the battles going on between our conscious and unconscious mind. Your subconscious may be urging you to go one way but your mind may want you to go another, and the emotional toll is represented by the crash."

Crash dreams may highlight "unforeseen events that might give rise to an outburst of strong emotions. As such, the turbulence may refer to a family member, parent, or romantic partner. Perhaps you or someone close is experiencing strong emotions that need controlling? Having a plane crashing nightmare may be warning you to face the issue head-on before the relationship falls apart." If it seems like this advice is in the discourse of fortune-telling rather than psychotherapy, there is perhaps a thin line separating them.

There are variant interpretations: "dreaming about a plane crash may also encourage you to become more persistent when dealing with life's challenges. Despite the ups and downs of the rollercoaster of life, it can mean that you'll succeed in becoming stronger than ever before." Sometimes the dreamers themselves are piloting the crashing planes. "You might be surprised to learn that if you are in charge of a plane which comes crashing down from the sky of your dreams, you should consider it a good signal. That's because these visions usually predict a happy love life or an unexpected encounter." Well, possibly, though they lose me as they go further around the bend: "In fact, you may meet your future spouse, and if you're married, a baby may be on the way." (You don't have to be married to have babies, I reflect, challenging one of the less absurd strains of this augury.)

The interpretations get granular: dreaming about witnessing a plane crash "can be a warning of danger on the horizon," which seems fair enough, and "can reveal the fact that you're struggling to finish what you started, or that the schemes that you set in motion aren't going to plan." Dreaming about surviving a plane crash could be "a positive sign highlighting your knowledge and ability to overcome challenging situations. Surviving a plane crash can mean you have abandoned a toxic relationship."[57]

Another such website—there are many dozens of them—offers even more specific exegeses. Being trapped in a crashed plane shows your desire to escape a difficult situation in real life. Dreaming of parents suffering a plane crash affirms your vital connection with them: "If you love your parents and fear losing them, you can dream of a plane crash with your parents inside" which represents "your true love and affection for your parents." Dreaming of a midair collision signifies "having disagreements with your loved ones. The subconscious mind here tells you to stay put as the circumstances will eventually change if you talk this out with the other person." Dying in a plane crash signifies "bad decisions that are coming back at you. The poor planning and carelessness you show are causing these ventures to fail." (Talk about blaming the victim!) Seeing a plane in flames "represents your repressed emotions. These negative emotions might have been piling up for years and must be resolved before they take a toll on your mental health."[58]

But more seriously: some non-Internet experts describe plane crash dreams as "existential dreams," which aligns with my own categorization of aviation disasters as existential crises. Compared with other types—"transcendental dreams" are uplifting and energizing; "mundane dreams" are self-explanatory—existential dreams feature striking "light/dark contrasts, ineffectual movement (fatigue), separation and loss, spontaneous affective shifts, and intense sadness during the transition to wakefulness," writes psychologist Don Kuiken. Compared to transcendental and mundane dreams, and plain old nightmares, study participants report that existential dreams produce more numerous incidences of feeling scared/terrified, despair/discouraged, angry/frustrated, lost/disoriented, vulnerable/helpless, nervous/anxious, inadequate/failed, and guilty/ashamed. (Those last dyads recall the mattress company's interpretation that dreaming about plane crashes means you are careless.) Existential dreamers report significantly fewer experiences of feeling powerful/competent, happy/joyful, hopeful/optimistic, or peaceful/calm.[59] These data support my intuitive sense that people who dream about plane crashes are existentialists, and if it were possible to solicit a second opinion from Kierkegaard, I think he would affirm my diagnosis.

4

The Day the Music Died

I'm scared shitless of what's coming next.
I'm scared shitless, these angels I see in the trees are waiting for me.
The engines have stopped now. We all know we are going down.
Last call for alcohol. Sure wish I could have another round.

Drive-By Truckers, "Angels and Fuselage"

Hurtle down the runway on a one-way trip to heaven
It's hell on wheels in a 747.

Cure for Sanity, "Nightmare at 20,000 Feet"

This plane is definitely crashing!

Modest Mouse, "Shit Luck"

✈ Leaving on a jet plane

Pop music is full of cultural debris fields: songs that may gawk gruesomely at a crash, or mourn it, or resist mourning with joyful noise to displace the tragedy's joyless silence, or pay homage to (or even sanctify) the victims, or in some other way transpose aviation disasters into some sort of rhythmic, poetic, vocal-and-instrumental artifacts that live on after the raw immediate grief dissipates.

Something about the inherent pathos, the irony, and the narrative hook of plane crashes makes them prominent subjects on the hit parade. Lyrics tend to be fairly concise—most songs are a few hundred words long—and crashes prove amenable to succinct, visceral narratives that unfold in a few quick verses. Like other cultural genres, music helps broach the unimaginable and ineffable, facilitating catharsis and healing. Sometimes these songs can be brutally dark, sometimes more comforting. Common tropes in song lyrics include angry screeds of denial, panic attacks, last words to loved ones, fear, resignation. These varied songs and styles often resemble dirges, or elegies, or eulogies, or requiems: songs of trauma and perhaps recovery, memorial songs.

If Martians needed to have plane crashes explained to them in six lines, Cure for Sanity's "Nightmare at 20,000 Feet" (1990) would serve well: "This is no joke, the thing could go up in smoke / Or plummet to the ground as the G-force pulls us down. / Flight! Fright! Get uptight!" Next verse: "Are you ready for a rough ride? This could be suicide. / Turbulence ahead, I think my lunch is on the uprise / . . . . It's not the car, or the bus, or the train. It's the plane!"[1]

If even that's tl/dr, Modest Mouse's 1997 song "Shit Luck" gets it in one: "This plane is definitely crashing!"[2] If that lyric might strike our aliens as merely descriptive rather than more deeply explanatory and illustrative, the indie-grunge-rock vibe as the lead singer (or lead screamer) shrieks the line at the song's opening, before the music kicks in, performatively conveys a pretty keen sense of what's at stake and how people feel when they utter such thoughts. The title, too, embellishes the context.

The Rolling Stones' 1966 song "Flight 505" presents a no-frills quick-and-dirty crash: "Well, suddenly I saw that we never ever would arrive / He put the plane down in the sea / The end of flight number 505."[3] Bassist Bill Wyman said they flew BOAC 505 from the UK to their first US concerts in 1964.[4] "Maybe the song was instigated by the kind of existence the Stones were leading," offers music critic Richie Unterberger, "taking airplanes all over the world for their tours, probably to the point where they sometimes weren't sure where they were or where they were going."[5]

"Flight 505," like many of the songs in this section of my report, brings to the surface (or at least *toward* the surface) an unsettling panorama of uncertainty, as Unterberger infers, that's often close at hand in crash songs, and stories, and art, and other cultural texts. Where are we? Where are we going? Will we get there intact, or will we perish en route? Such anxieties often begin to accelerate in tandem with the aircraft itself as it gathers speed in its takeoff roll: musical tempo tracks aviational tempo. As short as these songs are, they broach far-reaching fear and trembling, as Capt. Kierkegaard might say. (Imagine his existential PA announcement coming on during a Scandinavian Airlines city-hop, in a lugubrious Danish cadence: "When death is the greatest danger, one hopes for life; but when one becomes acquainted with an even more dreadful danger, one hopes for death. So when the danger is so great that death has become one's hope, despair is the disconsolateness of not being able to die."[6])

Even for people who aren't card-carrying existentialists, our psyches contend with some combination of claustrophobia, acrophobia, and other sensory disruptions: drier and heavier cabin air, unpredictable ambient temperatures, erratic jolts in equilibrium, motion sickness. Mobilities bring on modifications in our sensibilities, as we go places and do things we don't usually do. How exciting, or disorienting, or scary, or just … uncertain. Aeromobility, though less dangerous (per mile traveled) than automobility, carries the most spectacular psychological associations of what *could* happen. Bicycling and horse-riding too can lead to peril, but not on this scale, and not with such psychocultural intensity.

So otherwise-mild-mannered passengers may suddenly feel like woebegotten worrywarts as triggers erupt from the sounds, feelings, and thoughts of aviation. A great many songs capture this sudden angst that's sparked and accentuated by the prospect of a crash, the memory of other crashes, the fear of a potential crash—or perhaps just a disquieting noise, or a bump, or a smell, that gets apprehensions percolating.

Nada Surf's 2008 "Ice on the Wing" minces no words, describing a fighter pilot's imminent tragedy merely by singing, over and over, the crisis encapsulated in the title—ice is growing on the wing. Ice buildup is dangerous because it alters airflow, reducing the lift force that keeps the plane aloft and potentially causing a stall. (Remember Continental 1713, discussed in the Diversion, and Colgan 3407 from Chapter 1.) Even if wings ice up, though, there are still procedures to address and remediate the danger, as long as pilots can dodge what Modest Mouse calls "shit luck." (Should that phrase be incorporated as an official rubric for air crash investigations? It probably is, albeit in a euphemistically tamer timbre.) Fingers crossed that the crew runs the right checklist and the de-icing system works. "Ice on the Wing," is not precisely a crash-song, but rather, a *might*-crash song—it ends with the narrative suspense unresolved as, indeed, many of these songs do. Be careful, they say, things feel pretty scary and dangerous, but let's hope we don't buy the farm.

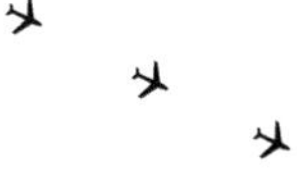

More scary-simple-scream-smash swan songs: *I'm scared of airplanes*, the Foo Fighters sing in their 1998 song "A320." (Me too, I sing along, sotto voce, though more audibly during panic attacks. Usually only a few nearby passengers hear in the noisy cabin. If they had any sense, they'd all be panic-singing along with me.)

I like how it feels being a person in the sky, they continue. (I know exactly what you mean! Paradoxically, despite all my anxieties, I like that feeling too.) *Looking out and seeing the ground, I don't believe gravity can pull me down from this height.*

As astoundingly dependable as I know aviation technology and pilot training are, and as much as I'd like to *believe* in them unconditionally, still, neuroses are irrational. (Gravity = "weight," in lift/thrust/drag/weight; it's hard-coded into the theorem, so—however counterintuitively—it's not going to pull anyone down out of the sky, at least not if lift/thrust/drag are doing their part.) In these quick-hit crash tunes, the lyrics may be pithy but they're not bland. The language is concentrated, crafted, pin-point precise: as powerfully true by humanist standards as the elements of aeronautical science are for their own audience.

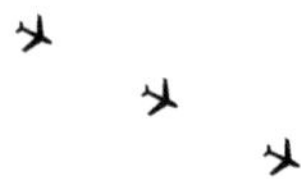

"From a Window Seat," a 2013 song by folk-rock band Dawes, offers a simple image—in sharply crafted polyphonic multimedia: musical, poetic, liturgical, terpsichorean—that has etched itself into my mind and will now etch itself into yours. The song opens as the singer/passenger settles in, watching flight attendants' departure preparations. *As they're pointing out the exits*, Dawes sings, *it looks more like a prayer, or some ancient dance their bloodline reaches through.* Since first hearing this, I have taken comfort on every flight—a mindful moment of relaxing succor, solemn, almost sacred—internalizing this safety-briefing-prayer and appreciating the compelling symbolic force of the cabin crew's "ancient" dance. Safety presentations, executed in a sort of robot-dance style, make the ritual seem especially powerful as it transposes age-old rites of protection into a modern spirit. The dance aesthetically demonstrates how we might cope with an overwhelming imminent adversity: a crash would visit destruction on every human body aboard. Before a flight alights, Dawes devotionally cantillates, flight attendants perform this choreography with their own bodies to ward off—primordially, magically—the peril of their passengers' corporeal annihilation. This dance situates art against chaos: art that resists and transcends pandemonium. It's a performative petition for the aircraft to resist the dangers of unencumbered gravity. Lift! Thrust!

The interplay between moving bodies and moving airplanes recalls the fundamental premise of mobility studies, which is that every movement—human or mechanical, fast or slow, systemically intricate or individually casual—is, by definition, a kind of mobility, all of which combine to comprise an overarching, interactive mobilities network. Veronika Zuskáčová describes aeromobility as embodied, that is, "practiced, enacted, and experienced through the body." Aeromobility "consists of the *physical journeys* of people that are *mediated* by the airplane"[7] [her emphasis], which is a nice way to think about how the flight attendants' dance invokes both aeronautic and kinesthetic movement: mobility/motility.

Conjuring ancient dance traditions, Dawes reminds me of Lord Shiva's ritual Tandava, which embraces eternal energies of preservation that couldn't be more keenly a propos in the moments before airplanes begin to hurtle toward heaven (or, in Hindu cosmology, toward *svarga*, the *devas* celestial abode). If this allusion may be unintended, still, Dawes reinvented Shiva's wheel: semiotic commonalities explain why such cultural patterns and expressions recur to facilitate the meanings they convey. Shiva's dance includes a specific moment that invokes protection: a hand movement (he uses his third hand) called *abhaya mudra*, a "fear-not gesture": holding the palm outward, fingers pointing up. This sign represents peace, a benevolence that dispels apprehension, encouraging us to forsake feelings of fear which obstruct the path of spiritual development. Think of it as a proleptic anticipation of "pointing out the exits."

Shiva's primal, natural indication of easy confidence and good intentions recurs in many cultures: such gestures demonstrate that one's hands hold no weapons; they cultivate better awareness of the present moment as they help to overcome dread. They make the dancer feel emotionally balanced and free of stress, calming the mind, displacing anxiety with strength, courage, and a deep inner security. Remember all this the next time your cabin crew point out the emergency escape routes—join in the dance yourself. In the worst-case scenario, if passengers *do* have to head for the exits, there's a dance routine for that too which flight attendants rehearse meticulously, designed to get everyone off the plane in a tightly choreographed ninety-second conga line.

"Plane Crash," a 1998 release by the band moe., depicts a fearful flyer's jitters blossoming:

> Yeah, they fly so high, 20, 30 thousand,
> That's pretty high.
> When they take off,
> my chest sinks,
> my ears pop,

I pray . . .
And to pass the time,
I hear tell my seat cushion is a flotation device,
Pray to god they ain't lyin'.[8]

Having personally spent many hours in the throes of panic attacks at 30,000 feet, I can confirm that this minimalist etiology captures it all. Oddly, this song is on my flight-panic-coping playlist, and even more oddly, it helps bring me back from the ledge. Dawes got me started praying during safety briefings, and then I keep praying, as moe. directs, that generations of aviators have pretty much figured out how to keep us alive. It calms me to think that this omnipotent terror (as it seems to moe., and to me) can be scored and sung so sprightly; listening to their vibrant energy overwrites my spiraling situational incoherence.

Again, it's art against chaos, order against disorder. The practiced, finished, compelling artifact of a good song (with its rhyme, rhythm, music, and imagery that lodges in your head, like a prayer, to be intoned again and again) combats the randomly horrible prospect of danger, failure, crash. When something so frightful is addressed in art, the sublime force of art itself provides a tranquility that counterpoints unartistic free-form neurosis. The cultural texts blaring through my earbuds embody control: lyrical arrangement. Control, pattern, and order are also lynchpins of safe flights, as is lyrical precision: pilots and air traffic controllers all have to say the exact right things, clearly enunciated in exactly the right ways. Planes crash when people get the lyrics wrong.

Performative artifacts—music, dance, art, poetry—embody in their balanced movements and repetitions an affirmation that displaces the specter of dread. Arguably (and this is admittedly radical humanism, but that's what they'd be paying me for if they hired me as a crash investigator) the art helps displace, even beyond the *fear* of danger, the *actual danger* itself. We can find in the art and culture of plane crashes, paradoxically, more of the energy that powers planes to do what they want: to fly. "Pray to god they ain't lyin" about aviation safety, moe. sings: we're dubious, but we *do* pray, and we *do* (almost always) survive. If this musical energy is more figurative than physical, it's still energy, and really, is there any reason to ignore any repository of power that might help keep airplanes in flight?

(God answers every prayer, my Rabbi was fond of saying, though sometimes the answer is no.)

✈ Pie in the sky

Besides singing so many crash songs, numerous musicians have themselves crashed, often while flying frenetically from concert to concert. Don McLean's 1971 "American Pie" was named one of the twentieth century's top five songs by the National Endowment for the Arts. "Almost all of us know the chorus of 'American Pie' better than we know our own national anthem."[9] Its manuscript (just some "scribble sheets for trying to figure out what I was going to say," McLean explained) sold for $1.2 million at auction in 2015[10]—a crass but credible indication of the song's "value."

I'll call it the most significant plane crash song in pop culture.

Like "An Irish Airman" and "High Flight," the plane-crash aspect of McLean's plane-crash song is subtle, sublimated. There's no explicit plane, no explicit crash, no explicit debris field—though the choral refrain is a perfect premonitory sign-off:

> This'll be the day that I die.

"American Pie" is full of quick, enigmatic allusions to a wide swath of people, culture, and history. Frequently asked to explain what the song actually means, McLean almost always refuses, telling fans to figure it out themselves. But its central reference, if not explicit, is undisputed: "The day the music died" refers to February 3, 1959, when Buddy Holly, Ritchie Valens, and J. P. Richardson (a.k.a. The Big Bopper) crashed into an Iowa cornfield—that I have visited—on an ill-fated late-night flight. Everyone knows this song is about that crash because everyone knows this song is about that crash. McLean was a thirteen-year-old paperboy when he heard the news—"February made me shiver, with every paper I'd deliver"—and revisiting that day a decade later, he characterizes it as not just a tragic crash but, more broadly, a crucial cultural turning point.

The Winter Dance Party—a 24-day, 24-stop tour across the Midwest—featured, besides the crash victims, Dion and the Belmonts, Frankie Sardo, Waylon Jennings, Tommy Allsup and Carl Bunch. On a tight budget, they traveled in shoddy school buses that kept breaking down, so poorly heated that everyone got sick; the uncomfortable arrangements left the bands increasingly exhausted. So Holly chartered a four-seater Beechcraft Bonanza after their eleventh concert, at Clear Lake's Surf Ballroom (which is still there, frozen in time, hosting a Winter Dance Party annually on February 3). It was supposed to be an hour-long 365-mile hop to Fargo, ND, just across the Red River from the next night's concert in Moorhead, MN. Holly hoped a few of the musicians (including himself) could get a good night's sleep, and he also needed to do a load of laundry.

There were last-minute passenger switches. Allsup flipped a coin and lost his seat to Valens (who said, "That's the first time I've ever won anything in my life"[11]). Jennings was supposed to fly, but offered his seat to the Big Bopper, who needed the sleep because he was coming down with the flu; Jennings also felt leery about the tiny plane. "The last time Jennings remembered talking to Holly, the frontman was chiding him for chickening out of the plane ride. 'I hope your damn bus freezes up again,' Holly said, smiling. Jennings replied with the words that haunted him for years: 'Well, I hope your ol' plane crashes.'"[12] Yikes.

Taking off in a snowstorm, 21-year-old pilot Roger Peterson—unfamiliar with the plane's newfangled gyroscope—thought he was gaining altitude when he was actually descending. The crash's probable cause was Peterson's decision to fly into black-out conditions for which he lacked instrument proficiency; a contributing factor was air traffic control's incomplete weather briefings.

The plane-crash elements of McLean's song are scattered and indirect. The story is sketchily elusive—

I can't remember if I cried
When I read about his widowed bride
Something touched me deep inside
The day the music died

—but potent if you tease it out: Buddy and Maria Elena Holly had been married for only six months when he died. Pregnant with their child, she miscarried from the shock of learning about the crash in the media (which led to the policy of notifying family before releasing names of the deceased). There's just a single brief crash image, and even this isn't all that obvious—you could blink and miss it:

The birds flew off with a fallout shelter
Eight miles high and fallin' fast
It landed foul on the grass

Flying birds symbolize planes—not a far stretch, but also not a literal depiction. The "fallout shelter," a backyard refuge from nuclear attack that evokes 1950s Cold War geopolitics, doesn't make much sense if we're parsing this passage as a crash allegory. How could birds carry that heavy structure: they "flew off with" it? Why? "Fallout" doesn't denote *falling out* of a plane, though if we're receptive to a kind of Joycean wordplay, it sounds as if perhaps it could (and when that *fallout* happens the plane no longer *shelters*). And then—"fallin' fast"—the incipient crash.

"Eight miles high" vastly exaggerates the Iowa flight's altitude: it never flew higher than a few thousand feet in the five minutes before crashing. But The Byrds—whom McLean admired, unlike most of the other musicians his song name-checks—had a 1966 song, "Eight Miles High," about a flight to Europe where their band would perform. That song was banned on US radio because the lyrics had druggy connotations: "'Of course it was a drug song,' band member David Crosby said. 'We were stoned when we wrote it. But it was also about the [plane] trip to London.'"[13] It's often considered the first psychedelic rock song, which McLean alludes to by describing the "high" plane as landing foul (illegal) on the grass (marijuana).

The Beechcraft "landed foul"—not illegal, but out of bounds: not where it was supposed to have landed. That strikingly arcane way of describing the crash exemplifies McLean's discursive technique. Sometimes we want the facts, the actual crash narrative, but sometimes it's nicer to have a more dazzling song instead, even if we have to work a little harder to figure it out. Though obsessed with the crash, McLean displaces it in favor of something less gruesome and easier to hum along to. In this song about the day the music died, what are we listening to? That's right: music! Music dies, but it also survives: it is reborn. "American Pie" is a phoenix rising out of the ashes of the debris, a common trope in so many cultural debris fields. The plane crash lurks as a palimpsest, but the song more prominently articulates the determination to move forward. McLean honors the victims by carrying on with their lifework, perpetuating the dynamism of the rock and roll music that was so important to them. If actual plane crashes are stark and unsubtle, McLean sings against that with the elegant impulse of his artful iterations.

McLean's crash scene, which began with birds (Byrds!) rather than an airplane as a figurative distraction, surrealistically transforms the debris field into a football field featuring a musical halftime show—powerful music: when the players try to take the field, the marching band refuses to yield! Does the musicians' refusal to acknowledge aviational discontent mean that the music negates the plane crash as long as it keeps playing?

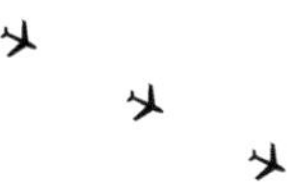

McLean's elusive references indicate its calculated ambiguity as a crash song. The songwriter "said he tried to simulate the feeling of a dream and 'capture something that you cannot express.'"[14] Some musicians *can* capture and express the essence of a plane crash in a sharp, searing phrase, an unmistakable and uncomplicated *YOU . . . are there* image: "Ice is growing on the wing"; "I'm afraid of airplanes"; "suddenly I saw that we never ever would arrive"; "This plane is definitely crashing!" But McLean rejects such straightforward representations of aviation disasters, writing instead in a complex, macrocosmic mode that emanates from the debris field but also ventures far beyond. This aesthetic, this modality, inspires my own efforts to venture far and wide probing symbols and suggestions, scouring debris fields for any connections they can offer, however elusive or enigmatic, to help understand and deal with the disasters at hand. Not all investigations will sustain such far-flung allegorical and semiotic readings, but some, like this one, absolutely will.

"American Pie" expresses McLean's nostalgic admiration for the music that died in Iowa, honoring its formative importance for his own career. In tandem, the song denigrates Elvis Presley, Bob Dylan, The Beatles and many more musicians, along with American culture writ large. The song depicts the US careening out of control, the traumatic plane crash resonating allegorically as the catalyst that presages and precipitates a much larger national trauma. Describing his ballad "as a morality song that charted the decline of America and its loss of innocence," Rob Crilly writes, McLean said that "Basically in 'American Pie' things are heading in the wrong direction."[15]

Like so many artifacts from cultural debris fields, McLean's far-reaching social critique draws strongly on existentialist angst. Children scream, lovers are crying in the streets; a generation is lost in space with no time to rediscover its path. Do we have faith in God? Church bells are broken, Satan laughs with delight. The Father, Son, and the Holy Ghost caught the last train for the coast; this'll be the day that I die. *Can* music save your mortal soul? Maybe once it could, before Buddy Holly disappeared. But now, a girl who sings the blues has no happy news and turns away. Not a word was spoken and the music wouldn't play, connoting a singer's existential paralysis: ineffability, silence. "For all its catchy sing-along jauntiness," writes Rob Walker, "there's little to really cheer about in 'American Pie.' It's devoid of hope." McLean called it "a farewell to the American dream."[16]

"This'll be the day that I die" is a refrain repeated thirteen (unlucky!) times throughout the song. The phrase seems to be spoken by Holly (to whom McLean dedicated the album, also called *American Pie*), or perhaps variously by all three musicians who died that night. A simple but powerful premonition of tragic fate, it recalls Yeats's language in Major Gregory's interior monologue. With eerie rhetorical effect, McLean channels Holly's inner consciousness just as Yeats voices what he imagines to be Gregory's final thoughts. Both Holly and Gregory might be embracing Thanatos, the death drive that fascinated Freud and courses rampantly throughout existential literature—or, they might not. McLean's line is adapted from one of Holly's own songs. "That'll Be the Day," released three years before his death, includes the nearly identical phrase: "That'll be the day when I die." Changing Holly's "that" to "this," McLean subtly counterpoints the otherwise-identical expressions. For Holly, his death lay out in the future: *that* day, while in McLean's rendition, the death is immediate, now: *this* day. It's still in the future ("This *will be* the day"), but the very near future, perhaps just moments away. Major Gregory's proleptic death-vision reflects a similar timeframe: the next breath beyond Yeats's ending could be his last.

Another dark line appears six times in "American Pie": "the day the music died" (obviously related to "This'll be the day that I die"). It is a subtle but significant expression of transference/displacement, or synecdoche, or metonymy, or syllogism (let's say all of them) of a type that recurs in many humanist crash investigations across other cultural media. Holly, Valens, and the Bopper made music; Holly, Valens, and the Bopper died; therefore, the music died. Of course people died too in that Iowa snowstorm, but what McLean explicitly memorializes is the music. This is no slight on the actual human victims—the people who made the music would certainly understand McLean's point. They were music.

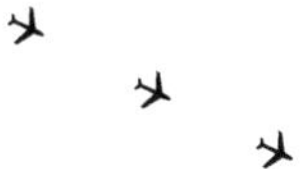

Beyond Anglophone culture there are many more musical plane-crash victims who didn't register prominently in the slice of the world McLean sang about, but left powerful legacies of loss and traumatic mourning in their own cultures. Bulgarian pop star Pasha Hristova, whose most popular song was "Edna bălgarska roza" ("One Bulgarian Rose"), died traveling from Sofia to an Algerian concert in 1971 when her plane's wing struck the runway during takeoff; the hull broke and ignited. Marília Mendonça was famous for her influence on Brazilian country music, *sertanejo,* a predominantly male genre until she stamped it with a feminist twist. In 2021, her Beechcraft King air taxi from Goiânia struck power cables and crashed into a waterfall on approach to Caratinga, where Mendonça was to have performed; 100,000 people attended her funeral.[17]

Pedro Infante, a macho Mexican ballad-singing musician/actor who performed "Te amaré vida mía" ("I Will Love You, My Darling"), died at the controls of his own airplane in 1957, having survived two previous crashes. As he flew to Mexico City from Yucatán, an engine failure shortly after takeoff sent his Consolidated B-24D spiraling to the ground, imbuing his signature song's final stanza with a macabre dramatic irony: As long as I can breathe and blood runs through my veins, he sang, I will love you. For decades after his death, Infante inspired the Mexican equivalent of Elvis sightings: some believed he somehow survived the fiery plane crash, got plastic surgery, and hid for years in Nicaraguan or Guatemalan jungles. Perhaps he wasn't on the plane—the debris field remains were too charred to identify. Fans refused to accept his death "insisting this national icon of the 1950s was driven underground by government persecution yet has managed to stage a quiet comeback."[18]

The melodies of all these dead musicians live on. Their own recordings continue to play in an infinite present, and other singers cover songs the dead performers made famous. The object lesson—simple, but crucial—is to scour debris fields, as McLean prompts us to do, not just for debris and people, but also for what the people did, what they created, what they contributed to the world. Of course this is just as true whether or not the crash victims are celebrities.

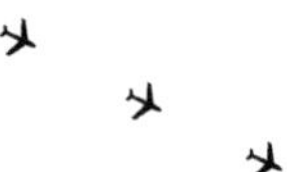

"American Pie" tops the rota of songs I listen to when I'm flying: my "most played" tab shows I've listened to it 137 times. I thought it was my own discovery to deploy crash songs as a protective spell against aviation disasters, until I read Mark Yakich, in *The Dangerous Book of Poetry for Planes*, reporting that others, too, are in on this scheme:

> The writer Sherman Alexie is fond of saying that in order to avoid crashing, he listens to a mixtape with songs by musicians who died in plane crashes. His logic is that he doesn't think God would be as ironic as to crash the plane he's flying in as he's listening to the tape.[19]

If pure irony is a fundamental factor in most plane crashes, perhaps it can be leveraged in this way, fighting irony with irony, to enhance safety. Alexie and Yakich favor songs *by* crash victims, while I prefer, instead, songs *about* crashes:

tomato/tomahto. Aviation safety experts seem to have overlooked this hack, which is exactly why they need humanist investigators on the squad.

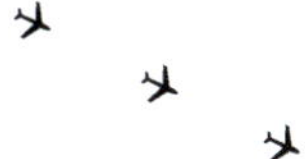

Approaching the Iowa cornfield/debris field where the Beechcraft landed foul, pilgrims drive along a remote gravel road until they come to a sculpture of Buddy Holly's trademark thick black-framed glasses—with 20/800 vision, he couldn't read the top line of an eye chart.[20] From there, they (ok, *we*) turn into the field and walk for close to a mile, not on a path but in the furrows between rows of stalks. It feels like the middle of nowhere, except every couple minutes someone passes by, listening to the song.

At a clearing, the point of impact features a hodge-podge of ramshackle markers: memorial offerings include beads, more sunglasses, plastic flowers, American flags, a rusty license plate, guitar picks, albums, a bumper sticker for the Rock & Roll Hall of Fame. The tableau, messy and random, looks not all that

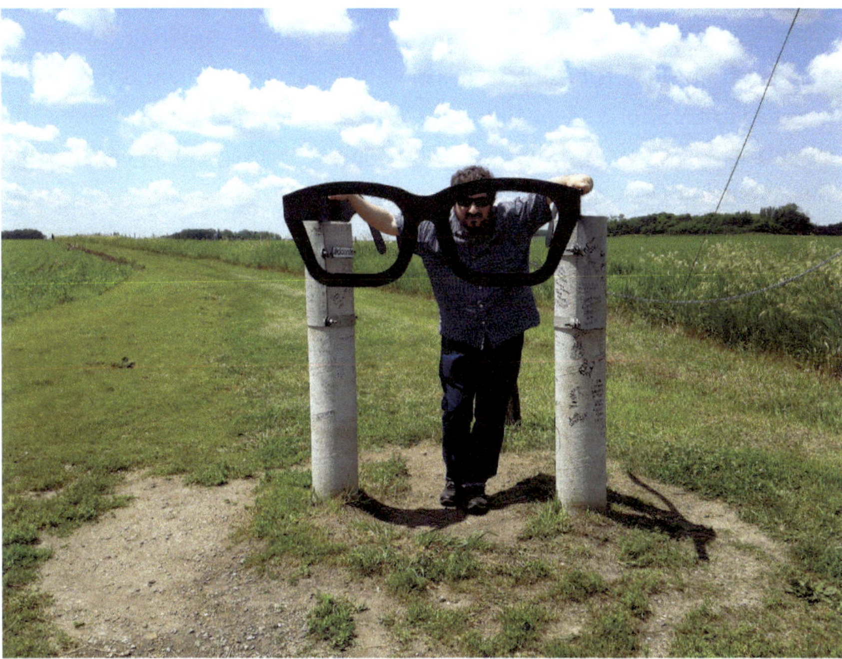

Figure 4.1 The humanist crash investigator in the field.

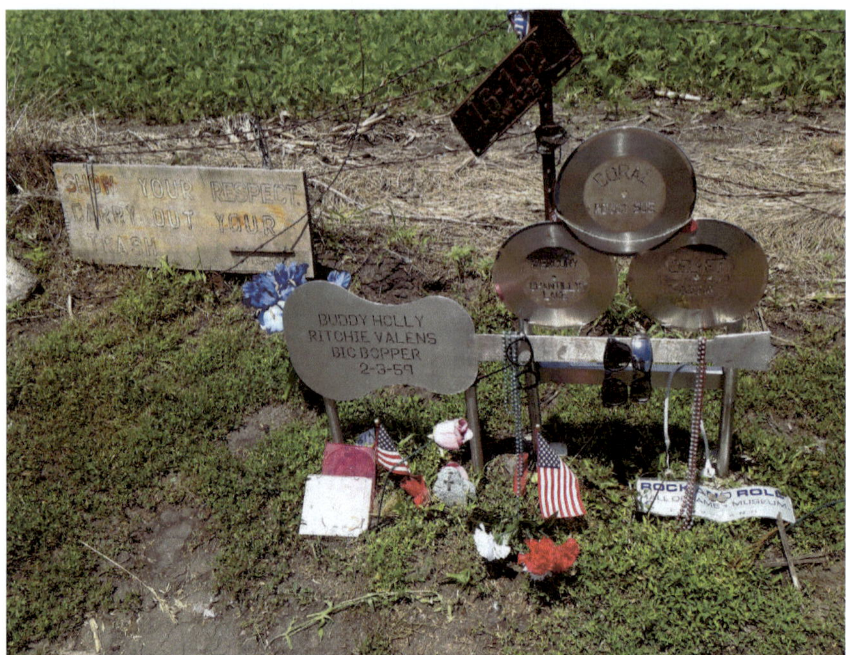

Figure 4.2 The day the music died: debris.

different from a debris field. The flags have fifty stars rather than, as they would have had in 1959, forty-eight: this is *our* debris, twenty-first-century residue (the albums are CDs, not vinyl) instead of the original wreckage, though at the same time it reiterates that earlier debris.

When I visited, it seemed cool, and strange, to be simultaneously experiencing both the cultural debris field—humming along to McLean's strains—and the literal one. I decided I preferred the song to the field as a memorial. Here's how the Civil Aeronautic Board's accident investigation described the debris field in their report from September 1959, seven months after the crash:

> The accident occurred in a sparsely inhabited area … Examination of the wreckage indicated that the first impact with the ground was made by the right wing tip when the aircraft was in a steep right bank and in a nose-low attitude. It was further determined that the aircraft was traveling at high speed on a heading of 315 degrees. Parts were scattered over a distance of 540 feet, at the end of which the main wreckage was found lying against a barbed wire fence. The three passengers were thrown clear of the wreckage, the pilot was found in the cockpit.[21]

McLean's investigative report took a dozen years, but it was worth the wait.

✈ Sweet Home Mississippi

Another "day the music died" song also memorializes several beloved singers whose plane-crash deaths rocked the world of music and American culture at large. Drive-By Truckers' 2001 track "Angels and Fuselage" is sung from the perspective of a man crashing toward his death. If Yeats's Major Gregory seems unimaginably placid as he anticipates his crash, the singer here is, well, more normal, which is to say, completely freaked out.

> Looking out the window, the trees are getting closer it seems. . . .
>
> And I'm scared shitless of what's coming next.
>
> I'm scared shitless, these angels I see in the trees are waiting for me.
>
> The engines have stopped now. We all know we are going down. Last call for alcohol.
> Sure wish I could have another round. . . .
>
> Friends in the swamp.
> Friends on the ground, in the trees.
> Angels and fuselage.[22]

The entire album, *Southern Rock Opera,* pays elegiac homage to Lynyrd Skynyrd. Like the Iowa cornfield crash, their flight was hopping from one show to the next. On October 20, 1977, the Convair CV-240 carrying the band from Greenville, SC, to Baton Rouge, LA, crashed in marshy terrain near Gillsburg, MS, due to "crew inattention to fuel supply"—i.e., they ran out of gas. When they realized their tanks were almost empty, the pilots tried to divert to an airport ten miles from Gillsburg; unable to make it even that far, though, they attempted an emergency landing in an open field, where the plane hit a tree and smashed into pieces. Twenty of twenty-six survived; the two pilots died along with lead singer Ronnie Van Zant, bandmates (and siblings) Steve and Cassie Gaines, and assistant road manager Dean Kilpatrick.[23]

Another *Southern Rock Opera* song, "Shut Up and Get on the Plane," is

> based on a bit of mythology about Skynyrd that claimed that on that fateful day Cassie Gaines had actually bought a ticket to fly commercial instead of getting back on the plane (which had had engine trouble in route to Greenville SC the

> night before). According to legend (and who ever knows what's myth and what's truth) Ronnie Van Zant persuaded her to sell her ticket and fly to Baton Rouge with the rest of the band. [Lyricist Mike] Cooley wrote the song from the point of view that it was still the right decision because "Living in fear's just another way of dying before your time." Wise words and probably the most important line.[24]

Fairly regularly in crash-aftermath tales, this attitude—don't let fear govern your life, live in the moment—is meant to fend off worrying about aviation disasters. One might reasonably argue that Cassie might have done better to lean into her fear in this instance, but Cooley's point is what we might call (h/t Doris Day) the *que sera, sera* philosophy of life and its mobilities. Perhaps this kind of fatalism is less about the tragedy that befell Gaines, more about our own ways of dealing with crashes and our anxieties about the next one. Yes, we could just stop flying—or we can continue to live our lives, accepting that whatever will be, will be.

A monument to Lynyrd Skynyrd, dedicated in 2019, features three large black stone markers containing portraits of the victims and descriptions of the band's accomplishments. There's also an oak tree—possibly one of the trees the Convair hit going down?—where visitors carve their condolences. "Free Bird," one of their most popular songs, is carved into that tree as well, so that it lives on, literally growing out of the debris field.

One of these stones includes a depiction that strikes me as morbidly unsettling, but at the same time, fascinatingly insightful into the semiotics of crash memorials. A posed group shot shows the band and techies getting ready to leave for their tour—sitting on their suitcases, excited for their adventure. That image is superimposed over a picture of the Convair, the actual one they flew (as confirmed by its tail number), sitting on the tarmac outside the hangar, ready to load and fly.

What exactly is this image saying? It's hard to see anything other than dramatic irony hitting us on the head so hard we might get a concussion. *We* know what happens next, but these poor happy souls don't. Possibly this image represents an attempt to somehow erase the crash by freezing the band in a permanent pre-crash moment that captures how much they loved going on the road to perform. I don't know: it seems extremely dark, which may be exactly what we should expect of crash memorials in debris fields.

Although this site has become one of southwest Mississippi's biggest tourist attractions, "It's very difficult to get to and there are no markings," said Bobby

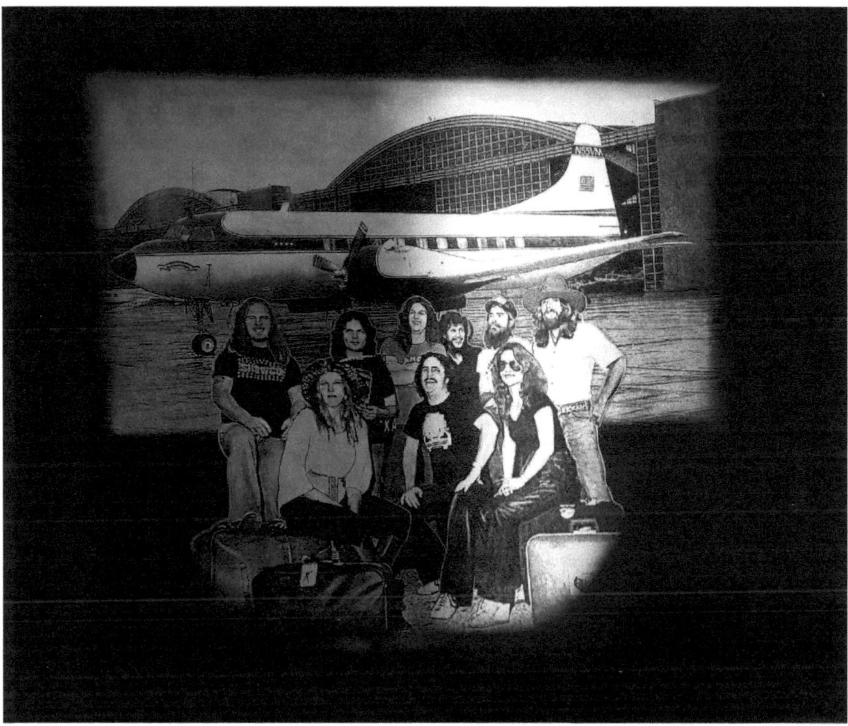

Figure 4.3 A macabre image of Lynyrd Skynyrd and the plane that would crash, killing four of them.

McDaniel, president of the Lynyrd Skynyrd Monument Project.[25] It's remote, like most debris field memorials, because planes usually crash in remote locations. (I've managed to visit only a dozen debris fields; I had hoped my research would take me to many more than that.) Even in our highly developed built world, most of the places planes overfly are far from any human settlement. The silver lining is that this minimizes ground deaths; rarely do population-centers become debris fields. Visitors to middle-of-nowhere crash sites will find an oddly peaceful sense of serene isolation.

"Angels and Fuselage": the song's title poetically juxtaposes two words, two entities, whose conjunction accentuates the irony of this (or any) crash. Each word's soft "g" whispers a connection between two very disparate aeromobilities. But working against that congruency, we also perceive the very different processes of angelic- vs. fuselage-enabled flight. The first is sacred, mysterious, smooth, effortless. If angels are merely imaginary, that makes their empyrean flights all the more astounding. "Fuselage" is a technical term for an aircraft's main body, from the French *fusil*, spindle, describing its shape. This sleek spindle with its resonance of technological prowess can cruise through the heavens too, but in hindsight, a fuselage (specifically, a *detached* fuselage, which is how the word presents in the song's title)—the centerpiece of most debris fields—looks like an accident waiting to happen.

✈ Flying on the ground is wrong

Punk rock band NOFX ("no effects": no fancy gimmicks, just raw hard music) released "Falling in Love" in 1997. It begins:

> Blast oxygen masks, smoke filled cabin
> Depressurize, don't be afraid, hold onto me.
> We're goin' down, but not our love.

I love that last line: Hope springs eternal—or, one might say, hope sings eternal. These sweethearts are literally "falling" in love!

> Death don't seem so bad
> When I'm with you, my only love
> So close your eyes, kiss me one last time
> We're gonna die, but not our love.[26]

A drawn-out electric guitar fade at the end goes on for so long that it feels less like part of the song, more like a mechanical drone—such as, say, a plane going down in the distance. It's a dark-punk version of what most would consider an unredeemably grisly tableau, but for NOFX, musical passion metaphysically transcends aviational carnage. (As crashing pilots might say, though with a different connotation, Fuck!)

Brad Paisley's 1999 country song, "If Love Was a Plane," describes how unlikely love is to succeed. Two young, aimless kids fall in love, get pregnant, get married, with no prospects for the future. (What could go wrong?!) If love was a plane, he sings, nobody would get on: imagine the pilot coming on the PA before takeoff, thanking passengers for flying with him but warning of a 60 percent chance the plane would go down. Finally, though, love conquers all: even knowing the odds are against them, Paisley sings, they line up at the boarding gate with their tickets. The Dispute's 2008 song "Such Small Hands" presents another metaphor of a crash as romantic failure: what sounded like a plane crashing was actually their passion snapping.[27]

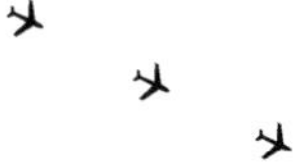

If some songs tend toward minimalism to render a plane crash in a phrase or two, "The Bronco Song," performed by the Fighter Pilots from Alconbury, presents hyperbolically graphic depictions as it parodies Glenn Miller's 1941 "Dear Mom," a WWII ditty in which a serviceman writes his mother a letter assuring her that everything is safe and pleasant: today was cloudy, your package arrived, everybody loved the cake. A few decades later, though, mom gets an unvarnished sense of the Vietnam War, to the tune of Édith Piaf's "Milord":

> Dear Mom, your son is dead, he bought the farm today
> He crashed his OV-10 on Ho Chi Min's highway
> It was a rocket pass and then he busted his ass,
> Mmm, mmm, mmm
>
> The fighters checked right in, gunfighters two by two
> Low on gas and tanker overdue
> They asked the FAC to mark just where that truck was parked.
> Mmm, mmm, mmm
>
> The FAC he rolled right in with his smoke to mark
> Exactly where that fucking truck was parked
> And the rest is in doubt 'cause he never pulled out
> Mmm, mmm, mmm[28]

The OV-10 Bronco, a light attack and observation aircraft, had the primary mission of forward air control (FAC). The refusal to prettify the combat, contrasting sharply with Miller's congenial, sanitized depiction in the song's original version, reflected the Vietnam War's more transparent and honest mediascape compared to past conflicts. By the 1960s, journalists, soldiers, and citizens on the home front came to expect the degree of accuracy that the debris field splayed out here exemplifies. "Bought the farm" in its original WWII iteration was a pleasant euphemism, but now that politeness, ironized, becomes casually macabre.

An extremely gory musical debris field appears in "Concorde" (2020), an odd, discomforting song from the Francophone electro-pop band Le Couleur. "Corps contra corps," it begins—"Body to body"—reprising the *embodiment* of aeromobility that Dawes foregrounded in their dance of the flight attendants. The passengers are crammed in body to body (for all its aerodynamic allure, the Concorde's cabin was notoriously tight and cramped), and in the debris field, too, it will be body to body, body against body.

Tu te fracasseras
En mille parties

Ce sera dans ses bras
Près de Roissy
Que tu emporteras
Ces rêves
Infinis

Leurs corps dans ton corps

(You will crash
In a thousand parts
It will be in his arms
Near Roissy
That you will take
These dreams
Infinite
Their bodies in your body)

Roissy, a Paris suburb, is home to Charles de Gaulle Airport, where the Concorde operating Air France flight 4590 took off for its tragically short flight on July 25, 2000. Le Couleur's song conjoins human and mechanical bodies. As in many other crash narratives, we think of the human bodies, in this case 109 of them (four more died on the ground) as they sat, orderly, in the body of the plane, in seats 1A, 14B, 23D, and so on. Then, juxtaposed with this when order became disorder, their bodies broke along with the Concorde's broken body.

Pilots often refer to "souls" rather than "bodies": reading out the final manifest to controllers before they leave the gate, they will report, say, 152 souls on board. This is done, in part, to identify the total number of people on the plane with one clear number, avoiding possible confusion about different categories of people (flight crew, cabin crew, deadheading jumpseat staff with no seat assignment, passengers, babes in arms, and so on). It's a holdover from maritime jargon, recalling how permeably the semiotics of marine and aeronautic mobilities mesh. An 1805 usage example appears in the *Virginia Argus* shipping news: "The captain went ashore at the block house, and got 11 volunteers, which made our compliment of men 29, as we had but 18 souls on board."[29] The New Testament used similar phraseology: "when once the longsuffering of God waited in the days of Noah, while the ark was a preparing, wherein few, that is, eight souls were saved by water" (1 Peter 3:20); on Paul's journey to Rome, "we were in all in the ship two hundred threescore and sixteen souls." (Acts 27:37).

An aviation website suggests another resonance:

> When an air traffic controller asks a pilot, during an emergency, for the number of souls on board, it communicates to the pilot that the controller and pilot are focusing extra hard together on solving the emergency successfully, and that one word tells the pilot that the controller is going to be marshaling resources to help in every way possible. "Souls" is a term full of life and caring. For rescuers, it communicates very quickly the total number of persons who must be found and saved.[30]

References to souls may be a superstitious way of thinking about the human bodies on board. Bodies are fragile, as Le Couleur reminds us, while souls are eternal, at least for believers (and just as there are no atheists in foxholes, I find there aren't many on airplanes either—though in debris fields, there are only existentialists). The word puts a brighter spin on a possible worst-case outcome: even if 152 bodies don't survive the flight, 152 souls will endure. It's a proactive way of sparing people (metaphysically, spiritually, imaginatively) from the debris field's ignominies: disembodying them, just in case, and disambiguating their bodies from the plane's body. Le Couleur shows what it looks like if bodies remain just bodies.

The lyrics in "Concorde" give way to a contrapuntal voice behind an instrumental track, a dialogue between the flight deck and air traffic control that is, eerily, sampled from the actual air traffic control recording of the conversation that took place just before, and just after, the plane caught fire (Figure 2.4):

> "Concorde pour New York en Echo 26. Il nous faudrait la 26 droite sur toute sa longueur." "Prévoyez la 26 droite. 4590 Piste 26 droite vent 090 8kt" "4590 Décolle 26 droite." "4590 vous avez des flammes derrière vous." "Reçu." "Vous avez priorité pour le retour sur le terrain. Concorde retourne sur la piste 09 en sens inverse." "Négatif on tente Le Bourget."

> ("Concorde for New York in Echo 26. We need 26 right for its entire length." "Plan for 26 right. 4590 Runway 26 right. Wind 090 8kt." "4590 Taking off 26 right." "4590 you have flames behind you." "Received." "You have priority for the return to the field. Concorde return to runway 09 in reverse." "Negative, we'll try Le Bourget.")

Le Bourget airport, ten miles from CDG on the other side of Paris, houses a Museum of Air and Space which today features a Concorde (intact): British Airways and Air France each had seven in their fleets, and many of the now-retired aircraft are popular exhibits in aviation museums around the world.

The spoken interlude adds "a harrowing layer of fear, but it's done so poignantly," writes Adrian Vargas, reviewing the song's "macabre sensuality." (It goes without saying that this dialogue, however horrific, is all intoned in the same cool, steady register throughout, as if the plane were *not* about to self-destruct.) The band "wanted to pay tribute to this mythical plane Concorde" by making their song like a romantic break-up. "These are the last moments of the plane, which remembers its memories, its image, its exploits. Like the last discussion when you break up, you remember our good times, trying everything to save the relationship but it ends and the name of this lover remains in our history, in our memory."[31]

"Concorde" celebrates the uniquely beautiful aircraft whose name will go down in history "Comme l'avion / Dépassant le son" (as the airplane beyond sound), but its sleek transcendent form contrasts trenchantly with its "fin spectaculaire" (spectacular ending). The music is disconcertingly at odds with the content. Its dreamy, ambient sound evokes a disco more than a dirge: "colourful synths and eclectic blend of vintage and modern sounds will have listeners wanting to twirl the night away on a lit-up dance floor," writes Jordan Currie, "only to be left feeling like they've stumbled into a living nightmare when further inspecting the lyrical content."[32] This jolt of stylistic discordance mimics the crash: what began as a lovely experience on the world's fastest passenger plane turned into a horrible break-up.

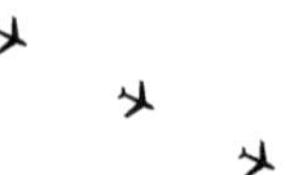

James Taylor's "Fire and Rain" (1970) typifies the strange, wonderful oxymorons of plane-crash songs. He sings of sweet dreams and flying machines in pieces on the ground: the image is no less potent for its brevity. Crashes are so large in so many ways, and one might accuse Taylor of trivializing them by reducing them to such a compact articulation, but of course I'd disagree. He does what so much music, art, literature, dance, and other aesthetic media aspire to accomplish: capturing immensely vast phenomena in a mode that is more easily accessible. The largeness of a crash overwhelms, while the achievement of encapsulating it in a single line makes it seem comprehensible. There are enough other sources that offer more exhaustive catalogs of aviation disasters; stylizing the diffuse, dispersed, devastating phenomenon of a debris field in a sweet, catchy line of music shows how we can resist its seemingly unyielding horror. It's lyrically creative—pleasantly distracting—when Taylor depicts the crash vehicle as a flying machine instead of a plain old plane. (I wonder if he knew the Wrights' 1906 patent, number 821,393, was for a "Flying-Machine.")

The line is an example of chiasmus—the same technique Yeats used in "An Irish Airman Foresees His Death"—oddly conjoining the figurative with the literal. Dreams lying in pieces on the ground describes a symbolic, emotional tragedy, while flying machines in pieces on the ground represents a literal aeronautical tragedy—two very different things, certainly, but in this song's imaginative space, listeners imagine that those crossed images are, if not identical, then comparable. The destruction of a dream, though it does not leave dead bodies in a scorched landscape, can still be quite traumatic. Taylor provocatively equates devastating emotion with literal physical devastation. He may or may not be right about this—but once again I'll say, approvingly, that it's a unique and interesting way to think about plane crashes, and to contextualize them in relation to other aspects of our lives, so . . . it goes into my investigative report.

Taylor's song mixes dreams and crashes, hope and failure, throughout. It describes friends who have suffered and died, alongside his own achievements and his own traumas. "Fire and Rain": life is full of paradoxes, reverses. The fires are horrible, but the rain will come and douse them. In 1966, Taylor's first band, which was mostly unsuccessful and disappeared quickly, was called "The Flying Machine," and lay in pieces after they broke up. The images of flying-machine wreckage also allude to Taylor's struggles with addiction and a friend's suicide, writes Elizabeth Maxham.[33] But whatever personal roman-à-clef Taylor presents here, it is still without question a plane crash, and I have to say it's one of my favorites: that line has become a mantra for me, a refrain. It embodies the stories and the spirit of my investigations, but delicately, aesthetically, even somewhat soothingly.

Taylor performed "Fire and Rain" for an episode of "The Simpsons" ("Deep Space Homer," 1994). Homer accompanies astronaut Buzz Aldrin (also playing himself) on the space shuttle, and Taylor visits mission control to sing for them. When he gets to the line about flying machines in pieces on the ground, he pauses, realizes the lyrics are inappropriate in this context, and revises: "Um, Sweet dreams and flying machines flying safely through the air." It's a good laugh line, but more than that, it acknowledges, in its reversal, the actual line's power as a haunting, minimalist description of aeronautical tragedy.

"Flying on the Ground is Wrong" is a song by Taylor's sometime-collaborator Neil Young from *Buffalo Springfield*, that band's first album. The song is not about planes—here, "flying" is a euphemism for getting stoned—but it's still a pretty good, succinct apothegm. Whenever possible, fly in the air.

✈ The sky plane caught fire

A stark contrast to Taylor's soothingly softened crash scene is Rammstein's 2004 German song "Dalai Lama," named for the spiritual leader who famously fears flying, though there is no other reference to him aside from the title. Rammstein spares no fraught details about the terrifying possibilities of flying machines that aren't flying as well as one would hope. (They use that exact descriptor, *Flugmaschine*, possibly as a shout-out to Taylor? And/or the Wright brothers?) A man sits on a plane with his child, falling asleep hours from their destination. All seems normal until the lyrics (translated here) turn suddenly dark:

Onwards, onwards into destruction
We must live until we die.
Humans don't belong in the sky.
So the lord in Heaven calls
his sons to the wind
Bring me this human child.

Onwards, onwards into destruction
We must live until we die.
And the child says to the father
Don't you hear the thunder?
That's the king of all the winds
He wants me to become his child.

From the clouds falls a choir
which crawls into the little ear.
Come here, stay here
We'll be good to you
Come here, stay here
We are your brothers

The storm embraces the flying machine.
The pressure falls quickly in the cabin.
A muffled rumbling drives the night.
In panic the human cargo screams.[34]

And then the father squeezes his child to death in this extremely unsettling song—to end his terror? So he can stay in "heaven"? It's a riff on Goethe's 1782 poem "Der Erlkönig" ("The Elf King"), in which the father and son's mode of mobility was equestrian, not aeronautic. It's all very strange, even creepier when you hear its ominous and relentlessly pulsing beat, and I'll just leave it at that. Songs about plane crashes seem to have a greater likelihood of being odd; as many as there are, it remains a somewhat bizarre thing to sing about.

Every song in this chapter's playlist has a line I can't get out of my head, especially when I'm up in the heavens myself and feel as if I'm flying onwards, onwards into (possible) destruction: here, the earworm is: "Der Mensch gehört nicht in die Luft" ("Humans don't belong in the sky"). Yes, one could certainly make that argument.

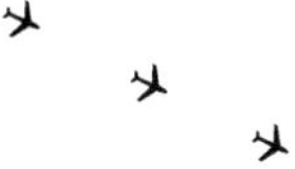

The phrase "On a wing and a prayer" belongs in any survey of musical crashes, or near-crashes. It's a common descriptor of how someone in a dire situation draws on meager resources and luck (not to mention the hope of divine intervention) to get out of it. In the 1942 film *Flying Tigers*, about US volunteers who fought the Japanese in China during WWII, John Wayne's character asks about desperately needed replacement pilots: "Any word on that flight yet?" A hotel clerk replies, "Yes sir, it was attacked and fired on by Japanese aircraft. She's coming in on one wing and a prayer." Songwriters Harold Adamson and Jimmie McHugh turned that line into a patriotic hit (sung by Bing Crosby) the next year, "Comin' in on a Wing and a Prayer," about a damaged warplane barely able to limp back to base:

One of our planes was missing, two hours overdue.
One of our planes was missing with all its gallant crew.
The radio sets were hummin', they wait for their word.
Then a noise broke through that humming and this is what we heard.

Comin' in on a wing and a prayer,
Comin' in on a wing and a prayer.
Though there's one motor gone we can still carry on,
Comin' in on a wing and a prayer.

What a show, what a fight,
Yes we really hit our target for tonight.
How we'll sing as we limp through the air,
Look below, there's a field over there.
Though there's one motor gone we can still carry on
Comin' in on a wing and a prayer.[35]

The expression that came from cinema and became a song then jumped back onto the silver screen: in 1944, Henry Hathaway's film *Wing and a Prayer* told the story of an American aircraft in the battle of Midway. The allusion to a stricken aircraft limping home may have drawn on the phrase "winging it," referring to actors struggling through parts they just recently learned in the theater's wings.[36]

The fraught plane in *Flying Tigers* supposedly had "one wing": flight isn't possible with only one wing, though there's an exception that proves the rule. In a 1983 training exercise, two Israeli Air Force aircraft, an F-15 Eagle and an A-4 Skyhawk, collided in mid-air over the Negev. The Skyhawk crew ejected safely and the F-15, despite having its right wing almost completely sheared off, managed to land at a nearby airbase. Realizing his plane was badly damaged when it "fell in a very tight spiral after a huge fuel leak from its right wing," the pilot regained control. Ordered to eject, "he decided not to bail out since he was confident he could land the plane at the nearest airfield, 10 miles away, even though the F-15 was flying on vapors. Then just before ejecting, [he] decided to light the afterburners, gaining speed and managing to somehow control the F-15 once again."[37] The airplane's lifting properties along with an overabundant engine thrust allowed the pilot to land his crippled plane on one wing and, I would imagine, a prayer.

The song's title highlights a crucial aeronautical element (wing) juxtaposed with something not included in engineering specs (prayer): something physical alongside something metaphysical, both of which work in tandem (if you believe in prayer . . . and in aerodynamics) to sustain flight. Wings keep planes aloft: most of the lift comes from the wing. Prayers are spiritually uplifting, and when aviation goes out of kilter, "uplift" might just work as an emergency replacement for lift.

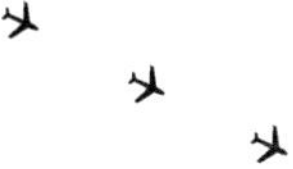

"El Vuelo 587" ("Flight 587"), later released as "El Avión" ("The Plane"), wasn't a crash song when it was released in 1997, but it became one when American Airlines flight 587 crashed in November 2001—just as John Gillespie Magee Jr.'s "High Flight" wasn't a crash poem until Magee subsequently crashed. When Kinito Méndez recorded the song, the Dominican merengue star "was singing of sheer joy," as captured in a 2001 news story headlined: "Plane crash changes meaning of a joyful song." Méndez was celebrating "the thrill of flying home for Christmas, of saving money all year for a blissful month of food and rum, dancing, and family. It's such a specific experience, so firmly etched in the Dominican consciousness, that he mentioned the most popular flight from the United States."[38] American's early-morning Airbus A300 JFK–Santo Domingo flight was a lifeline and a cultural phenomenon among New York's large Dominican community; Dominican movies often featured characters taking that flight, as Méndez himself frequently had.

Because the crash happened just two months after 9/11, and in New York, everyone initially assumed it was another terrorist incident. People were still enormously rattled, and it felt as if September's tragedy had happened again. Fairly quickly, though, terrorism was ruled out, and eventually the cause was identified as pilot error. The flight took off too soon behind a large plane that departed three minutes earlier, getting caught in its considerable wake turbulence. Bigger planes create greater turbulence, which dissipates if the next pilots wait a sufficient amount of time before starting their own takeoff roll; that's why planes sit and wait at the top of the runway. When American's crew realized what was happening, they responded too aggressively, as an aviation blogger recounts:

> As the plane encountered wake turbulence from a Boeing 747, the first officer overcorrected, then overcorrected in the opposite direction, over and over until the plane slewed so hard to the side that the vertical stabilizer ripped off in flight. How could this happen? Could a pilot really rip the tail off his own plane using

> nothing more than the flight controls? Who had taught him this deadly technique, and why?[39]

"Slew": turn or slide suddenly, violently, out of control. First Officer Sten Molin (final words: "Holy shit!") reacted to the turbulence with "unnecessary and excessive" use of the rudder, causing structural failure. The rudder swung back and forth four times in 7.5 seconds, the NTSB reported, noting also that Molin had been cited twice before for "overreacting" to wake turbulence.[40] Airbus, too, was found partly at fault because of flawed design.

A dreadfully bland memorial marks the spot where flight 587 impacted the Queens seaside neighborhood of Belle Harbor just two minutes into its flight, killing all 260 aboard along with five on the ground: the second-deadliest US aviation accident, not including 9/11. (Listmakers often cannot figure out exactly where to put 9/11.) Several dozen Belle Harbor residents, both office workers and firefighters, had died in the recent catastrophe at the World Trade Center;

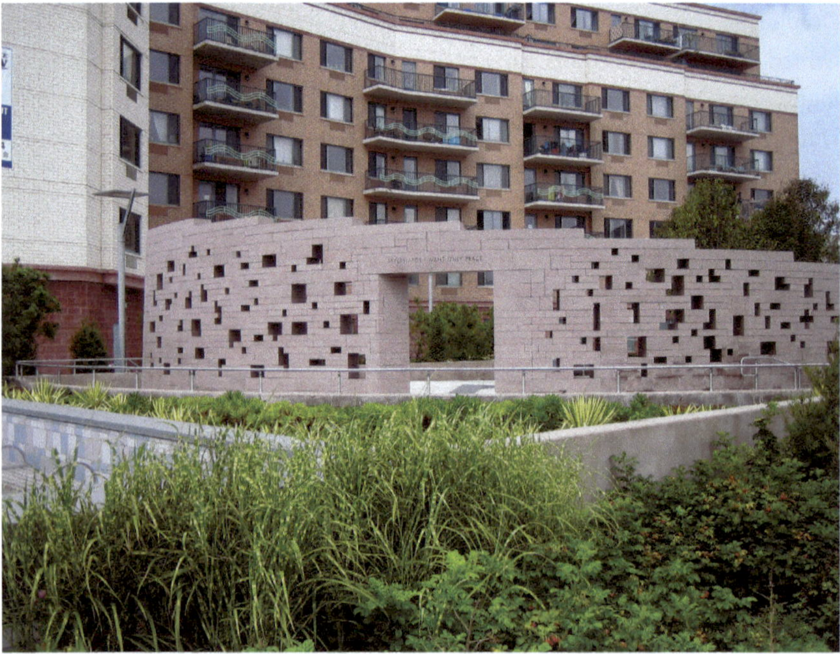

Figure 4.4 Freddie Rodriguez's monument features dull stones in a dull design that dully echoes the dull architecture behind it in Belle Harbor's Flight 587 Memorial Park. Gaps in the wall (obviously) symbolize the gaps left in people's lives when their loved ones died.

when flight 587 came down into their quiet community, the recurring trauma felt unbelievable, incessant.[41]

Until 2001, it was a sign that Christmas season had arrived when "El Avión" started playing on the radio every November. "It's full of hope, happiness, and gifts from the people who come," said disc jockey Miguel Espinal, loosely translating the lyrics that accompany the song's soaring horns and pulsing merengue rhythm. "The song describes a man who brings seven suitcases on the flight but still doesn't have room for all of the gifts he's carrying. It promises 'a spicy Christmas, like in times before.'" Méndez "wanted to write a song that would unite Dominicans living outside the country and those living inside."[42]

But the accident that brought down the plane also brought down the song, overwriting its exuberantly festive spirit with tragedy. "It's a very happy song," Espinal said, or rather, "It was. Now, I don't want to hear it." But Méndez has kept playing it: "I can't stop performing the song," he says. "I now think of the song as a remembrance and a tribute to all the Dominican people that disappeared on that plane." Soon after the crash, Méndez said he might revise the lyrics to acknowledge the tragedy,[43] though I have not found any indication that he ever did. He also said he might write a new song, "a slower song in tribute to all those who died,"[44] but again he does not seem to have done this. It's as if Méndez feels compelled to keep "El Vuelo 587" flying, so to speak, because flight 587 can no longer do so. (American still flies JFK-SDQ, but not nonstop: travelers now have to connect overnight in Miami, a sixteen-hour trip.)

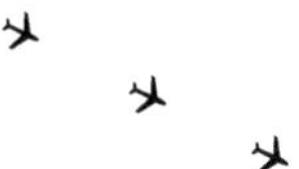

I wish readers could listen to all these songs, rather than just skimming my inadequate abbreviated extracts detached from actual music. (You *can* hear them easily, freely available on YouTube. I suggest playing them in the background while reading about how they illuminate these crash investigations—or, like me, collect them into an in-flight playlist.)

If your time is finite, and assuming you're familiar with "American Pie," please listen to, at least, "Concorde," "Dalai Lama," and Woody Guthrie's "Deportee," also known as "Plane Wreck at Los Gatos," a plaintive, powerful, 1948 ballad about a crash earlier that year in California's Central Valley. And you won't regret queuing up a dozen wonderful cover versions of this classic folk tune: Cisco Houston channels Guthrie's essence in his 1961 recording; Dave Guard & The

Whiskeyhill Singers, 1962, are pleasantly and slowly passionate. Judy Collins's 1963 version is piercingly beautiful in a folk-operatic mood. Odetta, the first Black singer to record "Deportee" (1964), gives a slow, dignified rendition which is one of the best of the bunch in terms of passionately conveying the story. Pete Seeger's 1967 version is of course perfect—his renditions of Guthrie's songs always seem like definitive reinterpretations, and this recording, with its simple twangy rhythms accompanying the powerfully ethical narrative, is perhaps Seeger's best cover of Guthrie's music. Listen also to the 1974 version by Woody's son Arlo (also sublime, with especially rich choruses), and Joan Baez's from 1971 (extraordinary too). The Byrds' 1969 cover has a dose more rock and Latin-inflected rhythms than the other versions, most of which hew pretty closely to Guthrie's folksy mode. Dolly Parton's 1980 version is perfectly Parton, and Bruce Springsteen sang it like The Boss at the 2021 ceremony where he received the Woody Guthrie Prize. Introducing it as "Woody's immigration song," Springsteen noted, "Deportee" is absolutely as relevant today as it was generations ago.[45] Listen also to Bob Dylan's rendition, and Sweet Honey in the Rock's, striking retellings of the tragedy in unique styles.

Guthrie's simple, soulful story about the dead workers is one of the most effective cultural performances I've come across, in any medium or genre, in terms of memorializing and humanizing plane-crash victims. "Humanizing" can be an offensive term, implying that the subjects would be less than human if not for the cultural intervention. In this case, though, people and mediascapes had consciously dehumanized the crash victims with racist, classist, and anti-immigrant prejudices; Guthrie's song intentionally and forcefully resists that. We might think of his intent, then, as anti-dehumanizing.

Guthrie was motivated to write "Deportee" after hearing about the crash, which killed all thirty-two on board—twenty-eight Mexican citizens who were migrant agricultural laborers and four Anglo victims: two captains, a stewardess who was married to one of the captains, and a guard from Immigration and Naturalization Service onboard to watch over the deportees. The DC-3 was overloaded as it departed Oakland for Imperial County Airport, twelve miles north of the border city of Mexicali. Outfitted for only twenty-six passengers, three more ended up sitting on the luggage. The plane slightly exceeded its takeoff weight limit, perhaps not enough to affect flight safety, "but it was a clue into the state of mind of the pilot and flight crew."[46]

News accounts Guthrie read about the crash did not list the Mexican victims' names, describing them simply as "deportees"—Mexican farm workers were deported back to their homeland every year after growing season, and most media coverage treated them as an anonymous cohort of fieldhands.

Indeed, crash victims (apart from celebrities) are often anonymized, if not dehumanized: they are almost always reduced to numbers, or described—if personal details are given—in terms of generic affiliations: nationalities, study-abroad students from a certain college, players on a particular team. Of all the people killed on 9/11, I can recall only two names: Todd Beamer, who led the passenger revolt on United flight 93—"Let's roll"—and Barbara Olson, a television commentator whose husband Ted argued the 2000 Supreme Court election case that put George W. Bush in the White House (but later redeemed himself with his outspoken advocacy for gay marriage).

Guthrie found the victims' names, which his lyrics recount intimately:

> Goodbye to my Juan, goodbye, Rosalita,
> *Adios mis amigos, Jesus y Maria*;
> You won't have your names when you ride the big airplane,
> All they will call you will be "deportees."[47]

"My Juan" was Juan Valenzuela Ruiz, a passenger whose body was never identified, and Jesus was Jesús Meza Santos. Maria Santana Rodríguez was the only Mexican woman onboard. There was a man named Rosalio Padilla Estrada, and perhaps Guthrie mistakenly (or artistically) transformed him into Rosalita. Tim Hernandez notes that the crash investigation team made many spelling mistakes rendering names and genders erroneously,[48] making Guthrie's investigative report all the more necessary.

The workers eulogized in "Deportee" were not regarded as having any value apart from their work of feeding Americans. Most people looked away (and still do) from migrant laborers' tenuous transient subsistence, but not Guthrie. His song imagines their own voices:

> Some of us are illegal, and some are not wanted,
> Our work contract's out and we have to move on.
> Six hundred miles to that Mexican border,
> They chase us like outlaws, like rustlers, like thieves.

Even before the plane crash, the deportees comprised a community of people who suffered and died in many other ways (as they do still today) trying to make a living:

> We died in your hills, we died in your deserts,
> We died in your valleys and died on your plains.

> We died 'neath your trees and we died in your bushes,
> Both sides of the river, we died just the same.

Finally, in the next-to-last stanza, Guthrie narrates the crash—with the concentrated minimalism that songwriters often use to render the unimaginably chaotic violence of a crash in a tight, smooth musical passage. The tragedy happens in just two lines:

> The sky plane caught fire over Los Gatos Canyon,
> A fireball of lightning, and shook all our hills.

The scene has a natural, stylized simplicity: fire, lightning, canyon, hills. "Sky plane" might seem like a redundant descriptor, or perhaps it foreshadows that the plane will not be in the sky for long. "Deportee" depicts bounteous nature, but the sky plane emphasizes discordance between the ethos of the natural world, the *sky*, vs. aeromobility in the service of villainy, the *plane*. The planes offend the natural world as Americans (ab)use the sky to expel Mexicans, exiling them from *our* Eden once they have served their purpose of harvesting our crops. We have transgressed against the landscape, and for Guthrie, this tragedy informs the specific tragedy of the plane crash. The racism, classism, and xenophobia he describes are even more tragic than the engine failure. As happens so often in plane crashes, multiple distinct failures precipitate the disaster; Guthrie's investigative postmortem spotlights ethical failure as its most egregious cause.

The song's stylized two-line crash is followed by an even more stylized, poeticized, one-line debris field, certainly one of the most delicate (yet no less terrible) that my investigations have uncovered:

> Who are all these friends, all scattered like dry leaves?

The simple, natural imagery is the antithesis of the fragmented, scorched mechanical debris that comprises actual crash sites. Friends scattered like leaves (friends of each other? Of Guthrie? Of the song's audience, after Guthrie has tried to fix our culture's ethical lapses?) connotes tragedy, but also an attempt to look at the crash scene in a way that eases the pain: they did not die alone.

I've said that the discourse of songs may provide less upsetting ways to conceptualize crashes: much of what stuns us about plane crashes is stripped away from Guthrie's account. There is dangerous violence in "Deportees," as there must be, but really in just one word: "fireball." (A bizarre piece of trivia: the charter airline whose plane crashed in Los Gatos, Airline Transport Carriers, was owned by a couple who previously ran a company with the worst name ever for an aviation operation—Fireball Air Lines! Did Guthrie know this?) Yes, the hills shake, the sky lights up, and the friends scatter like dry leaves: all this is disturbing, and is of course the consequence of the fireball, but still it's much less visceral than it might be. It's subdued, stylized, transposed into a musical voice that's more palatable than reality. Art is doing its job.

Compare Guthrie's account of the crash with a more factual, reportorial description:

> One hour and 35 minutes after the aircraft had departed from Oakland, it was observed flying over the hills east of Coalinga, California, cruising at an estimated altitude of 5,000 feet above the ground. At the same time, a trail of white vapor, 150 to 200 feet long, was observed streaming from the left engine of the aircraft. Ten to 15 seconds later, flames were then seen flowing from the left engine over the wing and back to the tail. Witnesses on the ground claim to have seen several people jump from the doomed airliner when, seconds later, the left wing broke free from the fuselage, and the airplane fell to earth, crashing in a spectacular fireball in Los Gatos Canyon, killing all aboard.[49]

Another account is based on reports from eyewitness Red Childers, who described it to his granddaughter:

> As Red ran closer he watched a thread of black smoke unfurl from the mountain pass, where a fragile seam between two worlds had ripped open. Everywhere he looked were articles of clothing, papers and documents, life's particulars blown across the canyon. He could smell fire. Rounding the bend, he spotted it. A burning sensation entered his lungs, forcing him to retreat. The tops of trees surrounding the wreckage were aflame. A chill ran through him when he discovered that what he first mistook for felled tree limbs weren't trees at all. The echoes of godforsaken screams cast out into the air just seconds ago were still reverberating in Red's ears. "Red saw seats with people still in 'em being thrown out the hole in the side of the plane," his granddaughter June recalled. "They were screaming until they hit the ground. There was nothing he could do but watch in horror."

Finally, images captured by local newspaper photographer Henry Stuart give one more perspective of the same moment. Tim Hernandez describes these photographs in *All They Will Call You*, his book about the song:

> Stuart photographed the wreckage up close, while the embers were still ascending. Then he went and stood atop the ridge and panned out as far as he

> could, in an attempt to capture the totality. He did his best to adjust the aperture delicately to document the angle of light just right, so that someone viewing these stills, six decades later, would get an idea, not only of the images, but of the sensory reality whole. But his heart was racing. His hands trembled. The work was compromised. Some of the images are nothing but smoke, as if in a cloud. Photographs taken too close. Strange abstractions. Blobs of black and gray. Empty spaces. Gaps that invite the mind to make their own meaning. If you look close, closer yet, you find shapes, objects amid the shadow and light. Like a Rorschach test, you come to discover the darkest recesses of your own imagination. A scrap of the engine's propeller, at first glance, suggests a human appendage. But no, it's a propeller after all. A skeletal gear. A bone of skyship.[50]

Guthrie's transformative lyrical distillation of all this into "friends, all scattered like dry leaves," preserves the essence of the scene's sensory intensity, while declining to describe the particular details of exactly what was actually *scattered* across the debris field: he omitted clothing and body parts, burning metal and smoke, blobs and scraps and gaps, from his investigative report. "A bone of skyship," as Hernandez describes one of the images: yes, that's certainly poetic in its way, and the photographs too have their own aesthetic intensity, but that's not the story Guthrie wants to tell or the way he wants to tell it. All these different perspectives convey, as we would expect, different ways of perceiving and rendering the debris field. The reportorial stories and images are sad, informative, important, moving; the photographs are haunting, resonant; Guthrie's song is timeless and transcendent. Redux versions of it appear continually, year after year, just as immigrants continue to be exploited year after year, and planes continue to crash, with declining frequency, but still, year after year.

The farmworkers were buried in Fresno, namelessly. A mass grave includes a bronze marker that reads: "28 Mexican citizens who died in an airplane accident." The cemetery catalog lists them as "Mexican national 1, Mexican national 2," and so on, up to 28. In 2011, Hernandez spearheaded a drive to raise funds for a memorial engraved with the victims' names, which he found in a long-neglected file from the annals of Fresno County's Hall of Records. Guthrie's daughter, Nora, blessed his effort: "My father believed in the importance of names. He would repeat them like a chant. Finding their names matters."

The monument was dedicated in 2013, etched with thirty-two falling leaves—a perfect tribute to Guthrie's imaginative depiction of the debris field. Four leaves bear only the initials of the Americans who died on the flight (since their names had already been reported),[51] and in the center are the names of the twenty-eight "deportees":

> Miguel Negrete Álvarez. Tomás Aviña de Gracia. Francisco Llamas Durán. Santiago García Elizondo. Rosalio Padilla Estrada. Tomás Padilla Márquez. Bernabé López Garcia. Salvador Sandoval Hernández. Severo Medina Lára. Elías Trujillo Macias. José Rodriguez Macias. Luis López Medina. Manuel Calderón Merino. Luis Cuevas Miranda. Martin Razo Navarro. Ignacio Pérez Navarro. Román Ochoa Ochoa. Ramón Paredes Gonzalez. Guadalupe Ramírez Lára. Apolonio Ramírez Placencia. Alberto Carlos Raygoza. Guadalupe Hernández Rodríguez. Maria Santana Rodríguez. Juan Valenzuela Ruiz. Wenceslao Flores Ruiz. José Valdívia Sánchez. Jesús Meza Santos. Baldomero Marcas Torres.

It is certainly one of the most poignant plane-crash memorials ever devised, inspired by one of the very best musical artifacts from a cultural debris field.

✈ I wonder when I'll hit the ground

There are dozens of tracks I call simply "going-down songs," which is pretty self-explanatory: that's what happens. We're about to crash, I'm scared, I don't want to die. (Most of these are not on my panic-alleviating playlist.) They express singers' fears in varied and interesting ways, and they're not bland or boilerplate, but they all basically say the same thing. Crash is a crash is a crash is a crash, as Gertrude Stein might have said if she'd been a humanist air crash investigator.

These going-down songs are a far cry (emphasis on *cry*!) from the more dulcet music of Woody Guthrie or Don McLean. "Death" (2008), by English post-punk revival band White Lies, typifies this sub-genre:

> I love the feeling when we lift off
> Watching the world so small below
>
> I wonder what keeps us so high up
> Could there be a love beneath these wings?
> If we suddenly fall should I scream out?
> Or keep very quiet and cling to my mouth?
>
> As I'm crying, so frightened of dying
> Relax, yes, I'm trying
> This fear's got a hold on me

Yes, this fear's got a hold on me

Floating neither up or down
I wonder when I'll hit the ground
Will the earth beneath my body shake
And cast your sleeping hearts awake?

Could it tremble stars from moonlit skies?
Could it drag a tear from your cold eyes?

Assemblage 23, an electronic body music/futurepop one-man band, sings in the 2004 track "30k feet":

Hello, if you're there pick up the phone
I'm calling from thirty thousand feet above you
The captain's just informed us that our plane is going down
So I'm calling for one last time to say I love you
I'm not certain how much time I might have left so I'll be brief
I'm sorry if this message only amplifies your grief
But I couldn't bear the burden of never having said goodbye
And the pain you feel I promise you will go away with time
I'm sorry I won't be there to see our children grow
Please tell them that I loved them more than they will ever know
Tell my family and friends how much I love them all as well
I'm sure that we will meet again but only time will tell
I'm sorry most of all I won't be there when you grow old
To be there by your side and keep you warm when you are cold
Forgive me but I think my time is drawing to a close
So I've one last thing to tell you now before I have to go
I . . .

The song ends there, cut off mid-breath (as if the plane just crashed—get it?!), followed by a creepy electronic squeal. It's less eloquent than the exquisitely composed ending of Yeats's poem, but perhaps more accurate, more authentic. Assemblage 23's title describes how far the plane will fall, an obvious but noteworthy detail. In an article headlined "What If You Fell out of an Airplane at 30,000 Feet," Pierre Köchel explains: "When you're in free-fall . . . it all happens so fast. From the moment you're outside of the plane, it's only about 170 seconds until you hit the ground. During that time you will be extremely cold, and deprived of oxygen."[52] Assemblage 23's song clocks in at 3:10, just 20 seconds longer than the time Köchel estimates the free-fall would last.

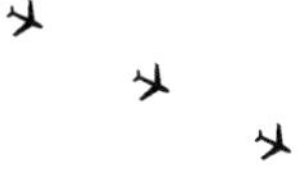

If I were Canadian, I'd have to include a much lengthier discussion of The Tragically Hip's 1993 song "Fifty Mission Cap," a tribute to Toronto Maple Leafs defenseman Bill Barilko. A few months after he scored the 1951 Stanley Cup's winning goal over the Montreal Canadiens—generally considered the team's most famous goal ever—he disappeared. He had flown off for a fishing trip in a single-engine Fairchild 24 floatplane that vanished without a trace. The Royal Canadian Air Force spent two months looking for it—the costliest air rescue search in Canadian history—but without success.[53] Finally, in 1962, the wreckage was found and Barilko was buried in his hometown. Auspiciously, that same year, the Leafs won the championship for the first time since 1951. "Fifty Mission Cap" is played during every Maple Leafs home game, and the team's locker room features a framed handwritten copy of it.[54]

But I need to wrap up this soundtrack, though it seems to want to keep playing on and on. If I don't turn off (or at least pause) the music, I'll end up with a book that's all about plane-crash songs, with no room for all the other interesting cultural whatnot I'm investigating. I'll play us out with a few final recommendations: Fall Out Boy's "Sending Postcards From a Plane Crash (Wish You Were Here)"; "Plane Crash Blues (I Can't Play the Piano)," by Car Seat Headrest; "Plane Crash," by Covey; "About A Plane Crash," by Suicide Silence; Lyrica Anderson's "Crashing Planes"; "Planes Do Crash," by The Raveonettes. "At the Bottom of Everything," by Bright Eyes, features an apology from the flight deck. In a spoken passage before the music starts, lead singer Conor Oberst sets the scene:

> And then, uh, suddenly there was this huge mechanical failure, and one of the, the engines gave out, and they started just falling thirty-thousand feet. The pilot's on the, on the microphone and he's, he's saying, "I'm sorry, I'm sorry, Oh My God, I'm sorry" and apologizing.[55]

Models of stoic discipline, pilots are eternally calm, graceful under pressure. As dire as things may get, they remain entirely focused on *not crashing*, so in real life they would have no mental space left to address an imminent tragedy the way Oberst describes. But even though a pilot would never in a million years say anything like this to their passengers, "At the Bottom of Everything" makes us wonder if perhaps they should? Aviation is science, science is truth: shouldn't that truth be absolute, or is there some rationale for reconsidering the standard operating procedure of feeding passengers white lies so they don't panic? I won't answer that question, but will simply record in my investigation that Bright Eyes raises the possibility of an alternate protocol, unconditional pilot honesty, that may merit further exploration. Here's an example of the status quo: just before Alaska Air flight 261 crashed off the California coast in 2000, Captain Ted Thompson made this placid PA announcement, as documented by the CVR:

> Folks we have had a flight control problem up front here, we're workin' it, uh, that's Los Angeles off to the right there, that's where we're intending to go. We're pretty busy up here workin' this situation. I don't anticipate any big problems once we get a couple of sub systems on the line, but we will be going into LAX and I'd anticipate us parking there in about twenty to thirty minutes.[56]

Nope. All eight-eight aboard the MD-83 died when the horizontal stabilizer trim system failed, due to excessive wear resulting from poor maintenance—insufficient lubrication—of a jackscrew. In its final moments, Alaska 261 was flying upside down (which inspired the opening scene in the 2012 movie *Flight* featuring Denzel Washington at the controls). Capt. Thompson's final words: "ah here we go."

In Rilo Kiley's "Plane Crash in C," nothing but the title has anything to do with a plane crash, although as we might expect, this song has a generally unnerving mood. The title reminds us that there are a great many plane crash songs—it's a genre, a tradition. Kiley is playing with the convention of classical music titles. Chopin's 24 Preludes, for example, indicate with their titles how they are all a bit different from each other but still, fundamentally of a piece: Prelude in F Minor, Prelude in D♭ Major. The one that scores my imaginary slow-motion plummet when I'm on a plane that I think might crash is Prelude in E Minor (which Chopin selected for his own funeral). Kiley suggests that we could assemble a similar assortment of plane crash songs in various keys. We might think of "American Pie" as Plane Crash in G Major, and "Deportee" as Plane Crash in D♭ Major, in Woody Guthrie's original version. The Highwaymen (Willie Nelson, Johnny Cash, Waylon Jennings, Kris Kristofferson), in a cover I don't much like, offer "Deportee" as Plane Crash in C Major, while Joan Baez's version would be Plane Crash in A# Major. Lots of songs, lots of styles, lots of keys, but unifying the whole playlist is a collection of perspectives and heuristics that resonantly illuminate cultural debris fields. Those of us who are busily scavenging through them appreciate the musical accompaniment.

5

Crashes in Art

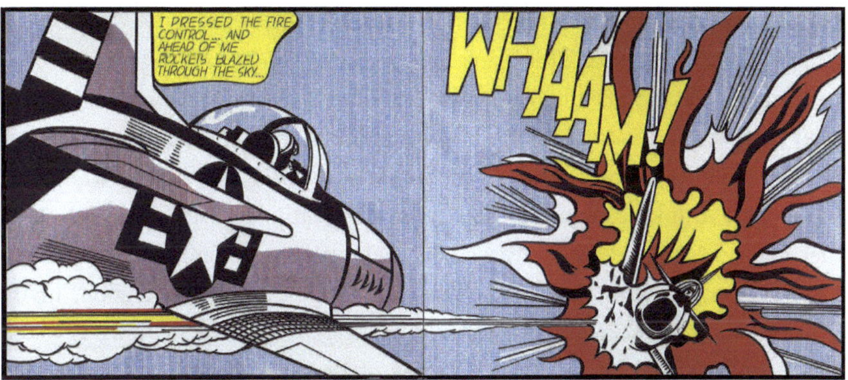

Figure 5.1 Roy Lichtenstein, *Whaam!* (1963).

The visual aesthetics of plane crashes

In September, 1923, Norman Rockwell went with his friend Dean Cornwell, an illustrator, to Atlantic City, NJ, to judge the Miss America contest. They were offered a free ride in a seaplane—it was the first time Rockwell had ever flown. The ride was bumpy but they landed safely and watched the plane go up again with other passengers. "Within seconds, everything turned catastrophic," writes biographer Deborah Solomon.

> The plane flipped over on its side, floated down like a spiraling leaf and crashed in a meadow, killing the two men inside. Later, Rockwell was surprised when Cornwell showed him some sketches he had drawn of the wrecked plane, a tangle of metal and debris. "It seems cruel, but this is how an artist looks at life," Rockwell later commented. "You realize the suffering, but you are always thinking, 'Would this make a picture, or wouldn't it make a picture?'"[1]

Aviation disasters appear less frequently in visual arts than in literature, music, film, and most other cultural media, though when they do turn up on canvas ... *WHAAM!* Is there something about the cultural resonance of plane crashes that makes such narratives more common subjects for novels and popular music, but less amenable to painting and sculpture? I'm sure there is—the data bear that out; the question is, *what*, precisely? Perhaps even in these tradition-shorn postmodern times, art is still generally considered patrician "high art," and plane crashes figure as more plebeian: fodder for action thrillers or dewy-eyed ballads rather than galleries? Fertile grist for television adventures but unworthy of painters' refined contemplation?

Plane crashes may lack the hook for sophisticated cultural engagement that museum-goers and art aficionados expect. They are simply depressing, messy. They may seem too obvious, though this is another reason why it's crucial to have a humanist crash investigator on the scene: *nothing* is straightforward after we're done thinking about it! If art is eloquently coherent, crashes seem inarticulate. Art has done pretty well for itself over the millennia hewing to the usual suspects: nudes, nature (flowers, landscapes, animals), religion, myth, history (war, violence, conquest), portraits, designs and abstractions. A plane crash could indeed be squeezed into one of these categories: landscape with plane crash (there are actually few of these in my gallery below), portrait of a nude victim (an improbable possibility). Art has profusely depicted combat, and there's some interesting military plane crash art, but it's a niche. For the most part, crash aesthetics have just a slender Venn-diagram-overlap with the established conventions and preferred subjects of traditional art.

In most visual media, artists would face technical challenges rendering plane crashes. The vocabularies of painted, sculpted, drawn, lithographed, kilned, sewn, forged, or woven artifacts are less suitable, less versatile than the technologies and lexicons of, say, cinematography, in terms of the ability to vibrantly capture all the complex elements of an aviation disaster: the moment of transition from safety to imminent tragedy; speed, noise, action, tension, terrified passengers inside the cabin juxtaposed with quick cuts to external visuals of the erratic aircraft bucking and bouncing. Film and music, which *move*, seem to be more amenable media than the static arts. Photography, though static, is a medium with properties keenly relevant to plane crashes; Andy Warhol and Paul Nash, discussed below, both created paintings that grew out of photography, and remember that the first fatal plane crash, an astounding event, was accompanied by C. H. Claudy's first plane crash photo (Figure 1.1), also astounding.

As fascinating as it would be to see crashscapes rendered in mosaic, tapestry, woodcarving, ceramic, or gesso, I have never encountered such art (and not for

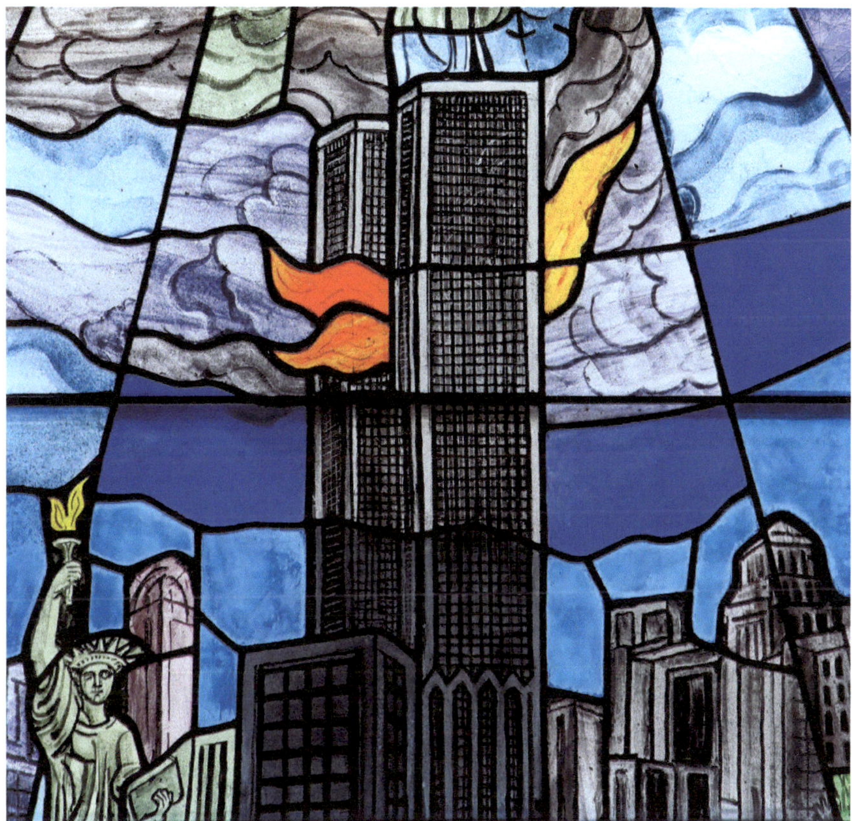

Figure 5.2 A Staten Island stained glass memorial, at Our Lady of Lourdes Church, depicts Lady Liberty's torch weirdly echoing the Twin Towers' flames.

lack of looking). I've found a few stained glass windows memorializing plane crashes, mostly 9/11; they tend to be mawkish.

Perhaps form and function are at odds: how can sculptors capture an aviation disaster's kinetic energy? What can a potter do to convey the brokenness? (*Kintsugi!*) But though plane crashes have many moving parts, there's also a point when the parts stop moving. Crashes should, then, be possible for painters to depict on canvas: to fix the aircraft's breakdown. Fix in art, that is, as in "capture, make stable"; not, alas, repair. Might plane crashes be disqualified as high art simply because the plane itself, when it impacts the ground, is no longer *high*? This may seem like mere quibbling, but in fact binaries of high and low are quite sharply inscribed—reified—in our cultural attitudes and perspectives. It is not preposterous to posit that the literal/spatial trajectories of crashes, their subject's inherent loss of elevation, somehow inflects their inability (or greatly diminished ability) to sustain the necessary altitude—highbrow—of high art.

Art is usually beautiful in some way, and plane crashes are usually not. It takes at least a bit of aesthetic perversity, resistance, subversion, for a painter to foreground a mangled hull in a debris field instead of a vase of flowers or a pleasantly serene landscape with cows.

✈ Painting war crashes

Pop art maestro Roy Lichtenstein's two-canvas painting *Whaam!* (1963) has an incomparably perfect title for plane crash art. He captures it all in a word, and I might offer my own critical response to his tour de force in a single word too: *Yep!* But prolixity being an occupational hazard for the humanist air crash investigator, I will elaborate.

Lichtenstein's title is inscribed, hugely, on the painting itself: a large, SCREAMING, eye-catching word—though actually it's more (or less?) than a word, closer to a sound, or a sound effect, as if we were watching a movie or reading a comic book rather than looking at a mere painting. Lichtenstein plays with a word—"wham"—which would be perfectly appropriate as is, but whaam is even better, and WHAAM is better than that, and WHAAM! is best of all. . . . or, I should say, *BEST OF ALL!* (The word, all upper case on the canvas, got turned down a notch for the title, *Whaam!*) If I were a little edgier, I might've called this book *WHAAM!* instead of *CRASH!* I have, actually, appropriated *WHAAM!*'s terminal punctuation for my own title, as an intertextual homage—I hope I don't owe the Lichtenstein estate copyright fees for that!

(In the early twentieth century, this figure of punctuation was known as an ecphoneme. It's easy to see why that didn't catch on, though another archaic term is much better, and I'd definitely support it for a retro reprise: "admiration mark" or "note of admiration," from the fifteenth century. Mid-twentieth century slang terms for ! were "bang," "shriek" or "shriekmark," and "pling," all of which are a thousand times better than *ecphoneme*, and snazzier than *exclamation point* too. "Bang" comes from the comics discourse that Lichtenstein draws upon—a gunshot would be represented by an exclamation point in the dialogue balloon emanating from the pistol. "Pling" and "shriek" are hacker/ASCII terms. Other aliases include "exclam," "smash," "cuss," "boing," "yell," "wow," "hey," "eureka," "soldier," and the one Lichtenstein adapts, "wham,"[2] along with "gasper," "screamer," "shout-pole," "slammer," "startler," and (!) "dog's cock."[3])

There's lots going on in *Whaam!*, undercutting my earlier assertion that it's difficult for a painting to capture all the sound and fury of a plane crash, but it's one of those exceptions that prove the rule. Lichtenstein portrays the noise, the collision, the explosive weaponry and smoke and fire: the beginning—the moment, frozen in a single visual image yet overbrimming with dynamism—of a process that will unfurl in time and space, transforming *flight* into *fall*, *airplane* into *debris*. I think Lichtenstein would have agreed with me that paintings (before *Whaam!*) mostly struggled to convey the essence of plane crashes, and his solution was to expand the vocabulary of painting by adding a multi-media dimension: including words on the canvas, which a few other painters, but not many, have done. Most of them thought that was cheating: if they have to add text, they haven't done their job of *showing* what they're supposed to represent in color, form, composition; words are seen as undercutting the purity of images. Lichtenstein transgresses this proscription resplendently, with a good word: an action word, a sound word, a comic word, a painted word. There are other, smaller words, on the canvas besides "WHAAM!"—denoting control and military/aviational precision: "I PRESSED THE FIRE CONTROL … AND AHEAD OF ME ROCKETS BLAZED THROUGH THE SKY … "—and they too will help with the crash investigation, but the story here is mainly WHAAM!

Lichtenstein cheated (or, let's say, *innovated*) in other ways too: interpolating pop culture into the world of museum art, postmodernistically reiterating the discourse of comics, using the medium and techniques of painting in ways that evoke a different medium and technique, animation. He rebukes highbrow culture, which may explain why the plane in this painting doesn't have to stay "high": it can crash.

At this moment of attack captured on canvas, the hull of the plane that was hit is still largely intact, but we can imagine what it will look like in a matter of seconds, as Lichtenstein has painted premonitory scraps of debris beneath its wing and hull. This image strikes me as uniquely insightful for understanding the split-second transformation from a unified airplane into a mass of wreckage. Rarely do we see a crash-plane as both whole and broken in the same moment; occasionally, today, a video-capture might record that, but *Whaam!* appeared decades before people were able to isolate that precise moment when a plane sat (flew) on the fulcrum of aviation and ruin. Lichtenstein pinpoints a crucial moment as he zeroes in on his investigative findings: things change.

Whaam! adapts a 1962 DC Comics issue—"All-American Men of War" volume 92—which includes a story, "The Battle Hawk,"[4] where WHAAM!-like expostulations explode profusely in nearly every frame: BAM! BLAM! VOOM! VOOMP! RATATAT! BRATATAT! CRAASH! POW! WHROOOOM! Choosing "cartoon to represent military action arguably also renders the scene ridiculous and juvenile," the Tate Museum explains in its analysis of Lichtenstein's work. While the DC comic's original intention "may have been to show glorious, action-filled images of 'All-American Men of War,'" Lichtenstein's quasi-absurdist treatment turns it into "a tongue-in-cheek male daydream of aggression, conquest and ejaculatory release." Painted as the Vietnam War was accelerating, "this deconstruction of military heroism could be read as a statement on the folly of war."[5] Like so many modern technologies, aviation could be used for the betterment of humankind or for the previously-unimaginable scope of destruction it facilitated.

If the WHAAM!-glee is sarcastic, that's a new and weird element of plane crash discourse—it resembles the sarcasm from "The Bronco Song" (see Chapter 4), which is exactly contemporaneous. Some viewers, though, will regard Lichtenstein's image without sarcasm, but rather, as a good crash—indeed, a wonderful crash: GO TEAM! This sensibility surfaced in W. B. Yeats's warplane crash poem "Reprisals," about Major Gregory ("Some nineteen German planes, they say, / You had brought down before you died. / We called it a good death"), but that was a bit more polite, restrained. Not now. In the post-atomic age, in a war that seemed more violently brutal than any before (perhaps because previous ones were not televised, but also because of deadlier weaponry), there's nothing subtle about the pleasure that Lichtenstein's crash may embody—again, for some: not for those in peace movements, or who feared being drafted for combat, or who were being bombed from above.

As humanist air crash investigators try to discover and reassemble stories out of the wreckage, in tandem with regular air crash folks digging for an etiology, we all need to find the right words. Their forensic analytic discourse is comprised of important terms, to be sure, but their texts are dry: clunky acronyms, offputting terminology, dull jargon. Pardon my indignation, but how can such tediously long-winded technical prose do justice to such gripping stories? What a mismatch of form and function, content and style, signifier and signified. I can understand why their reports read as they do and what their rhetorical premises are, even if I disapprove of them. But their turgidity makes my writing here all the more necessary to enable an all-encompassing investigation. We need to fill in the gaps, the culture, the humanity elided in their dispassionate subsections and data, maps and diagrams. They have missed the BLAM and VOOMP of it all, the ironies and tragedies, the heroism of most pilots, the stupid mistakes of others, the stories of what it's like to survive an aviation disaster, and how to deal with the devastation when loved ones perish amid the debris. Look at their crash narratives, and look at mine. Seriously: who's doing a better job of answering first officer Pierre-Cédric Bonin's query, "*Mais qu'est-ce qui se passe*!!?" Who's telling the more compelling story of what's going on?

Our humanist vernacular, WHAAM! and fuck, existentialism and irony and anxiety, superstition/prolepsis … freedom, fear, *flygskam* … flying machines, melancholy exits, wing and a prayer, tumult in the clouds, buying the farm, this'll be the day that I die: these are not just stylistic frippery or wry legerdemain or belle lettres—far from it. They are precisely the words we need to do our investigation here, studying these crashed planes as we sift through their cultural debris fields.

Revisiting those tiny pieces of *Whaam!*'s anticipatory debris from the plane that will soon crash: Lichtenstein does not depict a debris field in much detail, but he does show us the instant at which it begins to develop, up in the clear blue skies. (*YOU … are there.*) I have been discussing debris fields as places situated on the ground (or in the mountains, or seas). A basic point that I haven't made yet, and should, is that while they are, in large part, set in those terrestrial locations, Lichtenstein shows that they are also in the air: almost always, they start up above. A crashing plane could conceivably remain fully intact until it hits the ground, but more often fire, explosion, decompression, or some other mechanical failure will cause parts of the aircraft to fall off, becoming debris, as the plane is plummeting (and before it becomes nothing-but-debris). The primary visual attraction in *Whaam!* is a hit plane. It seems at first like a single thing, a unitary event. But if we look closely, as we are expected to do with art, we see the beginnings of the plane's dynamic transformation from a unitary object into multiple objects. Just beneath the right-side plane's hull and wing Lichtenstein paints a dozen larger pieces of debris breaking off, interspersed with many tiny dots suggesting smaller bits. An instant earlier, those black specks and fragments were part of the airplane, and now, with explosive speed and energy, they are hurtling toward the debris field.

During WWII, Lichtenstein served in an anti-aircraft combat unit, shooting down enemy planes from the ground. He began a flight training program, but it shut down because more troops were needed for ground combat. He ended up painting air combat, flying, and crashing, instead of doing it: I'd say the world is better off that he swapped art for reality. Lichtenstein painted several other canvases thematically and visually similar to *Whaam!* in the early 1960s: *Jet Pilot* (1962), *Blam!* (1962), *Takka Takka* (1962), *Brattata* (1962)—not to be confused with *Bratatat!* (1963)—and *Okay Hot-Shot, Okay!* (1963); the titles, obviously, all come from the same argot of comics. *Blam!* depicts a pilot ejecting after his plane has been Blammed. *Takka Takka* shows a ground-based anti-aircraft machine gun shooting at planes.

Some think Lichtenstein's art glorifies the hyper-masculine violence of air combat, while others believe the comic-book aesthetic and nonsense-words mock military braggadocio. I'll consider it ambiguous, ambivalent; from his wartime experience, Lichtenstein must have known first-hand that military warfare was both noble and futile, tragic and comic. He knew about aviation's fundamental ambiguity: a crashed plane was a plane that hadn't crashed, until it did. A plane that hasn't crashed is a plane that could crash. In *Whaam!* Lichtenstein depicts this binary, these two sides of the coin, with his two-panel painting of two fighter planes, one safe and one not: one victorious, one vanquished. It's a profoundly stark painting about the yin/yang of it, evoking the symmetries that Yeats's "An Irish Airman" presented more delicately. Instead of the text inscribed on Lichtenstein's canvas—which is perfect, no complaints here—he might have written: In balance with this life, this death. If aviation often embodies existential uncertainty, military aviation embodies this a hundredfold more starkly.

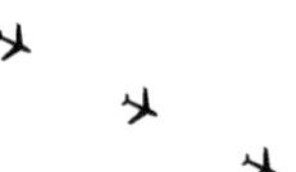

Whaam! is loud and violent. A WWI painting by US artist John Singer Sargent, and many WWII paintings by English artist Paul Nash, depict war crashes in softer, gentler ways. There must have been some kind of "WHAAM!" in these paintings' backstories, but Sargent and Nash sublimate moments of explosive crisis. Their crash paintings have a strongly, unexpectedly pastoral mood, which at least in part reflects the locations where they were set. Sargent's scene is in a gently rolling hayfield—yes, this pilot bought the farm. His painting, and Nash's from a rural series called *Aerial Creatures*, insistently frame crashscapes in England's hills and fields, beneath the countryside's clouds and skies. (Nash has other WHAAMier crash paintings as well, but in *Aerial Creatures*, the wrecked planes whisper rather than shout.) With such calming panoramas surrounding the debris fields, these tragedies seem temporary: the wreckage will be removed, and the scenes will endure, as they have for centuries, in their rural rhythms. It's a way of acknowledging the war, the risk of flying and aerial combat, but at the same time delimiting that risky danger. These crashes don't seem to do as much damage as they might. The images make me think of a continuum of debris fields arranged according to their levels of traumatic destruction. These, at the least disturbed end of the scale, strike me as the antithesis of lower Manhattan's Ground Zero, where the profusion of destruction seemed boundless and irremediable, leaving a debris field like none other the world had ever seen or even imagined.

Sargent's *Crashed Aeroplane* (1918) recalls a theme from Pieter Bruegel the Elder's sixteenth-century *Landscape with the Fall of Icarus*. In both, a flyer has crashed in the background, and both foregrounds feature a few humble earthbound field-workers whose compositional presence overshadows the crash sites. Bruegel shows hardly any of the watery debris field, just the feathered-flyer's tiny leg splashing and about to go under, while Sargent depicts the biplane's wreckage in a field behind the farmers, but if he gives his debris more space than Bruegel did, it is scarcely more significant. In both paintings, the point is that daily life, tending to crops, is more important than aviation. Those who choose flying over farming deserve what they get: it's not surprising that their aircrafts

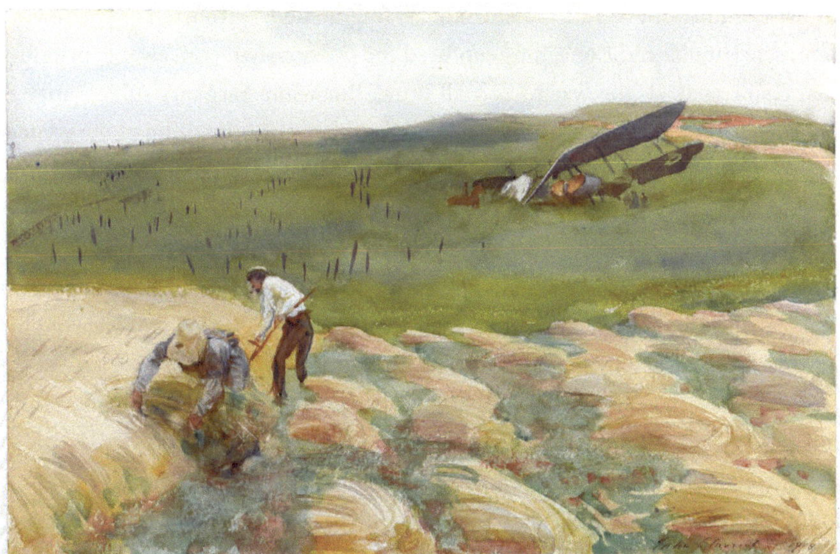

Figure 5.3 John Singer Sargent, *Crashed Aeroplane* (1918).

crash (for Bruegel, Icarus is himself the aircraft), and there's hay to gather, fields to plow, so the terrestrial characters are just not very interested in the so-called disaster. It's not their problem. As W. H. Auden writes in "Musée des Beaux Arts," inspired by Bruegel's painting, a plowman working nearby might have heard the splash, but for him it wasn't an important failure. Sargent's version includes a few looky-loos—we can just barely discern a person on horseback, and a few other dabs of paint depict wee distant onlookers by the wreckage—but he encourages his painting's audience to be inattentive, like the farmers, to whatever happened off in the distance.

Famous for his portraits of Spanish dancers, gondoliers, and the infamous Madame X, Sargent's aesthetic would not have seemed especially well suited to war art or plane-crash paintings: his work is more culturally refined, posed and poised. The word "insouciant" recurs in accounts of his artistic style. "The mood in the well-heeled society portraits that made his reputation is above all celebratory," writes Richard Cork; "he dotes on his own skillful ability to paint the splash of sunlight on his clients' privileged, carefully preserved faces,"[6] making his war paintings an unexpected turn.

He traveled to France and Belgium in summer 1918 as an official war artist, commissioned to commemorate joint efforts of American and British troops. The best early twentieth-century war artists, like Käthe Kollwitz, George Grosz, Anna Airy, and Otto Dix, forged a harsh, jolting new aesthetic: surreal/cubist/futurist, uncanny and disturbing, fragmented, ironized. Eschewing representational traditions, they captured the previously inconceivable brutality that characterized "the war to end all wars." But while Sargent's subject matter was new for him when he visited the front lines, he kept something of the genteel high-society style, a soft impressionist serenity that characterized his entire career.

His military art depicted scenes he had personally witnessed. *Gassed* (1919) depicts dozens of soldiers blinded by mustard gas being led to treatment. *Two Soldiers at Arras* (1918) shows two men lying in the grass, one still wearing his gas mask, overcome by a chemical weapon attack. *Camouflaged Field in France* (1918) and *A Wrecked Tank* (1918) are self-explanatory, though again one would not expect the soothing atmosphere of rural romantic landscapes to mitigate, as it somewhat does in these works, the horrors of WWI carnage.

In *Crashed Aeroplane*, this soothing aesthetic suggests ambivalence about what happened off in the distance, even denial—which could be coping strategies to mitigate the trauma of witnessing a crash, or might simply indicate that some people, like these farmworkers, don't care about it. The war doesn't seem to impact their lives, or at least they pretend it doesn't. It recalls the antipathy to militarism that Yeats imagines in his friend Major Gregory: all the Irish Airman cared about was Kiltartan, his village. Perhaps the Great War did not feel quite as immediate for Sargent as it was for the Europeans who lived in these places where planes flew and bombed and crashed; an American visitor might feel geopolitically detached.

But it seems like a dud of a reaction, disappointingly insubstantial for those of us who are more fascinated by the crash and want to investigate. It's as if he's saying: oh look, this happened, here it is; others have ambled over to check out the debris field, but not me. It is the diametric opposite of the high-intensity experience that draws viewers into *Whaam!*: Sargent's aesthetic is more of a *yawn*.

What was the battle? Or was it one of those ironic wartime non-combat accidents, like John Gillespie Magee's and probably Major Robert Gregory's? Who was flying? Why did the plane crash? Most other crash-texts would engage these central questions, but Sargent demurs. It's not even clear what country the biplane was flying for: some critics identify it as British, but without authoritative evidence. Did the pilot die, or escape? (There might be a white parachute draped over the wing, or there might not be.) I have to call this an unsatisfying image of what a plane crash looks like, both from an aeronautical perspective and a human perspective. At the same time, it's one of the least troubling crash sites I've investigated, and that's a notable data point. If it seems deficient (insouciant!) compared to other more forthright depictions, still, it stays with me.

Bruegel and Auden seemed, at first glance, unconcerned with Icarus, but they weren't. They had strong feelings about him: they thought he was a fool. Similarly, Sargent's tepid acknowledgment of the disaster *is* a response, an interesting one. By not getting very bothered about whatever happened across the landscape, he suggests how trivial a crash and its debris field can be. Presumably, in real life and closer up, this would have been a run-of-the-mill debris field, with big parts, small parts, charring, perhaps a casualty, splayed across the field, but we don't see that so we don't know. Those fuzzy first-responders are probably doing what they can to help, but like the farmers (and artist), they too seem not terribly bothered.

The grass is high, all the more reason the fieldhands can't go and investigate: make hay while the sun still shines. The tall grass down by the crash site helps obscure the wreckage. It seems like a parable: airplanes come and go, but the grass grows on. Think about the hay's vertical mobility: it moves (grows!) up and up, becoming more valuable and nutritious by the week. That natural, organic mobility is the one Sargent values, as opposed to the mobility-deficient airplane in the debris field.

I think a comparable aesthetic for a plane-crash picture today would be improbable (though of course I could be wrong). Remember that when Sargent saw this scene, aviation was only fifteen years old, and the number of plane crashes, even if high as a percentage of hours flown, was still a very small number compared to the roster of crashes we have now that aviation is so ubiquitous. Is there a naïveté in Singer's depiction? The trauma of plane crashes as we now experience them is at least partly a function of the fact that they have happened over and over again, and we have seen images—and cultural renditions—over and over again, which wasn't the case for Sargent. Also, these planes fell just a few thousand feet, whereas today's crashed planes might fall ten times that. Not that a few thousand feet isn't enough to do great damage: remember that the first fatal plane crash fell only 100 feet. But a crash will make more noise, more debris, more fire, more drama, the further it falls. The 1910s was a simpler time for plane crashes, which may explain Sargent's less-fraught mood.

And finally, if *Crashed Aeroplane* doesn't fit, doesn't seem to reveal or invoke the proper WHAAM! angst—well, more power to it. Artists don't ask professors how they should paint their pictures, nor should they. What if they gave a war and nobody came? What if a plane crashed and nobody cared? In the vast majority of plane crashes humanistically investigated herein, people care a lot: they get freaked out, as, I'd say, they should—but we might productively try to investigate what's going on in this rural English crash that *doesn't* rattle people; and as the entrepreneurs say, we might even try to bottle that. If Sargent (like his foreground figures) doesn't deign to acknowledge the violence, the damage, perhaps that's because he doesn't know exactly what to do with it, but more likely, I think, it's because he *does* know what he wants to convey: benign neglect.

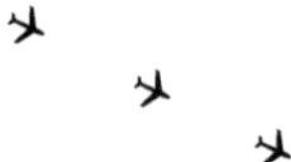

Paul Nash painted more plane wrecks by far—and better ones—than any other established artist of his time. In WWI, as an official war artist (along with his brother, John), he produced sharp, compelling images of soldiers, trenches, and ruined battlefield landscapes at the Western front. As WWII began, the War

Artists' Advisory Committee (WAAC) hired Paul Nash to paint for the Royal Air Force and the Air Ministry. But the bureaucrats, somewhat dense about contemporary art, decided they disliked his avant-garde style. They wanted to give the public what (they thought) it wanted, "faithful reporting of the facts,"[7] that is, straightforward realism. WAAC terminated Nash in December 1940, though they continued to buy his art freelance and many of these works became highly acclaimed.

Airplanes were "his chief subject of the war," writes Robert Hemmings. He spent his time with the Air Ministry in 1940,

> when the threat of German invasion was most imminent, pouring over magazines like *Flight* and *Aeroplane*, visiting airfields and crash sites, photographing, and sketching and painting airplanes. Through this scrutiny, he came to see airplanes as something more than material objects, more than mere technological instruments of war. They became quasi subjects recruited into the war effort.[8]

Battle of Britain (1941) depicts a scene from Germany's devastating assault on England in July–October 1940, the first military battle fought entirely in the air, which left thousands of soldiers and tens of thousands of civilians dead. Despite the heavy loss of life and aircraft on both sides, the British were considered victorious because the Luftwaffe failed to achieve their goal, destroying the RAF. Britain's morale improved, and the US, which had stayed out of the war in part because they doubted Britain could win, became persuaded of their fighting force.

"The painting is an attempt to give the sense of an aerial battle in operation over a wide area and thus summarises England's great aerial victory over Germany," Nash wrote.

> The scene includes certain elements constant during the Battle of Britain—the river winding from the town and across parched country, down to the sea; beyond, the shores of the Continent, above, the mounting cumulus concentrating at sunset after a hot brilliant day; across the spaces of sky, trails of airplanes, smoke tracks of dead or damaged machines falling, floating clouds, parachutes, balloons. Against the approaching twilight new formations of Luftwaffe, threatening.[9]

Displayed in 1942, *Battle of Britain* quickly became "an icon of British fortitude and stoutheartedness."[10] Nash combines the realism of his deft aerial panoramic overview with an equally potent strain of surrealism, which might be

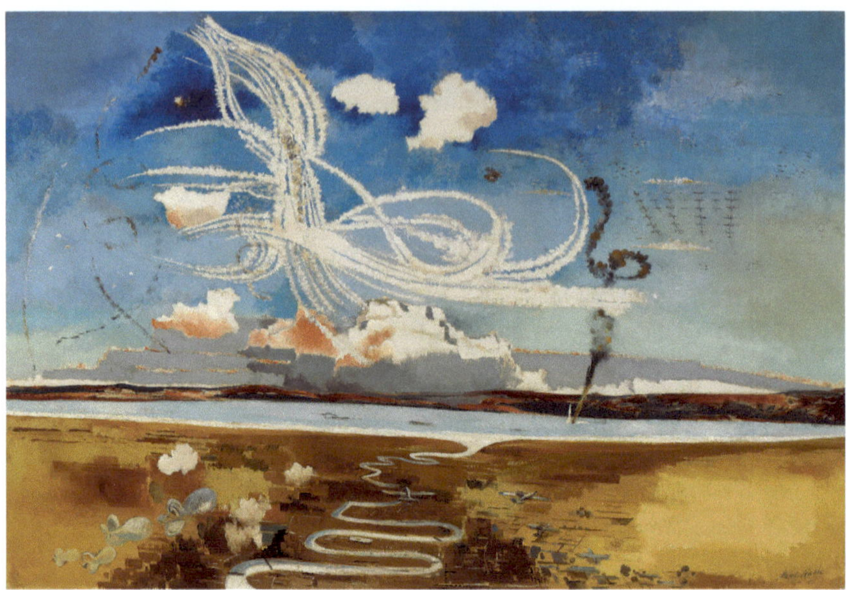

Figure 5.4 Paul Nash, *Battle of Britain* (1941).

taken as an existential commentary on the unceasing destruction raining down from the skies. The landscape, the skies, the air squadrons have a literal verisimilitude, but the canvas also manifests an eclectically fantastic energy, especially enhanced by the wonky contrails. If there is a cartoonish spirit—perhaps anticipating Roy Lichtenstein's comic air battles two decades later—Nash admired American animation, acclaiming "Walt Disney as the true voice of surrealism."[11]

There is a lot going on, aviationally: planes flying in patterned formation off in the distance, and in more chaotic dogfights at center. Other warplanes, near the bottom, seem to be flying up to aid their comrades in the pitched battle. Several barrage balloons at bottom left help protect ground targets against aerial attack. While representations of planes are always about mobility, we might elevate the kinetic smorgasbord of *Battle of Britain* to the throes of hypermobility, by which I mean: there is (very) much going on here mobility-wise, and it is happening (very) fast. The painting is extremely busy, and dizzy. Is hypermobility too much of a good thing? Should plain old (plane old) aeromobility suffice?

Hypermobility may represent the advantage, the winning strategy, for the air force that finally comes out ahead, and the other side, reviewing their game notes, may find that they were, comparatively, hypomobile. But airplanes have hard limits in terms of how fast they can fly, how high, how far on a tank of gas, and transgressing these ratings is a recipe for disaster. So yes, "hyper" can well signify *too much mobility, too much danger*. Yet the extreme predicament of war may excuse, even demand, pushing the envelope. The "envelope" denotes a set of performance standards that *may not be safely exceeded*, which is not quite the same as standards that *may not be exceeded*—try this at your own risk: it might work, it might not. If it does, you're a hero, flying faster farther longer. If not, you might crash. It's a binary: safety, staying inside the envelope, means (probably) staying aloft. Pushing the envelope means (possibly) going down, though perhaps in a blaze of glory.

In Nash's wild dogfight, it is contrails more than airplanes that catch our eyes and tell the story of flying and crashing. (Nash called them "vapour trails": the first *OED* usage citation of "contrails" is from 1945.) The battle-action contrails are mostly white; a few black ones, tracing thicker curlicues, indicate planes that are crashing. These contrails were a collaborative effort: when Nash's student Richard Seddon saw the painting at his studio, he "advised Nash to include more black smoke trails and painted an example on the canvas. When the painting was exhibited in London, Seddon's black trail was still visible on the canvas."[12]

A few black contrails on the left seem to show two or three planes in the process of spinning and going down, and a closer and clearer black contrail center-right leads to the moment of impact when a downed plane impacts the English Channel. I said before that it was harder for two-dimensional paintings, compared to more dynamic media, to capture the various stages of a crash. Nash, though, excellently conveys movement and temporal progression with his eclectic style, most keenly with the contrails that show (or imply) several minutes of aviation, greatly helping to propel his crash narrative through time and space.

Some planes in Nash's tableau are crashing and some aren't. Some will go down "beyond the frame" (beyond this canvas's geographical scope, or after the moments Nash captures here), and some won't. It's especially salient, and existential, to see both those conditions—flying, crashing—in a single image. It emphasizes a fact about plane crashes, and how we think of them, that is, at the same time, so very basic, and yet possibly the most vital insight discernible by the humanist air crash investigator: any given airplane might crash, or it might not. We can't get much more definitive than that. Compounding our uncertainty in Nash's account, we can't clearly tell, as we watch this momentous battle, which planes are on which side: from Nash's distant perspective, they all look pretty much alike. That's why we cue up the existential checklists: Nothing to be done

(*Waiting for Godot*). All we are is dust in the wind (Kansas). Hope for the best, expect the worst (Mel Brooks).

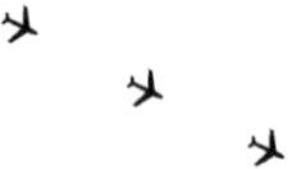

Nash painted a dozen watercolors in 1940–1 depicting Luftwaffe planes that had crashed in the UK, a series he called *Aerial Creatures*, a.k.a. *Raiders* and *Marching Against England* (from a German propaganda song "*Wir Fahren Gegen Engeland*," "We Are Marching Against England," which Nash ironizes, as the assembly of crash paintings shows that the Nazis are not marching, or flying, very well). *Battle of Britain* and Nash's other famous plane-crash painting, *Totes Meer*, both oil paintings, were not part of this sequence. Taken together, the watercolors are meant to affirm that British forces can defeat the aerial encroachers and defend their homeland. All the paintings contain some poignant element of English landscape juxtaposed with the wrecked planes, reiterating a point similar to Sargent's: landscapes frame the crashes, and contain (i.e., delimit) them. The wreckage is transitory; British hills and cliffs will endure. "The forces of good are identified with the landscape" in Nash's war art, writes Charles Hall.

Down in the Channel depicts a Dornier 18 flying boat that crash-landed on the sea. There is little evident debris, perhaps because Nash does not choose to gloat. (In military crash-art, more debris and destruction connote a more damning indictment of the enemy's failure.) Simply the fact that the German plane wallows immobilized in English waters is enough. Most debris fields are messy, unsightly, grotesque, strewn with an array of ruins. In these plane-crash watercolors, it's almost as if someone has done a clean-up before the painter arrived—and in fact, Nash "was never allowed to visit crash sites before they had removed the bodies and generally tidied things up a bit," Hall writes; "bodies, living or dead, are conspicuous by their absence in his work." Possibly Nash simply made a virtue of necessity by not depicting the debris that had been cleared away before he arrived on site, but I like to think it was an intentional aesthetic, emphasizing a compositionally simple contrast: a downed, defunct airplane, no need for accessorizing debris, in a sublime landscape. Some of his paintings in this series were based on photographs that did include human casualties, "all of which are scrupulously excluded in the final product."[13]

Bomber in the Corn shows a crashed German Heinkel He 111. There is a bit more debris visible, and the wreckage appears slightly more wrecked compared to other paintings in this series where the damage is hardly visible. But as the title indicates, the visual hook here is the cornfield. The fecund yellow farm in a vintage English landscape suggests that the attack was not very disruptive, and corn will soon grow over whatever scars the bomber inflicted, restoring pastoral tranquility. Another war artist, John Piper, lauded this painting for presenting "no summoning of melodrama, no wallowing in tragedy. A setting sun, some trees in a copse, decorate the stage from which these strange facts are announced simply."[14] This debris field is a temporary condition that seems as if it will quickly and easily dissipate.

In *Bomber in the Wood*—like *Bomber in the Corn*, except, obviously, set in the forest—a crashed warplane nestles in the trees just as the other one nestled in corn; it, too, will disappear as the scene eventually returns to pure woodland. The wreckage here has taken on the brown of the trees, just as the wreck in *Bomber in the Corn*, shaded yellow, matches the corn. I do not know if these planes were indeed simply abandoned, left to be overgrown by nature: I suspect they weren't: *Totes Meer* (Figure 5.6) shows the British didn't let anything go to waste. The scope of debris in *Bomber in the Wood* is, as in Nash's other scenes, minimal. A wing is bent, but not detached from the hull. There's a bit of tree-debris: nothing drastic, hardly any at all, but close inspection shows a few small branches that seem to have broken off as the plane came down. Again: yes, this debris field has debris, as seems tautologically necessary, but it is untroubling debris, easily dealt with.

Photos of the scenes Nash painted are archived on London's Battle of Britain Monument website[15]—some are his own photos, and sometimes when ill health prevented him from investigating crash sites he relied on other people's photographs of them. Since its invention, photography has been a powerful medium for documenting wars, violence, tragedies. Nash acknowledges and integrates its keen representational power as he produces his "covers" (as musicians would call them), his adaptations of plane crash photographs.

That Battle of Britain website also gives precise historical and military details about the scene depicted: what kind of British plane shot down the German plane, and sometimes even which RAF Airman made the kill; crash dates and locations; names of Germans killed or taken prisoner; the bombing mission, and whether or not it had been achieved before the plane was brought down. A plane crash is always much more than just the crash itself, and Nash did the digging to discover the backgrounds of the crashes he depicted.

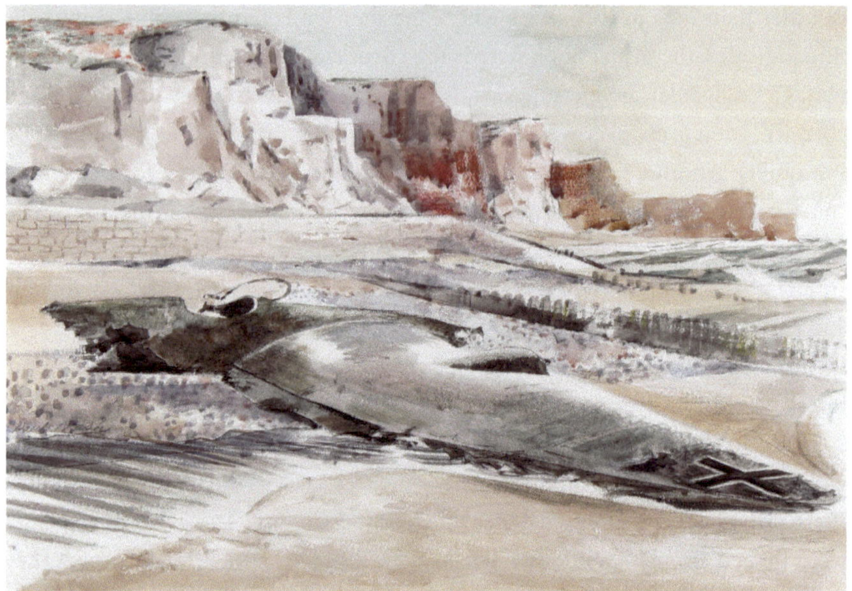

Figure 5.5 Paul Nash, *Raider on the Shore* (1940).

Other paintings in this series include *Under the Cliff*, *East Anglian Heinkel*, *Encounter in the Afternoon*, *Death of the Dragon*, *Messerschmitt in Windsor Great Park*, and *Raider on the Moors*. In many of them, the photographic archives reveal, Nash took artistic license: amalgamating some scenes, and reimagining some wreckage, mostly to make the surrounding landscape more picturesque. (If the NTSB found out humanists did things like this, I fear it might dissuade them from taking our investigations seriously.)

Raider on the Shore shows a Heinkel down on the beach, featuring—again—no messy debris or upheaval. The plane's color matches the shore's (as other planes blended into the trees or cornfields where they crashed), and looks as if it is being worn smooth, like driftwood, by the tides washing over. Like the other *Aerial Creatures*, it has hardly hurt the landscape, and nature's forces seem poised to transform the wreckage into something native and harmonious, rather than ominously foreign. "The rugged English landscape reigns over the enemy airplane's fallen materiality" in Nash's paintings, writes Robert Hemmings,[16] and Hall describes this motif as "naturalising and, as it were, neutralising the intrusion of the enemy." (Naturalising/neutralising: that's good.) The decrepit planes have a mythic resonance: they are like "ancient predators in the process of being absorbed into the landscape they sought to rule."[17]

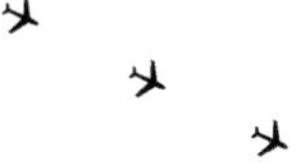

Conceptually, *Battle of Britain* and *Totes Meer*, each of which depicts dozens of aircraft, bookend Nash's individual watercolor portraits of crashed planes nuzzled in sentimental English landscapes. "Portraits" suits the *Aerial Creatures* series because Nash came to believe, after years of studying and painting military planes, that they had personalities, almost like soldiers and pilots. In a *Vogue* essay, "The Personality of Planes," Nash wrote that airplanes

> possessed each a personality, difficult to define and yet undeniable. It was not wholly a matter of mechanistic character. There seemed to be involved some *other* animation, 'a life of their own' is the nearest expression I can think of, which often gave them the suggestion of human or animal features.

The Vickers Wellington, for example, "is very human."

> It is jolly, it is on the plump side, I see that now. But when I first tried to stare one out of countenance, I was shaken. This baleful creature filled me with awe. Its chief characteristic is a look of purpose, of unswerving concentration upon its goal. Its big mammalian head and straight point wings, its proud fin and strong level flight, like that of an avenging angel, all make up a personality of great strength, a formidable machine, heroic and justly popular.[18]

The more plane crashes I investigate, the more I encounter perspectives that I had not seen before and that help me understand ever more deeply the totality of our cultural engagements with these mishaps. Nash shows that it is possible to see these mechanical constructions as human-like, in their living, flying state and in their demise as well. I haven't seen any other humanist crash culture that explicitly extends this anthropomorphic life-force to airplanes, but now that I think about it, it seems possible that the poets, novelist, singers, and filmmakers I've investigated might share similar intuitions. Aircraft embody the epitome of modern genius in their avionics, their engineering, their computer programs—is this human ingenuity or, in some sense, the airplane's own? Does the plane have sentience, will, desire? As pilots say (and devoutly believe), the plane *wants* to fly. It all seems pretty intelligent to me, pretty "human," whatever that problematic term now means. Is it silly to pretend, or imagine, that planes are (like) people?

For better or worse, anthropopathy happens when artists crash air-crash investigations.

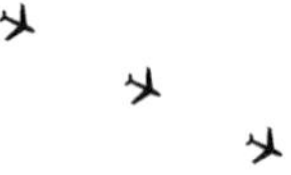

Totes Meer was "one of the few unquestioned masterpieces of the war," writes Charles Hall, "recognized as such as soon as it was exhibited at the National Gallery in May 1941." Eric Newton called its debut "one of the most important single events in British art for three-quarters of a century."[19] Critics described it as an "aeronautical graveyard,"[20] extending Nash's sense of airplanes as dead forms (the title means "Dead Sea" in German) that were once, as he had described in *Vogue*, figuratively alive. Nash discusses *Totes Meer* in a 1941 letter: the salvage dump

> looked to me, suddenly, like a great inundating sea. You might feel—under certain circumstances—a moonlight night, for instance, this is a vast tide moving across the fields, the breakers rearing up and crashing on the plain. And then, no, nothing moves, it is not water or even ice, it is something static and dead. It is metal piled up, wreckage. It is hundreds and hundreds of flying creatures which invaded these shores (how many Nazi planes have been shot down or otherwise wrecked in this country since they first invaded?). Well, here they are, or some of them. By moonlight, the waning moon, one could swear they began to move and twist and turn as they did in the air. A sort of rigor mortis? No, they are quite dead and still. The only moving creature is the white owl flying low over the bodies of the other predatory creatures, raking the shadows for rats and voles.[21]

Is the wreckage still or moving? Water or metal? Mechanical or mortal? Dead or alive? *One could swear they began to move and twist and turn as they did in the air*: are the planes crashed? Not-crashed? Both at once? Existential ambiguity pervades Nash's written description of the scene.

It may be viewed as a companion piece to *Battle of Britain*, painted the same year. As different as they are, both offer "cosmic visions of air battles."[22] There are roughly as many warplanes in each painting, but in *Battle of Britain* the planes are mostly aloft and here they are all grounded. If *Battle of Britain* depicted hypermobility, *Totes Meer* represents hyperimmobility. The cessation of flight Nash presents here is comforting to his countrypeople: in this debris field, a monstrously large formation of planes no longer endangers English people and cities.

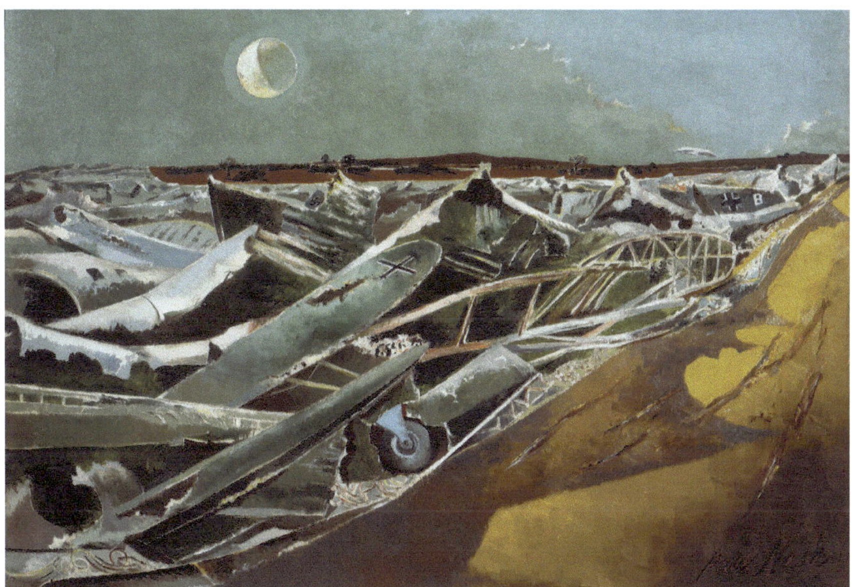

Figure 5.6 Paul Nash, *Totes Meer* (1941).

I've not seen any other debris field with *so many* crashed planes. One alone makes a big, scary, traumatic, destructive mess. Two (on the runway at Tenerife, over Park Slope in Brooklyn, at Ground Zero)—exponentially more. Here we have . . . dozens? Maybe a hundred? It is the debris field to end all debris fields. Again here, as in some of Nash's watercolors, the debris field has been moved. In the watercolors it was artistic license (Nash imaginarily depicted debris in different places and arrangements than it actually was), but in the scene from *Totes Meer* it actually happened: this debris was all relocated. Airplane wreckage from across the country was transported and agglomerated into debris writ large. This was done partly so debris wasn't scattered all across the UK: it was centralized in one large dump. More importantly, the planes were brought together so the wreckage could be salvaged to augment the war effort.

Cowley Dump, the site depicted in *Totes Meer*, actually contained English as well as German planes, but Nash invoked artistic license to depict a sea of only German aircraft. These Luftwaffe planes destroyed in England are destined to be recycled, reborn like a phoenix rising out of the ashes—and it's hard to imagine a more effective symbol for a debris-field phoenix than an actual new airplane.

As in all Nash's crash paintings, English countryside surrounds wrecked planes, framing the panorama with crests of hills, meadows, sky, making the simple but powerful statement that planes are transitory, as is war, but the landscape is eternal. "The inclusion of the moon in the background of *Totes Meer* adds incongruous beauty to the painting and in typical Nash style, suggests the unwavering power of nature, in spite of man's atrocities. The landscape beyond the broken sea of planes suggests that salvation remains a possibility and that the destruction, though horrific, is not total."[23] The ruins "are not only awesome as some kind of *memento mori*, but are in some sense portents of another order of existence, only dimly and occasionally perceived."[24] Amid the destruction, Michael Prodger notes, "there is just a hint of life; a white bird (an owl? a seagull?) that flies over and away from the wreckage like a departing spirit."[25]

In the most enormous debris field imaginable, filled with planes whose erstwhile violence represented an acutely existential threat to freedom, Nash is able to imagine a larger picture, a time-scheme in which this too shall pass. The landscape beneath and beyond the debris will somehow, eventually, endure and emerge triumphant. Despite this vast tranche of wreckage, countless piles of unfathomable ruin, still, Nash seeks—and finds—transcendence.

Cowley Dump, where Nash extensively studied debris to prepare for *Totes Meer*, was very near his flat: literally on the same street, Banbury Road, Oxford. How perfect that he lived in Oxford's debris district! I wonder if he became interested in airplane debris because he lived nearby, or if he moved to that house specifically because he was already so fascinated by plane wrecks? It's a great story either way. As he explored the debris field, he photographed many different views of it, and also took pictures of individual pieces he pulled out of the piles and propped against a fence.

Cowley Dump—officially, the Cowley Yard Metal and Produce Recovery Unit—was near a Morris car factory which switched to military production when war broke out. The debris was

> spread over 100 acres of farmland next to the factory, piled three metres high, and laid out along eight miles of "roads." Thousands of tons of high-grade aluminium and other materials, such as rubber, steel, and plastics, were reclaimed and reused. Samples of aluminium had to be taken from wrecked enemy aircraft, and carefully assessed in a laboratory before it could be reused.

Ten thousand Morris workers, mostly women, recycled debris into "aircraft components such as engines for the Lancaster bomber and the Bristol Beaufighter,

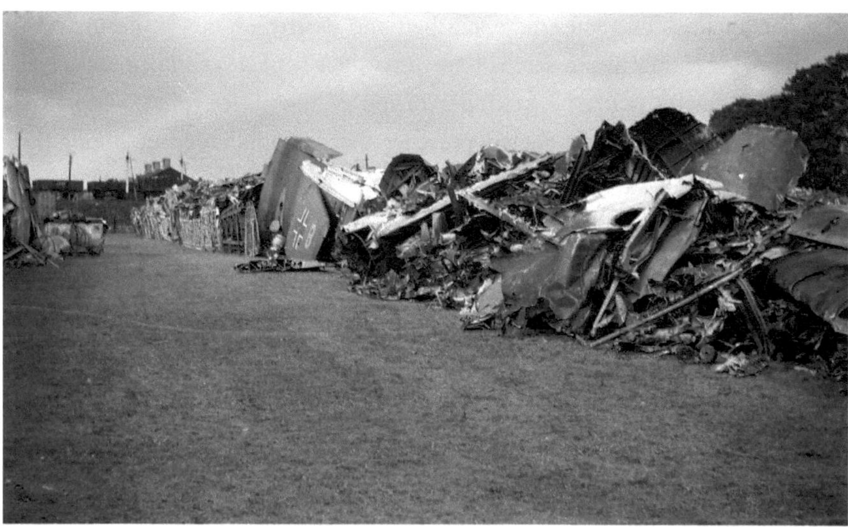

Figure 5.7 Researching *Totes Meer*, Paul Nash photographed crashed airplanes at Cowley Dump.

and wings and tail units for the Horsa glider." The plant also "cannibalized badly damaged aircraft of all nationalities, for parts and raw materials" to repair damaged airplanes.[26] During the Battle of Britain, destroyed aircraft arrived at Cowley daily by rail. In addition to debris from crashes in military engagements, a significant amount came from RAF training accidents. It is the most valuable debris (or, the most valuably repurposed) I have encountered throughout my investigations. If I had to identify a few specific cultural expressions that have animated my obsession with plane crash debris, *Totes Meer* would be in the top five.

Cultural debris fields often resonate with a strong impulse to cleanse and redeem the traumatic, messy chaos of brokenness, and *Totes Meer* accomplishes this feat exceptionally. Nash described his impressions of Cowley Dump:

> There lived here in death innumerable vehicles of destruction of different personality once all directed by human agency, some in the character of ships manned by crews, others as clearly bound up with man as a horse to its rider.... There was a persistent suggestion of a ghostly presence.... I do not mean the wraiths of lost pilots or perished crews were hovering near, it was nothing so decidedly human, but a pervasive force baffled yet malign hung in the heavy air.[27]

This is such an artistic, painterly expression—as we might well expect from a painter, of course. It's a perfect complement to his painting. Again he explains the personalities of planes: here, crashed and destroyed, they're dead, and yet Nash imagines they live in death. *A pervasive force baffled yet malign in the heavy air:* what exactly *is* that? Invoking a fusion of mobilities (plane, ship, horse, human), Nash describes a ghostly presence that one might expect among these machines in which (and because of which) so many people perished, but he also crafts an artistic vision that goes beyond the pilots and crews, the violence and ruin. He does not forget the battles (as demonstrated so vividly in *Battle of Britain*), but his art here aspires to understand and convey more, broaching that (existentially) *baffled pervasive force.*

Nash collaged his Cowley photographs and sketches together to create "a fragmented sea of battered remnants ... to illustrate the fate of the 'hundreds and hundreds of flying creatures which invaded these shores.' His unrealized vision was to distribute a postcard of this image throughout Germany as propaganda."[28] In a later iteration, Nash created an even-more-surreal version of the Cowley debris featuring Hitler's head superimposed, collaged above the damaged aircraft,[29] looking not unlike one of Terry Gilliam's Monty Python animations. The head sits on top of broken planes—even larger than the wrecked hulls, like one more piece of debris, however incongruous, tossed onto the pile.

His surreal Hitler is yet another debris field innovation on Nash's part. It wouldn't have occurred to me that a megalomaniacal dictator might belong amid the wreckage, but now that Nash has shown what it would look like, it makes sense. Rarely do cultural commentators invent additional elements to heap onto extant debris—what's already there is more than enough to make the point—but Nash colors outside the lines in so many ways in his highly researched (and also highly imaginative) debris fields.

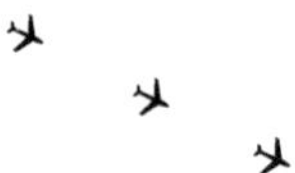

A year earlier, Frances Macdonald painted her own version of the same dump. When the War Artists' Advisory Committee did (occasionally) hire women painters, they were expected to focus on the domestic home front; Macdonald didn't. Her work at Cowley captures a sense similar to Nash's of chaotic debris strewn in big piles, but her *Graveyard: No. 1 Metal and Produce Recovery Depot, Morris Works, Cowley, Oxford*, makes the wreckage look like a big messy jumble of uniquely different planes, shapes, colors, while Nash's debris seems more

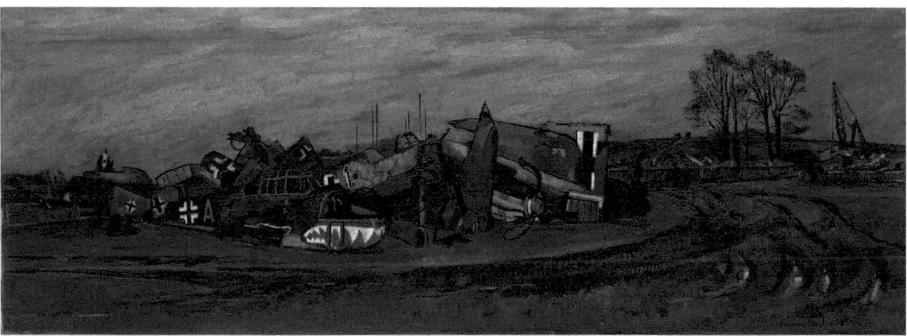

Figure 5.8 Frances Macdonald, *Graveyard: No. 1 Metal and Produce Recovery Depot, Morris Works, Cowley, Oxford* (1940).

uniform, a homogeneous array of colors and forms with an overarching unity, like the regularity of waves in the sea.

A large natural vista surrounds Macdonald's debris, like Nash's, but her landscape is less pastorally pretty, more a continuation of the derelict scene colored by the central debris. Her crashed planes are not redeemed, as Nash's are, by the English landscape. Note the face painted on the front of the Messerschmitt Bomber, nicknamed "Fliegender Haifisch" (Flying Shark), at the front. The Luftwaffe actually did paint their planes like this, which helps explain why Nash thought they had personalities. The industrial ugliness Macdonald depicts is not wholly dissimilar from what Nash shows, and yet one feels in his image of Cowley the attempt to soften it, to impose art on it—not to prettify or falsify in any way, but rather to bathe the scene with his aesthetic. Macdonald seems content to let the debris be debris.

Art is control, and Nash controls his *Totes Meer* scene imaginatively and ethically. Like so many war artists and war poets, Nash seems to have felt a conviction that art could control war—capture war, and in some sense rule over war: perhaps, even, overrule it. Discovering so much fodder for art in the debris fields he investigated, Nash teaches us that a crash is sad, a war is bad, but there is art to be found, art to be made, art to be conscripted in the war effort (and that "war effort" means fighting the war, but also surviving the war, and ending the war, and living beyond the ending). Paintings, music, poetry about plane crashes all live on, flying high even after the planes themselves have plummeted out of the sky. Culture survives disasters, perhaps with even more plangency as we mull the ironic conjunctions of art and tragedy. (Would Buddy Holly's talent have blazed quite as brightly in our musical heritage if he hadn't crashed into the cornfield?)

"The material debris of modern warfare becomes raw material for the beauty of Nash's painting," Robert Hemmings writes, affirming my contention that as artists enter and then emerge, productively, from debris fields, art vanquishes chaos. "No longer agents of ruin-making as bombers over British skies,"

> the German airplanes become in *Totes Meer* the very objects of ruin. Instead of producing British architectural ruins through air raids on British cities, the material thingness of these German objects, dislodged from flight, produces directly the mechanical ruins that are enfolded and contained by Nash's landscape. By embracing the landscape genre—"the cornerstone of the English pictorial tradition"—Nash participates in a larger movement during the Second World War that imbued in landscape painting the power to defend Britain and its heritage.[30]

The debris and the field are usually one unified entity, a debris field, but they may also be two separate presences at odds with each other: an agon. In *Totes Meer*, as in Sargent's *Crashed Aeroplane*, fields prevail over debris.

6

Art in Crashes

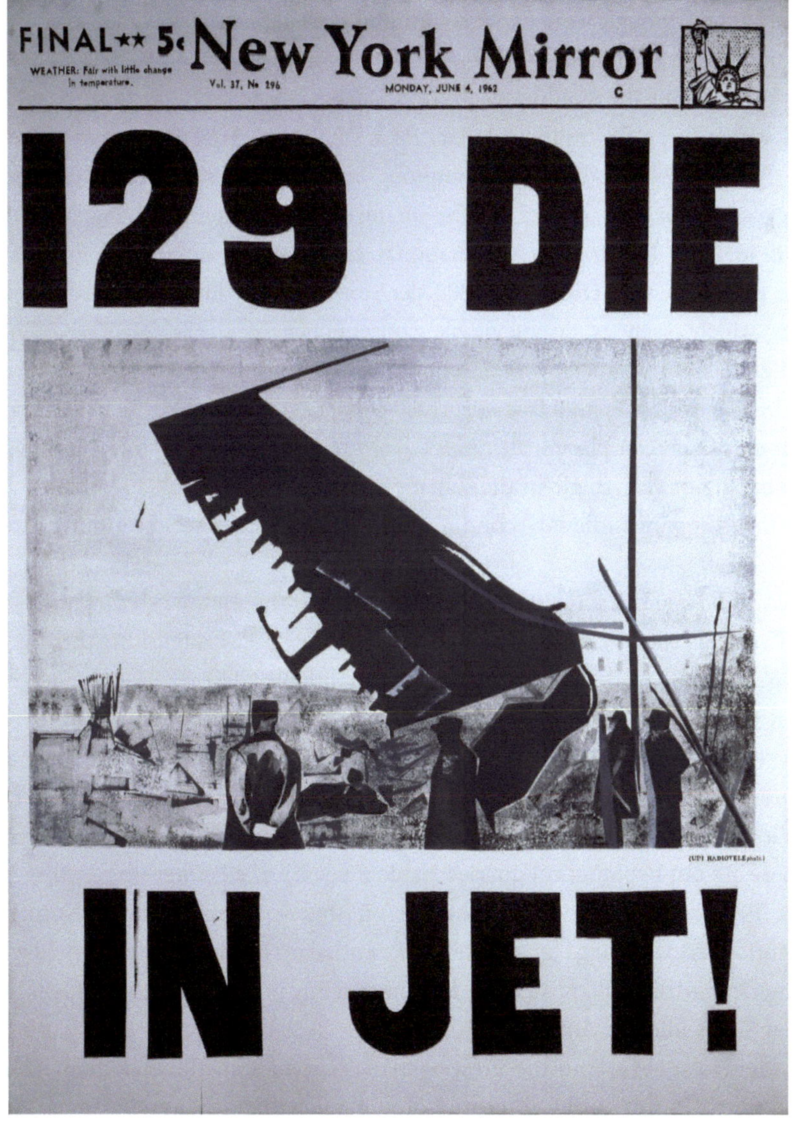

Figure 6.1 Andy Warhol, *129 DIE IN JET!* (1962).

How tragic is any given plane crash, and why? It may seem trivial, profane, "academic" in the worst way, to quantify tragedy, but the fact is that some crashes are (or *seem*) worse than others. The crash of a wide-body airliner carrying a few hundred people is probably worse than that of a turboprop with only—only!—a dozen passengers and crew. The deaths of "innocent" people on the ground may make a crash feel more tragic, but aren't the airline passengers also innocent? Circumstances that make crashes more newsworthy may also make them seem more tragic, though we're on shaky ground if we let media coverage shape such moral and philosophical facets of our investigations.

What about the nonhuman toll of a crash—how tragic is that? Airplanes are expensive: a few million dollars for a small one, $100,000,000 or more for an Airbus A340 or Boeing Dreamliner. Someone loses lots of money when they crash—is that tragic? It'll be an insurance company paying out—does that make it less tragic? Multinational corporations sometimes founder in the aftermath of a crash: the 2003 decision to close down Concorde's routes was widely seen as an inevitable consequence of the 2000 crash. Boeing suffered, both financially and reputationally, after two 737 Max crashes in 2018–19, which sparked widespread concerns about their deficient safety standards and complacent attitudes toward regulations. Their stock plummeted, probably not very tragic in the scheme of things; many workers lost their jobs as the company suffered economic turbulence, which seems unfortunate, if not tragic.

And how about art? I have been investigating the multifaceted relationships between art (poetry, music etc.) and crashes. How do we adjudicate the loss, the tragedy (?), of art that a plane crash actually, literally, destroys? How much does that matter, and why? Certainly it is regrettable. Is the destruction of artworks, say, 10 percent as tragic as the death of people? One percent? Does it depend on the art in question? Is the loss of a Picasso painting more tragic than the loss of a Gorky? How about a single work by Picasso compared to multiple Gorkys? These are not hypothetical queries: Pablo Picasso's *The Painter* was destroyed in the 1998 crash of Swissair flight 111 off the Nova Scotia coast. Numerous paintings and drawings by Arshile Gorky ended up in a watery debris field when American Airlines flight 1 crashed in Jamaica Bay in 1962, just after takeoff from New York's Idlewild Airport.

I find losses of art more interesting than tragic, or, sometimes, both interesting and tragic. In this quirky enterprise of humanist air crash investigations, I have undertaken the complicated task of figuring out what a plane crash means, how people feel about it, how we respond to it, what we do with it, and especially what the cultural realm makes of it: what "goes in" to the minds/experiences/imaginations of artists who create culture from, and after, debris fields, and what "output" emerges? The fate of actual art in plane crashes provides one more point of deliberation for all my other humanist inquiries. If this might seem like an insignificant and inconsequential niche, well, there's a lot more art in crashes than you might initially imagine, and it turns out to be a pretty potent plot-element of crash narratives.

I like art immensely and value it highly: I have dedicated my life to studying and propagating the arts. When I say I value it, I like to think that I do so in different ways from how Sotheby's values art, though I acknowledge that if we dug down into their value system and mine, there would be some (but certainly not complete, or even extensive) overlap.

I feel extremely sad, even mournful, when an artwork is stolen, or vandalized, or accidentally destroyed, or in some other way malevolently disrespected. I believe such a loss makes the world a bit less beautiful, and less interesting, and I think our culture has failed when we are unable to keep art safe and intact. Some of the most egregious losses include the Taliban's destruction of ancient Bamiyan Buddha statues; the 1990 heist of the Gardner Museum's paintings, especially Rembrandt's self-portrait and Vermeer's *The Concert* (my favorites: yes, obviously, this is subjective); the Nazi destruction of "degenerate art" and their exorbitant thefts of innumerable other treasures from museums and private collectors; imperialist plunder of the Benin Bronzes, Parthenon marbles, and Ishtar Gate. (If you don't consider these pillaged artworks "lost," check your privilege.) Certainly, after any such losses, plenty of art still remains. I try to console myself with that thought, and also with the hope that people will work harder to take better care of art after seeing what harmful things can happen to it—just as, after a plane crash, engineers and aviators work diligently to prevent a recurrence, and to take better care of airplanes after seeing what devastating things can befall them.

The loss of some art is, arguably, more lamentable than the loss of other art: if the art is "better," however we come to make that assessment, it seems more upsetting. The same calculus is not applicable to people—the death of a certain person is no more tragic than the death of another one, though that said, the deaths of Buddy Holly, Sally Ride, and Kobe Bryant certainly carry a denser sociocultural construction than the demise of other, unfamous, people who experience aviation accidents. If deaths of famous victims are not actually more tragic, perhaps they seem to be? And "seeming tragic" may be the same, at least on some level, as "tragic"?

I explore several debris fields that include art to explore how these case studies help illuminate the larger general question at hand, the most basic aspect of these investigations that I have broached repeatedly but still not yet answered definitively: how do we feel about plane crashes?

Beauty in flames

Aviation was both muse and destroyer for Arshile Gorky, the Armenian-American painter acclaimed for his early and strong influence on mid-twentieth-century Abstract Expressionism. His art often portrays airplanes and other aspects of aviation, always in a wonderfully wonky, wobbly mode. One of my favorites, *The Mechanics of Flying* (*c.* 1936), depicts a flight deck, but not one that any pilot would ever deign to set foot in. The essence of an actual flight deck is its precision, its regularity. The stabilizer trim wheels are to be found precisely *here*, not a few inches away, and the co-pilot's corresponding device is, symmetrically, right *there*. The control yoke, airspeed indicator, throttle levers, are exactly where they are. But not for Gorky: his view of a cockpit (the now politically incorrect term—see Chapter 7—he would have used) embodies perversely fluid asymmetries. To use slightly anachronistic descriptors, it is trippy, groovy; it looks the way a cockpit might appear to a drunken pilot—who we would not want at the controls of our airplane, it goes without saying.

It's a terrible cockpit aeronautically, but outstanding aesthetically. It's exciting and eclectic, a wonderfully liberatory reflection of every other cockpit's plodding homogenous design. (Are the humanities again at odds with aviation? It seems as if my chances of actualizing this air crash investigator gig are getting slimmer by the minute.) Gorky captures the imaginative and emotive essence of what flight meant in the 1930s in his idiosyncratic iteration of lift/thrust/drag/weight.

If Gorky's vision bears little resemblance to an actual working flight deck, it depicts much more closely what that cabin might look like in the unfortunate event that it turns up in a debris field. I'm not suggesting Gorky had any premonition of a plane crash when he painted this mural—commissioned for an airport terminal, a crash would be an atrocious choice of subject. I don't think he consciously meant to color *The Mechanics of Flying* with the chaotic unruliness

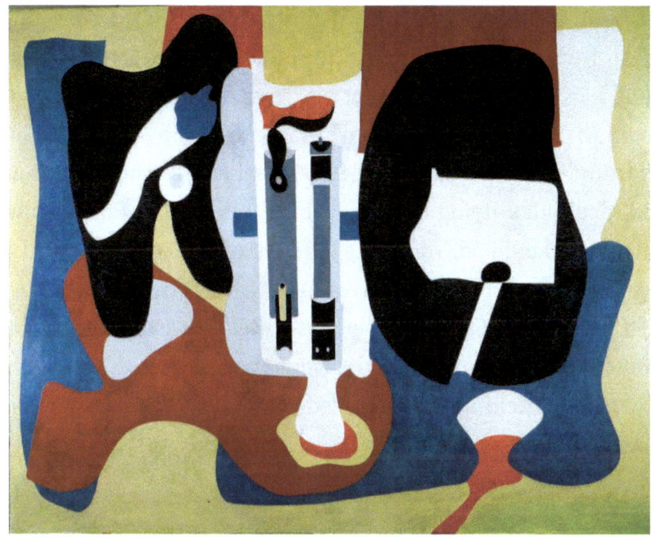

Figure 6.2 Arshile Gorky, *The Mechanics of Flying* (*c.* 1936).

of a debris field, which transforms the precision and regularity of the flight deck (and every other part of the plane) into something more jumbled. But I propose that Gorky's painting exemplifies my idea (Freud's idea, really) that any thought includes its antithesis. A flight deck's raison d'être, not crashing, somehow, sort of, subconsciously, includes crashing—if only in the sense of *don't let this happen!*

The Mechanics of Flying was one of ten murals Gorky painted for Newark Airport's Administration Building. The series, "Aviation: Evolution of Forms under Aerodynamic Limitations," was one of the first mural projects commissioned by the New Deal Works Progress Administration (WPA) in its Federal Art Project. Presaging Gorky's fraught interaction with aviation, these murals were later lost: eight were destroyed, while two others, including this one, were reclaimed from near-destruction in 1973, exhumed from beneath fourteen layers of paint.[1]

Gorky lost many other paintings in non-aviational mishaps: several were destroyed in a relative's house fire in 1934; a 1946 fire in his Connecticut studio ruined 20 more; yet another fire, at the New York Governor's mansion in 1961, burned a painting of his on display there. Were the cosmos trying to tell him something?

The trove of paintings and drawings that draw Gorky into my air crash investigation were being transported from Idlewild Airport (now JFK) to LAX in March of 1962, fourteen years after his death. New York's Allan Stone Gallery loaned them to Everett Ellin Gallery for an exhibition—"Arshile Gorky: Forty Drawings from the Period 1929 thru 1947"—scheduled the following month. "It has been difficult identifying the works that Stone sent to Ellin that were lost in the crash," said Parker Field, Managing Director of the Arshile Gorky Foundation. "Details are scarce and reports have noted that between 10–15 works were onboard. It may be that the number is smaller, however. In February [1962], Stone wrote to Ellin to confirm that he would be sending seven works," of which only two have been definitively identified.[2] One of those, *Picasso Woman* (1932) portrays a meditative woman in a style that, as its title promises, resembles Picasso's.

The crash of American flight 1, killing all ninety-five aboard, was probably caused by a wiring short circuit in the automatic piloting system. Flaws in the system's manufacturing process led to "rudder control system malfunction producing yaw, sideslip, and roll leading to a loss of control from which recovery was not effective." Visiting the plant where the suspect systems were assembled, inspectors found workers using tweezers to bind up bundles of wires, thereby damaging them, though the company denied responsibility for the flaw.[3]

Aside from Gorky's art, the crash claimed several famous passengers: a retired Chief of Naval Operations, an Olympic sailing medalist, a close personal friend of President Dwight D. Eisenhower, and Louise Lindner Eastman, whose daughter Linda would later marry Paul McCartney. A fictional character also died on the flight: the father of Pete Campbell from the television series *Mad Men*.[4] When his ad agency, Sterling Cooper, tries to recruit American Airlines as a client, Pete seals the deal by leveraging his grief, winning the executives' sympathy by informing them that his father died in the recent crash. Pete's weaselly character shines as he leans into the task the firm is contracted to perform: helping to mitigate the PR disaster and rebuild the public image of the airline that killed his own father. I haven't found much information about whether airlines really do this, quietly "managing" such tragedies to minimize financial fallout in the aftermath of aviational fallout, but it wouldn't surprise me.

As Kafka wrote, the meaning of life is that it stops. The tragic irony of a plane crash is that it cuts people's lives shorter than they were supposed to have been, than they otherwise would have been had they not taken that flight. And the meaning of art, or one of its meanings, is that it is eternal: "not for an age, but for all time," as Ben Jonson lauded Shakespeare's legacy. People always die, but art, at least *great art,* isn't supposed to. The death of art might then be regarded, in some quibbling sense, as a more shocking loss than a person's life. Gorky's art could have lasted forever (if it hadn't been on that flight). We may appreciate art (and also, people) more, for having lost them too soon. And perhaps the loss makes us appreciate other art (and also other people) all the more, realizing anew how fortunate we are to have them in our lives.

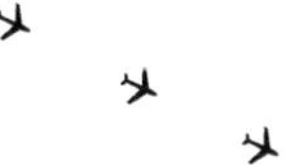

Swissair flight 111, JFK-GVA, crashed off Nova Scotia on September 2, 1998, killing all 229 on board. The catastrophe began with a fire in the flight deck started by materials later found to be flammable, which shouldn't have been used (and now, of course, are not). In addition to the human toll, many other valuables were on board: 110 pounds of cash (by weight, that is, not £), four and a half pounds of diamonds, a large container of gold. Swissair did not provide an exact valuation,[5] but Lloyds of London eventually paid $300 million compensation. The massively valuable cargo reflected New York City's wealth and Geneva's banking infrastructure.

The recovery operation in the watery debris field was one of the largest, longest (four years), and most expensive ever. Remains from every victim were recovered, along with 98 percent of the debris: over 300,000 pounds of it, about two million pieces, retrieved by a "suction-dredge vessel" equipped with a giant vacuum to collect wreckage from the sea floor. (Was the lengthy recovery operation related to the enormous amount of potentially-recoverable wealth from the debris field? That seems like a safe bet: follow the money.) But the cash, diamonds, and gold were never found. There was (and is still) robust interest from amateur and professional treasure-hunters, but Nova Scotia's Special Places Protection Act, implemented a few years after the crash, makes it illegal to conduct salvage operations there out of consideration for victims' families.[6]

The crash destroyed another valuable shipment: two paintings. Swissair described one as "unknown"—no information available. The other was Picasso's *The Painter*, which Sotheby's was delivering from seller (unnamed) to buyer (unnamed). Picasso created at least six versions of this painting (in French, *Le Peintre*) in 1963. Sotheby's would not confirm which was on the plane, but the most likely candidate is one they had sold two years earlier for $867,000. It was insured for $1.5 million—nothing to sneeze at, but certainly in the low-to-middling range of Picasso's catalog. "*Artnet Magazine* described 'Le Peintre' as 'a decidedly mediocre late Picasso,'" writes Anthony Depalma.[7] It depicts an artist staring contemplatively at his canvas

> as he lifts his brush to the surface. There is intensity in his brow line, and his expression is serious. Wild lines make up his beard, adding an element of frenzy to the creative process. The hand of the man also contains movement—Picasso has layered multiple outlines of the hand to create this motion to and fro across the canvas.[8]

The artist's sweater, a Breton stripe, makes it likely a self-portrait.[9] Some critics see the artist's beard, in some iterations, as more of a goatee, which makes them cringe: goatees have not stood the test of time.

Would it have been more tragic if the lost painting had been Picasso's portrait of Gertrude Stein, or *Guernica*? I have to say, yes, it would have been much worse, sadder, more of a loss, if a truly excellent Picasso painting had been lost. How do we rank or compare the loss of several works by Gorky a few decades earlier with this incident? Was losing a somewhat-interesting Picasso more tragic than losing a hoard of cash and diamonds? I'm inclined to say yes: cash can be replaced, while the painting, even if it is just ok, cannot. (But there *are* five similar versions that survive, so maybe we could do without the sixth?) We can imagine how we might begin to handle such assessments and comparisons of value—indeed, the folks at Lloyds make these kinds of calculations every day. I do not suggest that this exercise helps us to appraise, to value, the importance of human lives lost in crashes: it simply doesn't, and it feels sordid even broaching the premise of "valuing" a human casualty even just to reject it.

But even if such actuarial exercises do feel squalid, too soulless for this investigation, it is nevertheless common to calculate plane crash payouts—compensation for human deaths—based on how litigators calculate an airline's or manufacturer's malfeasance and liability. At some point, the value of a human life *is* actually quantified, and these quantities are different for different victims, based on cultural, geographical, political, and economic data points. It is inevitable—and wrong—that calculations of human "value" may resemble, at least loosely, calculations about the value of art and diamonds.

Boeing avoided criminal trials after two 737 Max planes crashed in 2018–19 by settling for $500 million, shared by 346 crash victims' families, which received about $1.45 million each.[10] After USSR air-to-air missiles shot down Korean Air flight 007 in 1983, families reached individual settlements with the airline—the largest was $10 million, while others ranged from $75,000 to $6 million.[11] Presumably some lawyers represented their clients more successfully than others. The USSR accepted no responsibility and offered no reparations, blaming the incident completely on KAL's navigational error that led the 747 into prohibited Soviet airspace.

A 1998 study confirmed inconsistent compensations to crash victim beneficiaries. Assessing twenty-five major air disasters between 1970–84 resulting in 2,198 payouts, RAND's Institute for Civil Justice found survivors received, on average, $363,000, but 8 percent won over $1 million while 25 percent got under $100,000. "The bottom line is that compensation is neither adequate nor fair," said RAND economist James Smith. "People who suffer identical losses are treated very differently" based on a variety of factors ranging from how laws differ state to state, to the number and wealth of passengers on board.[12]

It is repellent that some lives are assigned greater monetary value than others. Financial accounting is a profoundly imperfect way of calculating the value of human life, yet that's how this process plays out. If there are other ways of solving this quandary in terms that are more humanist, philosophical, ethical, spiritual than dollars and cents, they are also more elusive, more ambiguous. (At the same time, though, a simple solution seems blatantly obvious: equity!)

The *coup de grâce* of the Swissair Picasso story: there are reports, sketchy but (for me) astounding, that a fragment of Picasso's painting was actually recovered from the debris. "Small pieces of the painting, about 20 centimeters, were recovered in the search effort, Operation Persistence," according to media reports.[13] Really? What are the odds of that? How disappointed the moneybags must have been to find scraps of canvas instead of the other more fungible treasures. A Picasso snippet is interesting, sure, but not a resource that could be monetized, its lost value magically restored, as the diamonds or gold could have been if Operation Persistence had persisted until those treasures were found. The diamonds would have retained not only their original value, but an additional premium—a pretty significant bump, I'd venture—by leveraging their debris field backstory. The gold, of course, would have been fine, and even the cash could probably have been ironed or hung to dry to recoup its value.

I have so many questions about the Picasso debris. How many "small pieces" were found? (Were they 20 cm each? Five by four? Ten by two? Or did the scraps sum to 20 cm square?) How were they identified as scraps of the painting? What sort of toll did the crash, and the ocean, take on these canvas fragments? *What did they look like?* Did the colors hold? Was it possible to detect any recognizable segments of the painting (like the goatee?!) on the scraps? Did the scraps prompt searchers to try to find more scraps? Imagine if they had found them all: it would have been a miraculous cluster of debris, and then imagine some fascinating reassembly project—*kintsugi*-style, for sure!—by restoration specialists. Lloyds and art historians probably consider the Picasso debris worthless, nothing more than an ironic reminder of a lost masterpiece (or semi-masterpiece). Boy, would I like to have seen that fragment. I think there is absolutely a value that inheres in it—I can't speak to the cash value, but the imaginative value, the humanist value, seems overwhelming. Imagine displaying it next to one of the other five extant versions of *The Painter*. I'd be honored to write the museum's object panel:

> This fragment was recovered from the debris of Swissair flight 111, which crashed off Nova Scotia's coast. It is from one of at least six similar works Picasso painted in 1963, all with the same title, and we display it here alongside another (intact) version. Certainly this scrap betokens a loss, even a tragedy. (But how does this tragedy compare to the human tragedy of the passengers and crew who lost their lives on that flight?)
>
> We think of art as everlasting: curators oversee extravagant security, surveillance, climate control, in earthquake-proof, fireproof venues. We take great care of it with the most failsafe protection imaginable. But just as people move from place to place via mobility networks, so too, sometimes, do paintings. Usually the people, and the paintings, arrive safely; very occasionally, they don't. This fragment embodies the worst-case scenario that may befall art (and people) when they move through the world.
>
> In its last moments as a unified work, The Painter was boxed up inside an MD-11 that plummeted out of the sky, engulfed in flames, nearly upside down as it crashed into the Atlantic Ocean. Was the art world derelict in allowing this to happen? Should art be banned from airplanes? (Should people?)
>
> Artistic debris may be considered worthless, though the ancient sculptural and architectural remnants in our entrance gallery suggest otherwise. Sometimes these fragments seem all the more fascinating because we have to—we *get* to—imagine what they looked like when they were complete: it's almost as if we become collaborators with the artists ourselves. When something is displayed in a museum even though it's only a fragment of the whole, that prompts us to imagine how incredibly amazing the intact artifact would have been, and even though we can't see that unmolested artwork, still, we can cherish our imagined amazement thereat.
>
> Battered by its unfortunate journey from one anonymous wealthy collector to another, this reclaimed scrap of art may prompt viewers to be grateful for all the other works in this gallery, and in the world at large, that have not succumbed to

plane crashes, or avalanches, or molasses factory explosions. We try our best to sustain things that are of great value, and even in our failures to do so, we may laud the effort, the impulse to keep things safe.

To the best of our knowledge, only one other Picasso painting has since been destroyed in a plane crash.

✈ 9/11

The plane crashes on September 11, 2001, took far more human lives than any crashes ever before. They also destroyed far more art than any other crash. A spokesperson for AXA, one of the art insurance companies that handled 9/11 claims, called it "the biggest single disaster ever to affect the industry."[14]

When the Port Authority of New York and New Jersey planned the World Trade Center, they allocated 1 percent of the budget for public art. The crashes of United flight 175 and American flight 11 destroyed numerous pieces of public art on the surrounding plaza and other nearby sites as the towers collapsed. "Public art" is an admirable concept—it is out in public, for the public, who don't have to visit a museum or go out of their way to experience a moment of inspiring beauty. But just as public art flourishes amid a flourishing public culture, 9/11 showed that so too will it suffer in the throes of public suffering.

Roy Lichtenstein has a reprise here: several works from a series displayed in a public area of the towers were destroyed. "Entablature," a project from the 1970s depicting an assortment of lower Manhattan's architectural facades and ornamental motifs, was as demure as *Whaam!* is explosive. The array of embossed screenprints emphasized "texture, surface, relief, and reflectivity," according to the Whitney Museum. Lichtenstein's title refers to the horizontal structures that sit atop classical Greek columns. The series presented "a distinctly American derivative, one based in revivalist, industrialized architectural imitations that were built en masse in the early twentieth century." He saw these designs as "clichéd symbols" of "imperial power" and "the establishment."[15] The fragments of early twentieth-century buildings featured in these artworks eerily prefigures the fragments of the late twentieth-century buildings that would comprise Ground Zero. The World Trade Center's massive arches, piazzas, and fountains that filled lower Manhattan's panorama of ruin were (just like the "Entablatures") modern American reinterpretations of classical European forms. As these real building elements intermingled with Lichtenstein's artistic representations of earlier ones, the debris field formed a macabre pastiche of architectural traditions.

Another Lichtenstein work, a 1990 sculpture called *Modern Head*, was damaged but survived. The Public Art Fund had installed the vibrant blue 30-foot-tall pop-art bust in Battery Park City, a block from the World Trade Center. Media images after the attack showed the sculpture covered in debris but still standing; the FBI used it as a message board during its investigations at Ground Zero. (The term "ground zero" first appeared in 1946, according to the *OED*: a point "directly at, above, or below an exploding nuclear bomb." It had been lower case, but usage convention now is to capitalize specific references to the WTC debris field.) Removed later in 2001, *Modern Head* is now installed outside the Smithsonian's main building in Washington, DC, where the story of its 9/11 endurance figures prominently in the museum's description of the artwork.[16]

Other sculptures in nearby Zuccotti Park—Isamu Noguchi's *Red Cube* and Mark di Suvero's *Joie de Vivre*—were also damaged but repaired.[17] Alongside those was John Seward Johnson II's 1982 sculpture *Double Check*, a blandly realistic bronze depiction of a businessman bent over a briefcase getting ready to go into the office, double-checking that he had everything he needed.

> On 9/11 the statue was mistaken for an actual person, and many on the scene ran towards the statue to ask if it was alright. Photos of the statue covered in debris became iconic emblems of New Yorkers' post-September 11 resilience, as the statue remained standing despite being heavily pummeled by shrapnel and became a symbol of strength and a memorial following the attacks. The very realism for which it had been previously criticized became a venerated icon.[18]

After the sculpture was cleaned up, people began leaving things near it: flags, flowers, a hard hat, a hose from the NY Fire Department, crucifixes, stuffed animals—a random assortment of memorial debris that replaced the crash debris.

Double Check "became a symbol of the World Trade Tower victims, murdered for simply going to work," writes Tim Miller. "The statue represented the common, working guy in a suit who died trying to make a living for his family. It gripped the hearts of New Yorkers." Johnson later moved the sculpture to his studio, casting a duplicate "adding the objects left by mourners—now bronzed—and giving the statue a gray patina. The new sculpture received the fitting title *Makeshift Memorial*." Johnson also refurbished the original statue, leaving the damages caused by the crashing debris, and returned it to Liberty Plaza Park where the businessman now sits on a granite bench facing the site of the Towers.[19]

Other destroyed public art included James Rosati's stainless steel sculpture *Ideogram* (1967); Masayuki Nagare's black granite *Cloud Fortress* (1975); Joan Miró's *World Trade Center Tapestry* (1974); and Louise Nevelson's large black wooden sculpture, *Sky Gate, New York* (1977–8). Like many of the public artworks commissioned, Nevelson's featured a direct engagement with the Twin Towers: she called *Sky Gate* a "night piece," a silhouette representing her rendition of the city's skyline.[20] It seems perverse but also appropriate that the art—meant to complement the WTC's lofty architectural bravado with a corresponding measure of humanist bravado—ended up, in its own destruction, mirroring the destruction of those buildings and of over 2,600 victims who died inside them.

Elyn Zimmerman's memorial fountain for the victims of an earlier attack, the 1993 World Trade Center bombing, was mostly destroyed, but a piece that was recovered is on display at the 9/11 Memorial Museum. Zimmerman inscribed the six 1993 victims' names on her fountain—one was John DiGiovanni. The surviving debris fragment reads just "John"; I wonder how many 9/11 victims were named John. In its destruction, Zimmerman's art ironically became more expansive in some sense, albeit unintentionally, now honoring not just one, or six, but many dozen victims by name. The art uncannily echoes the cycle of terrorist brutality at that site: violence/memorial, violence/memorial.

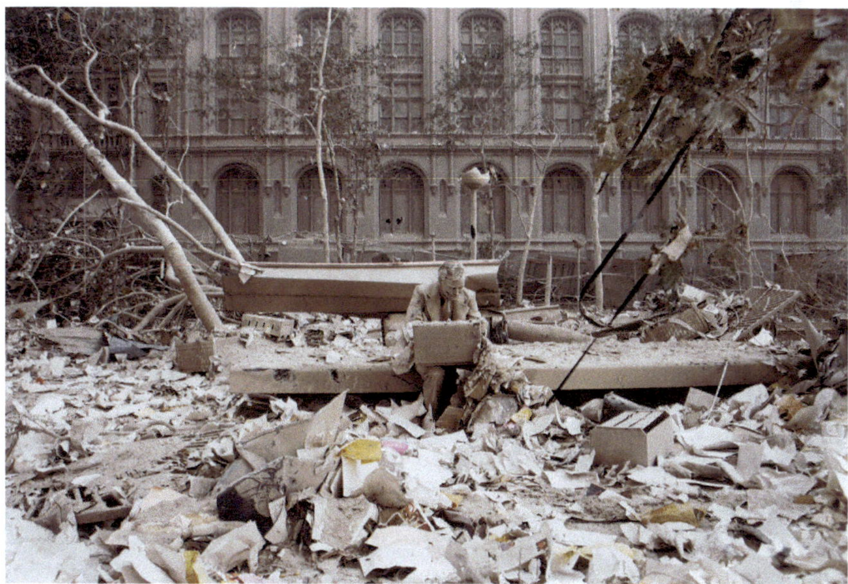

Figure 6.3 John Seward Johnson II, *Double Check* (1982), shortly after 9/11.

The Sphere, Fritz Koenig's abstract 25-foot-tall bronze sculpture, stood on the plaza between the Twin Towers. Resting above a ring of fountains and rotating once every twenty-four hours, it was meant to symbolize world peace through world trade. It survived the collapse but was seriously disfigured. Its extensive damage serves perfectly—and again, uncannily—as a memorial homage to the attack's overarching impact, illustrating how art adapts over time to reflect a changed reality. The sphere evokes a globe, as befits the *World* Trade Center, and also, after 9/11, the *global* scourge of terrorism, the *global* impact of those plane crashes. The damaged art-globe mirrors the damaged world. Koenig spoke at the ceremony where *The Sphere* was rededicated, a few blocks away, in 2002: "It was a sculpture, now it's a monument. It now has a different beauty, one I could never imagine. It has its own life—different from the one I gave to it."[21]

Alexander Calder's red steel sculpture *World Trade Center Stabile* (1971) was also heavily damaged. About half was excavated from the ruins and is now, like the debris from Zimmerman's fountain, on display in the 9/11 Memorial Museum. Looking at them there makes viewers think about art in debris, art as debris, and the toll plane crashes take on important things besides people. Saul Wenegrat, the director of the Port Authority's art program who commissioned WTC's public art, said in 2002 that Calder's sculpture "cannot be restored, but its pieces may come back to life in a different form."[22]

The Calder debris was, at first, just barely identifiable as part of the sculpture that had stood outside 7 World Trade Center. The parts were twisted and torn, scorched, covered in dirt. Alexander S. C. Rower, Calder's grandson and director of the Calder Foundation, circulated a flyer among clean-up site workers in the weeks after 9/11, and foundation officials were on the scene constantly, searching for the sculpture in the ruins. Rower knew the damage would be extensive: "You can assume that it kind of blew apart as No. 7 fell on it."[23] He described finding the debris: "I was there when they pulled some of the parts out of the ash. This was October 11. The steel was still red hot, which was shocking to me. The heat, the intensity of that devastation was so incredible."[24] Rower said the sculpture was easier to identify because its metal is a half-inch thick, and no other major structural element of the World Trade Center had the same dimensions; also, zigzag patterned bolt-holes running along its edges made it more clearly distinctive.

World Trade Center Stabile had a stunning informal title—which was again, at the risk of overusing this descriptor, uncanny. Its official title, like Miró's *World Trade Center Tapestry*, acknowledges the commission, but Calder himself referred to the piece (and this was of course before the crashes: he died in 1976) as *Bent Propeller*—wow!—which is the title critics now generally use. The sculpture is composed of three sheets of metal curved gracefully like bird wings, or, as Calder suggested, a bent propeller.[25] It seems ridiculous, but … did he somehow imagine what might happen to his sculpture, and to the Twin Towers? I suppose I don't believe that this is really likely, or even possible, but—and please excuse my rampant humanist license here—does a great artist somehow anticipate things that the rest of us don't? (I think: yes.) Every building built is a building that could fall; every plane flown is a plane that could crash. Calder's sculptures celebrate industrial power and energy with their large, bright, luxuriant sweeping forms. The "propellers" in this sculpture fit with that feature of his art: but why "bent"? Propellers bend only if their planes crash.

Calder probably didn't literally know what would happen, but his art suggested, intentionally or coincidentally, that something might happen in the future that would fulfill the prophecy, if you will, of bent propellers. (There were obviously no propellers on the two Boeing 767s that crashed into the Towers, which may make my prophetic reading of his sculpture seem inconsistent aeronautically, but it poses no problems semiotically or aesthetically.) It recalls for me another piece of 9/11 culture written decades before the attack: a poem that wasn't meant to be a 9/11 poem (unless we indulge the same idea of fortuitous artistic prophecy that I'm suggestively attributing to Calder), but is now. Auden's "September 1, 1939," marking the beginning of WWII, is set in September, in New York, just because that's where he happened to be on that day: sitting in a bar, getting drunk.

The poem about that day's global tragedy—a moment so awful that the date alone connotes its terror—is filled with spine-tinglingly proleptic lines about skyscrapers—"this neutral air / Where blind skyscrapers use / Their full height to proclaim / The strength of Collective Man." Auden describes "the folded lie … of Authority / Whose buildings grope the sky." And most ominously, "The unmentionable odour of death / Offends the September night." Anyone familiar with this poem felt instantly, when the planes crashed into the Twin Towers, that those lines incomparably described the occasion, no less powerfully because its creation predated the moment by decades. Like Calder, Auden couldn't have known that this precise event would happen, but did he guess that something like it could? His poetry, like Calder's sculpture, stood ready when needed to help people deal with and give voice to that terrible day. It may or may not provide some comfort to realize that the humanists had seen this, or something like this, coming. The unmentionably offensive odour of death reverberating among the New York skyscrapers that Auden felt in September of 1939 was not, he knew, a one-off. We are a predictable crowd, we humans: the feelings his poetry conveyed at the outbreak of WWII would be felt again by "later other"—another Audenesque phrase, meaning . . . us.

Civilization flourishes alongside its discontents. Art and plane crashes are coterminous, and sometimes, I'm discovering, even symbiotic. Art happens in a world in which crashes, too, happen.

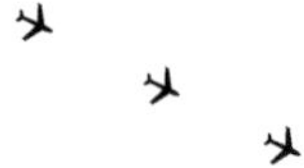

When terrorists crashed American flight 77 into the Pentagon's western side, killing 125 who worked there along with fifty-nine passengers and crew on the plane (and themselves), we probably wouldn't have expected any art in that debris field. But there was: twenty-four artworks were destroyed and another forty sustained substantial damage in collections of the Army, Navy, Air Force, and Marine Corps. There is a unique irony in the Pentagon's art-debris: their art about war was lost in an act of war. The eight paintings destroyed from the Army's Center for Military History include Gary Porter's *O.D. One Each* (1967), which depicted a US soldier in Vietnam with his O.D. ("olive drab"-colored) duffel bag, helmet, and sleeping bag. Another, *The Knucklebusters*, artist unidentified, showed three soldiers in camouflage struggling to fix a broken M-1 tank—"knucklebusters" is military slang for mechanics. Ten Air Force paintings were burned, all (extra-ironically) of aircraft, along with seven works from the Marine Corps collection. Marine art curator Jack Dyer described the artwork lost that day as "cultural casualties,"[26] a perfect phrase to describe the subject of this chapter's investigations.

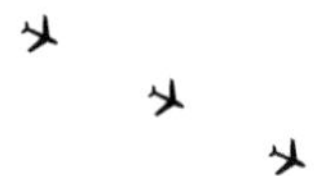

The most awful part of the 9/11 art-debris field came from destroyed artists' studios. Fifteen artists from South Korea, Singapore, Austria, Australia, Iran, Israel, Jamaica, Japan, England, Colombia and the US, were participating in Lower Manhattan Cultural Council's artist-in-residence program on the North Tower's 91st and 92nd floors. This "World Views" program was an inspired concept for this cultural community that was so *worldly*, with studios offering such stunning views of the *world* (as its artists were creating *World* Views) from the *World* Trade Center. The residency, scheduled from May–November 2001, was supposed to culminate with open studio viewings of projects completed during artists' time there.

That show did eventually take place, a couple of months delayed, in SoHo's New Museum of Contemporary Art, near where the WTC had stood. It was dedicated to the lone World Views artist killed on 9/11, Jamaican sculptor Michael Richards, who arrived in his studio the previous evening and worked through the night on a series of sculptures commemorating WWII's Tuskegee Airmen.[27] Richards had spent many years on this project, creating several figures. "Aviation and flight are recurrent themes in the artist's practice," notes art critic Victoria Valentine, "and in a tragic turn ultimately factored into his untimely death."[28] In one of his best-known works, *Tar Baby vs. St. Sebastian* (1999), a gold-painted figure of the artist in an airman's uniform is pierced by multiple small airplanes"—eighteen miniature P-51 Mustangs, to be precise—"linking a figure from Southern folklore and a Christian martyr, as the title suggests, as well as the story of the Tuskegee Airmen and the artist's own Afro-Caribbean identity. 'The idea of flight relates to my use of pilots and planes,' he said, 'but it also references the black church, the idea of being lifted up, enraptured, or taken up to a safe place—to a better world.'"[29]

The sculpture Richards was working on when he died, according to colleagues who had seen it, was another life-size figure of himself—many of his works were self-portraits—"dressed in the airmen's uniform, astride a falling meteor ablaze with flames."[30] *A falling meteor ablaze*: stunning, eerie. This sculpture of a profoundly heroic Airman falling, ablaze, must have fallen itself, ablaze, as a consequence of unspeakably evil Airmen. I cannot help but imagine the artist and his art falling together: the man and his sculpture of a man, of himself. Richards's mission, and his life, were unfinished—like the long-term project, the ongoing series of transcendent Black pilots, he worked on during his final hours.

This idea of Richards and his sculpture so intimately conjoined, however horribly, conveys a sublime lesson about the creator/the creation, life and art. It also reminds us how cycles of war violence recur generation after generation, and how Richards tried to understand that, and temper that, and teach his audience something valuable about it by creating a sculpture depicting a man falling like a meteor ablaze—the very creation of which resulted in the artist's reenacting this gruesome fate. It is a kind of infinite regression of people dying

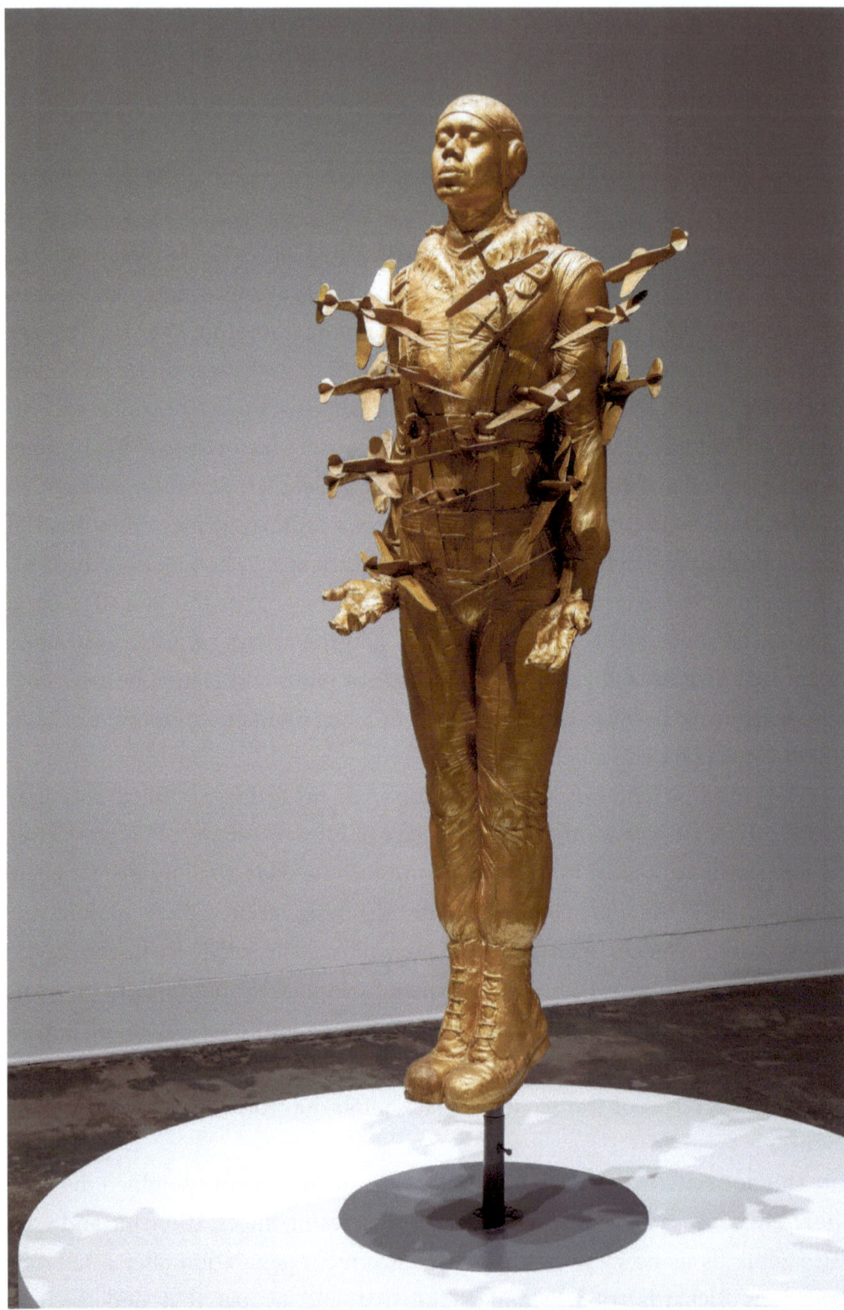

Figure 6.4 Michael Richards, *Tar Baby vs. St. Sebastian* (1999), in which the figure, a likeness of the artist, hauntingly anticipates his fate in a WTC art studio two years later.

from warplanes (American flight 11, a Boeing 767, was not a warplane . . . until it was), crashing stupidly into lives that were full of talent and determination: lives of mid-twentieth-century airmen who fought racism and fascism in one fell swoop, and of the twenty-first-century artist who celebrated and sustained cultural memories of those aviators' heroism.

Is it too simplistic to suggest that the most complex and cognitively overwhelming debris field in the history of aviation, Ground Zero, could be pretty succinctly summarized in Michael Richards's compact tableau investigated here? His personal contribution to the colossal debris field, his own microcosmic inscription therein, offers a valuably comprehensible perspective on the macrocosmic, incomprehensible catastrophe. Coincidentally—prophetically?—Richards conjoined human creativity about historical violence, inscribed in the fierce determination of the Tuskegee Airmen's stories, with the aleatory violence of 9/11—a previously-unimaginable perversion of aviation that happened to crash into the sculptor's studio that morning.

Richards's anticipatory depiction of aviation tragedy in *Tar Baby vs. St. Sebastian*, and his subsequent engagement in his own real-life aviation tragedy, is ineffably harrowing, and ironic, and also amazing. It is, quite simply, art in its purest and most powerful manifestation, inextricably entwined with aviation in its most awful and dysfunctional manifestation. My rubric of "Crashes in Art"/"Art in Crashes" is merely clever wordplay until artists like Richards fill it in, make it real, with his art, his crash, his art of crashes, his art in crashes.

Richards's world views ended in that moment on 9/11 as he, his studio, and his art became debris, all mixed together. The dead artist, like all that day's 3,000 other crash victims, left behind world views of some sort that survive their deaths, that are enriched (as well as ruined) by what they left behind. Richards used himself as a model in his art, perhaps somehow sensing that he might not be on earth for long enough, and wanting to leave "himself" behind to endure—"himself" comprising his art, as well as his physical likeness—with the confidence that if it was good art (it is!), it would survive him. His works still appear prominently in art exhibitions and public art installations: a recent one, "Are You Down?" took its name from another of his sculptures

> featuring three life-size human figures surrounding a target, which represent the artist in uniform as a Tuskegee Airman. The three parachutists appear to have fallen from the sky, sitting discontent on the ground in what appear to be puddles of tar.[31]

We may ask not just of the art but also of the artist, are you down? Yes, Michael Richards is down, but also, in another sense, no, he's not. His Tuskegee Airmen, as depicted in that installation, are also down, and also not. They still fly high—metaphorically, aesthetically, historically—in the eternal present of Richards's art, which still survives (except for the sculpture destroyed on 9/11). Of the 996 Black pilots trained at Alabama's Tuskegee Army Air Field, 148 died in combat crashes or training.[32] They, too, went down into debris fields; and they too flew high, and still fly high.

When the World Views show had its delayed opening on December 1, 2001, most of its exhibitions were recreations of projects conceived before 9/11, destroyed and subsequently remade. "A few pieces that predate the destruction of the trade center appear in their original form," Holland Cotter writes, including "a series of cartoonlike watercolors titled 'But Buildings Can Talk' by Carola Dertnig, which she finished last summer and stored in her apartment rather than in her trade center studio. In them, the twin towers are turned into identical sisters and play ambiguous roles in a morality tale about commerce and greed." Some artists reworked their residency projects after 9/11: "Kara Hammond recreated from memory a group of architectural drawings, including one of her World Views studio. She also added a new drawing to the series. Titled 'Cenotaph,' it shows a slim, tapering tower rising from the Lower Manhattan skyline where the trade center had been."[33]

The Lower Manhattan Cultural Council's offices and records were totally demolished, along with 150 artworks in their collection and another 424 pieces from their studios.

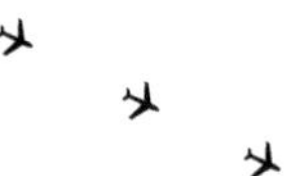

Other art lost in the Ground Zero debris field included some of the Broadway Theatre Archive's "35,000 photographs that captured great moments of the American stage and approximately 40,000 negatives of photographs by Jacques Lowe documenting the presidency of John F. Kennedy," stored in a Five World Trade Center safe-deposit vault. Another vault in Tower Two contained a rare antique rug collection—twenty-five hand-woven kilims, heirlooms passed through generations of Muslim families from the Middle East, North Africa, and Southeast Asia—valued at over $500,000.[34]

And buildings—at least, good ones—are also art. Numerous architectural landmarks were destroyed: foremost, obviously, Minoru Yamasaki's astounding 1972 Twin Towers. Initially, they faced a tough reception: fellow architects considered them "a monstrously over-scaled inhuman blight on the city."[35] Architect Dale Gyure explains how their most trenchant critic, Ada Louise Huxtable, described the buildings as "the world's daintiest architecture for the world's biggest buildings," echoing those who favored the "masculine" bare bones, steel-and-glass wing of contemporary architecture.

> 'Dainty' wouldn't be the only dubious epithet of a gendered nature to be directed toward Yamasaki's work: a comprehensive list would include terms like 'frilly', 'precious', 'prissy', 'saccharine', 'lacy' and 'epicene'. Such descriptions were firmly connected in the public mind with women and their 'frivolous' obsession with decoration.[36]

Throughout his career Yamasaki faced such misogynist, and also racist, reactions to his work. But the World Trade Center's tall, simple elegance grew on New Yorkers and the world. The loss of the buildings themselves was hugely mourned after the planes destroyed them, their artistic force finally appreciated in their death if not in their life. The musician Moby wrote a "eulogy for the twin towers":

> i know that people are more important than buildings, and that the loss of a single life is more tragic than the loss of some buildings, but nonetheless i want to try to write my own remembrance of these buildings. from my rooftop the twin towers were the only buildings that dominated the skyline. in fact from all of lower manhattan they were the only skyscrapers that you could always see. they were always there, always pointing the way south. if you would ever come up out of the subway and feel disoriented all you would have to do is to locate the twin towers to gain your bearings. . . . every morning they would be waiting for me. i would go up to my roof and see them quietly standing there. they were so unique. like a brother and sister. ancient and modern at the same time. two giant sentinels standing silent watch over manhattan and all of new york. the most amazing thing about the twin towers was that they cast shadows on each other. and passing clouds would cast shadows on them. it was so beautiful to see. i would oftentimes sit on my roof and watch big clouds floating by and casting shadows on the twin towers. the towers would stand there silently and the clouds would float by and gracefully cast shadows on the towers simple exteriors.[37]

Besides exquisitely conveying their beauty, Moby extols their architect's creative force:

> i can't help but think that yamasaki . . . saw them as having an almost zen quality in their lightness and stability. and how could buildings be 'bad architecture' when they were familiar to every single citizen of the world? how could they be 'bad architecture' when millions of us looked at them every day, casting shadows on each other and reassuring us? aesthetically i really loved them. i loved that they were a pair. i loved that they stood at strange angles to each other. i loved to go up close to them and touch them. i loved to sit at their base and look up and get instant vertigo.

And speaking of admiration marks and shout-poles (as I was back in Chapter 5), a *New York Times* letter-writer called the Twin Towers "New York's punctuation: two exclamation points."[38]

Other damaged architectural treasures nearby included the Barclay-Vesey building (1927), considered the world's first art deco skyscraper; the Beaux Arts-style West Street Building (1907) with its striking "wedding cake" mansard roof; the small Greek Orthodox Church of St. Nicholas (1922), converted from a private nineteenth-century home, all the more distinctive *in situ* because it had survived the twentieth century in its understated original form while the financial district brusquely shot up around it; and the Federal Hall National Memorial (1842), a Greek Revival building that stands on the site of George Washington's inauguration and the first US Congress meeting-place. Except for the Church, these buildings have all been laboriously restored; the Barclay-Vesey renovations took three years, costing $1.4 billion. A new Church of St. Nicholas, featuring Santiago Calatrava's sleek modern design—much flashier than its humble predecessor—opened near its original location in 2022.

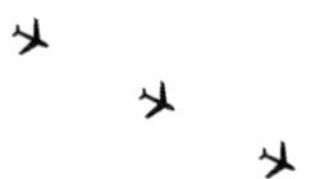

Much public art is sited outside, or in indoor public spaces like lobbies, freely and easily accessible for everyone. Public art can also live inside, in museums, though this might more accurately be called semi-public art: anyone can see it, but often not for free, and not as easily as if it were out in the world.

And then there's private art, held by rich people and corporations in places accessible only to those who own it, and their friends and clients. Art in homes and offices, the plutocrats probably think, is all the more rarified precisely because it is so minimally available to the public. It's as if seeing art is somehow zero-sum: the fewer people see it, the more each person can enjoy it—the Louvre's infamous *Mona Lisa* scrum is a counterexample. But if only a very small number of people have access to a work of art, each of them reaps a large percentage of the beauty and pleasure it disperses into the world. A way for wealthy people to bask in their privilege, it is nonetheless a ludicrous and devious proposition. I resent privately held art because I am offended by the vast inequality of wealth it celebrates; because art vanishes into solitary confinement, which must be as crazy-making for the canvas (and for the progenitor, the artist) as it is for a person similarly isolated; and because it is usually protected and conserved less effectively, less professionally, than art in the public domain. A vast amount of such exclusive art from WTC offices—much larger in scope than the public works discussed above—became debris on 9/11.

Would these private collections have survived if they were in museums rather than offices? In retrospect, we realize the art was in an insecure venue: an office building that (previous experience had shown, in the 1993 WTC attack) was a target because it epitomized, for terrorists, the excesses of Western wealth and power. True, a plane could crash into a museum as well as a corporate complex, but that hasn't happened. Should we evacuate art from places that terrorists are likely to target? I'm inclined to say no, because then the terrorists win; but also, I don't know: maybe?

Auguste Rodin is the star in this branch of the art-crash investigation, the most prominent artist with the most privately held art and the most captivating debris narrative, but this strand of the case also includes work by Cindy Sherman, Romare Bearden (two paintings), Jacob Lawrence (five paintings), Le Corbusier, Paul Klee, David Hockney, Currier & Ives (numerous lithographs). If these works had been collected in a museum show rather than a debris field, we'd call it a blockbuster exhibition. Once again—reprising Swissair's 1998 crash—a Picasso painting was destroyed on 9/11; which one, specifically, was never publicly revealed, thanks to the privacy and secrecy surrounding private art. I wonder if it was "better" or "worse" than *The Painter*. Theoretically, it could actually have been *The Painter*: remember, Picasso painted six versions, so even after the Swissair crash, five survived. Wouldn't that make an amazing crash story? It certainly would increase people's interest in that undistinguished painting.

John Bachmann's mid-nineteenth-century *Bird's Eye View of New York and Brooklyn* hung in Citigroup's WTC offices: a clever curatorial choice (do private collections even have curators?) as it depicts the exact location where the Towers

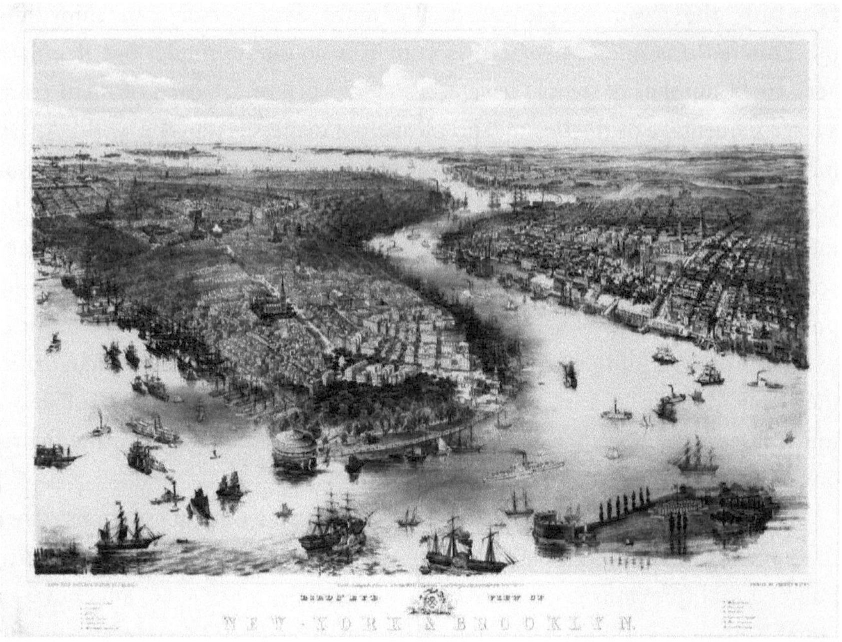

Figure 6.5 John Bachmann, *Bird's Eye View of New York and Brooklyn* (1851).

would rise. It has a cunning anticipatory energy, depicting exactly where viewers would have been standing when they saw this print more than a century after it was composed. Bachmann in the 1850s (like Yamasaki in the 1960s) was inspired to imagine Manhattan from above: as if from a skyscraper, though such things did not exist then, or an airplane, which also did not exist. ("Although bird's-eye views appear to be captured from above the city," writes Hanna Kinney, "they were mathematically compiled on a map or a grid of the city based on hundreds of sketches made on the ground."[39])

The cunning anticipatory energy I described above works only for viewers who saw Bachmann's print during the four decades between the World Trade Center's construction and destruction. After 9/11, that nineteenth-century image changed again. Now, when I see the open space Bachmann depicts at the bottom of mid-nineteenth-century Manhattan, it strikes me as an ominous (and uncanny!) anticipation of how it would look after the Towers fell. Since that day, whenever I see a view of the city's skyline that includes the bottom tip, I'm aware of what *isn't* there: the WTC. I see what happens when planes crash into buildings. Like many other prophetic artworks, *Bird's Eye View* seems to provide an aesthetic premonition about something that he couldn't possibly have known—or could he?—would happen in the future. (Proposal to the cadre of conventional crash investigators: hire someone to survey art and literature from previous generations, to suss out other predictions of crashes that haven't happened yet. I would be happy to help craft the warning notice explaining that people have to evacuate because a poet who died decades earlier intuited a lurking danger.)

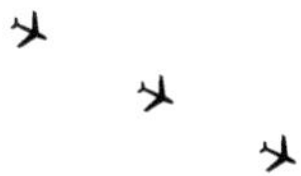

There were a lot of Rodin sculptures in the private-art debris. It's interesting to think about how we arrange and characterize and enumerate the elements of a plane crash: there were a lot of workers from Cantor Fitzgerald (658) and Marsh McLennan (295), a lot of NYC Firefighters (343), a lot of British (67) and Greek (39) and Dominican (47) victims, a lot of art: the Rodins may be considered another community that suffered destruction. Art soothes us in times of trauma, and art itself, as we see at Ground Zero, actually experiences these traumas in terms of its own physical materiality. This phenomenon seems especially salient for human sculptural forms, as in the case of John Seward Johnson's *Double Check*, Michael Richards's World Views residency work-in-progress, and the Rodin sculptures. Any maimed art is upsetting, but maimed art in bodily forms haunts us—and this was especially true on 9/11—in a way that is more directly incisive, more painful, than wrecked architectural prints or antique rugs.

The fate of nonhuman bodies in plane crashes, like Rodin's, Richards's and Johnson's, makes me think about aviation safety and forensic exercises where crash-test "human" dummies experience remotely controlled flights and crashes. These drills are rare: complex, expensive, and potentially dangerous to carry out. In 2012, a multinational team in Mexico equipped a Boeing 727 with cameras, dummies, and instruments to measure the crash impact. Investigators studied the data and the debris field to better understand exactly what happens to planes and people in crashes.

Passengers up front would have been most at risk in such a crash, they found: "Nobody would have survived from Row 7 forward. Seat 7A catapulted 500 feet from the plane." People closer to the wings would have suffered serious but survivable injuries, like broken ankles; the test dummy near the tail section was largely intact, suggesting passengers there might have escaped serious injury. The brace position was found to minimize concussion and spinal injuries, but created additional loads that could result in fractured legs or ankles. "'Upright dummies near the front and in the back both suffered severe stress to their lower backs, but the braced occupant didn't,' said Cindy Bir, one of the test crash engineers who set up three $150,000 crash-test dummies with 32 sensors on each."[40]

Somehow, in a way that may or not make sense, I think of the human sculptural forms destroyed in the WTC plane crashes on a continuum that has, at one end, crash-test dummies, and at the other end, actual human crash victims. As investigators study dummies that experience a crash, I think we can also examine the Rodins and other human-like artworks that experienced a crash to learn something about human beings who experience a crash.

"Cantor Fitzgerald, a bond-dealing firm that lost more lives than any other in the tragedy, also suffered the biggest artistic loss," writes *The Economist*. "Its offices on the 105th floor of One World Trade Centre housed a collection of sculptures by Auguste Rodin. It is still uncertain how many Rodins were in the building, and thus destroyed. Estimates range from dozens to several hundred,"[41] exemplifying the laissez-faire stewardship of privately held art: owners are not compelled to maintain or share even the most basic information about their collections.

Artworks destroyed on 9/11 have "never been fully documented or commemorated," writes art critic Adrian Wilson. "In many cases, not even a record or photograph remains. The reasons may be a lack of information, a respect for the human loss, or even the fact that poor decisions were made. Because of the complete losses, or reluctance to share information, it has been impossible to collate all the items." Numerous organizations "attempted to compile a full inventory but without success. Not only the art, but the paperwork to prove much of provenance vanished."[42]

Cantor Fitzgerald's chairman, Howard Lutnick, "refused to discuss in any depth the loss of its art collection," write Dan Barry and William Rashbaum. "What did any of that matter when 658 of the company's 960 employees working in the building—including Mr. Lutnick's brother, Gary—perished in the collapse?"[43]

I think it does matter: not nearly as much as the human death toll, but . . . it matters.

Amid the wreckage a quarter-mile away from Ground Zero, several fragments of Rodin's sculptures surfaced. They were transported to a recreated debris field in Staten Island atop Fresh Kills landfill, the world's largest when it closed its operations in March, 2001. Rubble from Manhattan, 1.6 million tons, had been brought there for sorting to help clear out the site where the Towers had stood. In a small trailer on that site, clean-up crews stored a dented bust from *The Burghers of Calais* (1884–9) and two of the three anguished figures from *The Three Shades*—Rodin's 1886 interpretation of the scene from Dante's *Commedia* depicting damned souls just outside the gates of Hell, all hope abandoned—broken almost beyond recognition; a foot was severed, and the bodies were decapitated.[44]

"It's just absolutely astonishing," said Clare Vincent, a Metropolitan Museum specialist in European sculpture. "It really is incredible to me that they could have survived that sort of inferno, even remotely in recognizable form." At the risk of belaboring a painfully obvious point, Dante's fourteenth-century Hell, as reiterated by Rodin in the nineteenth century, served well—uncannily so—as a macabre analogue for New York City's twenty-first-century Hell. The "bodily" damage to Rodin's sculptural forms parallels and evokes the casualties that people suffered. What are the odds of these particular infernal figures being destroyed in these particular crashes? Perhaps, once again, it is not a question of random happenstance, but rather, some mystical knowledge about the future (or instinct, or guess) that uniquely inhabits the artistic consciousness. Artists seem to anticipate tragic horrors that will happen beyond the ending of their books, beyond the frames of their paintings, after they have cast all their sculptures, and indeed, after they have shuffled off their own mortal coils.

One more Rodin fragment appeared soon after the planes crashed, and then vanished again: a cast of Rodin's most famous work—featured in Cantor Fitzgerald's logo—*The Thinker* (1904). 1904: remember that the Wright brothers first flew in December, 1903. I wonder what *The Thinker* was thinking? It is not chronologically impossible that he was thinking about an airplane, or even a crash. Investigators believed the Rodin cast "may have been stolen, after having been recovered by a firefighter at the disaster site," write Barry and Rashbaum.

Cantor Fitzgerald said they planned to use the remnants of their Rodin collection to create "an appropriate memorial to lost friends and colleagues"[45]—though I found no evidence that such a project was ever undertaken; perhaps it was, super-privately. There is so much that remains unknown (or if people know, they won't tell me) about the fate of private art from Ground Zero. Can you imagine not being told how many people were lost, or what their names were? I know, it's not the same thing, but I cannot imagine the rationale for this refusal to share information that crash investigators (whether humanist investigators or real ones) should be able to have for the sake of conducting the best possible inquiries and determining, as fully as possible, exactly what happened, and what happens next.

Dietrich von Frank, President of AXA Art Insurance, described seeing damaged remnants of Calder's and Koenig's sculptures, which reminded him that "art, and especially art publicly displayed, helps us to connect to the world we live in. As both works of art have been rescued from the debris, their damaged and nearly destroyed condition will be the perfect vehicle to remind the public in the future of what has happened, and, therefore, will remain true public art, art for everyone to remember." These public artworks have become *even more public*, von Frank suggests, and I agree. And I'd add, as nebulous and subjective as this sounds, Calder's and Koenig's works have become *even better art* as well: in the time since they were originally created, they've soaked up even more of the world, and they contain/convey even more aesthetic and sociohistorical power—not to mention irony!—than the artists had originally instilled in them.

✈ Art(lovers) in crashes

When I moved to Atlanta in the 1980s, locals regularly bemoaned an underwhelming arts scene, relative to the city's size and national prominence. The excuse was that the cream of Atlanta's art community was lost back in the 1960s—in a plane crash, obviously, or why else would I be writing about it?—and cultural organizations never recovered from that blow. It's a unique twist on art-in-crashes, also featuring a vivid crash-in-art cameo appearance by Andy Warhol.

Air France, trying to establish a presence in the US southeast, developed an alliance with Atlanta's art crowd, offering a free trip to Paris as a prize for the Art Association's auction. The event grew into a full-blown month-long tour/fundraiser: a chartered Air France jet would take a planeload of art aficionados from Atlanta to Paris, London, Amsterdam, Lucerne, Venice, Florence, Rome, back to Paris, and then home. The travelers included upper-crust art patrons, opera fans, Atlanta Symphony Orchestra volunteers, Junior League members, artists (professional and amateur), and supporters of the High Museum of Art, for whom a "first-hand glimpse of the world's masterpieces" would dispel the image that Atlantans were culturally bereft, writes Ann Uhry Abrams in *Explosion at Orly: The Disaster that Transformed Atlanta.*[46]

Recently elected Mayor Ivan Allen championed a "Forward Atlanta" campaign—boosterism always flourished at the core of Atlanta's ethos—hyping the city's cultural potential in the interest of attracting new business. Branded as "The city too busy to hate," promoters tried to project Atlanta's distance from pervasive Southern racism by embracing, basically, anything else that didn't smack of segregation and prejudice. The delegation, "a distinctive coterie to represent their city in Europe," went "with an understanding that they would be spreading the word about Atlanta. They were determined to demonstrate that Atlantans could be more cultured and worldly than other Americans, and perhaps even match Europeans in their urbane sophistication." Mayor Allen was on hand with local media to bid the group farewell on May 9, 1962.

After a busy and successful tour, Atlanta's art pilgrims prepared to come home on June 3. Air France flight 7 was scheduled to fly to New York, where it would land for refueling and passenger transit through customs before continuing to Atlanta. During the takeoff roll, the pilot noticed a signal indicating that the Boeing 707's tail stabilizers were not working properly. He had passed V1, the maximum speed at which a takeoff can be rejected (sometimes called Go/No-Go). After that point, according to universal safety protocol then and now, an airplane simply has to take off despite whatever problems have arisen, and try to deal with those issues in the air while making an emergency return to the airport.

But the Air France pilot attempted the impossible, reversing the engines in an attempt to abort takeoff. All eight tires burned out, causing the craft to veer. At the end of Orly's runway 26, a hill sloped down and the plane plunged into the gully, crashing through a row of concrete posts topped by approach lights. Light poles punctured the wings, tearing open fuel cells. The engines fell off, the tail blew away, and the fuselage became a fireball. Most passengers were killed instantly and nearby houses in the village bordering the airport, Villeneuve-le-Roi, were badly damaged, but there were no ground fatalities. In terms of the trial-and-error theory of aviation safety, this crash made it even more blatantly indisputable that pilots simply cannot ever fudge the protocol mandating takeoff after reaching V1. (If you recall another V1-snafu investigation, you've been paying attention! Continental flight 1713, discussed in my first "Diversion," also tried to abort after V1, suffering the consequences of that impossible maneuver. That happened twenty-five years *after* the Orly crash; there are exceptions, though not many, to the rule that aviation constantly becomes safer as pilots learn from other pilots' mistakes.)

Abrams described the crash as Atlanta's version of 9/11 (she was writing about it forty years on in 2002) in terms of its vast impact on the city.[47] The death toll, 130 passengers and crew, included 106 members of the Atlanta tour. It was, at the time, the most people ever killed in a plane crash. Three flight attendants—their job titles were gendered in that era: two stewardesses and one steward—were blown out the jet's tail when it exploded. The stewardesses were the only people aboard the plane who survived; the steward succumbed to his injuries.

Commonly when I was young, parents flew separately so their children would not become orphans in case of a crash. Even today, it is not uncommon for companies to arrange that when a large group of employees travel together for a meeting or site visit, they're not all on the same flight. A plane crash is (or seems) more devastating if an entire family or community or team is lost. The deaths of Atlanta's art patrons caused—in addition to so much individual loss and grief—the stultification of the city's cultural establishments.

✈ Art(lovers) in crashes . . . in art

The day after the Orly crash, newspaper headlines announced 129 fatalities, not 130: Marcel Lugon, the steward rescued from the runway, had not yet died. The body count of 129, though ultimately inaccurate, has become famous: figuratively, etched in stone—or, what is perhaps the same thing, etched in art. News of this crash caught Andy Warhol's attention, and he turned it into the "crashiest" piece of art I've come across—see this chapter's epigraph, Figure 6.1—by which I mean that it *really* evokes a crash, and richly conveys my own fascination with the debris field as the place we go to get the story, to finish the story, in all its tawdry/tragic pathos. I've found no other cultural artifacts representing any debris fields that so strikingly foreground the exact number of victims (albeit incorrectly), another reason I regard Warhol's *129 DIE IN JET!* as "pure crash."

For all the mobilities infrastructures, aviational complexities, and investigative energies that comprise the discourse of a plane crash, the *Mirror* front page and

Warhol's recirculation of it tell the whole story in a very small number of small words (and a numeral) and a straightforward shot of a debris field that pretty clearly says it all. Less is more.

But perhaps I contradict myself: while Warhol's image looks like a literal, simple crash and nothing but, it's actually not, and by now you've probably figured out that it never is: there are plentiful, if subtle, artistic tweaks (as there always are). Warhol's subject is, as one would presume, taken directly from a tabloid newspaper, and if you look at the newspaper[48] and the art side by side they'll appear nearly identical at first glance—indeed, they seem to *Mirror* each other!—but then you start playing spot-the-difference.

Unlike many of Warhol's best-known works, this one was completely drawn by hand: Warhol hadn't yet adopted the methods (he would soon) that employed mechanical processes of reproduction. His drawing omitted a small-print line at the bottom of the tabloid that informs: "Stories on page 3. Other photos, page 3, centerfold." The *Mirror's* readers may have wanted more information, but Warhol's viewers don't: everything we need is there in his drawing, which is why the newspaper's photo caption, too—"Tail section stands upright amid smoldering wreckage after a N.Y.-bound Air France jetliner crashed on takeoff near Paris"—was superfluous, so Warhol left it out. A piece of small-print text from the tabloid that Warhol did retain is the photo credit, "UPI RADIOTELE photo," duly acknowledging his collaboration with United Press International's photojournalism; he also preserved the newspaper's date, issue and volume numbers, its sale price (5¢) and the masthead's weather blurb ("Fair with little change in temperature").

The tabloid's small print is mostly omitted, I think, because it would have been hard to reproduce and might have looked a bit messy. Yes, obviously, this is an overwhelmingly messy scene as it is, but Warhol's aesthetic is to present the mess (paradoxically) more neatly and sharply: artistically. To that end, Warhol gives the photo a kind of airbrush treatment to make some of its background a bit better-focused while some is removed, leaving a cleaner image with better contrast.

The human figures, too—the crash scene's first responders—in sharper contrast, are more ominous in Warhol's image than in the *Mirror* photograph. As small as they are, Warhol drew them more prominently than in the original. Mired in a haunting miasma, they remind me of the onlookers in Edvard Munch's existential scenes. In Warhol's adaptation, "the policemen watching the grim labours of rescuers have become shady and secretive, more like Gestapo than gendarme," writes David Pascoe.

In the further reaches of this debris field, the tabloid photograph depicts several more people picking through tangled wreckage, but Warhol omits them. Perhaps he thought they made the scene look too busy, distracting attention from his creepy bystanders in the foreground. He altered a fallen tree on the right side: "a birch sapling, snapped in half by the explosion, becomes, in Warhol's representation, a stark cross, or gallows." And Warhol has taken some small (but significant) liberties with the plane debris too: in his rendering of "the charred empennage," Pascoe writes, the "expensive delicate ribbing clearly visible in the UPI image has been painted out, to create a monolith. Where the photograph showed the tail attached to the rear of the fuselage, which rested on the ground, in Warhol's reproduction it seems to float, a questionable shape—a black void—flagging the finality which is officially announced on the newspaper's masthead,"[49] where "FINAL" (edition) is in all caps, like the headline.

Warhol's artistic license with the human figures spotlights his concentration on the viewers: both those within the frame, and those outside it—that is, us—viewing the debris and the in-frame viewers. I feel certain that the questions in Warhol's mind, as he conducts his own artistic air crash investigation here, are the same the ones I have myself been posing: What does this mean? How can we describe it? What do we do with it? How do we take in the tragedy, and the trauma—how do we make sense of it? What sort of a failure are we presented with here? How do we adjudicate and remediate the mechanical failure? And also, the failures of society and civilization? These people who died in Paris came for art, and their fate was death; what sort of a world does that betoken?

129 DIE IN JET! initiated a series of about 70 images Warhol created between 1962–4 called "Death and Disaster." His ten categories had mostly self-explanatory titles: *Ambulance Disaster, Electric Chair, Suicide (Fallen Body), Race Riot.* Some, like *Green Car Crash* and *Orange Car Crash 14 Times*, commence his famous technique involving identical multiple monochrome images in garish hues. One, *Tunafish Disaster*, depicts a double-image of a can of tuna above a double-image of two pleasant looking middle-American middle-aged suburban housewife types. True story (like the plane crash, and all his other visual narratives in this series): the women died of botulism poisoning from tuna sandwiches they ate while watching their children play.

Warhol's point: Death and Disaster are everywhere. The Cuban missile crisis, President Kennedy's assassination, and Birmingham's 16th Street Baptist Church bombing occurred during the period Warhol was producing this series, along with crashes including, in addition to Air France flight 7, American flight 1 (Gorky artworks); Eastern flight 512 (twenty-five killed during a go-around in thick fog at Idlewild airport when a wing struck the ground, sending the plane crashing into a marsh); United flight 297 (crashed on descent near Baltimore, all seventeen aboard dead after a birdstrike, two whistling swans, spurring enhanced "bird-proofing" safety measures)[50]; Continental flight 11 (forty-five dead in Missouri when a passenger ignited six sticks of dynamite in the lavatory hoping an insurance company would pay out a premium to his family, which it didn't);[51] and many morc.

Art audiences in the 1960s were becoming "enculturated to accept the near-constant barrage of images from far-away places and too-horrible-to-comprehend situations," writes cultural technologist Paul Boshears. Mass media were instruments of "constant phantasmagoria"; reading newspapers "is a schizophrenic affair," and in that vein Warhol's painting embodies "the horror of living in a society that simply cannot stop itself from revisiting and reproducing absurd violence."[52]

A plane crashes: it seems aeronautically simple and straightforward (but it's not!), and also perceptually straightforward (but it's not!). A stabilizer broke, the pilot reacted unwisely, 129 (and then one more) died. What was supposed to be a scintillating and culturally educational trip ended up tragic and terrible. That's the thumbnail version, but you know by now that there is so much more investigating required to get the full story here, and Warhol, too, knows that it's not nearly as obvious as the *Mirror* makes it seem. His aesthetic alterations, subtle as they seem, are vital signs that cultural creators need to enter into the debris field and do their work. Like Paul Nash and so many other cultural creators whose art starts in naturalism and realism but doesn't end there, Warhol cannot leave the debris field bereft of the artist's touch.

Rodin redux

The Atlanta arts community's growth over the decades was certainly slower than if this crash had not devastated its ranks. Much wealth that might have been donated was not; much energy for sustained cultural campaigns, just starting to percolate in 1962, vanished. But when the art scene eventually flourished, Atlantans took pride in the triumph: it seemed like that well-worn post-crash trope, a phoenix rising out of the ashes (which is actually depicted on Atlanta's seal, alongside the word "Resurgens," celebrating how the city rose again after it was burned to the ground in the Civil War). A committed movement to fulfill the crash victims' ambitions culminated in the 1968 opening of the Woodruff Arts Center, a twelve-acre campus housing an art museum, a theater, and an orchestra: bare-bones operations at first, but after a few decades of arduous development, these enterprises have become world-class. As devastating a setback as the plane crash was for arts organizations and patrons, there was a way to rebuild, to rise again. To make an obvious but important observation, it may mitigate the intense sense of irretrievable loss that families and communities inevitably feel after a plane crash if something concrete can be done: a cause, a restoration. Building enduring legacies counteracts the debris field's pervasive existential nihilism.

Art and crashes, crashes and art—they overlap: not all that often, but when they do it's astounding. As a humanist who studies crashes and also studies art, I cannot overstate the fascination of debris fields that include elements of both: unlikely bedfellows, more power to them. Entwined in ways that provocatively unsettle conventional ideas about crashes, and about art, they embody intriguing dyads: beauty/ugliness, unity/wreckage, life/death. Quiet contemplation/frenzied horror. Both are rare phenomena: an exquisite painting, a crashed airplane. A work of art is not as valuable as a human life, but they are not mutually exclusive. We can have both people and art; we can lose both people and art.

Auguste Rodin makes a reprise in art-crash art: As a memorial to the Orly victims, the French government gave Atlanta's High Museum of Art a figure from a casting of *The Shade*, renowned for its disfigured, anatomically distorted rendering of the human form. Rodin's tortured pose evokes the hellscape of a plane crash debris field, the horrific violence wreaked on the bodies that suffer in that violent chaos. His sculpture provides a vicarious experience of the crash: *YOU … are there.* (Yes, Air France 7's disaster must have been imagined proleptically in 1886. Remember—artists know things!) *The Shade* is a strangely interesting focal point for a plane-crash memorial monument. I have come across few others that so explicitly transport viewers to the debris field's harshest moment of trauma, especially the human perspective thereof. As Dante described, shades are dead souls who are nevertheless in some sense animate, sentient: even in death, they are still with us. In the debris field, most of the literal wreckage does not remain with us—it is cleaned up or blows away, or is gathered for inspection and eventually discarded. To guarantee that an element from the wreckage endures, make sure it comes from the *cultural* debris field. It should be fabricated from an extremely durable medium like bronze (though actually, poetry will do just as well), and imbued with a plenitude of insight, power, and—however paradoxical, however macabre—beauty, so people will not be able to stop looking at it.

7

Race, Crash, and Gender

Here is the secret to surviving one of these crashes: Be male. In a 1970 Civil Aeromedical institute study of three crashes involving emergency evacuations, the most prominent factor influencing survival was gender. . . . Adult males were by far the most likely to get out alive. Why? Presumably because they pushed everyone else out of the way.

Mary Roach, *Stiff: The Curious Lives of Human Cadavers*[1]

The Wright sister

Katharine Wright, the third woman ever to fly, was an integral part of her brothers' work, and was also integrally entangled in Orville's 1908 crash. There were two older Wright brothers as well: Reuchlin was barely involved with the aviation business, while Lorin occasionally helped publicize Orville and Wilbur's accomplishments, and ran the bicycle shop when they were otherwise engaged, but it was Katharine who became a fully fledged member of the team. Yet while this genial Wright sibling was somewhat prominent in the early twentieth century's society pages (often standing in for her perpetually morose, socially awkward brothers), she has disappeared from history.

The serious injuries sustained by Orville in the first-ever fatal plane crash changed his life forever. The same was true for Katharine—his afflictions changed her life as well. She did the womanly things a crash demands: "Without a second thought, Katharine rushed to help immediately," writes Milena Evtimova. She took a leave of absence and boarded the train from Dayton to Washington. "'School can go and my salary, too,' Katharine wrote to Wilbur. 'Little brother shall not be neglected as long as I am able to crawl around.'" Katharine deeply loved her teaching job, which was important also because "she was the only one of the five siblings in the Wright's family with a stable income."[2] She was not cut out to be the angel of the house—outgoing and outspoken, she supported women's independence fervently. But when traditional feminine duty called, she abandoned her own career to sustain those of her brothers.

During Orville's long convalescence, she rarely left his room, and he later said he would have died without Katharine's aid. She began serving as the brothers' social secretary. "After she helped to negotiate a one-year extension of the Army contract, the brothers knew they needed her"; that deal marked the beginning of their company's financial security. Her worldly brio, her "intelligence and zest, made her unique. These qualities came in handy when the brothers found themselves surrounded with fame and suddenly submerged in an environment of European and world elitism they were not familiar with."[3] The proverbial woman behind the men, Katharine provided plentiful emotional labor and public-facing support that weighed heavily in the success of the inventors/entrepreneurs known as "the Wright brothers," a gendered designation of the family business that elided her existence.

"I get so [heated] up over living forever in a man's world, with so much discussion about what kind of women men like and so little concern over what kind of men women like," she wrote in a letter. "If you ask me, there was no reason, and never has been, why women should sit around and wait for men to turn up. I've always lived with men and don't look on them as such a wonderful treat!" Yet Katharine sacrificed herself for her brothers. After two decades supporting their enterprises, she finally began to envision a life apart from them, marrying Harry Haskell in 1925. "Katharine feared Orville's reaction to this relationship [Wilbur had died in 1912]—her fear was justified. Orville thought the marriage to be a betrayal to him and the family. He relied on Katharine to be his connection with the outside world. He refused to speak to his sister and never saw her again until Katharine was on her deathbed."[4] The first fatal plane crash was the defining event of Katharine Wright's life. Although she was hundreds of miles away at the moment of impact, still she ended up, metaphorically, in its debris field.

✈ White skies and the phallomobilities of the cockpit

Ancient Romans believed the atmosphere was gendered female. "The air, lying between the sea and the sky," Cicero writes in *De natura deorum*,

> is according to the Stoic theory deified under the name belonging to Juno, sister and wife of Jove, because it resembles and is closely connected with the aether; they made it female and assigned it to Juno because of its extreme softness.[5]

Hera, Juno's Greek equivalent, became the goddess of the skies and heavens. She could fly, and could bless mortals with clear skies or curse them with storms. Throughout early history, in different cultures, air was sometimes thought of as masculine, and sometimes feminine. Egyptians considered the atmosphere "male where it is windy, female where it is cloudy and sluggish,"[6] Seneca wrote. Other philosophers also read various dimensions of the sky, and the world at large, as either masculine or feminine. Such "cosmic anthropomorphism" waned in the eighteenth century, Clive Hart writes, as astronomers, "wanting to write crisply about physical facts, felt obliged to begin by clearing away all talk of male/female as superstition."[7]

But as air became more scientifically important (and in tandem, more commercially important), this de-gendering of classical and Renaissance symbolism gave way to a re-gendering in which the semiotics of the sky were ineluctably masculinized. Aeromobilities became, fundamentally, phallomobilities. Women, for example, did not go up in balloons. Sophie Blanchard, Napoleon's "Aeronaut of the official festivals" at his wedding to Marie Louise, was an exception who proved the rule. At the end of an 1819 Paris pyrotechnics performance which she called the "Bengal Fire" demonstration, she became the first woman to die in an aviation crash when her balloon caught fire and fell to the ground.[8] Some admired her pioneering courage—a sentiment that recurred over the generations as more women crashed. Others read her demise as a cautionary tale, a sign that women did not belong up in the air—and this attitude, too, persisted alongside the development of flying machines. "A woman in a balloon is either out of her element or too high in it," Grenville Mellen moralized in his 1828 collection *Sad Tales and Glad Tales*.[9] Charles Dickens was still tsk-tsking about her demise thirty-four years after the fact in *Household Words*: "It was the sixty-seventh ascent Madame Blanchard had made. The jug goes often to the well, but is pretty sure to get cracked at last."[10]

During the twentieth-century invention and expansion of commercial flight, the masculine ethos—characterized by physical and mental courage, aggression, autonomy, mastery, and technological skill—became a central feature of aviational culture, and was indeed "more important to pilot identity than consuming the newest and safest technology," writes Erin McComb. Pilots were "the personification of manliness"; technological advances that made flying easier and safer actually "threatened their identity as men and pilots" because they diminished the aspects of skill and risk. The old guard believed that "technology only led to unqualified people flying and more accidents in the sky. Safer technology and automatic controls meant passivity . . . and pilots equated passivity with femininity."

When airport compounds—"masculine space in which outsiders were not welcome"—started to become less grungy, their denizens "fought against the beautification of their hangars that might attract new pilots such as women and 'sissified' men," McComb writes, illuminating the joint deployment of misogyny, homophobia, and gender panic. Pilots trying to sustain their hegemonic privilege argued that diversity and inclusivity in their ranks only led to more unqualified people flying and therefore more accidents in the sky: "flight classes for women simplified the technological aspect of flight, while real men relished the technological complexity." (This objection directly contradicts the assertion that men *eschew* technological complexity to fly by the seats of their pants; sexism is nothing if not opportunistically inconsistent.) Resistance to women pilots took the form of "language, images, and organizations used to keep women apart from the masculine community of flying. This included scathing editorials that mocked women pilots."[11]

Even in our own enlightened times: "The cockpit of an airliner is no place for a woman," began the note scrawled on a napkin left behind by a WestJet passenger in 2014. The pilot, Capt. Carey Steacy, posted the note on her Facebook page, generating enormous support from her airline, other women aviators, and the public at large. You can't really say things like that today, which feels like a victory, and yet people *do* still say such things, which indicates there is still more work to be done.[12]

Cockpit: Consider how that word's profane resonance complicates women's struggle for inclusion and equity in the pilot's seat. It probably derives either from a London cockfighting theater torn down to make room for buildings that housed King Charles I's cabinet, thus a control center, or a nautical term for where a boat's cockswain—a person who rows a cockboat, "a small or light boat . . . carried on board or towed behind a larger vessel"[13]—sat to steer.[14] Both are seventeenth-century usages, as is the word's vulgar denotation, signifying a vagina,[15] envisioned as a pleasure hole for a penis: a pit for a cock. This etymological stinkbomb makes it easier to drivel, as generations of chauvinists have done, that a woman doesn't belong in the cockpit—because she *is* a cockpit (get it?). Ann Pfau captures the phallogocentric freeplay of planes/penises in her study of WWII soldiers: a sexually charged feeling of power, common among many airmen in training, "is evident in some of the names with which airmen christened their assigned planes—*Big Dick, Cock O' the Sky, Nine Yanks and a Jerk, Purple Shaft*. The boast 'big dick' graced at least five Eighth Air Force bombers."[16]

"Cockpit" now rarely appears in official aviation discourse—pilots substitute a nonsexist nonoffensive phrase in their announcements "from the flight deck"—though down in the gutter, such blather is harder to extirpate. A recent Reddit thread[17] channeled masculinist-panic by asking what cockpits should be called now that there are, alas, women pilots. Ovary office? Womb Room? Hen Den? appeared alongside many far more repugnant suggestions.

In the twenty-first century, air remains a largely male preserve. It is racialized, too, as white, and classed, as upper. Consider the wildly expensive Concorde fares, ensuring that the fastest passengers were the richest passengers; billionaires' obsessions with penetrating space in their phallic rockets; the obsequious deference paid to those in the First Class cabin—which Virgin, getting points for transparency, actually calls Upper Class. Like so many other aspects of the natural world, the sky is hegemonically construed with default settings for the usual white male VIP clientele.

In 2021, according to the Bureau of Labor Statistics, 93 percent of US airline pilots were white and 96 percent were men.[18] Things are changing, albeit surely not at supersonic speed, but the skies are gradually moving toward diversification: one might say there's no place to go but up, demographically. Groups such as Fly for the Culture, Sisters of the Skies, and You Can Fly work to encourage more heterogeneous pilot training pipelines. The *New York Times* was confident enough about future trends to declare "The End of the All-Male, All-White Cockpit" (presumably the headline writer missed the "flight deck" memo) in a 2022 article about airlines' efforts to recruit underrepresented aviators:

> Few women and people of color aspire to fly planes because they rarely see themselves in today's flight decks. The cost of training and the toll of discrimination can be discouraging, too. Now there's urgency for the industry to act. Pilots are in short supply, and if airlines want to make the most of the thriving recovery from the pandemic, they will have to learn to foster lasting change.[19]

A small number of talented, determined women and people of color broke barriers a half-century ago (following on the epaulets of an even smaller cadre of pioneers in the half-century before that). Marlon Green and David Harris were the first Black pilots to fly for major commercial airlines, hired by Continental and American respectively, after the Supreme Court's 1963 ruling that Green had experienced unlawful discrimination. The state of Colorado, home of Continental's headquarters, ruled that Green was qualified to be a pilot but had not been hired because of racial discrimination. Continental appealed, arguing that while they were not racist themselves, many other people they dealt with were, thus making it impossible for them to hire Green. The airline "argued that having a Black pilot onboard their aircraft would be burdensome as it might upset passengers," writes Amanda Laughead, and also "that they would not be able to find hotels for Black pilots"[20] in segregated parts of the US. Continental thought Green's civil rights were trumped by the civil wrongs of bigots who would be put off by a Black man in the flight deck, and racist hoteliers. After the Court rejected the appeal, Green was hired as a pilot in 1964 (with full seniority and retroactive pay from 1957, reflecting years of discrimination) and flew for Continental until his 1979 retirement.[21]

David Harris, a US Air Force captain who flew B-52 bombers for six years, had an easier time getting hired in 1964, while Green's case was moving through the courts. He applied for several positions, but only American Airlines responded. A light-skinned African American with green eyes, Harris was often mistaken for white, writes his biographer Michael Cottman, so "during the American Airlines interview, Harris went out of his way to set the record straight. "He stopped them and just said, 'Hey, look, I just want you to know, before we proceed, that I'm Black,' writes Cottman, 'Because he is so proud of his heritage that he didn't want to pass as white.'" The recruiter responded: "You know, I really don't care if you're Black, white or chartreuse, can you fly an airplane?" He could, and he did. Within three years of his hire, Harris was promoted to Captain—the first African American to reach that rank at a major US airline—and flew thirty years for American.[22]

A decade after Green and Harris began their careers, Frontier Airlines hired Emily Howell Warner as the first woman pilot for a major US passenger airline. Rampant sexism and racism still pervaded the aviation industry. Airline advertisements in the 1970s and 1980s almost exclusively depicted pilots as white men, said Alan Meyer, a historian whose book *Flying While Black* examines the slow pace of racial integration. These ads, alongside numerous other cultural stereotypes, "continue to reinforce this image," Meyer said, "this often subconscious association between whiteness and maleness and technical competence." Some progress—not a great deal—was made over the generations since Green's 1963 victory, but things seem finally poised for improvement: in 2020, United "launched a flight school with the aim of hiring thousands of pilots in the years ahead, at least half of them women or people of color, writes Niraj Chokshi, and "other carriers have launched similar initiatives, too."[23] The industry, keenly aware of entrenched racial and gender disparities at every level, says they're committed to rectifying them. Maybe they truly are—we'll see.

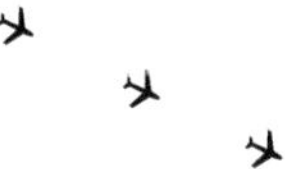

The default white male profile for pilots extends to just about everyone else in aviation, with the exception of flight attendants, who for decades were costumed, socialized, and merchandised as eye-candy for straight male passengers, belying their extremely important roles in safety and crowd management. (That corps is now more diverse, with significant numbers of male flight attendants—mostly gay, showing how demographic pigeonholing can be both overcome and sustained at the same time.)

Masculinity, class, and race inflect the social construction of aeromobility in the passenger cabin as well as the flight deck. "The sideways looks I get when boarding a plane make me question whether I belong up there. Flying in first is a psychological experiment for me," writes Mitchell Jackson, a Black man who constantly feels under suspicion by predominantly white cabinmates: he perceives such unspoken thoughts as "Why are you up here? What do you do for a living? Are you famous? Do you think you deserve what I deserve?" In *Traveling Black*, about the history of and resistance to travel segregation, Mia Bay explains that the message is "that African Americans cannot be truly first-class people. They can't be on the first tier of Americans in terms of traveling in that elite space." When R&B singer Lyfe Jennings's status as a first-class passenger was questioned multiple times between checking in for a flight and boarding it, he posted on Instagram: "Sick of this shit!!! lady asked me 4 times did I know this was the 1st class line I told her yes everytime. I can't tell yall how many time a white man or white woman has asked me to step out of line to ask if im supposed to be flying first class."[24]

Woody Guthrie's "Deportees" describes how Mexican plane-crash victims became invisible in the aftermath of their tragedy because they were not white. That song, discussed in Chapter 4, provides salient evidence of how, even in debris fields, the prejudices people faced in life persist unabated in death.

When a passenger had to be bumped from an overbooked flight in 2017 to accommodate repositioning airline staff and nobody volunteered, not even for $800 vouchers, was it just coincidental that 69-year-old Dr. David Dao was designated for removal? United never explained why they selected him. If it had been a white man protesting that he had to be on duty at his hospital the next day, would the airport security team have yanked him out of his seat, struggling and screaming? Was his Vietnamese-American ethnicity a factor in the decision to drag him, unconscious and bleeding, down the aisle and off the plane?[25] (Their erstwhile slogan, "Fly the friendly skies," seems to have fallen by the wayside.) I find some vindication in the fact that the security officers were fired immediately after the story went viral, and Dr. Dao's settlement compensation from United, while confidential, was assumed to be in the mid-seven- to eight-figure range. Just as causes of crashes are scrutinized so modifications can be made to ensure they will not recur, we may hope that the foot soldiers of aeromobility, too, learned from this "boarding accident" and will do everything necessary to avoid another similar fiasco. United has promised—and again, time will tell if this racist malfunction has really been fixed—that they have implemented systematic reforms to correct the process that resulted in Dr. Dao's egregious maltreatment.

Orthodox Jewish men commonly refuse to sit next to a woman passenger for fear she might impinge upon their holiness by touching them, even accidentally. An El Al flight from New York to Israel "was delayed for over an hour due to the refusal by a number of ultra-Orthodox men to sit next to women," the *Times of Israel* reported. The men "boarded and refused to take their seats, as they were next to women, causing the protracted delay." One man, "particularly devout and ascetic," boarded "with his eyes closed and [kept] them shut for the duration of the flight in an apparent effort to avoid looking at any woman on board." El Al often quietly accommodated such prejudices; recently they announced that their official policy is no longer to do so, but chat boards indicate it still happens. Other airlines, too, have accommodated various misogynistic attitudes in the interests of smoothing things over so flights can take off.[26] The men who cause these disruptions seem confident that the airlines' path of least resistance is obliging their sexism.

When news stories reported Dr. Tisha Rowe's removal from an American flight in 2019 for what flight attendants deemed inappropriate clothing (a sleeveless romper), many others came forward—almost all women and mostly, like Dr. Rowe, women of color—with accounts of similar experiences. Dr. Rowe, a family medicine physician, was told she would be allowed to fly only if she covered herself with a jacket or a blanket, conditions she refused. On Facebook she wrote:

> WE ARE POLICED FOR BEING BLACK. OUR BODIES ARE OVER SEXUALIZED AS WOMEN AND WE MUST ADJUST TO MAKE EVERYONE AROUND US COMFORTABLE. I'VE SEEN WHITE WOMEN WITH MUCH SHORTER SHORTS BOARD A PLANE WITHOUT A BLINK OF AN EYE. I GUESS IF IT'S A 'NICE ASS' VS. A SERENA BOOTY IT'S O.K.[27]

Soon after businesswoman Jessica Leeds sat down in her first-class seat in the 1970s, a stranger in the next seat lifted the armrest, moved toward her, and began to grope and kiss her for several minutes until she was forced to move to another seat far away from him, back in coach. "There was no conversation. It was like out of the blue," Leeds testified. "He was trying to kiss me, trying to pull me towards him. He was grabbing my breasts. It was like he had 40 zillion hands. It was like a tussling match between the two of us."[28] Confronted with this charge decades later, the man, who was running for the US presidency (which he went on to win), responded, "'Yeah, I'm going to go after you,' dismissively, waving his arms," implying that she was not attractive enough for him to molest. "'Believe me—she would not be my first choice. That I can tell you. When you looked at that horrible woman,' he continued, in a singsong voice 'you said, I don't think so.'"[29] *She would not be my first choice*: imagine a man boarding a plane and calculating an ordered list of candidates to assault: best prospect over there in seat 5B, second choice right behind me, honorable mention to the one over by the . . . Yes, I think many women can imagine exactly such a scenario, every time they fly.

The number of midair sexual assaults doubled between 2017–19, and spiked even higher in post-Covid air travel as travel frustrations rose and social inhibitions against offensive behavior diminished. Melanie Cox writes in "Flight and Fight" about a 22-year-old woman flying from London to Seattle. "After taking antinausea and antianxiety medication and drinking wine, she faded in and out of consciousness. She remembers another passenger wrapping his legs around hers, lying facedown in her lap, squeezing her breast underneath her bra, and touching her vagina. The FBI later found that man's DNA inside the woman's underwear.[30]

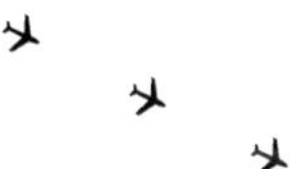

What does any of this have to do with plane crashes?

If white men are aviation's normative figures, and everyone else is marginalized, my premise is that debris fields too (both the literal and cultural versions) will reflect these inequalities. Race/class/gender dynamics in airplanes and in the industry inflect similar iterations of dis/empowerment in plane crashes.

The term "intersectionality" describes how systems of discrimination overlap with each other across persecuted groups and throughout myriad social experiences. Kimberlé Crenshaw's coinage seems especially apropos for mobility studies, as transportation involves negotiating and navigating literal intersections. If being groped, harassed, racially profiled, disrespected, or dragged down the aisle aren't quite as dangerous as actual crashes, still, they set the scene. If pilots from underrepresented demographics find themselves microaggressed, macroaggressed, limited in their access to training and support, perceived by colleagues and passengers as less competent than white men, facing constant streams of racism and sexism despite their accomplishments, there may well be some very toxic mojo up in the air. Even before anyone boards the aircraft, there's a pervasive zeitgeist of hegemony and bigotry, like a fog thickly settled over the airfield. This fog cover (please don your metaphorical humanist-investigator thinking caps here) is one of those situations that might not cause a crash in and of itself, but could well be one of a few elements that combine to create a crash-inducing "perfect storm."

Race, class, and gender are indelibly imbricated in a crash when the pilot is not a white man. Consider the newspaper headline after Chelsea Infanger's Cessna 208B crashed in Heyburn, Idaho, in 2022: "Pilot killed in plane crash was 'adventurous, beautiful' woman who 'brightened the room with her smile.'"[31] Such discourse reduces the pilot's character to stereotypical gender-constructs of appearance, relegating to irrelevance her professional identity. (No crash story about a male pilot has ever praised his winsome dimples.) Hegemonic networks constantly expand their own power, diminishing in tandem the centrality, or aspirations to centrality, of everyone who is already attenuated. The rich get richer, the men fly higher; the women are expected to smile more brightly, fulfilling the implicit sexist presumption that "femininity" is mutually exclusive with proficient aviation.

An academic study titled "Comparing pilot-error accident rates of male and female airline pilots" finds gender has no discernible impact on accident rates (controlling for time in service: less-experienced pilots are more likely to crash, and men tend to have logged more flight hours than women). "After adjusting for variables included in the model, accident rates of males and females were not significantly different," K. L. McFadden writes. "These findings suggest that neither males nor females are a safer pilot group."[32] An earlier study, "Pilot-error accidents: male vs female," found that "Males had a higher rate of accidents than females, and a higher portion of the male accidents resulted in fatalities or serious injuries than for females."[33] Male and female pilots crash for different reasons, Susan Baker found: males "are more likely to crash due to inattention or flawed decision-making, while female pilots are more likely to crash from mishandling the aircraft."

> Mishandling aircraft kinetics, such as incorrect use of the rudder, poor response to a bounce, or inability to recover from a stall, was the most common error for both sexes, but was more prevalent among females (accounting for 81 percent of the crashes) than males (accounting for 48 percent). Males, however, appeared more likely to be guilty of poor decision-making, risk-taking, and inattentiveness, examples of which include misjudging weather and visibility or flying an aircraft with a known defect. Females, though more likely to mishandle or lose control of the aircraft, were generally more cautious than their more venturesome male counterparts.[34]

Women crashing

There were numerous prominent early women aviators—not a massive number, but still an impressive corps given the prejudices of the times. Raymonde de Laroche earned certification from Aéro-Club de France in 1910, becoming the first licensed female pilot; born Elise Deroche, her *nom de vol* was sometimes preceded by "Baroness." An instant star also known as *la femme-oiseau* (the bird-woman), she competed in meets around Europe, inspiring many other women to pursue their licenses. The next year Amelia (Melli) Beese became the first German woman to earn a license and Harriet Quimby became the first US woman to do so. Denise Moore was an early pioneer who flew without a license. Moore was a pseudonym: she didn't publicly use her real name, Jane Wright (no relation to the Wright brothers . . . or sister), because she didn't want her family to know of her career.

Mathilde Franck, a Frenchwoman, planned to fly across the English Channel in 1910. Suzanne Bernard, another young Frenchwoman, learned to fly in 1912. Cheridah de Beauvoir Stocks, a charter member of the Women's Aerial League, earned a Royal Aero Club Aviator's Certificate in 1911. Blanche Scott, known as

"The Tomboy of the Air"—her mannish style helped blunt concerns about women flyers—is credited as the first female test pilot and also the first daredevil female stunt pilot, for which she earned thousands of dollars a week in the 1910s. In her most popular feat, the "Death Dive," she dropped from 4,000 feet with the throttle retarded, pulling up 100 feet from the ground.

Julia Clark, the third US woman to earn her license, embodied the feminist spirit that most of these pilots shared. Within a month of beginning her training, writes Eileen Lebow in *Before Amelia: Women Pilots in the Early Days of Aviation*, "Julia was flying as well as any of the men. She sensed that 'the men do not fancy my flying' because 'they hate to admit or have it proven that a woman can do anything a man can.'"[35] Bessie Coleman—known to her fans as "Brave Bessie" and "Queen Bess"—was the first Black and Native American woman to earn a license, in 1921. Since US flight schools wouldn't accept Black students, Coleman moved to France, acquiring her international license from the Fédération Aéronautique Internationale. Returning to America, she performed dangerous routines as a stunt pilot in flight shows—she was famous for her "loop-the-loops" and figure 8's—but her dream was to open her own flight school which would provide women and people of color access to aviation. She fought racism as she built her career: for example, she refused to perform at venues where Black and white people had to use separate entrances, becoming "famous for publicly standing up for her beliefs."[36]

You may not be unduly surprised to learn that all these women crashed.

Not all the crashes were fatal, though most were. There were, of course, early women aviators who didn't crash, but they are not my subject here. Lots of men, too, crashed in those risky early years of flying when aircraft were flimsy assemblages of fabric and wood and there were few best practices of aviation to draw upon. This first generation of pilots pretty much invented the plane as they flew it.

Prejudices and stereotypes made it harder for women to fly than men. Did that make it easier for women to crash? Did they have to take greater risks? Bessie Coleman and other women aviators had to contend with aircraft that were inferior to men's planes. Their access to the infrastructure of aeromobility, and especially to formal training, was restricted. Frequently they had to resort to strategizing and subterfuge in the face of social resistance to women flying. Considering how demanding aviation was, these extra "tasks" for female flyers would have made the job all the more difficult. When Melli Beese earned her license in 1911, she passed her flight test despite "considerable efforts by male comrades to sabotage her with lighthearted practical jokes [*sic*] like draining fuel from her tank, loosening control wires, or replacing fresh sparking plugs with clogged ones."[37] Early women aviators faced significant additional pressures alongside all the other challenges of balancing lift, thrust, drag, and weight.

A woman's death in an aviation mishap "was viewed as more tragic than that of a man, because it was outside the normal expectation," Lebow writes, noting also that there was often "condemnation of parents who permitted their daughters to pursue such dangerous activity." So there was both extra sympathy and extra blame. Some reacted to these crashes with admiration for what the pilot—a mere woman!—had tried to achieve; others saw them as a sign that her reach had exceeded her grasp, and women should stay home where they belonged.

Mathilde Franck crashed but survived. At a 1910 airshow in Sunderland, UK, Franck flew a Farman biplane above thousands of spectators. "A boy on the ground was killed"—fifteen-year-old Thomas Wood, the first ground death I've discovered in the history of plane crashes—"when Franck's aeroplane caught a flagstaff and flipped over onto the ground. The motor fell on the boy, several spectators were injured by other parts of the machine, and Mathilde suffered a broken leg," Lebow writes.[38] She never flew again.

Cheridah de Beauvoir Stocks, too, survived a mishap at a British airshow, this time at Hendon, as a passenger in a plane that spun out of control and crashed. Unconscious for six weeks, she was partially paralyzed when she finally regained consciousness, and, like Franck, never flew again.[39]

Tomboy Blanche Scott survived several crashes. During one of her daredevil Death Dives (the catchphrase seems to audaciously tempt fate!), her carburetor flooded and the plane wouldn't pull up.

> Pulling the stick back quickly, the machine hit tail first. The pilot walked away because, she believed, she was wearing a lucky red sweater. The proof was, another time, without the sweater, she landed nose down in a swamp and broke several ribs, her collarbone, and left arm. Blanche was fond of saying she had forty-one mended bones in her body, the result of numerous crack-ups and two that were serious. She must have forgotten the sweater more than once.[40]

After her second serious crash, caused when a throttle wire broke on her Red Devil in 1913, she took a year off to recover, but returned to the skies once again. She retired in 1916 "because of the lack of opportunities for female engineers and mechanics," writes Hannah Chan. "Additionally, she was bothered by what she perceived as the public's disturbing interest in air crashes."[41] (Mea culpa.)

Raymonde de Laroche survived the first, but not the second, of her crashes: coming in for landing on a windy day in 1910, she misjudged the height of poplars near the airfield, and "the tail of her machine brushed a tree branch before she could pull up," causing her to drop twenty feet to the ground. She was thrown from her seat and the plane lay in pieces, but de Laroche, "at first unconscious, received only a broken collarbone and bruises." Nine years later, soon after setting a women's altitude record by climbing to 15,300 feet, she was inspecting airplanes at Le Crotoy airfield in the Somme when a test pilot, M. Barrault (history has not preserved his first name), invited her to fly with him as he tried out a new airplane. She strapped into the rear seat with Barrault up front. "It climbed quickly, its operation vastly different from the prewar models she knew. The pilot turned and headed back toward the field, the aeroplane moving gracefully. As it lowered for a landing, it was seen to swerve to one side, lose speed, and go into a spinning dive before crashing heavily."[42] The first people to reach the scene found de Laroche and Barrault lying dead amid the debris field.

Like de Laroche, Bessie Coleman survived her first wreck but not her second. In 1923, her airplane engine suddenly stopped working mid-flight and she crashed. Badly hurt, she suffered a broken leg, cracked ribs, and cuts on her face. But fully healed from her injuries, she returned to perform air tricks in 1925. In 1926, Coleman took a test flight with a mechanic, William Wills, who piloted while she took the passenger seat. At 3,000 feet,

> a loose wrench got stuck in the engine of the aircraft. Wills could no longer control the steering wheel, and the plane flipped over. Coleman was not wearing a seatbelt. At the time, airplanes did not have a roof. Due to her un-fastened seatbelt, when the plane flipped over Coleman fell out of the open plane. She did not survive the fall. Wills crashed the aircraft a few feet away and also died in the accident. Her death was heartbreaking for thousands of people across the world. At her funeral in Chicago, famous activist Ida B. Wells-Barnett delivered her eulogy.[43]

Black newspapers gave the crash front-page coverage and Black communities honored her heroism, but the mainstream press barely noted Coleman's death, focusing instead on Wills, who was white.[44] Coleman's dreams were fulfilled posthumously: Lieut. William Powell, a Black engineer whose applications to flight schools and the Army Air Corps had been rejected, created the Bessie Coleman Aero Club in 1929 to promote aviation awareness among Black women and men; in the 1930s he founded the Bessie Coleman Flying School and Bessie Coleman Aero, the first Black-owned airplane manufacturer.[45]

Like de Laroche and Stocks, Coleman was a passenger, not a pilot, in her crash. Perhaps their names should have asterisks on female pilot death-lists to indicate that men were flying.

Of all these early female aviators, Coleman is probably the best known today. Mae Jemison, the first Black female astronaut in space, carried a picture of Coleman on her 1992 mission; a US stamp and commemorative quarter honor her. Beryl Bain wrote and starred in a one-woman play, *The Flight* (2023), about Coleman's ground-breaking achievements. Also that year, Mattel issued a Barbie® doll honoring Coleman. The box features a quote from her—"I made up my mind to try, I tried and was successful"—and celebrates her career:

> Barbie® recognizes all female role models. The Inspiring Women™ Series pays tribute to incredible heroines of their time; courageous women who took risks, changed rules, and paved the way for generations of girls to dream bigger than ever before. At the age of 23, Bessie Coleman left Atlanta, Texas, and moved to Chicago to build a better life for herself and pursue an education. It was there in the windy city when she decided she wanted to learn to fly. At that time in the United States, Bessie could not obtain a pilot's license because she was a woman of color. Not giving up, Bessie learned French and traveled to France where she ultimately fulfilled her dream. As a pilot, she was so passionate about encouraging people of color to pursue aviation that she wanted to open a flight school of her own.[46]

Many such motivating accounts of Coleman's career end here, without noting her crashes. (Mattel's website copy omits the crashes, though the box does go on to acknowledge the fatal one.) I can see why that omission might make sense, both to elevate her historical importance—a crash generally reads as a failure—and also to avoid traumatizing young admirers, but I think it's a mistaken impulse. Crashes happened, and they were a fundamental aspect of aviation. There are fewer crashes now because there were more at the beginning: part of what a crash is about is not crashing the next time. One might invoke Samuel Beckett's existential wisdom: "Ever tried. Ever failed. No Matter. Try again. Fail again. Fail better."[47]

I want to problematize absolutist perceptions of plane crashes, with the accompanying stench of blame, fault, ineptitude. Yes, a crash is always sad (unless, as I discuss in Chapter 9, it's karma). But especially early on, there were simply a great many things that could go wrong, many situations that had never (or hardly ever) happened before. What I most appreciate about Coleman's character and fortitude is that she knew crashing was a significant possibility, and she experienced one, survived it, and returned to the skies. She died for her cause, for her passion. Not only should we resist sweeping it under the carpet, but perhaps we lead with this. Or perhaps not. I am not an expert in child psychology or doll marketing, but Queen Bess was indeed an amazing woman and it feels inappropriate to bowdlerize her career.

Denise Moore died in 1911 when a wind gust flipped her airplane over in Étampes, France; headlines called it "Aviation's First Female Sacrifice."[48] Melli Beese survived the crash of the plane she was flying as she applied to renew her pilot's license in 1925, but soon afterwards committed suicide; her motto was, "flying is everything, living is nothing."[49] Suzanne Bernard, too, crashed during her pilot's license test in 1912: her Cauldron biplane was caught in a wind and capsized, crushing her to death beneath it.[50] Julia Clark was the first US woman to die piloting an airplane: in 1912, coming in for a landing, her Curtiss struck the treetops (as had happened to de Laroche) and fell to the ground, "turning turtle, pinning the pilot underneath" (as had happened to Bernard). "Her skull was crushed, there were several serious breaks, and Julia died a few minutes after reaching the hospital, never regaining consciousness." A macabre detail from the crash site: "Her plane was gathered up and shipped to the factory, but Mrs. Clark's remains did not fare so well. She was abandoned at the morgue . . . dead, unclaimed."[51] Debris field protocol was rudimentary in 1912; perhaps it seemed more compelling to conduct a forensic examination of the airplane's remains rather than the pilot's.

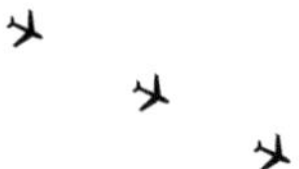

The Blériot XI Harriet Quimby flew at the 1912 Boston Air Meet was fast but difficult to control. Balance was crucial: if there wasn't a passenger, a sandbag was needed in the back seat to offset the pilot's weight. Leslie Kerr calls it "a fragile, problem-ridden, and unforgiving aircraft even for experienced flyers like Harriet," noting that a dozen or more Blériot pilots died in crashes caused by loss of control.[52]

Airshow organizer William Willard won a coin flip (with his son) to be Quimby's passenger. "He was a large man," Don Dahler writes, "tipping the scales at two hundred pounds or more. Friends described him as somewhat spontaneous in his enthusiasm"—put a pin in that detail. "As the assembled crowd teased the widower about venturing skyward for the first time with such a beautiful guide"—*hmmm*—"Leo [Stevens, Quimby's manager] stepped close and warned him to 'sit tight' once they were in the air lest he throw off the plane's balance." The forty-minute flight around the spectacular setting, late afternoon sun glinting off the plane's white wings, "was one of the most beautiful performances I ever saw Miss Quimby or any other aviator make," Stevens said. "At all times she had the Blériot under splendid control."

As Quimby approached for landing, the plane suddenly bucked and began to dive. "The next instant we saw a body hurl itself upwards out of the machine, apparently leaping 50 feet in the air, describe an arc, then come plunging down," Stevens recalled. Willard had been thrown out of the plane. (Some Blériots had lap belts and some didn't, but even in those equipped with them, they were not commonly used—that changed after this crash.) Quimby wrestled with a plane that had become unstable, Dahler writes:

> Suddenly freed of its two-hundred-pound ballast, she was in a losing battle against physics and gravity. For the briefest of instants, the pilot righted the machine and it appeared she would regain control. But there came a violent shudder, and the monoplane dipped again, its tail flung into a perpendicular position, before turning completely upside down. Bill Willard had not yet hit the water when Harriet, too, was catapulted from the plane, arched clear, and began to fall, her purple flight suit silhouetted against the setting sun. Both bodies reached terminal velocity within seconds, before slamming into the concrete-hard tidal flats two-hundred feet from shore and sinking deeply into the mud.

In what must have been a haunting sight for the thousands of spectators, the Blériot, after ejecting pilot and passenger, "regained its flight trim and descended in gentle spirals until the wheels touched the water and flipped over on its back relatively undamaged." (*The plane wanted to fly!*)

Formal air crash investigations did not yet exist in aviation's early years, but knowledgeable people in the industry always, instinctively, tried to figure out what went wrong, with the hope of fixing the problem—this was the germ of the standardized crash investigations instituted after Knute Rockne's 1931 crash. Sometimes experts published their thoughts in scientific journals. Some others (most conspicuously, the press), unimpeded by their lack of aviational expertise, nonetheless contributed their two cents as well. If crowds of spectators witnessed the disaster, an even larger cadre of ad hoc crash investigators would weigh in.

There were rumors that Willard had intentionally leapt from the plane, suicidally despondent over his wife's recent death and financial pressures from his airshow, though most people found that far-fetched. Equipment failure was

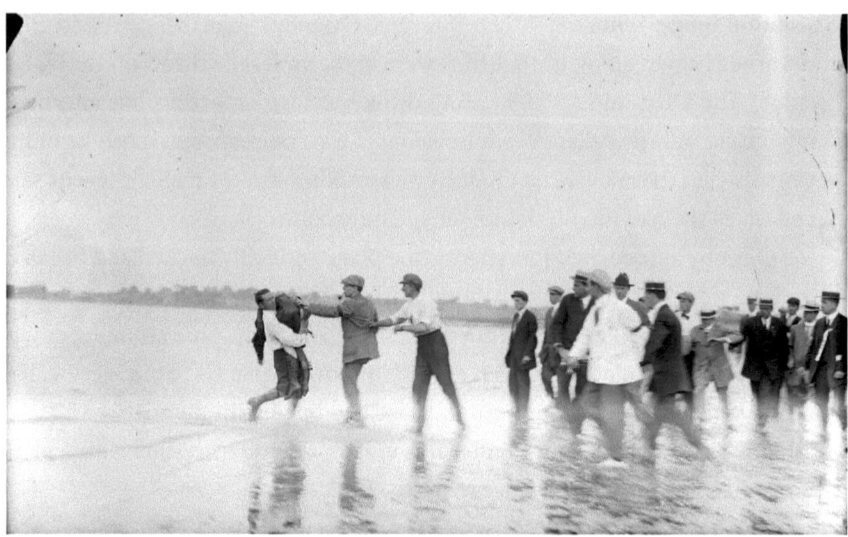

Figure 7.1 Spectators carry Harriet Quimby's body out of Boston Harbor after she fell from her Blériot.

always a likely conjecture, especially in those early days of so many new and relatively untested models; pilot error, too, was a common supposition. One pilot who saw the crash, Lincoln Beachey, was "almost positive that Miss Quimby fainted in the air. She was coming down at a high rate of speed and her semi-conscious control caused the machine to lurch. When she recovered it was too late."[53] (Beachey himself would crash three years later, also in an airshow exhibition and also into water. He survived the actual crash, the autopsy showed, but subsequently drowned in San Francisco Bay. Unlike Quimby, he *was* wearing restraints—ironically they prevented him from escaping the submerged wreck.[54])

Another pilot who witnessed Quimby's crash, Earle Ovington, thought the plane had a design flaw. He sent his conclusions to *Scientific American*: "When we reached the wreck, I scrambled on top of it, and the first thing I saw was the rudder wire caught over the lower end of the warping lever. If you examine my sketch"—again, early aviators anticipated the forensic processes of crash reports—"you will see that by the wire catching as indicated the rudder would be thrown to the left and the monoplane turned toward the left as it plunged downward."[55]

Misogynists presented their own "investigative" conclusions. Aviator Claude Grahame-White deduced that her crash illustrated the unsuitability of women pilots: "Women are temperamentally unfit for flight because they are prone to panic. When calamity overtakes women pupils as eventually I fear it will, I shall feel in a way responsible for their sudden demise." (It's not clear to me why Grahame-White felt personal responsibility for all the dead women pilots: perhaps because he did not forcibly remove every one he encountered from her airplane?) A *New York Sun* writer concluded that the sport of aviation competition "is not one for which women are physically qualified. As a rule, they lack strength, presence of mind, and the courage to excel as aviators. It is essentially a man's sport and pastime."[56]

Quimby's manager came up with his own conclusion, which I'm inclined to endorse if only because it makes such a brilliant story. (Yes, humanist air crash investigators must be cautious about the allure of a delicious narrative; I suppose it's a good idea to keep engineers and aviators on the team, to balance out our lurid literary propensities.) Rejecting other people's conclusions about faulty aircraft design or piloting—"I know her to be a woman of great coolness and judgment and an operator of extraordinary ability"—Leo Stevens wrote to the journal *Aeronautics* blaming the crash on William Willard:

> My last warning to Willard before he entered the machine and even after he had climbed aboard was not to leave his seat under any circumstances. This warning I was very particular to give because I knew him to be a man of sudden impulses. I was fearful lest under sudden impulse and effervescing enthusiasm he should suddenly lean from his seat to communicate with Miss Quimby. This I knew would be an exceedingly dangerous thing to do.... Now then, this is what I believe really happened. I believe that as the flight drew to its conclusion, Willard, enthusiastic over Miss Quimby's splendid performance, for a moment forgot the danger of moving, and suddenly stretched forward over the deck to shout a word of congratulations. Miss Quimby, unable to see what was going on behind her, had no warning of Willard's movement until his shifted weight caused the machine to dip and the tail to flip upward. With Willard's weight gone—a weight absolutely necessary to the control of the monoplane—she was pitted against a circumstance over which no aviator, no human ingenuity, or knowledge, or skill or practice could have control.[57]

I cannot restrain myself from hazarding a footnote. I wonder if Willard did indeed stand up, precariously, unwisely, just as Stevens hypothesizes—but not to congratulate Quimby. Could he have been performing the rhetorical intervention we now designate as mansplaining? I propose that it is circumstantially possible—nay *probable*, in the spirit of Occam's razor—that an important and highly strung man riding in a monoplane piloted by a brilliant woman in 1912 had something to tell her: something important enough to nullify Stevens's caution about staying put; something (about flying?!) he thought he knew and she didn't.

Whatever particular insight he might have mansplained, if this is indeed what transpired, has been lost to history.

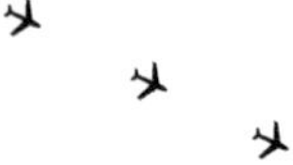

Blanche Scott ("Death Dives") was flying at the meet where Quimby died: in the air at when Quimby crashed, she "had a difficult time finding a clear place to land; unruly crowds were everywhere, and her nerves were not steady. With much anguish, Blanche got her machine down and, reportedly, fainted."[58] (Those woman aviators were *always* fainting . . . reportedly . . .) Later, reflecting on the traumatic experience of witnessing Quimby's death, Scott said, "If aviators choose to stay in the game, the reality is we may die. We all know this and that's why all flyers are fatalists. We accept what will be, will be."[59]

Just before her final flight, Quimby wrote a letter to her parents that concluded: "If bad luck should befall me, I want you to know that I will meet my fate rejoicing."[60]

"Lady Lindy"

One of Harriet Quimby's great admirers, Amelia Earhart, often avowed how the pioneer aviator inspired her. "To cross the English Channel in 1912"—Quimby was the first woman who did that—"required more bravery than to cross the Atlantic today," Earhart said in 1932 as she prepared her own transatlantic flight. "We must remember to always pay respect to America's first great woman flyer's accomplishments."[61]

Exemplifying how masculinity was pilots' default identity, Earhart's nickname was "Lady Lindy." If she wasn't quite as amazing as Charles Lindbergh, the sobriquet implies (because otherwise her own actual name would have sufficed), she came as close to his aviational prestige as *a lady* could. She hated the nickname, devised by her husband (and manager/publicist), George Putnam. Earhart actually somewhat resembled Lindbergh: like Blanche Scott, she presented as a "tomboy," looking like "an adolescent boy who had chopped off his own hair," writes Judith Thurman: "lanky and nonchalant, with no hips or breasts—no visible womanliness—to speak of. She flew wearing men's underpants (they were apparently superior to a woman's for the purposes of a quick pee). In her flight gear—a jumpsuit or jodhpurs ('breeks'); flat, lace-up knee boots; a white shirt and a man's tie; a bomber jacket or a leather coat—she seems, at least by the codes of this century, flagrantly androgynous."

She codeswitched, strategically navigating a continuum of gender performance: "Earhart—whose intention was to stay aloft both as a pilot and as a celebrity—projected a confusing mixture of traits with such an aura of virtue and assurance that she disarmed received ideas about femininity." She was "the antidote to those shameless flappers" with their air of "harlotry"; she "will become a symbol of new womanhood," a contemporary writer declared, embodying "the clean mind and the strong body." In photo spreads, though the tomboy-aviator was dominant, there were also "pictures of the well-bred lady in a long skirt, a fur wrap, a girlish middy, or an evening gown, her arms full of flowers." Thurman writes that "the press, and, no doubt, Earhart herself were aware that there was something troubling about her appearance"—presumably, a butch affect—"that had to be neutralized."[62]

Like every female pilot I have investigated, then and now, Earhart had to confront and overcome an entrenched skepticism about whether women could *really* fly. From the very beginning of aviation, some women have always managed to do so. But also, from the beginning (and still today), aviation's demographics reveal that the corps of women pilots, while extant, has been significantly constrained by sexism. When a woman crashes, her gender always surfaces in the mediascapes and in the popular imagination as at least one possible/likely element in the combination of circumstances that leads to aviation disasters.

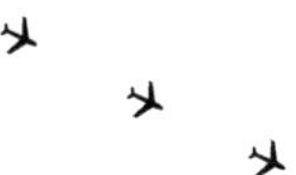

No debris field was ever found for Earhart's presumptive crash. Some claim to have discovered bits of metal and bone that they believe came from Earhart's flight, but I think they are grasping at straws. People are always desperate for debris—for evidence that frames the story and the aftermath. We crave the closure and the certainty that a debris field facilitates. Saintly relics bolster religious belief and faith, making metaphysical phenomena at least somewhat physical. So too, debris field relics help people grasp, palpably, the existentially incomprehensible reality of crashes. In both cases, relics concretely memorialize the martyrdom of saints or passengers. The etymological root of "martyr" is "witness," and the debris-relic is the vehicle for such witnessing, such homage.

The place I have most powerfully experienced debris-as-relic for the purpose of witnessing and metaphysical understanding is at New York's 9/11 Memorial Museum, which archives 74,000 debris field artifacts.[63] That day's crashes were arguably the most existentially confounding traumas of our age. The curators realized people needed to witness, and to be figuratively doused with, the wreckage—flattened FDNY firetrucks, caps worn by first responders, smashed public art, scorched dusty wallets, pieces of the World Trade Center façade, steel columns recovered from rubble, the North Tower's 360-foot-tall radio/television antenna—to process what happened. The absence of debris for Earhart's flight is one of the most distinctive aspects of one of the most compelling plane crashes ever.

A final word on 9/11 debris and the importance of debris for truth, memory, and understanding: In the twisted conspiracy-movements that plague contemporary ideoscapes, the 9/11 crashes are among the most significant delusional paradigms. Never happened, say the whackos who call themselves "9/11 truthers." The purported lack of airplane debris is Exhibit A in their Big Lie: "Remember that day when 4 planes crashed but zero plane parts were found?"[64] The buildings were destroyed in false-flag operations, they blather, the result of carefully placed explosives, or perhaps missiles fired by the US, rather than commercial passenger jets.[65] (In fact, crash investigators impounded much, though not all, of the airplane debris recovered around lower Manhattan—an engine, landing gear, a wing, black boxes, fuselage fragments, seatbelts—for forensic investigation.) I wish it wasn't necessary even to acknowledge deranged conspiracy-theorists, but it is. By negative exemplum—denying the existence of the debris and the reality of the crashes—they help illustrate why debris is necessary: why debris is true.

In Earhart's case, as for another famously vanished flight, Malaysia 370, the lack of debris keeps crash investigators—especially *amateur* crash investigators—all the more invested in working the mystery. In the absence of wreckage to support one of those long, tediously formal investigative reports, anything might have happened. (Malaysia's 777 actually did generate a small amount of bona fide debris, confirmed by serial numbers, that surfaced years after its 2014 disappearance—not enough to figure out what happened, though sufficient to prove it actually crashed.) For Earhart, the more absurd suppositions include: being captured by Japan because she was on a US spy mission, reappearing years later as WWII propagandist Tokyo Rose; somehow surviving a crash, moving to New Jersey, changing her identity, living happily ever after as a housewife; being captured by aliens; faking the crash, eloping with her navigator and, again, living happily ever after.[66] Professional crash teams are quite good at determining exactly what happened, but when they occasionally can't, then—to fill the void of existential uncertainty—it's game on, and the public intervenes at will, unfettered by contraindicative evidence, with crowdsourced "investigations" and hare-brained theories.

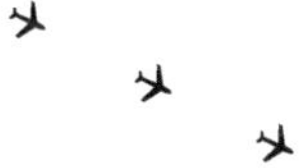

After departing Lae, New Guinea, in July 1937, Earhart's Lockheed Model 10 Electra vanished. It failed to land as scheduled on Howland Island; the 2,500-mile flight—the longest, most dangerous leg of her adventure—was near the end of her attempt to circumnavigate the planet. She and her navigator (and lover?!) Fred Noonan would have achieved a unique accomplishment: six other male pilots had previously circled the globe, but by shorter routes, while Earhart's 29,000-mile planned itinerary kept as close as possible to the equator. She had completed 22,000 miles when they arrived in Lae, and would have made it to 24,500 miles at Howland, leaving just two legs (Howland to Honolulu to Oakland), 4,300 miles, to go.

What happened to her? The dominant assumption then, and still today, was that she ran out of fuel, likely because of navigational and communication errors, and ditched or crashed. Earhart's amazing adventures were widely acclaimed and publicized—not merely because she was a woman, though that was the *pièce de résistance*. Who knew women could undertake such brave, manly explorations? But was her death a sign that she had overreached—that maybe women shouldn't be circumnavigating the earth? Questions and slights emerged. For men, too, the hubris of Icarus often inflects a crash's investigative aftermath: did they push the envelope, flying too high, too far, too fast? Alongside mechanical mistakes, crash investigators (professional as well as amateur) also keep an eye out for moral failures, and as we have seen, some considered flying-while-female such a transgression. Women's crashes can be taken (by sexists) as confirmation of gender inferiority—proof that there are some things women can't do, at least not as well as men can. Such knee-jerk misogyny can accommodate pretty much any new or unconventional activity that any woman ever performs, especially something as spectacular as Earhart's aviation.

In 1940, several bones were found on Gardner Island (now Nikumaroro, in Kiribati, the island nation 400 miles southeast of Howland), but a 1941 forensic examination determined the bones were from a male. Those bones subsequently disappeared, leaving only the examiner's notes and measurements. A 2018 study, however, reviewing those 1941 notes, found that analysis incorrect, hampered by cruder forensic knowledge than we have today—meaning the bones could have been female. (Were scientists back then so blinkered by patriarchy that they couldn't see a woman even when they held her remains in their hands?) The recent research compares the 1941 measurements with Earhart's clothes (preserved in a Purdue archive), finding support for a match. Others, though, critiqued a conclusion that relied on those 1941 data by a scientist who, we now know, committed numerous errors and lost his samples.[67]

Attempts to match DNA from a small finger bone found on Nikumaroro to Earhart's living relatives were unsuccessful. A few possible airplane debris fragments have surfaced in recent years, none conclusive. A small, indistinct photograph from the period seems to show two white people in the Marshall Islands near a Japanese ship, persuading some that Earhart and Noonan were captured. The controversies about what happened are still fought fiercely. The object lesson here (or, more properly, lack-of-object lesson) is that a plane crash without a debris field is unsettling, unfinished, inadequate, cognitively dissonant. It helps us appreciate all the other debris fields from all the other plane crashes, and understand why these sites attract so much attention, time, forensic resources, and inquisitive energy.

Ric Gillespie, a crash investigator who has made a dozen expeditions to Nikumaroro, where he believes Earhart landed and lived as a castaway, calls this planeless plane crash the "Holy Grail of aviation mysteries."[68] Earhart epitomized for her era the feminist cause of embarking upon extraordinary enterprises that were previously the sole purview of men. But amid much praise, Earhart also experienced pushback, a kind of scrutiny commonly deployed against women and people of color who rejected and subverted the doctrine that white men do everything first, and better. Earhart took great risks, like both men and women who are heroes, pioneers, adventurers, dreamers, but women face a great deal more resistance. Men are brave, women are foolhardy.

Earhart hired Noonan, one of the world's most proficient navigators—whose experience and skills covered both sea and air, appropriate to the task at hand—as her assistant in the second seat. But he had a reputation as an alcoholic, which Earhart's transmissions confirmed: twenty hours before their plane lost contact somewhere over the Pacific, she said, "'He's hitting the bottle again and I don't even know where he's getting it!' . . . Earhart, whose faith in Fred Noonan was wearing thin, now faced the possibility of having to do more of the navigation on her own, even though her navigator was aboard. During much of the crossing, Fred 'dozed,' according to Amelia. Those who knew Fred wondered if he was hung over."[69] As voyage leader, Earhart may deserve blame for having taken on (and kept on) someone who was not completely dependable.

Her aviation skills were not perfect. On her first attempt at the circumnavigation, she crashed on takeoff from Honolulu's Ford Island airfield. (Many men, too, crashed many planes pursuing firsts in early aviation.) She didn't know Morse code, lacked technical skills in navigation and communication, and failed to bring some crucial transmission equipment on her round-the-world flight. Some believe Earhart was overrated, "a martyr to her own ambition," writes Mara Gay in "Why Amelia Earhart Just Isn't All She's Cracked Up To Be," calling her "a good pilot in a time when there were great pilots." Earhart "liked to hog the spotlight" and was considered "something of a show-boater, a fame-lover, whose PR and connections helped her eclipse the achievements of less glamorous and more dedicated female pilots."[70]

Critics accused Earhart posthumously of "embarking on a capricious joyride that ultimately cost taxpayers millions of dollars, the estimated tab for a huge rescue mission authorized by President Roosevelt, Earhart's fan and friend," writes Thurman. "Even some of her staunchest admirers disapproved of the last flight," saying she was "caught up in the hero racket."[71]

It is a complex task to scrutinize our heroes, warts and all, under history's harsh spotlight. Recall that "Man Lindy"—as nobody called him, because of course he was a man—became rabidly enamored of Nazis in the 1930s, endorsed eugenics, accepted the Service Cross of the Golden Eagle from Hermann Goering (on behalf of Hitler) in Berlin in 1938, tried to keep the US neutral in WWII to bolster Germany's advantage, and blamed Jews for dragging the US into war. Compared against Earhart's shortcomings, hiring an alcoholic and not knowing Morse Code, and considering it a draw on grandstanding, I'd say Lindbergh wins the award, hands down, for most dislikable pilot of the generation, and Earhart, despite her unfortunate final flight, nevertheless sustains the admiring praise she earned and deserved in her career full of dignified, heroic accomplishments. (Lindbergh crashed four times in the two years before his 1927 transatlantic solo—parachuting out of each plane, he walked away from them all: Lucky Lindy.)

Red Tailed Angels

For the Tuskegee Airmen, at the intersection of aviation and racism, tallying plane crashes—downed German aircraft and safeguarded Allied missions—quantifies victory over prejudice. Segregationist military institutions forbade Black aviators and soldiers from serving alongside white forces. An 1925 American War College report, "The Use of Negro Manpower in War," characterized Black people as "a subspecies of the human family," concluding that they "were deeply superstitious, and filled with a common abundance of moral and character weaknesses. 'Petty thieving, lying and promiscuity are much more common among negroes than among whites. In physical courage it must be admitted that the American negro falls well back of the white man and possibly behind all the other races.'"

Blue Skies, Black Wings, Samuel Broadnax's book about early Black aviators, describes implacable resistance to integrating flight schools: as aviation "began generating strong interest in America, Blacks were summarily turned away or blocked from any aspiration of learning the art of flying." Only the very best characters could learn to fly, and white supremacist prejudices held that "a lineage leading back to former slaves could not be considered the best. To even hint that the descendants of slaves would occupy the same spectacular air space would taint and tarnish a highly exclusive avenue that few could tread." There was "too much sparkling prestige and perceived power attached to flying to permit inferiors to bask in the same golden glory." Exposing hypocritical racist anxieties, Broadnax writes, "When the Army Air Corps excluded Blacks from even the most subservient of roles it was not from the espoused belief that any admitted would fail to reach the high standards demanded by flying; it was just the opposite. It was the latent fear that they would succeed and in doing so forever dispel the promoted notions of racial inferiority."[72]

Black aviators, categorically excluded from existing flight training programs, were grudgingly permitted to form their own training unit at Alabama's Tuskegee Institute, a historically Black college. It was clear that even though this track was segregated and its pilots were sure to be called to serve in inferior roles, it was the only way Black aviators could get any assignments at all. Enrollment in Tuskegee's program was, therefore, profuse and enthusiastic. As the first African-American military aviators, the 332nd Fighter Group and the 477th Bombardment Group of the US Army Air Forces, the Red Tails (referring to their fighter planes' livery) were charged with protecting bombers from enemy fighters.[73] The corps was also known as the Red Tailed Angels, and sometimes, by Nazis, "red-tailed devils" because they shot down so many German aircraft.[74]

Although Tuskegee pilots first "had to fight their own country in order to help fight the enemy," they excelled in their mission of keeping American planes from getting shot down and attacking the Luftwaffe brutally. Despite white pilots' initial prejudices, Broadnax writes, "the truth finally emerged":

> Red Tails were not losing bombers to enemy fighters. As a bomber pilot your best chance of surviving your sitting-duck bombing runs and returning, even in crippled condition from ground fire, would be in having the Red Tails as your escorts. This led the former skeptics—those who had ridiculed the idea of there being Black fighter pilots—to request that the Red Tails be their escorts whenever the opportunity arose.[75]

Women athletes

I noted in Chapter 1 that many sports teams have experienced plane crashes. Here's another way to investigate gender inequities and male hegemonies strewn about debris fields: tally athletes' bodies and you'll find almost all men. The victims of such tragedies skew heavily male because men's sports are better funded and higher profile than women's. There are more men's games than women's—e.g., the WNBA plays forty-game seasons while the NBA's is more than twice as long, eighty-two games. And when a women's team, college or professional, travels from game to game, it is much more likely to be on a bus than a plane.

Major sports crashes of male teams include that which befell, in 2016, Brazilian soccer club Chapecoense, a backwater squad "in the middle of a fairytale season,"[76] near Medellín, Colombia, killing nineteen players (three survived) and the coaching staff; in 2011, Russia's Yaroslavl Lokomotiv Hockey Team crashed, killing twenty-seven players, two coaches and seven club officials; in 1993, Zambia's National Soccer Team, flying to Dakar for a World

Cup-qualifying match against Senegal, crashed into the Atlantic, killing eighteen players and five team officials. In 1987 a Navy plane carrying Peru's soccer team Alianza Lima, returning to the capital from a game in the jungle city of Pucallpa, plunged into the Pacific, killing sixteen players and the coach. In 1977, a chartered DC-3 carrying the University of Evansville basketball team crashed and burned after takeoff in heavy fog and rain, killing all players and its coach. A Uruguayan Air Force charter carrying members and supporters of Old Christians Rugby Union Club from Montevideo to Santiago, Chile, crashed high in Argentina's Andes Mountains in 1972. That tragedy became one of the most famous and macabre plane-crash narratives: the story inspired Piers Paul Read's book *Alive: The Story of the Andes Survivors*, and Frank Marshall's film, *Alive*. The crash stranded twenty-seven survivors in frigid conditions at 11,000 feet, but when rescuers finally arrived seventy-two days later, only sixteen were ultimately rescued—they had survived by cannibalizing their fellow passengers' frozen bodies. In 1949 a plane slammed into a mountain peak outside Turin, killing twenty-two members of Torino Soccer Club, regarded as one of the best of its era: the psychological effects were felt so strongly that a book about it was titled *The Day Italian Football Died*.

So many dead male athletes. The single major aviation disaster involving women athletes—actually a mixed team, men and women—was the 1961 US Figure Skating Team crash. Flying from New York to Prague's World Figure Skating Championships via Brussels, Sabena flight 548 plunged into a Belgian field, killing the entire team of nine men and nine women skaters, along with sixteen other family members, coaches, and skating officials, and everyone else on board as well as one on the ground.[77] The investigation was inconclusive, though flight control mechanism failure was considered the likely cause.

The tragedy stunned the US; media outlets covered it extensively and President John F. Kennedy, an old friend of team member Dudley Richards, issued a statement: "Our country has sustained a great loss of talent and grace which had brought pleasure to people all over the world. Mrs. Kennedy and I extend our deepest sympathy to the families and friends of all the passengers and crew who died in this crash."[78]

Just the previous month, when the Figure Skating Championship was nationally broadcast for the first time, television audiences were enthralled. "Americans got to see these people, understand these athletes," said Barb Reichert, director of the sport's governing body, "and then a few weeks later, they opened their newspapers to find out that they'd all perished in the plane crash. These people who probably weren't household names became household names from that weekend of competition," she said. "You see the real people, you see their personalities. You could see the exuberance of these young people. It was quite a big deal."[79]

Laurence Owen, sixteen, known as "the queen of the ice," was "truly America's brightest star coming out of those games," Reichert said; she could have been not only "the best skater in America but perhaps on a world stage, as well." Owen had made the cover of the *Sports Illustrated* issue published only two days before the crash. It's impossible to rank-order all the pathos from all the plane crashes, but I'd say *Life* magazine photographer Stan Wayman's debris field image (Figure 7.2) has a pretty strong claim as the most haunting, poignant, ironic, and simply overwhelming artifact imaginable.

Wayman's image quintessentially embodies everything I'm trying to get into my investigative reports about the essence of a debris field. Although she died, Owen's image survived—badly singed, but intact—in the debris field, as did her legacy, her moment of triumph. Amid the harsh, awful wreckage, a token of life (*Life!*) endures. Owen got on the plane to be a champion; the plane didn't make it, and neither did she. Knowing the outcome, we wish we could go back in time to change it. But as we look at this photograph and try to understand it, and come to terms with the debris field, I think we realize that Laurence Owen, and Sabena 548, had to try to do what they did, to get to where they were going. We're left with a tragic story, but also a pretty incredible story, about a plane crash but also about a great deal more.

Black athletes

The skating tragedy was the worst US sports crash until it was surpassed, nine years later, by the crash of Marshall University's football team. On November 14, 1970, a Southern Airways DC-9, flight 932 from Kinston, NC, to Huntington, WV, clipped the tops of pine trees on approach and crashed into a mountainside, killing all seventy-five on board including thirty-eight members of Marshall's Thundering Herd squad returning home from a game (which they lost 17–14) at East Carolina University. The NTSB report lists the probable cause as "descent below Minimum Descent Altitude during a nonprecision approach under adverse operating conditions, without visual contact with the runway

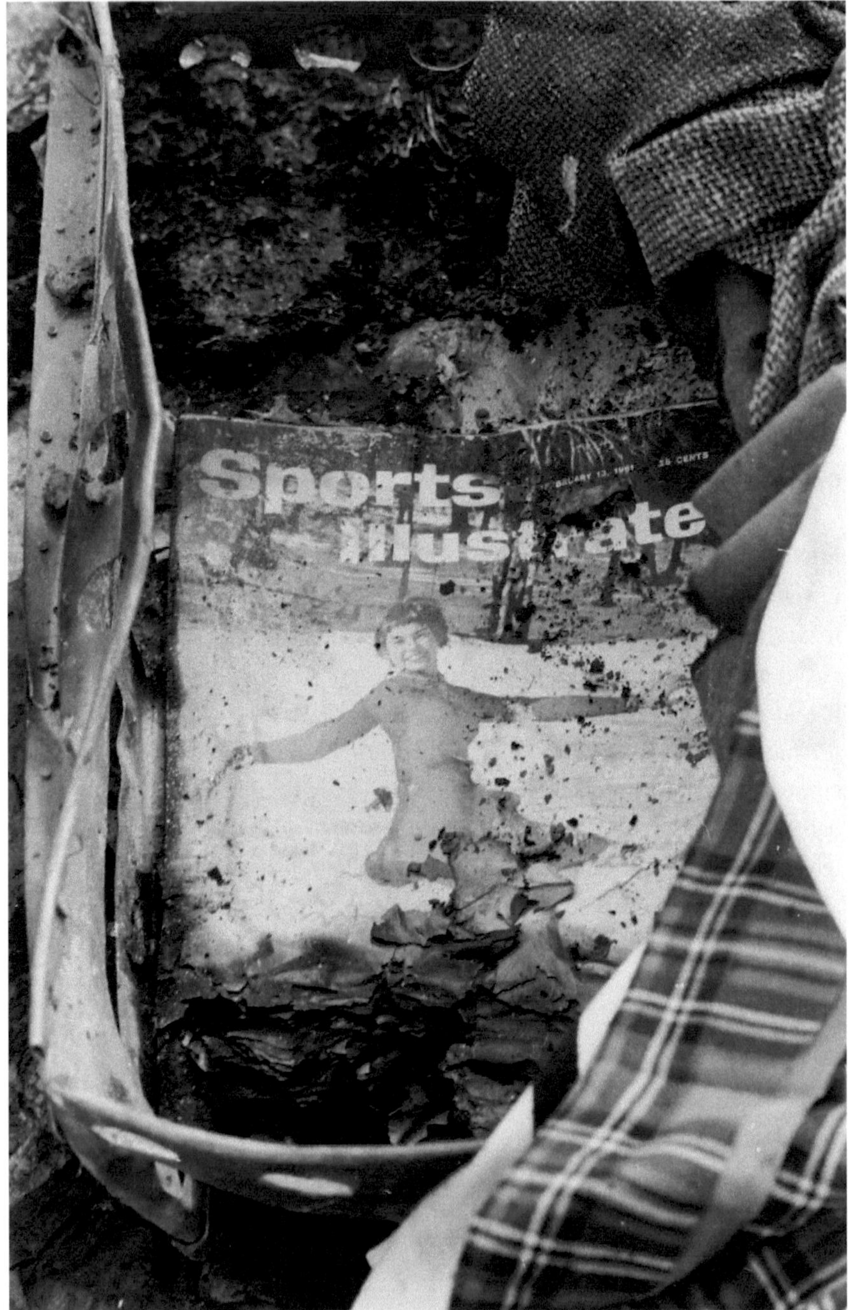

Figure 7.2 Laurence Owen appeared on the cover of the *Sports Illustrated* published just before her crash, a copy of which ended up in the debris field.

environment," likely due to either "improper use of cockpit instrumentation data or an altimetry system error."[80]

We Are Marshall, a 2006 film starring Matthew McConaughey, David Strathairn, and a largely white cast, presented a Hollywood version that focused on the team's feel-good comeback the season after the tragedy. It "deserves kudos for effectively tugging at people's hearts," writes Craig Greenlee, but it was "clueless about the truth," prompting him to write his own account, *November Ever After*. "The story is such a marvelous story," he said. "Why would you doctor it? Just tell the story." A Black sportswriter, Greenlee was recruited for Marshall's 1968 freshman football squad, which went undefeated. Though he quit the team before the crash, "I knew most of the guys on that flight."

The Thundering Herd, 2–18 over the previous two years, had just hired a new coach who overhauled the team by signing mostly Black players, many from the Deep South. It was unusual, though it would soon become common, for majority-white schools to recruit large contingents of Black players. In a school of 7,000 with only 125 Black students, Greenlee writes, they stood out on campus. Huntington, too, predominantly white, left the Black cohort having to face many "cultural adjustments" in "a chilly racial climate," Greenlee writes.

The campus was on edge Friday night before the crash, following a melee after an intramural football game between the Black United Students' team Greenlee coached and an all-white fraternity whose members brandished Confederate flags. "Racial tensions reached a fever pitch that day, raising the likelihood an ugly race riot might occur." One of the Black players, Larry Brown, helped quell the conflict just before the team left for East Carolina: "Brown helped keep the peace, coaxing an angry crowd to calm down in the aftermath of the fight; by eight o'clock the next night, Brown was dead."

> Given what happened on Friday the 13th, many of us believed we were on the brink of a full-blown race riot at Marshall University. But before the night of the fourteenth ended, moods, emotions, and outlooks changed dramatically. Everybody suffered indescribable losses that transcended race and heritage. Nobody was thinking about any racial beefs. It was as if the Friday fights had never happened. Folks were too busy grieving and making plans to attend funerals. This wasn't a Black thing. This wasn't a white thing. This was a death thing, and death does not discriminate.[81]

Greenlee reports the tragedy had a silver lining, helping to heal racial discord: a singular, poignant illustration of how we learn things from plane crashes.

Despite widespread coverage at the time, the Black angle on this crash was barely acknowledged until a Black writer finally reported the story a generation later, which makes me wonder if there are other crashes—I'm *sure* there are!—where, blinded by white-male hegemonies, we fail to detect richer stories, and more diverse stories, lurking in debris fields.

✈ "Crash" as a metaphor for racism

"Crash" (2001) is part of a sequence Elizabeth Alexander calls "dream poems," in which she "turned from history to describe another avenue of inspiration—dreams. She uses these subconscious journeys for twists and turns of language, for substance, and for 'the fabulously logical illogic of nighttime dreams.'" Dreams help transcend familiar ruts of composition: "I wanted to make sure that language was always *surprising*—that the journey to write a poem was never *inevitable* in any way" [emphasis mine].[82] Although Black women like the speaker in "Crash" are drastically underrepresented in aviation, the poem presents a *surprising* defiance of *inevitably* white male pilots. And it's not insignificant that Alexander's pilot survives the crash, with brio.

> I am the last woman off of the plane
> that has crashed in a cornfield near Philly,
>
> picking through hot metal
> for my rucksack and diaper bag.
>
> No black box, no fuselage,
> just sistergirl pilot wiping soot from her eyes,
>
> happy to be alive. Her dreadlocks
> will hold the smoke for weeks.
>
> All the white passengers bailed out
> before impact, so certain a sister
>
> couldn't navigate the crash. O gender.
> O race. O ye of little faith.

Here we are in the cornfield, bruised and dirty but alive.
I invite sistergirl pilot home for dinner

at my parents', for my mother's roast chicken
with gravy and rice, to celebrate.[83]

This crash didn't actually happen—it practically couldn't, with so few sistergirl pilots in flight decks. But Alexander asks us to imagine if it did, as poetry often invites readers to imagine things that do not literally exist: if poetic license is not the same as a pilot's license, they figuratively converge in this particular investigation. What would happen if this woman *were* flying this plane and unexpected dangers arose, Alexander dreams, is that the disaster would be not a mechanical defect or engine failure, but rather, racism. White people would bail out, presumably to their deaths, before what they assumed would be the troubled flight's crash. And then when the pilot lands safely—as most manage to do in most in-flight emergencies—the passengers of color who remained on board, who did not abandon her simply because she was a Black woman, would survive: disheveled but intact, and having earned a delicious, nurturing, family dinner to celebrate the adventure.

Alexander subverts conventional (white-male) crash narrative traditions as her dreadlocked pilot navigates and survives what white people thought she couldn't. ("Passenger error" is the term I'd use in my humanist investigative report.) It's a shot across the bow to advance racial and gender equity in the trope of crash literature, and it works: it's not a tragedy after all, but a disaster averted, a poem of jubilation. Usually the cultural debris field is somber and morose, but Alexander's version culminates in a resounding twist appropriate to her subversive reimagining. From all the cultural debris fields I've investigated, Alexander's "Crash" is the only artifact I've found which presents that lone titular word and nothing else (Lichtenstein's *Whaam!* is close). How striking that it is also the happiest and most triumphant crash poem I have discovered, illuminating the value of resisting entrenched cultural templates, or, to put it more frankly, sexism and racism.

After an incident, air crash investigators investigate, poking and prodding, and publish their findings in the richness of time, but Alexander has no patience for that process to unfurl. She comes to a conclusion pronto: immediately after the crash, in the poem's last short couplets, she moralizes; she chastises. She heckles the disbelievers, the cynics, the bigots: "O gender. O race. O ye of little faith." (At the risk of overreading parallels between my investigations and

NTSB's, Alexander's "O" reminds me of an NTSB report's bullet-point—and, of course, I like hers better.)

Passengers, especially in the throes of aviation emergencies, are indeed expected to embrace an immediate, firm sense of *faith* in their flight crew, their airplane, and the general science of aviation. Most of the times a flight encounters unexpected problems, however dire, the pilots calmly explain that there's an issue and they'll deal with it; if necessary, they'll divert. The plane nearly always manages to land safely, confirming that our faith was justified: standard protocol, the spiritual equivalent of bracing for impact. Assuming faith is like assuming the crash position.

(*Assume Crash Position*, a 2010 album by Konono N°1, features an Afropop sound they call Congotronics and a style they describe as Bambozo trance music. Bambozo refers to communities in the Bas Congo region, and "trance" invokes "a variety of images and cultural phenomena, including ritual and a mystical, hypnotic effect," writes ethnomusicologist David Font-Navarrete.[84] The long, repetitive tracks have a vigorous staccato tempo, generating an "amazing sound of electric likembes (metal thumb pianos) playing through fuzzed-up amps and jury-rigged mics," writes Douglas Wolk.[85] It's not completely clear to me, especially since I don't understand the Kikongo and Lingala lyrics, how this album represents or simulates the emergency protocol in its title, but it is nonetheless a top hit on my airplane-anxiety playlist. Its funky electronica trance does indeed make me feel less fixated on the possibility of an imminent crash. In the throes of my most persistent fearful flying neuroses, there was a period when I actually would assume the crash position as we approached for landing, just because, I felt, it couldn't hurt. I found it caused more difficulty than comfort, though: my peccadillo seemed to agitate fellow passengers and cabin crew, so I tried listening to *Assume Crash Position* instead of actually assuming the crash position, which was a satisfactory alternative: I have never been injured in a landing. As humanists often find, art generally works as well as—if not better than—reality.)

For Alexander, surviving the crash in "Crash" seems like a metaphor for surviving America, surviving white supremacy. The characters end up bruised and smoky, but alive. In an interview about "Crash," Alexander wonders: "What would it mean for more people to put their faith in Black women? What would it mean not to be underestimated? What would it mean to be turned to? What would it mean to see us as heroes?"[86] What fascinating questions, and how powerfully provocative of her to explore these ideas through a plane crash, an event loaded with vivid fear and tinged with existential despair, but also inspiring faith and prayer. (In my humanist credo, poems are prayers.)

Flying, and crashing, are contingent upon both mechanical and human dependability, Alexander suggests, and our faith in that dependability. In so many other facets of life, too, it behooves us to have faith in the "pilots" (doctors, teachers, bus drivers, artists) to whom we have delegated responsibility for whatever figurative "flights" we may be taking. Alexander's moral is that abandoning faith in a sistergirl—which is illogical, unethical, dysfunctional—comprises a metaphorical "crash" that is as awful as an actual crash. (Do those who lack faith in people because of their race or gender deserve to suffer, or even perish, like the white passengers who bailed out? Would it be a kind of karma? I don't think that's an unreasonable extrapolation of Alexander's ethos.)

The debris field in "Crash" resembles many others we've encountered—sooty, hot metal, backpacks strewn around—but its contours are sketchy and minimal, and almost as soon as it is depicted, it disappears: "No black box, no fuselage." Is that because this is a dream, a poetic fancy? Or because Alexander metaphorically suggests that some people (sexists and racists) surveying the debris field of this "crash" will perceive a different reality than others? White passengers saw an inevitable failure, but the poem's Black perspective displays a Sully-esque triumph, a good landing (Chuck Yeager: one that "you can walk away from"), a miracle. The poem's debris field, finally, is comprised not of metal wreckage, but instead, of chicken, gravy, rice, family, community, friendship, support, creating a final scene resonating with gleeful affirmation, faith, that a Black woman pilot can—or, *could*, if airlines would hire more than a handful of them—perform the amazing feat of surviving a breakdown, a potential aviation disaster.

In 2020, fewer than 150 Black women were US pilots with commercial, military or flight instructor certificates, and only a small percentage of them flew commercial airliners. "Sometimes they don't think women should be flying, let alone a woman of color," said Capt. Stephanie Grant. "So we have to go in—just as, I would say, even more prepared to prove that we can do it." Grant staffed the flight deck with Capt. Rachelle Jones on February 12, 2009, when Delta flight 5202 from Atlanta to Nashville became the first commercial flight ever piloted by two Black women. Sistergirl pilots confirm the obvious truth of Alexander's poem: "You can feel like an impostor," First Officer Joi Schweitzer said. "You go through with society telling you that this isn't your career, 'You shouldn't be here,'" Capt. Monique Grayson said, remembering one of her male classmates who told her "she might as well join the circus." Capt. Alexis Brown encountered people who said, "Oh, you're the actual pilot? Like, you did the takeoff and the landing?"[87]

In her interview, Alexander posed questions about the aftermath of a crash that people survive: "What does it mean to escape? The narrow escape—what does that teach you? How do you carry that? How do you process that?" Her poem offers answers: you celebrate surviving the wreck, with traditional rituals and comforts, food and family, and beyond that—beyond the ending—you also celebrate surviving other disasters, other tragedies, like racism. You leverage a single, prototypical, amazing instance of survival into a longer-term macrocosmic determination.

Alexander's pilot makes me think of the organization Sisters of the Skies (SOS), working "To increase our sisterhood [of Black women pilots] through scholarship, mentorship, and outreach. Our vision is to develop pathways and partnerships to increase the number of Black women in the professional pilot career field."[88] Their mentorship program "was birthed out of the need for role models and representation—'If YOU can SEE it, YOU can BE it!'" SOS and Elizabeth Alexander are moving on different flightpaths toward the same destination. It takes a village, a Black village, to raise a Black pilot. The Black community, like the Black passengers, will survive and advance, and the sistergirls will find and uplift more sistergirls. The crash in "Crash" is not a disaster, but a step on the way to aviational equity—crashing barriers—and beyond that, social equity at large.

✈ The symbolism of women's crashes

Is it essentialist to suggest that women's crash narratives seem more inclined than men's to be symbolic rather than factual? Two works—Dani Shapiro's short story "Plane Crash Theory" and Eiléan Ní Chuilleanáin's poem "Deaths and Engines"—present crashes that are not actually crashes but, rather, metaphors for more intimately human situations. Since debris fields marginalize women, it seems intuitively reasonable that women's writing about crashes may be less literally realistic than that of most men. For male writers, artists, and singers, a crash is a crash: yes, certainly, with metaphorical/symbolic/philosophical resonances, but not as pervasively symbolic as it sometimes seems for female cultural creators. I am generalizing from an n of two (O humanists!), which we could expand to three if we think of Elizabeth Alexander's "Crash" as being about faith, race, gender, and soul food, not a crash, and even to four if we add Alice Oswald's "Swan," from Chapter 2, where the titular avian dies *as if* she'd been in a plane crash.

Women experience (and consequently depict) crashes as being overshadowed/ overwhelmed by the hegemonic dominance that is always-already encoded into aviation from the erectly-poised manpilot to the male-gaze-worthy fly-me-to-Miami stewardess. As Mary Roach writes in the epigraph to this chapter, men are prone to trample women in an emergency evacuation: perhaps while women are *following the instructions* ("Come this way. Stay calm. Step out."), gathering up children or people with impairments, performing emotional labor? Or maybe women simply forsake any hope of reversing the course of masculinity in a moment of chaos, ceding exit-door access to manly men? The trampling, which is certainly literal, may also be figurative. Perhaps, then, women writers prefer (or are resigned) to envision crashes in a more allegorical mode, since they get squeezed out when it comes to the real thing. Perhaps women belittle a crash, anticipatorily, before it belittles them.

The title of Dani Shapiro's 2001 story, "Plane Crash Theory," led me to assume it would be useful for my investigations—which it is, though not in the way I initially thought. It turns out to be about family life, a childcare crisis (how feminine!). The single reference to a plane crash symbolizes how she and her husband have extremely different ways of gauging the world's dangers. "Things don't go wrong all at once," she muses, considering the hazards of daily life.

> There are small things—invisible things—that constantly go wrong. Wires fray inside a wall. A van speeds through a yellow light. Someone leaves a Q-Tip in the baby's crib. These small things almost always just scatter and disappear. Big wind comes along and—poof!—they're gone. But once in a while, they start sticking to each other. If this happens, you find yourself with a big thing on your hands.
>
> Whenever we're on an airplane taxiing down the runway, I ask Michael to explain this to me. He calls it Plane Crash Theory. I know he wonders why I need to hear it again and again. But I do. His theory is simple, scientific: in order for a commercial airliner to crash, many things have to go wrong in sequence. Many unlikely things. No single thing causes an accident. It is the sheer coincidental accrual and velocity of these failures that sends two hundred people plummeting into the ocean. This makes Michael feel better. He finds comfort in these odds as he settles into his seat and cracks open a newspaper as the jet takes off. Me, I think it's as likely as not that I'll be on that particular plane.[89]

Michael's theory is right (I've described it elsewhere as a "perfect storm"), and Shapiro's narrator is also right that people may be comforted, or may not be, by realizing how many things have to happen at once for a plane to crash. As interesting as this passage is, it is not about a plane crash per se, but instead, a plane crash as a template for a crisis that happens in a domestic sphere, nowhere near an airport or a debris field. (As the story unfolds, the babysitter accidentally drops the couple's young son down the stairs; it's very scary, but in the end he's ok.)

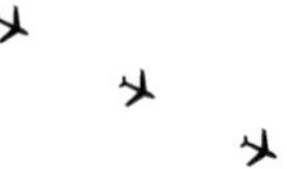

Eiléan Ní Chuilleanáin's 1972 poem "Deaths and Engines" uses a crash as a metaphor for merely death, as opposed to airplane fatalities; is that overkill? (Haha.) Written around the time of her father's death, a friend's suicide, and escalating violence in Northern Ireland, the poem's premise is that life, in difficult times, is like a crashing flight. Ní Chuilleanáin presents keenly realistic debris field images, even though they are "only" metaphorical:

> We came down above the houses
> In a stiff curve, and
> At the edge of the Paris airport
> Saw an empty tunnel
> —The back half of a plane, black
> On the snow, nobody near it,
> Tubular, burnt-out and frozen.
>
> . . .
>
> No sound came over
> The loudspeakers, except the sighs
> Of the lonely pilot.
>
> You will find yourself alone . . .
> And know how light your death is;
> You will be scattered like wreckage,
> The pieces every one a different shape
> Will spin and lodge in the hearts
> Of all who love you.[90]

I am struck by a small but incisive poetic touch, wreckage comprised of pieces that are not uniform. When the flight began, of course, every piece *was* uniform, unified: a given part on one side of the plane would exactly match the same part on the other side, and on every other aircraft of that model. A plane crash, though, generates artifacts marked by difference, disorder, abnormality—antithetical to aviation engineering norms, where precision, uniformity, and exactitude to specs are paramount. Ní Chuilleanáin's metaphorical crash imagery asks us to recall the precise visual/physical aspects of scattered wreckage, and understand her aesthetic of debris as a symbol of mortality more generally: the moment when our engines start to fail, and our once-uniform pieces devolve into the deformities of illness and death.

Ní Chuilleanáin's narrative is about personal mortal decline; Oswald's, a dead bird; Alexander's, racist prejudice; Shapiro's, an injured baby. All these events are, in some (very) loose way, *like a plane crash*. The crashes are the vehicles, not the tenors, of these similes—the tenor is the thing being described, and the vehicle is the figurative language used to describe it. These writers decenter what tends to be a male obsession (to which I am extremely susceptible myself) with the crash as the main event, spectacular—WHAAM!—in its gory, lurid intensity. Perhaps these women are telling me(n) to step back from fetishizing debris fields. They are correct, of course, that an airplane is a vehicle.

Diversion

UTA 772 Memorial

No other plane-crash memorial was as difficult to create as the one in the Sahara Desert's Ténéré region, commemorating Union de Transports Aériens (UTA) flight 772. All 155 passengers and fifteen crew died on September 19, 1989, flying from Brazzaville, in the People's Republic of the Congo (now Republic of the Congo) with a stopover in N'Djamena, Chad, onto UTA's homebase in Paris. When a suitcase bomb exploded on the second leg, the DC-10 crashed in Niger. Six Libyan terrorists were tried and convicted, in absentia, in Paris; the motive was presumed to be revenge against France for supporting Chad's political-military conflicts with Libya. (Libya resented the US, too, for taking Chad's side during the 1978–87 Chadian-Libyan wars, which likely motivated Libyan agents' 1988 destruction of Pan Am flight 103, also brought down by a suitcase bomb planted onboard.)

I find this monument more moving than any other I've investigated. The extremely challenging project shows the benefit, the payoff, of facing and overcoming the many complexities that are always inherent in such an undertaking, but were especially tough here.

Nearly impossible to reach in person, the memorial is best visible from the sky (and on Google Earth, at 16°51′53.748″N 11°57′13.362″E). There are camel caravan routes nearby, so it is possible to encounter it that way, but most who see it are flying overhead—some following the same route UTA 772 had taken. No other airplane-crash monument is designed to be seen primarily by airplane passengers: that's innovative, and edgy.

Many plane crashes happen in remote locations, a fact this monument foregrounds. Nearly all other monuments for remote crashes are more conveniently located, usually in the flight's departure or arrival city. I understand the reasons for choosing more accessible venues, and yet once I learned of this one, which accepts and leverages the tragedy's remoteness, it struck me as inarguably suitable: perfect.

Figure 7.3 High above the UTA 772 memorial, viewers can appreciate the relationship between the plane that crashed and the place where it crashed. The desert milieu, unsettling and overwhelming, is also peaceful, beautiful.

The airplane's silhouette, life-size, is inscribed in a circle—a symbolic compass—seventy meters in diameter, pointing in the direction of Paris, the intended destination. The silhouette is set against a background of large black stones brought in (not easily) from seventy km away. On the perimeter are 170 mirrors, smashed, one for each victim. The design references early-twentieth-century air mail service Aeropostale, which arranged stone circles as points of reference for navigating across the Sahara; flying over the desert by sight is difficult without landmarks because pilots cannot gauge how high they are.

The desert is dynamic: "The sand is playing on the stones," designer Guillaume Denoix de Saint Marc says. "You cannot expect it to look the same—it is alive more or less. It's like land art."[91] (The Institute for Public Art includes this installation in its web-archive, an eclectically-curated assembly featuring hundreds of worldwide artworks—many sculpture parks, environmental and urban renewal projects, community-centered happenings, but no other plane-crash memorials.[92])

The memorial deftly connotes both the airplane's presence and its absence. Jutting out at the northern point, like a sundial, stands the right wing (specifically, the starboard half of its horizontal stabilizer)—so the plane *is* here, at least a piece of it, though most of it is missing. An earlier makeshift monument was erected at the crash site by colleagues of three Exxon employees who died in the crash: they raised the wing and attached a plaque with their co-workers' names, but it was not well anchored and fell over. "They had tried to make their own monument," said Denoix de Saint Marc. "I was so touched that I wanted to keep it," so the upright wing became an integral part of his design. He planned his memorial six miles away from the main debris field, to retain the sanctity of the crash site, and also to locate it directly on the flightpath so it would be easily apparent to airplane passengers overhead. (For obvious reasons, wreckage often, as it did here, lands some distance away from the flightpath.)

The project took nearly two decades to complete because of the enormous obstacles: pragmatic difficulties involving the construction of a large, complex design in a nearly-inaccessible location, but added to this were large, complex geopolitical difficulties. In 2007, Denoix de Saint Marc, whose father, Jean-Henri, died in the crash, traveled with two other victims' families on a 400-mile convoy through the Ténéré Desert. It was a dangerous trip: temperatures reached 120° F, and water was extremely scarce—the team had to dig their own well on-site. There was a Toureg rebellion at the time—an armed insurgency among local

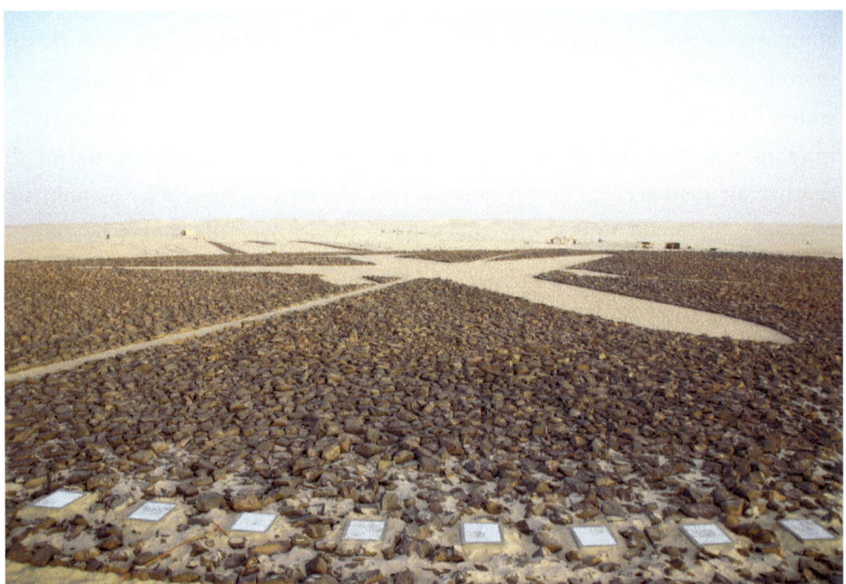

Figure 7.4 The UTA 772 memorial at ground level, near the end of construction.

nomadic communities—and Al-Qaeda Islamic Maghreb was also active in the region. With 140 workers from Niger, the team spent six weeks building the memorial.

The process, perhaps even more than the completed memorial itself, was an act of devotion. For Denoix de Saint Marc,

> the physical contact with what remained of the plane was very important. In his book he describes being summoned to identify his father's body, only to be dismissed again because dental records had confirmed his identity. He never saw the body—a fact that haunted him for years. He salvaged a UTA security belt which he always carries with him. "It's completely scratched and broken and it still has some sand in it," he says. "It symbolised security—unfortunately it was not enough. It reminds me of how fragile life is."[93]

The resonance of debris, and the importance of palpably touching it, is what drew Denoix de Saint Marc to undertake this extraordinary project. When he arrived at the crash site, "My first feeling was anger. We were astonished. We could not speak. We were just walking between the debris. It was crazy, seeing all these parts, it was 100 km square, parts of plane." When traces of explosives were found in 1989, French authorities removed fifteen tons of debris that carried the most clues—flight deck, wheels, luggage—but the rest remains where it fell. Handling the pieces made it real, Denoix de Saint Marc said. He even brought some debris back to France so other victims' families, unable to travel to Niger, could still have some tangible contact with the wreckage.[94]

Bringing victims' relatives to disaster scenes can be an effective treatment for shock and grief, according to Lars Weiseth from the Norwegian Centre for Violence and Traumatic Stress Studies, a counselor for people who have lost family members in plane crashes, weather disasters, and terrorist attacks. He finds that undertaking such journeys makes survivors less susceptible to post-traumatic stress responses. "The profound urge to undertake such trips is first and foremost about gaining an understanding of what went on before someone's death," he says, but there are other motivations too:

> The second factor is the nearness to the dead person. The site of death is almost like the grave and gives you a very strong sense of physical closeness to the deceased. A third factor is the almost duty-like sense you have. A sudden, violent death means there is no time to bid farewell. When I talk to people who have done this, I really think it's almost a religious sense of duty. You have to overcome a resistance and a fear—it's really an effort—and I feel you do this for the missing family member. Then there is also finally an anti-phobic thing, you overcome

your fear by doing something with others. There is this cohesion, this sense of mutuality, and on the site you can carry out some symbolic rituals.[95]

Creating this monument was not the only way Denoix de Saint Marc processed his grief. In the years he spent coming to terms with his own personal pain—in the wake of his father's death, his marriage dissolved and his career foundered—he founded the International Federation of Associations of Victims of Terrorism (IFAVT), an organization that supports people whose lives have been overturned by terrorism. It was "born out of the idea of connecting victims of terrorism around the world. While those victims might have different nationalities, cultures and beliefs, they go through the same struggles and can find strength in numbers." The group wanted to create "a network strong enough to stand against the spread of radicalisation" by countering "extremist discourses which may lead to radicalisation, intolerance and sometime terrorism." Their mission statement affirms: "while terrorists call for a partitioned humanity, we now stand as one, as a family of all races and fate, sharing our pain, and acting together toward a same goal: honouring victims' memory and denouncing all acts of terrorism."[96]

IFAVT arranges and curates terrorist victims' testimonies—victims who were injured but not killed, and also families of people who were maimed or

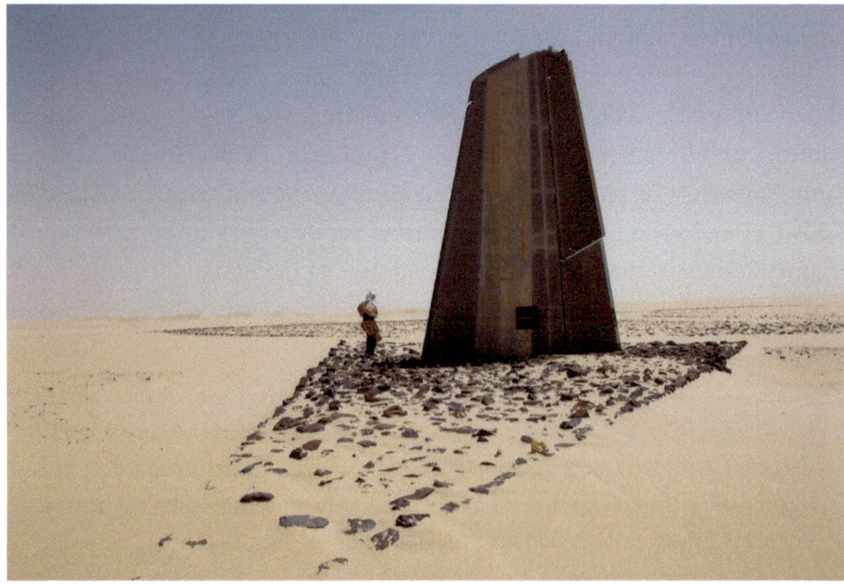

Figure 7.5 A desert traveler contemplates UTA 772's wing.

killed—which model non-violent responses to terrorism. Victims, Denoix de Saint Marc writes, had usually not been personally targeted by terrorists: like his father, they were randomly unlucky. But survivors can easily develop feelings of martyrdom and anger, which can lead to their own eventual embrace of violence. "My personal experience has shown me that another path is possible: a path of resilience through action and testimony. I was 26 years old when I lost my father in the attack perpetrated by the Libyan secret services. What followed for me was an erratic and complex personal journey."

This amazing man created an amazing monument. It's so good because of how meaningful it was for Denoix de Saint Marc, and thus, contagiously, for anyone else who encounters it. His thoughtful, passionate determination to *do something* after the crash, to *make something* out of the debris field, rubs off on us—and this is true whether or not we know all the details of the memorial's backstory, and of his own. This installation is so powerfully restorative because it's one piece of a much broader set of responses and processes. (I don't have time to go into the long story of how Denoix de Saint Marc got Saif Qaddafi—son of Muammar Qaddafi, the Libyan dictator who orchestrated the terrorism—to pay for it all!) He worked so hard, for so long, on so many interconnected projects involving the aftermath of the plane crash, and the UTA 772 memorial resonates with the energy of all that. It's a prototype of all the things that need to be done after a crash. It's about planes and violence and death and remoteness, and acceptance, and building something important, something new, out of the debris field—something you couldn't have had if you didn't have the debris field first. We've seen how crashes make aviation better, and so do debris fields, especially cultural debris fields. The Sahara sand-plane is a great monument, but it's also part of a memorial process, a monumental process (!), that resonates with the vastness, the far-reaching problems, and pain, and healing, and solutions, that are necessary to move beyond a plane crash, and that document how people have done that.

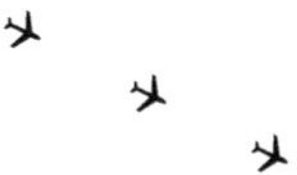

In November 2023, thirty-four years after the crash and sixteen years after the memorial's creation, it was destroyed. You might think something so far from the madding crowds would be protected from human folly—you'd be wrong; you might imagine a cultural creation that already embodied such profound evil, violence, and pain would be immune to any further indignities—again, you'd be wrong.

The ruination is extensive. Photographs posted on social media look like something I have never seen elsewhere: the debris of debris. Debris-squared.

"Une profanation odieuse," Denoix de Saint Marc called it—an odious desecration—precipitated, he believes, by the July, 2023, coup in Niger. Its instigators were hostile to Niger's French affiliations, suggesting a motive for destroying this testament to international cooperation. He said it seemed like "an act directed against France, committed by Russian militiamen Wagner," the infamous mercenary troops who collaborated with the overthrow of Niger's government, "with the approval of the putschists"[97]

The military junta's spokesperson, Lieutenant Colonel Abdramane Amadou, addressed that accusation with a laughably ludicrous denial, stating that "the monument was not the subject of vandalism, but that it was just degraded by time and desert erosion."[98]

Denoix de Saint Marc vows to rebuild another cenotaph on the site.

8

I Will Survive

And then all of a sudden I was outside the plane. I was suspended in mid-air, suspended in my seat. It was not so much that I had left the plane but rather that the plane had left me. It simply wasn't there any more. I was all alone with my row of seats. I sailed on through the air and then I tumbled into a fall. I spiraled, face downward. The seat belt squeezed my stomach and I couldn't breathe any more and in this moment I realized with absolute clarity what had happened to me. But I had no time to be afraid because apparently I lost consciousness. I can still see the jungle beneath me, a deep green, like broccoli.

Juliane Koepcke, *Wings of Hope*

Surviving a plane crash is quite possible. "Approximately 90 percent of aircraft accidents can be categorised as survivable or technically survivable," finds a 1996 Transport Safety study.[1] A 2001 NTSB report gave a higher figure, 95.7 percent,[2] and a 2020 update hiked that to 98.2 percent.[3]

Imagine surviving a crash, mustering up your courage and rationality, getting back onto another plane, and then that plane crashes too. Many military pilots have survived multiple crashes: Sir Laurence Olivier, who survived two commercial flight crashes alongside his wife, Vivien Leigh, crashed another two planes he flew as a lieutenant for the Royal Navy's Fleet Air Arm. A pilot "of notorious incompetence," he was finally relegated to target-towing and recruitment demonstrations.[4]

Aurelia Grigore, a flight attendant for Romania's TAROM Airlines, survived two crashes on flights she was working. When a 1980 flight from Bucharest to Nouadhibou, Mauritania, missed its landing approach, the Antonov An-24 ditched in the water, breaking apart just short of the runway; Grigore helped conduct a largely successful evacuation with only one fatality. In 1986, a TAROM Tupolev Tu-154 flight deck erupted in fire after a hard landing in Bucharest, killing three pilots, but thanks to Grigore's calm implementation of the evacuation plan, everyone else—fifty passengers and both flight attendants—survived. Grigore resumed her job *again* after the second crash, closing out her thirty-year career in 2004 without any more incidents. "The Stewardess Who Cheated Death Twice," as a newspaper headline labeled her, "was nicknamed the 'black cat,' which meant bad luck. She was seen as a liability, and some pilots were scared to fly with her."[5] Personally, if she'd been staffing a flight I was on, I'd be more inclined to regard her presence as a good omen rather than a liability. By the same token, I can't imagine passengers would worry if they saw Capt. Chesley Sullenberger at the controls: I'll take a crew who've survived a crash any day.

Tuula Hyvärinen survived two crashes, in a small plane, and then in a helicopter—*both* on December 18, 1979. The Finnish woman had been working in Iceland and took an aerial sightseeing trip in a small Cessna before returning home for Christmas. "I remember we flew into a cloud that was totally white. It was like flying in milk," Hyvärinen said. The pilot tried to turn the plane around, and "What I remember next was that we crashed on the ground. I could feel pain in my lower back. The plane was upside down and I was hanging from my seatbelt. I felt something had broken in my lower back."[6] A rescue helicopter arrived an hour later, bringing Hyvärinen on in a stretcher. "Then I felt we were going up, and then I felt we were on the way down again. I felt the crash again. It was unbelievable. This cannot be happening again," she said, as the helicopter crashed 800 meters from the Cessna wreckage. Hyvärinen managed to free herself from the stretcher and leave the helicopter, where one of the rescue workers said to her, "Við hittumst aftur, elskan" (We meet again, my dear). This time she refused to board another aircraft, insisting on ambulance transport.[7]

Hyvärinen and Grigore have quite the stories. Other crash-survivors who made it out of the debris field relatively intact and with great narratives to boot include Antoine de Saint-Exupéry, whose 1935 crash in remote North Africa during a Paris–Saigon air race inspired his beloved story about a little prince from asteroid B-612 who encounters an aviator—an incarnation of the author himself—wandering through the Sahara Desert. Saint-Exupéry crashed (and survived) again in 1938, attempting to set a world record from New York City to Tierra del Fuego. Too heavy to climb because the fuel load was miscalculated (confusing US and British gallons), his plane crashed on takeoff from Guatemala City. His next crash came in 1943, just after he joined the Free French air corps as a reconnaissance pilot; and once again Saint-Exupéry returned to the flight deck. He crashed again the following year, this time fatally, on a reconnaissance flight over Southern France ahead of the Allied invasion. As no debris field was found, he was declared missing in action for over half a century. Finally, in 1998, a French fisher found Saint-Exupéry's identity bracelet in the ocean near Marseille, and two years later divers discovered the wreckage from his P-38 Lightning.[8]

Juliane Koepcke, seventeen, the lone survivor of a 1971 Peruvian jungle crash who walked eleven days until she reached a small village, tells her story in Werner Herzog's 1998 documentary *Wings of Hope*. Roald Dahl's near-fatal 1940 military crash, a trauma he inscribes and revisits in many works, was the enabling inspiration for his writing career. Ernest and Mary Welsh Hemingway survived two crashes over two days in 1954. When everyone dies in an aviation disaster, forensic investigations can provide many significant insights, but a good deal of what happened remains indeterminate. Survivors, on the other hand, can give breathtaking first-hand accounts of the experience and the aftermath of crashing. Nothing else from debris fields matches the overwhelmingly real immediacy of these stories that survivors themselves tell: *THEY . . . were there!*

Look at Hemingway's crashes

Ernest Hemingway documented (and monetized) his crashes with typically jaunty-macho panache in a splashy magazine spread. *Look* had invited him to write a boilerplate piece about his African safari adventures, but after he and his wife crashed on January 23 *and* 24, 1954, his editors suggested he write about these instead, increasing his contracted commission with a hefty $20,000 bonus.

The Hemingways were touring the East African Congo Basin in a Cessna 180 while Ernest took a break from his safari assignment. The low-flying plane caught its wheel on a telegraph line (possibly) and went down near Murchison Falls. The crash landing was relatively smooth: the pilot navigated into a thicket of brush to soften the impact. After they spent the night outside, a passing launch brought them to Butiaba, Uganda, the next day. Hemingway claimed it was the same vessel featured in John Huston's film *The African Queen*, though we should always take his too-good-to-be-true details with a grain of salt. Mary and Ernest arranged to fly to Entebbe in a de Havilland Dragon Rapide, which caught fire during takeoff and, again, crashed. "The incredible happened," writes Anthony Burgess in *Ernest Hemingway and His World*, "proving that lightning always strikes the same tree twice."[9]

After a plane overflying the first crash's wreckage spotted no survivors, word spread that the Hemingways had died. Obituaries appeared, providing Hemingway the treat of reading them while he was still alive—an experience he called a "strange vice" that "could become extremely destructive to one's general equilibrium and cause one, perhaps, to lose one's status as a completely well-adjusted person."[10] His obituaries "must have invoked an odd experience of trauma and fascination," writes Selma Karayalçin—they "painted an entire life of the artist and 'man of action,' which not only fed his ego and gave him much to live up to, but also made him feel aware of his own mortality."

Hemingway published his double-crash narrative, "The Christmas Gift"—the sightseeing flight had been his present to Mary—in two installments. The kicker read: "The story of a husband's gesture which led to a BRUSH WITH DEATH." Karayalçin sees in the story a man "in denial concerning the physical and psychological effects of both plane crashes," presenting "a calm and collected persona who is cavalier about his experiences. This account, embraced by various biographers and critics, has become legend," though it "is rooted in a pose Hemingway had carefully maintained during his career." He recounts his afflictions in a letter:

> major concussion, rupture one kidney, damage liver, collapse of intestines, Paralysis sphincter, ¾ lost sight in one eye (left) (never any good anyway), Burns head, Brush fire = burns on lips (light), left hand severe, right forearm ditto, abdomen (light), legs (Light).

Hemingway's concussion came from forcing open the plane's door with his head to escape. Though his tone is flippant, Karayalçin writes, "Hemingway reveals in the same letter, almost parenthetically, that they were 'the worst days [he] ever saw.'" Mary's journal, too, gives a dire account of his pain: "His kidneys were seriously damaged. The urine samples he keeps in glasses in the bathroom are bright, dark red with an inch of sediment, the wound on the leg not good, hearing bad in burned ear, eyes bad, the new glasses uncomfortable because of the broken or bruised bone at the ridge of the nose."[11] The injuries marked the beginning of declining health that worsened until his suicide seven years later; so if these were not precisely fatal crashes, they were also not *not* fatal.

After describing adventures flying across Tanganyika in "The Christmas Gift," Hemingway gets to the first crash, narrated as if it were just another day on the job. After circling Murchison Falls ("very beautiful" in his sleek sparse prose: "a cataract which descends in various levels") and diving to avoid hitting a flock of ibis ("A bird of this type can easily go through the Plexiglas and could eliminate the pilot of an aircraft of this type"[12]), a meandering imperialist/racist strain creeps into the narrative.

> At this point, having deviated through no fault of our own from our proposed course, we encountered a telegraph wire on an abandoned line. This telegraph had been abandoned when the radio network was set up and nearly all the wire had been removed for the benefit of the natives, who wore it in circular coils in their ears. This small section of the line remained, as it was inaccessible to the natives, who are more or less allergic to Murchison Falls. This might be due to the presence of the various beasts which we had observed.

(Dim-witted natives! Scared of "various beasts" and blind to the splendor of the natural world, which only a white American can truly appreciate; ignorant of the real value of technology, which they plunder for their barbaric fashions.)

> The aircraft had encountered the wire with its propeller and its tail assembly. It was temporarily uncontrollable and then was so obviously damaged that it was necessary to land. There was a choice of going into what we refer to in RAF parlance as "the drink" which was directly below.
>
> However, the drink which was carefully observed and had already been scouted ... contained too many crocodiles to make landing advisable. Also, as you know, one does not land an aircraft with nonretractable wheels in the water. Water is one of the hardest substances on which to land an aircraft and unless you can make a belly landing the ditching will not be successful. The action of the unretracted wheels when coming in contact with the water will almost inevitably precipitate the aircraft forward so that the pilot and the passengers will find themselves upside down and under water.
>
> If this water is occupied by the crocodiles this maneuver is considered by experienced defiers of the laws of gravity to be extremely inadvisable. [Pilot] Roy Marsh chose the simpler and better course of swinging sharply to the left where there was solid land observable. This land was covered by heavy bush but a Cessna 180 can land at a speed of approximately 40 mph. Roy Marsh, who found that his flaps were working, laid her down very sweetly in the softest bushes which were available. These bushes were medium-sized trees. There was the usual sound of rending metal which is audible in a forced landing, but everything was intact. We observed the damage to the aircraft and to Miss Mary who had previously not participated in this sort of thing.... we decided that we would have to make our way very slowly up to the high ground to avoid the elephants who were already starting to comment audibly on our presence.[13]

Karayalçin suggests Hemingway invented his account of swerving away from the large birds and getting entangled in the telegraph wire. The more mundane and likely truth was that the Cessna hit an anthill (which was, to be fair, a hard clay structure 20 feet tall). In Hemingway's defense, we should probably not get too bothered when fiction writers deploy fictional embellishment.

There is nothing very traumatic or dire about the situation as Hemingway depicts it. Instead, with a studied irreverent poise, he focuses his concern on rationing the beer and whisky. The Hemingways spend an interesting night watching a herd of elephants ramble through their campsite, just the sort of thing he would have been doing anyway in his planned safari, suggesting that the crash only minimally disrupted their plans. (When an elephant who shows up the next day turns hostile, Hemingway paints that encounter as more dangerous than the crash.) The story is "full of humor and understatement in the light of very real danger," in Karayalçin's appraisal. "There is no terror, no surprise, as such experiences are understood to be taken in the author's stride," and the persona is "a hardened veneer that Hemingway has placed on the events as a form of self-protection."

After more drinking and exploring, and a cruise on (possibly) the *African Queen*, the Hemingways make their way to Masindi and take off for Entebbe.

> When we were one third of the way down the alleged airstrip, I was convinced that we would not be airborne successfully. However, we continued at the maximum rate of progress of the aircraft which was leaping from crag to crag and precipice to precipice in the manner of the wild goat. Suddenly, this object which was still described as an aircraft became violently air-borne through no fault of its own. This condition existed only for a matter of seconds after which the aircraft became violently de-air-borne and there was the usual sound, with which we were all by now familiar, of rending metal.
>
> Unfortunately, on this second occasion flames were observed coming from the starboard engine which was burning. The right-wing tank, which was fully loaded for the considerable flight to Entebbe, had also caught fire and due to the wind these flames were coming toward the rear of the aircraft. There is very little in an aircraft which is inflammable, but as the gasoline comes out of the tank it bathes the side of the aircraft and it burns in the direction in which the wind is blowing.
>
> At this moment when the crash of the aircraft had gone into Technicolor, I remembered the old rule that in a twin-engined aircraft you get out the same way you came in. I therefore went to the door through which we entered and found it jammed by the bending of the material of which the aircraft was

> constructed.... I opened the door by pressure exerted by my head and left shoulder. I mounted the left wing of the aircraft which had not yet taken fire .... Some people are under the impression that the aircraft burned in a sudden burst but I can testify honestly that I have never seen a kite burn more slowly. It must be a very rugged species of aircraft and she did not ignite completely until everyone was at a reasonable distance.

(Always on the lookout for new ways to characterize plane crashes, I tip my hat to Hemingway for "violently de-air-borne.")

At the moment of a plane crash, Hemingway explains, drawing on his now-considerable experience, "your only thoughts are of technical problems. Your past life does not rush through your brain like a cinema film and your thoughts are purely technical." You are in a state of shock, and when a plane crashes at takeoff "the shock is considerably greater and you cannot sort it out much at the time and so attempt to behave in a completely normal manner. This is quite easy to do and fools most people completely."[14]

Part one of "The Christmas Gift" ends with a teaser for the next installment that promises to show "what thoughts boil from the brain of a famous novelist who has suffered a concussion in a plane crash,"[15] and part two delivers that with a strong dash of vintage Hemingway, including another reference to his head injury: "This thought is conditioned by the fact that the so-called thinker has suffered a major concussion and therefore is not responsible for his thoughts. This type of concussion induces the type of thinking which sometimes tends toward violence. I believe this violence is a phenomenon of concussion due to the violent demise of the aircraft." While official crash investigation reports, too, describe survivors' injuries, Hemingway's humanist iteration does so in a poignant (though still calculated) personal voice. His scars and pains are not isolated details, but rather, part and parcel of his personae (both his literary characters and his authorial self-invention). He tells a compelling story, and a major goal of my investigation is to find good stories, good crash narratives; Papa and I coincide in our interests here.

Hemingway read his obituaries as he recuperated: "Most of the obituaries I could never have written nearly as well myself," he writes, implying that they are (like his own writing) subjective and at least quasi-fictive—certainly in this case, as Hemingway was not in fact dead. Almost all the obituaries "emphasized that I had sought death all my life," a theory he ridicules. "Can one imagine that if a man sought death all of his life he could not have found her before the age of 54?" He goes on to describe many ways of easily actualizing a death-wish, a haunting passage in light of his subsequent suicide.

Media coverage contained "glaring inaccuracies," Hemingway notes; someone claimed he had himself been piloting the plane, trying to land it on Mount Kilimanjaro to find the leopard carcass described in his story "The Snows of Kilimanjaro," which also features a plane crash as a minor plot detail.[16] The obituary's intertextual interweaving of "Kilimanjaro" again testifies to the literariness of Hemingway's crash, and the ways in which crashes infuse literature, and literature infuses crashes. In Dahl's and Saint-Exupéry's texts and crashes, too, there is a freeplay/interplay between writing and crashing—because a crash is full of such extraordinary narrative energy, and what would a writer do with narrative energy other than writing a narrative?

Finally, "The Christmas Gift" discusses the crash investigations, which were thorough because "the loss of a *Ndege*"—the word "means bird and is the African name for an aircraft," Hemingway explains—"involves loss to the insurance company or to the company owning the aircraft and in order to see if any negligence can be proved on the part of the pilot the investigation is profound and exhaustive." Capitalists care little about human tragedies, he writes, only financial implications. He calls the process an "Inquisition" designed to trip people up with some indiscretion that might eliminate the insurer's liability. "An interrogation is not difficult when you have a true story to tell," Hemingway explains, "but you must be most careful about technical details." A pilot who is crashing focuses on three things: first, self-preservation; second, the ethical responsibility for passenger safety.

> The third thing you are doing when you crash is to do it so it will look good to the insurance company. To have it look good to the insurance company, you must make this sort of triple play with extreme speed and accuracy and later must remember everything including in larger planes such things as propeller pitch. We had excellent photographs which would have borne out all our statements, but unfortunately these burned in the crash of the second aircraft. It was therefore a question of a long, both exhaustive and exhausting test of one's veracity and technical language.[17]

For Hemingway, crash investigations are an intrusion, a bureaucratic charade, noteworthy merely because they keep him from doing what he most likes to do in Africa: drink, swagger, write. Insurance companies are indeed major players in crash aftermaths, reminding us that crashes cost somebody lots of money in terms of repairing/replacing the aircraft and compensation settlements for casualties. I have found no other references to this facet of crashes in my investigations, nor in official investigations: it is apparently not *comme il faut* to discuss business and risk management when it comes to aviation disasters, and I give Hemingway points for reminding us that insurance policies and practices are in fact very much entwined with plane crashes.

Broadly popular in his time, Hemingway's literary reception has dwindled of late, and his snotty mockery of plane-crash investigations confirms that he is not my cup of tea. But he does tell a memorable and idiosyncratic crash-survival story, for which he gets a few more points.

"A Piece of Cake"

Roald Dahl barely survived his 1940 crash. Flying across Libya in a ramshackle Gloster Gladiator, the RAF's last remaining biplane, he was running low on fuel and daylight, unable to find the Egyptian airstrip where he was supposed to rendezvous with his squadron. When he attempted an emergency desert landing, his plane hit a boulder and collapsed, knocking him out. Biographer Donald Sturrock writes:

> The smell of petrol stirred his consciousness. He tried to open his eyes, but he could see nothing. Moments later both the Gladiator's fuel tanks exploded and the craft itself caught fire. Blinded and numb, Dahl contemplated what seemed to be a certain death. "All I wanted was to go gently off to sleep and to hell with the flames," he wrote later. But something forced him to act, to extricate his damaged body from its parachute straps, push open the cockpit canopy, and drop out of it onto the sand beneath. His overalls were burning too, but he put out the fire by rolling on the ground.
>
> It was not bravery, Dahl later noted, simply a "tendency to remain conscious" that saved him from being burned to death. "The world about me was divided sharply down the middle into two halves. Both these halves were pitch black, but one was scorching hot and the other was not." In terrible pain, Dahl crawled slowly away from the burning wreckage. But he was not yet out of danger: "My face hurt most. I slowly put a hand up to feel it. It was very sticky. My nose didn't seem to be there. I tried to feel my teeth to see if they were still there, but it seemed as though one or two were missing. And then the machine guns started off. I knew right away what it was. There were about 50 rounds of ammunition left in each of my eight guns and, without thinking, I had crawled away from the fire out in front of the machine, and they were going off in the heat. I could hear them hitting the sand and stones all round, but I didn't feel like getting up and moving right then, so I dozed off."[18]

All the bullets missed him. Infantrymen inspecting the wreckage later that night found Dahl barely conscious but still alive. His uniform was burnt and his face so disfigured that he was almost unrecognizable. Soldiers carried him to an underground Field Ambulance Station.

After a fraught period of rehabilitation, Dahl recovered from his burns, a concussion, and weeks of temporary blindness brought on by massive swelling in his brain. Sturrock calls it "the plane crash that gave birth to the writer," exemplifying how constructive, restorative creativity emanates from debris fields. Dahl's RAF career gave him "the need to write as well as something to write about," Sturrock writes.

> Indeed, it is impossible to imagine any of Dahl's first stories being written without his experience as a flyer. All of them are intimately bound up with it. Many touch on the ecstasy of flying itself. Others deal with the confused tangle of human emotions he experienced in that short but intense four weeks of aerial combat. Most reveal a deeply fatalistic streak, so much so that one is tempted to wonder whether writing them may initially have been a kind of therapy, a way of making some sort of sense out of the muddle of conflicting emotions to which he had been exposed.

Sturrock calls Dahl's recovery "a time of existential crisis"—remember from Chapter 3 how resonantly existentialism inflects plane crashes. "For almost a month he inhabited a hazy world of total darkness, uncertain of time or surroundings. Concussed, blind and isolated from family and friends, he was disoriented and helpless."[19]

Dahl wrote four stories featuring plane crashes, and the leitmotif of aviation recurs even more widely throughout his oeuvre. After his recovery, Dahl's "sense of fantasy heightened," Sturrock writes, "while his desire to shock became even more pronounced. He emerged from his crisis more confident, more determined to make a mark." His brush with death made him "more aware of his vulnerability, more reflective, yet also intensifying the sense of himself as a survivor, as a figure of destiny. This heightened sense of self was closely linked to the very act of flying."

In *James and the Giant Peach* (1961), the protagonist abandons his cruel family to find shelter inside an enormous peach, standing on its surface as it flies high above the ocean carried by a flock of seagulls. "Clouds like mountains towered over their heads on all sides, mysterious, menacing, overwhelming.... the peach was a soft, stealthy traveler, making no noise at all as it floated along. And several times during that long, silent night ride high up over the middle of the ocean in moonlight, James and his friends saw things that no one had seen before." It might seem paradoxical that a plane-crash victim would write so eloquently and empoweringly about the mysterious awe of flight, though Dahl also notes,

> Traveling upon the peach was not in the least like traveling in an airplane. The airplane comes clattering and roaring through the sky, and whatever might be lurking secretly up there in the great cloud-mountains goes running for cover at its approach. That is why people who travel in airplanes never see anything.[20]

In *Charlie and the Chocolate Factory* (1964), Charlie receives Willy Wonka's magical gift as he is flying high over the factory in a glass elevator. And in *The Minpins* (1991), Little Billy "flies on the back of a swan into a dark and magical nocturnal landscape, filled with fantastic natural wonders. Here, fifty years after he himself last flew on his own, Dahl powerfully evokes that sense of separation between the solitary flyer and the rest of humanity."[21] While he would inscribe many traumatic aspects of his crash in his fiction, he also writes *against* that anguish, reimagining and reclaiming sublime aviation experiences. Dahl depicts flying as astounding and life-changing; it is risky, but the dangers are survivable, and the reward is a richly experiential, even metaphysical, awareness of the world's opulence, a perspective that undergirds the magical appeal of his fiction.

Dahl credits C. S. Forester, known for his military adventure novels—most famously the Horatio Hornblower series—with launching his literary career. In 1942, Forester interviewed Dahl about his crash for a propaganda story (that Forester himself planned to write) in the *Saturday Evening Post*. Finding it difficult to recount the story in person, Dahl proposed instead writing down some notes to send Forester. "Then you can rewrite it properly yourself in your own time," he explained in his essay "Lucky Break," about how he became a writer. "Wouldn't that be easier? I could do it tonight."

> "A splendid idea," Forester said. "Then I can put this silly notebook away and we can enjoy our lunch. Would you really mind doing that for me?"
>
> "I don't mind a bit," I said. "But you mustn't expect it to be any good. I'll just put down the facts."
>
> "Don't worry," he said, "So long as the facts are there, I can write the story. But please," he added, "let me have plenty of detail. That's what counts in our business, tiny little details, like you had a broken shoelace on your left shoe, or a fly settled on the rim of your glass at lunch, or the man you were talking to had a broken front tooth. Try to think back and remember everything."

Dahl later avowed: "That, though I didn't know it at the time, was the moment that changed my life." His notes impressed Forester enormously:

> "You were meant to give me notes, not a finished story. I'm bowled over. Your piece is marvellous. It is the work of a gifted writer. I didn't touch a word of it. I sent it at once under your name to my agent . . . You will be happy to hear that the *Post* accepted it immediately and have paid one thousand dollars. . . . the *Post* is asking if you will write more stories for them. I do hope you will. Did you know you were a writer?"[22]

Dahl called the story "A Piece of Cake," though the *Post* changed the title to make it more bluntly dramatic: "Shot Down Over Libya." Published anonymously, because Dahl could not identify himself or his fighter unit due to military security, the story carried a headnote: "The author of this factual report on Libyan air fighting is an RAF pilot at present in this country for medical reasons."[23] Dahl was not in fact shot down—this crash narrative accommodates significant poetic license. His plane in the story, a Hurricane, is not what he was flying when he crashed. He was, as the note informs, "at present in this country" (the US), but not for medical reasons: he was on assignment to the British Embassy in Washington, a position he hated and soon quit. What the *Post* called a "factual report" was not really that at all except for the description of the crash itself, which does hew closely to Dahl's other accounts of it. "The Hurricane dipped its nose and dived toward the ground, and there wasn't a thing I could do," the *Post* story describes.

> I was doing about 250 miles an hour, so I suppose it took, roughly, two seconds to hit the deck, but it seemed a long two seconds. I remember looking down the nose of the machine at the ground and seeing a little clump of camel thorn growing there all by itself, and my stomach felt as though someone were using it as a pincushion for rusty hatpins.
>
> And then I knew I was still alive, because I could feel the heat around my legs, but I couldn't see a thing. I remember trying to get out, and catching hold of my straps and pulling away at them, but they wouldn't come. I couldn't for the life of me remember where the quick-release pin was placed, and all the time the fire was roasting my legs and hands. Maybe that's what stimulated my brain, because suddenly I remembered it. Of course, the pin was just down in front below the chest, holding all four straps together, and all one had to do was pull it out. I released it and tried to get out again, but there was something else there weighing me down, and I couldn't move. Once more I sat still and thought, and I could see a lot of red circles going around inside my head, and once more it came back to

> me suddenly. The parachute. Twist the release and press it in, and now let's get out of this fire.[24]

Official crash reports, though their subject matter is inherently thrilling, often seem flat—they are, after all, written by engineers and bureaucrats. Dahl's account poignantly combines overwhelming fears of pain and death alongside such small, keen close-ups as *where is that pin?* He took to heart Forester's basic but crucial advice about attending to specificities: "plenty of detail."

After freeing himself, Dahl continues, he still felt as if something was burning, so he rolled around in the sand and crawled away from the burning wreckage. Fictional details are mixed in about his comrades tending to each other's wounds (Dahl was alone when he crashed) and Italian snipers continuing to attack them (didn't happen), but the essence of Dahl's experience is rendered authentically: "And then it started to get cold. It always gets cold at night in the desert. . . . I kept spewing a lot of blood . . . I don't know how long we stayed there—maybe four or five hours . . . And then two or three British soldiers came up . . . I don't remember much more, except that I was shoved about a lot, and someone kept saying 'Take it easy.' I believe someone had some morphia."[25] That part is real.

This is the kind of document, the kind of discourse, that the humanist crash investigator valuably contributes to forensic analysis of debris fields. Dahl later published the original version of "A Piece of Cake," which describes the crash in the same general way as in "Shot Down Over Libya" but with a compelling interior monologue, befitting the fact that Dahl was actually on his own (and thus completely inside his own head) in the debris field.

> There was nothing to worry about. Nothing at all. Not until I felt the hotness around my legs. At first it was only a warmness and that was all right too, but all at once it was a hotness, a very stinging scorching hotness up and down the sides of each leg.
>
> I knew that the hotness was unpleasant, but that was all I knew. I disliked it, so I curled my legs up under the seat and waited. I think there was something wrong with the telegraph system between the body and the brain. It did not seem to be working very well. Somehow it was a bit slow in telling the brain all about it and in asking for instructions. But I believe a message eventually got through, saying, "Down here there is a great hotness. What shall we do? (Signed) Left Leg and Right Leg." For a long time there was no reply. The brain was figuring the matter out.
>
> Then slowly, word by word, the answer was tapped over the wires. "The-plane-is-burning. Get-out-repeat-get-out-get-out." The order was relayed to

> the whole system, to all the muscles in the legs, arms and body, and the muscles went to work. They tried their best; they pushed a little and pulled a little, and they strained greatly, but it wasn't any good. Up went another telegram, "Can't get out. Something holding us in." The answer to this one took even longer in arriving, so I just sat there waiting for it to come, and all the time the hotness increased. Something was holding me down and it was up to the brain to find out what it was. Was it giants' hands pressing on my shoulders, or heavy stones or houses or steam rollers or filing cabinets or gravity or was it ropes? Wait a minute. Ropes–ropes. The message was beginning to come through. It came very slowly. "Your–straps. Undo–your–straps." My arms received the message and went to work. They tugged at the straps, but they wouldn't undo. They tugged again and again, a little feebly, but as hard as they could, and it wasn't any use. Back went the message, "How do we undo the straps?"
>
> This time I think that I sat there for three or four minutes waiting for the answer. It wasn't any use hurrying or getting impatient. That was the one thing of which I was sure. But what a long time it was all taking. I said aloud, "Bugger it. I'm going to be burnt. I'm. . ." but I was interrupted. The answer was coming—no, it wasn't—yes, it was, it was slowly coming through. "Pull–out–the–quick–release–pin–you–bloody–fool–and–hurry."[26]

Dahl's two accounts, both gripping, offer keen insight into the narratology of a crash: the same material appears similar-but-different in different contexts. Dahl's multiple survival accounts resemble the kind of multi-perspectival forensic examination that crash investigators perform on mechanical debris to see what attributes—stresses, weaknesses, failures—they may reveal under different circumstances of flight and impact. Did a piece fail because of weather? Faulty design? Flawed maintenance? How does the fuel booster pump from one tank compare to the same pump from the other tank, and what can we infer from any difference? In Dahl's stories we can investigate such parallel questions as: is it difficult for the pilot to figure out how to remove the pin because of physical injury? Trauma? Disorientation? Inadequate training? The curious device of inserting dashes between every word in the telegraph-like messages between brain, arms, and muscles attunes our forensic spotlight to the precise meaning and resonance of each morpheme, just as engineers would isolate and examine every circuit and breaker in a crashed plane's wiring. If we are trying to figure out what went wrong in a crash, and how to survive it, it behooves the literary investigator to do just as Dahl's prose directs us: look–at–every–word. We must appreciate how vital it is for the mind to communicate and execute a strategy to emerge from the disaster, and Dahl's dash-dialogue emphasizes how a plane-crash narrative literarily reenacts the process of coping with a crash and escape.

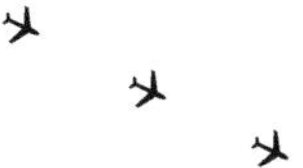

Dahl's 1943 book *The Gremlins* adds a quirky perspective on crashes. Gremlins were mythical creatures that, according to RAF pilot superstition, caused mechanical problems on aircraft. This is actually true: not that gremlins actually make planes crash, I don't think—though there are more things in heaven and earth than are dreamt of in my philosophy!—but that pilots imagined/pretended they did; Dahl didn't invent that. Gremlins crashed warplanes as revenge because their forest home had been destroyed, razed to build an aircraft factory.

When pilot Gus has the misfortune to see his aircraft's wings strafed with what appear to be bullet-holes, Dahl informs that the real culprit is "a little man, scarcely more than six inches high, with a large round face and a little pair of horns growing out of his head," wearing "shiny black suction boots, which made it possible for him to remain standing on the wing at 300 miles an hour," grasping "a large drill, almost as big as himself," busy "boring holes in the Hurricane's wing." Gus executes a few rolls trying to dislodge him, "but the suction boots held and the little man took no notice. He just went on boring, with a look of the purest concentration on his face. When he had done about four holes, he slung his drill over his shoulder, waddled up the wings, clambered onto the engine cowling, and bored a neat hole right through and into the magneto. The engine coughed; it sputtered; then it stopped."[27]

The gremlin attack forces Gus's plane down, though he manages to land smoothly. On his next mission they bring him down again (blow-torching his gas tank until it explodes), and again Gus survives, parachuting to safety. The story has a happy ending: Gus convinces his pesky little antagonists to join forces with the pilots against a common foe, the Germans. The RAF retrains them to repair rather than sabotage their planes: de-icing wings, mending punctures, straightening out bent propeller blades. I like the notion—as Dahl too must have—that pilots could eliminate crashes by reasoning with the forces that cause them, and coopting those forces to ensure safe flight.

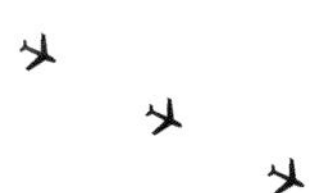

Dahl revisited his crash again in "Beware of the Dog" (1944), about a British pilot's recovery after he had been shot down. Still dazed from his injuries, hospital staff lead him to believe he is recuperating in Brighton, but when he crawls across the room and looks out the window, a sign that reads "*Garde au chien*" reveals that he is actually in Vichy France, and the nurses are spies trying to debrief him. In the story's last sentence, he tells them simply his name, rank, and serial number.

What I find so fascinating about this story is its opening passage, another hallucinatory-yet-vivid account of his desert crash (resituated, fictionally, to the European theatre). Like Yeats's poem about Major Gregory's crash, Dahl's crash-narrative has an eerie calm to it: an aestheticized escapist vision, an imaginative and surreal otherworldliness. The flight begins smoothly: "Down below there was only a vast white undulating sea of cloud. Above there was the sun, and the sun was white like the clouds, because it is never yellow when one looks at it from high in the air . . . It was quite easy. The machine was flying well, and he knew what he was doing. Everything is fine, he thought. I'm doing all right. I'm doing nicely."[28] The pre-crash moment, serenely beautiful, sets up the striking juxtaposition with what is about to happen. (Remember, keep your eyes peeled for the peripeteia, the reversal, that is inevitable in crash narratives.) Dahl doesn't describe what must have been an attack, but the next paragraph informs:

> He glanced down again at his right leg. There was not much of it left. The cannon shell had taken him on the thigh, just above the knee, and now there was nothing but a great mess and a lot of blood. But there was no pain. When he looked down, he felt as though he were seeing something that did not belong to him. It had nothing to do with him. It was just a mess which happened to be there in the cockpit; something strange and unusual and rather interesting. It was like finding a dead cat on the sofa.
>
> He really felt fine, and because he still felt fine, he felt excited and unafraid.

The calmness from the opening sentences continues here nearly unabated, although obviously something catastrophic has happened. The detached tone suggests that the pilot, in shock from the attack, doesn't immediately feel the pain—at least momentarily, he steps out of his own corporeal tragedy. Perhaps Dahl continues the story's peaceful pace because the plane is still aloft: it has not (yet) crashed, so it still embodies the smooth, exhilarating aerodynamic energy that comes from flying an airplane through the sky. But the reality soon becomes clearer: the pilot saw

> the sun shining on the engine cowling of his machine. He saw the rivets in the metal, and he remembered where he was. He realized that he was no longer feeling good; that he was sick and giddy. His head kept falling forward onto his chest because his neck seemed no longer to have any strength.... I'm going to pass out, he thought. Any moment now I'm going to pass out.

He realizes his plane is going down and he will have to bail out; he is significantly impaired. Seeing that he is over the English Channel, he turns sharply so he will fall out into the sea.

> As he fell he opened his eyes, because he knew that he must not pass out before he had pulled the cord. On one side he saw the sun; on the other he saw the whiteness of the clouds, and as he fell, as he somersaulted in the air, the white clouds chased the sun and the sun chased the clouds. They chased each other in a small circle; they ran faster and faster, and there was the sun and the clouds and the clouds and the sun, and the clouds came nearer until suddenly there was no longer any sun, but only a great whiteness. The whole world was white, and there was nothing in it. It was so white that sometimes it looked black, and after a time it was either white or black, but mostly it was white. He watched it as it turned from white to black, and then back to white again, and the white stayed for a long time, but the black lasted only for a few seconds. He got into the habit of going to sleep during the white periods, and of waking up just in time to see the world when it was black. But the black was very quick. Sometimes it was only a flash, like someone switching off the light, and switching it on again at once, and so whenever it was white, he dozed off.[29]

It's a fascinating literary touch, the visual alternation from white to black, to white, to black, and so on. Though I've never seen any comparable sensory description in official investigation reports, I feel certain that Dahl's insight here is keenly relevant to understanding a plane crash. Despite the danger that this black/white dissipation of flight indicates, there's still something almost reassuring here, a continuation of the aviational bliss that began the story, and begins every flight, and that endures throughout Dahl's fiction, in *Giant Peach* and *Charlie and the Chocolate Factory* and elsewhere, oddly unsullied by his own near-death experience. His memory of that experience is sometimes crisp, sometimes fuzzy and foggy, possibly a trauma-induced protection, which may explain how he can tell his crash story over and over without apparently retraumatizing himself. The process of crashing in "Beware of the Dog" is almost like a dance through the sky as he falls through it. It is represented not as overwhelming and terrifying (as I strongly imagine it would actually seem, at least to me), but rather stylized, simplified, aesthetically calm(ed). It is so gentle that he falls asleep. It strikes me that if one had to experience a crash and could choose how that would feel, Dahl's version would be a pretty good choice.

What is it, finally, that allows someone with such harrowing injuries to survive agonizing bodily and emotional trauma? Dahl poses that question again and again: is it innate human instinct? Personal perseverance? Luck? (It was not bravery,[30] he had said.) How are those vital impulses to escape near-death "telegraphed" through a body in traumatic pain? (He answers parodically in "A Piece of Cake": "The–plane–is–burning. Get–out–repeat–get–out–get–out.") This basic question of how one survives resonates too in Hemingway's writing; in Herzog's cinematic account of Koepcke's story, as well as in her own memoir; and in Saint-Exupéry's meditations on a crash that did not kill him. If the writer-survivors have not comprehensively or definitively answered this (fundamentally existentialist) question, they've done the best they could, and I will not presume to add anything more concrete than what they tell us: I defer to them.

✈ *The Little Prince*

In Antoine de Saint-Exupéry's beloved 1943 fable, an aviator narrates his adventure of crashing in the Sahara, where he encountered a charmingly quizzical boy who had also fallen out of the sky (from asteroid B-612). The pilot becomes enraptured with the little prince's stories of picaresque travel across the galaxy where he met such characters as a businessman who thinks he owns the stars he counts and a frenzied lamplighter on a tiny planet where dawn and dusk recur every minute. The pilot is taken with his new friend in this paean to childish wisdom and curiosity, imagination and folly, though he also worries whether the prince may be naively oblivious to the world's dangers.

The prince and the aviator are somehow linked, paired. Possibly the prince represents the child that the aviator once was, or wishes he had been. Or perhaps the adult aviator, especially as he is overwhelmed by his recent crash, wishes to integrate this quirky boy's spirited resilience into his present self. On some level the prince is merely a fantasy: an apparition, a delusion, that the pilot wills into being (consciously or unconsciously) to accompany him as he deals with being stranded.

The aviator's crash itself is minimally discussed. On page three, Saint-Exupéry recounts the incident:

> So I lived all alone, without anyone I could really talk to, until I had to make a crash landing in the Sahara six years ago. Something in my plane's engine had broken, and since I had neither a mechanic nor passengers in the plane with me, I was preparing to undertake the difficult repair job by myself. For me it was a matter of life or death: I had only enough drinking water for eight days.[31]

The pilot has two (related) problems here: his plane has crashed, and he is lonely—alienated. The six-year flashback-frame implies that the pilot eventually finds his way out of the desert. *The Little Prince* shows how the pilot solves both his problems at once, transcending both geographical and psychological isolation. His encounter with this delightful child allegorically depicts how to survive a nonfatal crash, and the allegory is all the more potent for its sketchy elusiveness. The story focuses squarely on the prince's explorations, his philosophy, and his personality, rather than (as in almost every other crash narrative) the actual crash. The debris field, such as it is, manifests no engine or hull wreckage, but instead, quirkier artifacts: a silly ermine-mantled king, a cross-sectioned boa constrictor who has eaten an elephant, an ineffectual geographer who has never gone anywhere, a fecund baobab forest, a narcissistic rose.

After that quick passage at the story's beginning laying out the crash, it appears only twice again, in the briefest of asides. In the story's twenty-fourth section (out of twenty-seven), the pilot says, "It was now the eighth day since my crash landing in the desert, and I'd listened to the story about the sales-clerk as I was drinking the last drop of my water supply." The reference to the crash, and the prospect of imminent death as water runs out, appear as little more than sidebars to the prince's beguiling yarns. The clerk to whom he refers has invented a pill that satiates people's thirst for a week, thereby saving fifty-three minutes. The prince wonders what one would do with those extra minutes: "I'd walk very slowly toward a water fountain."[32] The pilot's crash landing and his ticking timeline are subordinated to the prince's story—which informs, in the mode of make-believe, how one might survive the desert without water: obviously, extremely pertinent to the pilot's crisis. Yet *The Little Prince* is nevertheless a bona fide crash narrative, albeit a kind of shadow-crash-narrative, a displacement of a more conventional crash narrative. The aviator created this imaginative young fellow to help handle his own situation: to keep from going crazy in the desert; to keep his mind working, percolating, without fixating unduly on the trauma at hand.

The crash story resolves in part twenty-six, the penultimate section, as the prince tells the pilot:

> "I'm glad you found what was the matter with your engine. Now you'll be able to fly again . . ."
>
> "How did you know?" I was just coming to tell him that I had been successful beyond all hope!
>
> He didn't answer my question; all he said was, "I'm leaving today too." And then, sadly, "It's much further . . . It's much more difficult."[33]

I suggest that the prince is "leaving"—he arranges to be bitten by a snake, which may somehow return him (alive? postmortally?) back to B-612 to tend his rose—because he is no longer needed now that the pilot has solved his airplane problem.

The Little Prince is Saint-Exupéry's oddly delightful explanation of how to survive a crash that hasn't killed you. How do you keep yourself going? How do you suppress the fear that you could still die? How do you rise up out of the wreckage? His answer is: in your imagination. Invent a happier world to displace the conventional debris field and perhaps, somehow, wishing will make it so. (I've cited Vera Lynn's wisdom already: she's a font of insight for humanist crash investigators. I've never seen NTSB reports address *wishing* as a safety technique, but obviously, since many people do it in the throes of aviation catastrophes, it should be prominently acknowledged: you heard it here first.)

The strengths and hopes of children, of yourself as a child, can sustain you when grown-up qualities falter. Adulthood (including such "adult" enterprises as aviation) has failed the pilot, as Saint-Exupéry was left bereft in the North African desert. The point of this debris field, filled with selfish roses, lamplighters, and sheep-eating foxes, is: mind over matter. This is a common thread in the other survival stories I investigate as well. Non-fatal crashes pose significant physical and aviational challenges, but also, crucially, psychological challenges. It behooves survivors to do what they can to keep their minds calm and nimble. I suggest that a copy of *The Little Prince* is as important as flares and first aid supplies to stock in a crash-survival kit. A very slender volume, it won't take up much space.

✈ *Lord of the Flies*

Lord of the Flies (1954) precipitated literary and cinematic narrative traditions of stories that all pretty closely rehash William Golding's basic template. The term given to such stories, *robinsonade* ("a story about being marooned on a desert island or some similarly inhospitable place"[34]), shows Golding's own formative influence in Daniel Defoe's eighteenth-century *Robinson Crusoe*, and also offers another salient example of how shipwrecks palimpsestically underlie plane wrecks (as discussed in Chapter 2).

In this genre's modern iteration, an airplane crashes in a remote location; some passengers survive, often many, though usually not the pilots. It seems unlikely that the stranded passengers will be rescued quickly, if at all, so they must cobble together some kind of community, constrained by scant resources available in an isolated site. They will have to draw on their pre-crash social experiences, values, and skills, but unfortunately those tend not to translate well to present circumstances. A lush island/jungle/mountain setting may initially seem enchanting but soon becomes hostile and even terrifying.

The survivors establish a society that might seem utopian early on, though it always deteriorates. The dystopic (crashed) airplane is a good metaphor for the dystopian community that emerges in the wake of that crash as they contend with their devastating alienation from mainstream society. The pilots often die in these stories because factually, a nose-down crash, the most common kind, is likely to kill those in the very front. But also narratologically, dead pilots highlight the castaways' leadership vacuum, increasing the pressure on them to organize quickly (which often exacerbates social dysfunction: Rome was not built in a day). The pilots, fit and sensible ex-military types, likely could have offered guidance about survival skills; without them, the survivors are on their own. In Golding's novel, there were other adults on board besides the flight crew—one boy remembers a man with a megaphone—but they, too, have disappeared.

Although it would seem self-evident that survivors in these narratives would be better off if they formed mutually supportive fellowships, there are usually forces (greed, fear, short-sightedness, hubris, anxiety, secrets) that instead encourage divisiveness and totalitarianism. The survivors often hunt, which should be a way to enhance survival prospects, but instead, often descends into wanton brutality and bloodsport, doing the community more harm than good.

Cannibalism occurs not infrequently in these societies, from *Robinson Crusoe* to the real-life story of Andes survivors in another book that resonates with *Lord of the Flies*, Piers Paul Read's *Alive* (1974). Uruguayan Air Force charter flight 571 from Montevideo, Uruguay, to Santiago, Chile, crashed in the Andes on October 13, 1972, due to pilot error—losing situational awareness, they flew into a mountain. Initially twelve died and thirty-three survived, but when they were found two months later, only sixteen remained alive; the others were . . . dinner.

(Golding's boys didn't quite get around to eating each other, but it seems like it wasn't far off.)

Mysterious monsters, real or imagined, are ubiquitous: *Lord of the Flies* features "the beast." Television series *Lost* and *Yellowjackets* depict especially florid monsters, embodying the omnipresent unknown dangers in an unknown place. As these kinds of stories unfold, the act of survival comes to feel horrific: ironically, existentially, it starts to seem as if it might have been better had everyone just perished on impact.

The dysfunctional milieu in this tradition, exemplified by the English schoolboys' Hobbesian devolution in *Lord of the Flies*, is an implicit consequence of the crash itself. A plane crash is terrible, and even if it doesn't kill everyone right away, the harrowing tragedy still haunts the tableau. The torment unfolds at a slower pace than when the crash kills all aboard, but there is nonetheless an abyss of depression, confusion, crisis, trauma, and dread (unless you strike up a friendship with an imaginary little prince to distract you from the funk). *The Wilds, Manifest, Departure, Lost, Yellowjackets, Wrecked*, and *Flight 29 Down* are among the many redux versions of *Lord of the Flies*, which was itself cinematically adapted by Peter Brook in 1963 and Harry Hook in 1990. Game Jolt created a *Lord of the Flies* video game in 2014. Musical reiterations include Rupert Lally's *Notes from the Island* (2018) and U2's 1980 "Shadow and Tall Trees" (named after a chapter from the novel).

In *Lord of the Flies*, like most other works in this genre, precise details are elusive about why the plane went down. The narratives offer little that would aid a conventional crash investigation report. We know Golding's boys were evacuated from England after the outbreak of World War III with its anticipated nuclear destruction and impending global apocalypse—or possibly the nuclear attacks had already begun? It's unclear from the novel as it now stands. Golding's editor removed a lengthy prologue describing the atomic warfare from which the children took refuge, because he felt the context of why the plane was flying to wherever it was going didn't need to be part of the story; it's all about what happens on the island. Numerous proposed titles emphasize the primacy of setting: They Came to an Island; Island Refuge; The Isle Is Full of Noises; Beast on the Island; Beast in the Jungle (already taken!); Smoke on the Island; Trouble Island; Let's Play Islands; Offspring of an Island; Island Trouble; Island Story; My Island.[35] The novel was about the island, not the plane. The point of the aircraft, a *deus ex machina*, was simply to get the boys to the island.

But though Golding and his editor didn't feel the plane was important, I do. Did the plane crash as a result of nuclear combat? Did it run out of gas? Engine fire? Pilot error? We have no idea. A good way to signal an existential narrative is to open with a plane crash and then give no clue about what is certainly our first question, how it happened.

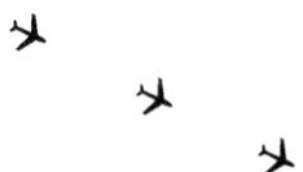

Debris fields in crash-survival narratives are usually near the constructed communities. Yet surprisingly (to me) in *Lord of the Flies* and its offshoots, characters pay little attention to how the crash site lingers near their new society. They are often marginalized or ignored, perhaps because the debris reminds survivors of the past, while they now must focus on the future. Debris fields represent ground zero, the farthest place from safety and civilization. It might make sense to stay near the wreckage because if and when rescuers did eventually show up, they would be looking for that spot, easier to detect from the air than a few makeshift tents or firepits. But survivors in these stories usually want to get away from the debris, perhaps so the symbolic and literal milieu of failure doesn't jinx their own hopes for success.

The crashes always happen early on—the *deus ex machina* is ironized because the machine, a malfunctioning airplane, is diabolical rather than godly. (*Diabolus ex machina*: is that a thing?) They are establishing shots, and the stories proceed from there. But I will linger on the wreckage, and the haunting presence of the shattered aircraft that brought them to their godforsaken destinations. Though sublimated, the debris fields nevertheless claim our attention—they always do: we can't look away.

In *Lord of the Flies*, the debris field is there but not there. It is described literally—and only sparsely—early in the novel. In the opening pages two boys walk around after escaping from the wreckage, trying to figure out what happened.

> "When we was coming down I looked through one of them windows. I saw the other part of the plane. There were flames coming out of it."
>
> He looked up and down the scar.
>
> "And this is what the cabin done."
>
> The fair boy reached out and touched the jagged end of a trunk. For a moment he looked interested.

> "What happened to it?" he asked. "Where's it got to now?"
> "That storm dragged it out to sea.'"

The first boy, who turns out to be Piggy, repeats later: "The plane was shot down in flames. Nobody knows where we are. We may be here a long time."[36] Apart from such brief references, though, the debris field is ignored (with one compelling exception, which I will investigate in a moment). There must have been many airplane pieces, equipment, luggage, and body parts, but the boys don't see these, or if they do, they don't talk about it. Even if the wreckage was swept out to sea, still, the plane would have broken into thousands of parts, large and small, and it's highly improbable that the storm could have removed all of that, leaving the scene spic and span. In any event, for the rest of the novel nobody mentions the debris, or the crash itself. Perhaps it's too traumatic to feature more emphatically in the narrative, or perhaps it's just not the point: it happened, and now they have to move forward.

Other stories in the *Flies* tradition, too, tend not to linger on the crash—neither the event nor the debris—but instead go on to develop whatever communities and adventures their narratives will present. Fair play, though if it were up to me, I'd focus much more on the debris field . . . but it would be a dull world if we were all alike. I will note, though, that Damon Lindelof's *Lost*, which went on (and on and on) for six seasons, 2004-10, in the shaggiest shaggy-dog-story that ever emanated from a debris field, was unwatchable by the end. As it doused viewers with "The Others" (the island's malevolent occupants who were there before the crash), the Dharma Initiative hatch (an extensive underground world full of guns, medicine, and way too many subplots), time travel, and so many other supernatural and supranarratorial phenomena, it became incoherent. Pardon my biases, but I think a plane crash is enough to sustain a series all on its own; it doesn't need hyperplotting.

Golding's debris field is evanescent except for one compelling detail: that scar in the ground made as the plane impacted the island. Because it's so minimalist compared to the usual crash site aesthetic, it is all the more powerful as a symbol—it's all that remains of the debris field, and we know how keenly investigators (including novel-reading investigators) need debris fields.

Golding introduces the scar at the very beginning, before revealing that a plane has crashed:

> All round him the long scar smashed into the jungle was a bath of heat. . . . The undergrowth at the side of the scar was shaken and a multitude of raindrops fell

> pattering. . . . In the middle of the scar he stood on his head and grinned at the reversed fat boy.

After Piggy's brief account of the crash and the ensuing scar, that mark in the earth recurs frequently throughout the novel. It is strikingly discordant compared to the rest of the island's landscape:

> The shore was fledged with palm trees. These stood or leaned or reclined against the light and their green feathers were a hundred feet up in the air. The ground beneath them was a bank covered with coarse grass, torn everywhere by the upheavals of fallen trees, scattered with decaying coconuts and palm saplings. Behind this was the darkness of the forest proper and the open space of the scar.

It remains a point of reference to the story's origin:

> "That's where we landed." Beyond falls and cliffs there was a gash visible in the trees; there were the splintered trunks and then the drag, leaving only a fringe of palm between the scar and the sea. . . . Ralph sketched a twining line from the bald spot on which they stood down a slope, a gully, through flowers, round and down to the rock where the scar started.[37]

Note the reference to "where we landed" rather than "crashed," another sign of how they erase everything having to do with the crash except for the scar.

What does the scar mean? Wiser minds than mine have mulled this question: cue up hundreds of term papers (sorry, "study guides") available for purchase from sites like gradesaver.com when you Google "What does the scar mean in *Lord of the Flies*?"

> What, exactly, does the scar represent in *Lord of the Flies*? Beyond physical accidents and injuries that will happen on the island, it is an indicator of fear, pain, trauma, and the inability to heal perfectly. The symbol of the scar appears throughout the novel as the boys wreak havoc on the island, and on each other.[38]

> The scar is both a figurative and literal scar used in the literary devices of personification and allusion. The image of a giant scar, the long gash in the jungle's landscape left by the boys' crashing airplane, is one of the book's most powerful symbols. The scar appears periodically throughout the novel and reinforces many of the novel's overarching themes. On a very basic level, the scar is the path that the boys' wrecked plane has cut across the island. Besides its literal (actual) meaning, the scar is also a symbol, and we can interpret the scar figuratively (symbolically). For example, the word "scar" brings to mind bodily trauma: deep cuts and bloody gashes. Scars typically refer to wounds on humans

or animals, but in *Lord of the Flies*, the injury appears on the island itself. In this sense, the novel attributes human characteristics to the natural world. In literary studies, we call this technique personification. We can also interpret the scar as an allusion to original sin and mankind's fall in the Bible.[39]

A rip in the forest caused by the crash landing of the boys' plane on the island. The scar symbolizes that man, and his savage nature, destroys paradise merely by entering it.[40]

In William Golding's *Lord of the Flies*, symbolism is used to depict a greater meaning within the objects that appear throughout the novel. One of the recurring symbols is the scar created in the story. The scar is created when the plane that the boys were in crashed onto the island. This was meant to represent man destroying nature simply by entering it. When the plane crashed it left a scarce amount of what was previously there. The plane is created by man and destroys the nature that it tore through. This creates a deeper understanding to what the novel is depicting.[41]

The scar symbolizes the boys' violent intrusion into the natural world and their destruction of it. As the story progresses, the scar takes on deeper meaning, representing the boys' increasing savagery and their descent into darkness. When the boys first arrive on the island, the scar is seen as a potential source of rescue, a place where they might be spotted by passing ships or planes. However, as the boys' behavior becomes more violent and primal, the scar is forgotten and left to heal on its own. It is a powerful symbol of the boys' loss of civilization and their descent into savagery.[42]

The scar is literally the dent the boys' plane put on the island. This island was an Eden, a perfect setting. The scar represents men's or boys' presence on this perfect place. The scar is the only visible imperfection on the lush island. This imperfection represents man and his very imperfect nature.[43]

Not bad, plagiarism factories: the diction is a bit stilted, but we get the point. If I may synthesize all this (with my own thoughts—I didn't pay for these): the scar, left by the fuselage of the crashing plane that was subsequently swept out to sea, marks the crash site, but one that is weirdly devoid of all the debris that normally comprises such a setting. It is literal, reflecting the crashed plane's physical impact and imprint, and symbolic, representing human fallibility and violence, but it's also an aporia, an elision. The scar marks where something isn't: the trees, and also the airplane.

The boys might have chosen to grapple with the debris field and try to come to terms with it. Instead they mostly miss or suppress the significance of the crash and its aftermath, turning their attention to what they consider more pressing issues. By the novel's end they have done an awful job of whatever they hoped to achieve, so the lesson would seem to be that they should have spent more time reflecting on what the scar meant. Because they did not discover or attribute their own meaning to the scar, the world at large (i.e., the author, Golding-as-God) inscribed it with meaning, as all the "study guide" investigations reveal.

I'm not sure this is Golding's moral, but it's certainly mine: *Figure out what a plane crash means.* Don't get distracted by conches and bonfires, egos and social experiments. Everything ended in the debris field, and everything begins in the debris field. Attend to the scars—*both literally and figuratively*—which denote as plainly as possible what is damaged, and what needs to heal. (And then after that, of course, go on and transform the debris into cultural artifacts that facilitate restoration.)

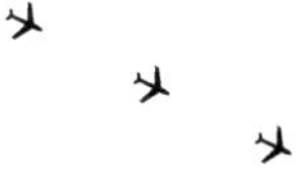

The debris field is a scar: a wound. Scars fade, probably … eventually … somewhat. But still, they're always there, reminders, even if barely visible. A scar is (literally, bodily) a site of pain and violence, but also of regeneration. Many people wear their scars proudly, testimony to what they have survived. A scar on the earth caused by a plane-crash impact may be a sacred site, a burial ground of sorts. Its sacredness is partly ironic, because it is simultaneously profane. It could be a pilgrimage destination, or a site of dark tourism. Visiting a crash site intentionally—as I have done myself in the course of my investigations—contrasts disconcertingly, if you think about it, with the crash victims who "went there" unwillingly.

Tim Lambert's family owned a plot of land where he fished and picked blackberries as a boy, in Shanksville, PA, the site of United flight 93's crash on 9/11. In the following months and years, Lambert returned—"There was just a burned out pit in a field and a charred line of trees"—to help victims' families comb the woods, the debris field, for anything they might appreciate recovering. When he began these missions, "Charred pieces of a paperback book slowly drifted by as a breeze picked up. Another strong whiff of jet fuel." But five years after the crash, Lambert writes, "when I stepped out of the car at the crash site, the air smelled like sugar maples and wildflowers" instead of jet fuel. "The ground was healing. The crash site, once so brown, barren and charred, was now a vibrant green. The grass was back, tall and lush, and so were the wildflowers. The surviving hemlocks stood tall, although they still bore scars from that day, missing branches from base to canopy." Today, "a field once scarred by a smoldering crater," is now "a living tribute to the forty passengers and crew who likely saved the US Capitol and hundreds of lives through their attempts to retake the cockpit." It is a *living tribute* because the trees that were scorched have come back to life, and because the people who died there enabled others to survive, to live.[44]

For years, "reminders of the devastation from the September day still surfaced. I came across a large piece of insulated wiring resting at the base of a tree," Lambert writes. "The land was still telling the story of Flight 93. But it was also healing—just like some of the families." Lambert visited the scarred/sacred ground with Ken Nacke, whose brother Joey died there. Ken struggled to cope with Joey's loss, and "it was in this field where Kenny felt he really turned a corner in his grief."

> As we stood near a 17-ton sandstone boulder placed at the point of impact, Ken told me about his brother. He was 42 years old, a weightlifter with a Superman tattoo on his arm. Ken gestured around us. Here, he told me, was the place he'd been able to finally subdue his grief. One day, he said, he'd been sitting on a bench, soaking in the wildlife and beautiful surroundings. The smells. The peacefulness.
>
> A pair of bear cubs wandered out of the woods. Maybe 200 yards away. Stopping short of the impact site, they started roughhousing. Wrestling. Rolling around. Swiping at each other. Chasing each other.
>
> He was fascinated and just watched. His mind went to a time when he and Joey would battle. In family rooms. In the grass. In a way only brothers can. He believed it was a message from Joey. He felt like it was a kick in the ass. Cherish the memories you have but move forward and honor your sibling by living your life.
>
> As we headed back to our cars, a baby deer trotted on the road in front of us. It stopped and watched. It took one tentative step in our direction and then bolted into the trees. Ken smiled. The healing continued.[45]

This 9/11 story has little to do with Golding's novel except to make the point that scars are painful, but eventually they heal. (In *Lord of the Flies*, the "healing" manifests as the boys burn down their dystopian forest and the British navy finally rescues them from the terrible community they have created, possibly—but possibly not—extirpating the social and moral darkness they cultivated on the island.) Perhaps the Shanksville crash narrative does not fit in this chapter about crash survivors since everyone on that flight died. But scars happen, and heal, for those who survive in another sense: the loved ones who survive the victims, those who grieve. Their scars will never vanish, but may become less raw and painful. Tim Lambert's grass and flowers and hemlock trees embody this healing, as does Ken Nacke's appreciation of the natural beauty, the rambunctious bear cubs. A debris field represents pure destruction: littered with burnt paperbacks, jet fuel, corpses, it is a macabre archive of all that has been ruined. And yet there also can be—there *will* be—innocent animals, and sugar maples, and sunlight, and peace.

Wings of Hope

There but for the grace of God . . .

President Theodore Roosevelt was (possibly) supposed to be flying with Orville Wright the day the first fatal plane crash killed, instead, Wright's passenger Lt. Thomas Selfridge. Reba McEntire was planning to be on the plane that killed eight members of her tour when it crashed on the way from San Diego to Ft. Wayne, but skipped the flight because she'd been sick and still felt weak. William Willard "won" (but in a very real sense, *lost*) a coin flip with his son to fly on Harriet Quimby's ill-fated Blériot. Tommy Alsop lost (*won!*) a coin flip that gave Ritchie Valens his seat on Buddy Holly's charter flight the day the music died, which Waylon Jennings, too, might have been on, but wasn't.

In his 1998 documentary *Wings of Hope*, German director Werner Herzog recalls that he crossed paths with that film's lead character twenty-seven years earlier in the very airport terminal where the film opens. Juliane Koepcke, then seventeen years old, took Lansa flight 508 from Lima Peru, headed to Pucallpa, deep in the Amazon, with her mother on December 24, 1971. Her parents, originally from Germany, worked at a remote conservation outpost they had established called Panguana. "This is a film that lay dormant in me for many years," Herzog says, "because I myself had almost been part of this very catastrophe."[46] Herzog's earlier flights were canceled because Lansa was short on airplanes, not yet having replaced one that crashed the previous year. Koepcke recounts in her own version of this crash narrative, *When I Fell From the Sky: The True Story of One Woman's Miraculous Survival*:

> In the crowd, jostling for boarding passes, is the filmmaker Werner Herzog, who has already been trying indignantly for twenty-four hours to get seats for him and his film crew on a plane to Pucallpa, for his flight the previous day was canceled too. He has to get to the jungle to shoot scenes for his movie *Aguirre, the Wrath of God*. He puts up a fight to be able to fly in our plane, and he is really angry when he cannot. In all the commotion I take no notice of him. Only many years later will he tell me that we might even have directly encountered each other that day.

Fate smiled on Herzog: flight 508 crashed halfway to its destination after a lightning strike, killing 91—the world's deadliest lightning-strike disaster in aviation (so many lists and categories!). The accident report faulted the pilots' decision to fly into hazardous weather they should have avoided. On the day before Christmas, they were probably suffering from get-there-itis: conversations captured on the CVR revealed that they "chatted about the upcoming Christmas celebration, about their children and families and how they hoped to return to Lima as quickly as possible." (Is it coincidental that Tuula Hyvärinen's and Ernest Hemingway's crashes were also Christmas-adjacent? Do pilots cut corners in anticipation of the festivities?)

The plane, a Lockheed Electra turboprop, looked "as good as new," Koepcke wrote.

> However, it's far from it, as we'll later find out. This type of airplane was actually designed for use in desert regions and had already been taken out of service in the United States for years. Because it has trouble withstanding turbulence—for its wings were, unlike those of other airliners, fastened firmly to the fuselage—a turboprop could not be less suited for a flight over the Andes. No, it was not new, but assembled entirely from spare parts of other airplanes. Of course, we didn't know that at the time.[47]

Everyone died except Juliane, who miraculously survived the airplane's plunge into the forest and then walked for eleven days until she found help. Growing up at Panguana fostered an intimate knowledge of the jungle, allowing her to navigate terrain most would have found impassible.

In *Wings of Hope*—its German title was *Julianes Sturz in den Dschungel* ("Juliane's Fall into the Jungle")—Herzog and Koepcke return to the crash site with a film crew as the director plumbs her memories and reconstructs her experience. They fly the same route Juliane took twenty-seven years earlier, though this time on Aero Peru; Lansa, which had an abysmal safety record, ceased operations a week after the crash. She doesn't love flying: "Since then, I have lost confidence in pilots and airplanes," she says in the film. "I listen to every noise. And especially on a flight over mountains, because of the frequent turbulence."[48]

Telling Herzog her story (on the plane! while flying over the Amazon! sitting in seat 19 F, the same one she'd been in on Lansa that day!), she remembers that the first 25 minutes of her 1971 flight were fine, but then it became very cloudy and dark. Her mother grew anxious when she saw the storm front approaching. "It was frightening how the clouds streaked by, as if they were living creatures." The sky turned pitch black, broken by streaks of lightning. She had never experienced such terribly rough air, she remembered. Christmas presents flew out of the overhead bins.[49] "The pilot does not avoid the thunderstorm, but flies straight into the cauldron of hell," Koepcke writes. She saw a blinding light on the right wing, as if lightning had struck an engine:

> With a jolt, the tip of the airplane falls steeply downward. Even though I'm in a window seat all the way in the back, I can see the whole aisle to the cockpit, which is below me. The physical laws have been suspended. It's like an earthquake. No, it is worse. Because now we're racing downward. We're falling. People are screaming in panic, shrill cries for help; the roar of the plummeting turbines, which I will hear again and again in my dreams, engulfs me. And there, over everything, clear as glass, I hear my mother say quite calmly, "Now it's all over."[50]

The film's English title, much better than the German one, comes from an inscription on Pucallpa Airport's monument to the crash victims reading *ALAS DE ESPERANZA* (wings of hope), featuring angels—who are immune to aviation disasters—surrounding a map of the region. An arrow points to *ZONA DONDE SE ENCONTRO A "LANSA"* (the area where the Lansa was found) marked by a bas-relief figure of a crashing plane. The motif recurs when Koepcke speaks of her eventual rescuer: "He was the first person I saw, and it was as if an angel were coming toward me."[51]

Herzog films Koepcke seeing this monument for the first time as they arrive in Pucallpa. "It touches me strangely considering that I emerged as the sole embodiment of hope whereas all the others remained without hope in this disaster," she remarks, reading what she calls the monument's "highly emotional inscription": "Brethren, we are united here through our longing to reach the warmth of the sacred heart of home. Christmas 1971 we were on our way hither.

But instead we were cast into dark eternity."[52] Herzog presents a uniquely charged intertextuality he has arranged between the crash narrative and the monument—what we might call the memorial narrative—that I've found in few other artifacts from cultural debris fields. It's not just that Herzog takes his title from the monument, but also that he opens the film with it, and his story unfurls—spatializes—the memorial's static geographic/aeronautic map. *Wings of Hope* is so detailed, in Koepcke's own voice, her striking demeanor (reserved, precise, Germanic) with her own recollections, and her memories of enduring (albeit not crippling) trauma—and it's all filmed *in an airport, at a crash memorial, on an airplane*, and *in a debris field*. You can imagine how resonant, and unique, a humanist crash investigator considers this cinematic creation: if you like my book, you'll love Herzog's film.

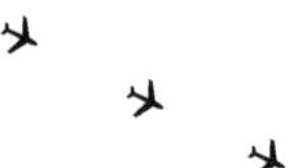

A half-century after the crash, Koepcke and her husband carry on the work in Amazonian conservation her parents began at Panguana, Peru's oldest ecological research station. Having seen how drastically the forest has changed in her lifetime due to agricultural deforestation and development, she made it her mission to reverse that destruction and preserve as much of the forest as she could. "People wonder with amazement how I manage to get on airplanes time and again," she writes. "I manage it because I have to if I want to return to the rain forest. But it's hard."[53]

How did Koepcke survive the two-mile fall? She has three theories, and she believes her amazing story probably involves a combination of all three. First: thunderclouds are subject to dramatic updrafts (rising wind). If her plane got caught up in these air pockets, it could have significantly slowed its acceleration as it fell toward impact. Second: she remained strapped into her seat during the plunge, and thinks the row (19 D/E/F), detached from the airplane's body, might have been spiraling, as falling maple seeds would; that too would have slowed her rate of descent. And third: when she ended up on the ground, the forest above her was full of tall trees densely intertwined with vines that might have acted like a net, slowing and softening her fall.

The media—wrongly, in her opinion—described the crash scene as the "green hell of the jungle."[54] But Koepcke loved the forest: "The jungle caught me and saved me," she said. "It was not its fault that I landed there."[55] The jungle saved her not just because the tree canopy broke her fall, but also because her intimate knowledge of the biota—its plants and ecosystems, its rivers and pathways, its many aids to survival for people who know what resources there are and how to use them—helped her find her way out. "I went to the school of the jungle. There I got to know its rules; the jungle became my home, and I learned which dangers loom in it and which don't."[56]

"If you ever get lost in the rainforest," her parents had advised her, "find moving water and follow its course to a river, where human settlements are likely to be." Walking away from the crash site she saw a creek, which became a stream and then eventually a river. After eleven days, she stumbled into a camp of forest workers who fed her cassava and poured gasoline into her wounds to flush out maggots that protruded "like asparagus tips." They brought her to a village, and then on to safety.[57]

While Juliane was walking through the Amazon, investigators conducted the most exhaustive search in Peruvian aviation history, but the jungle seemed to have swallowed the wreckage: they found nothing until Juliane emerged. Rescuers were then able to discover the crash site because she recognized a plant that was growing nearby, allowing local residents to pinpoint the location. After a difficult journey through the jungle, rescue teams finally made it to the debris field three weeks after the crash. There were no other survivors, though they ascertained that fourteen people had not died immediately in the crash but perished sometime afterwards.[58] The highlights of this story, which has been retold many times, are Juliane's survival and her walk to safety. (Koepcke finds all the accounts apart from Herzog's inaccurate and facile.) As fascinating as that part of the story is, I'm going to cover it just briefly, to get to what most captivates *my* interest for this investigation, which is, of course, the debris field.

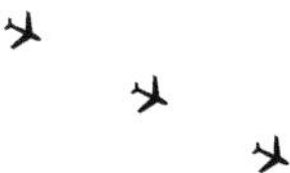

When she came to, Juliane crawled around looking for her mother but soon realized she was alone. She had lost her glasses and had only one shoe; she had a fractured clavicle and a deep cut on her calf. She remembers finding a bag of candies and a big Peruvian Christmas cake. She decided it would have been futile to remain at the crash site waiting for help, so when she saw a spring she followed it. In *Wings of Hope*, as she reenacts this trip, we see the intense resilience and rationality that she must have had as a teenager: she's cool as a cucumber.

She saw planes circling for a few days, but when they stopped she believed the search was done and she was on her own. Four days into her walk, she came across another row of seats, with three dead bodies. "It was the only contact I ever had with anyone from this plane. The seats were stuck in the ground. They were literally drilled three feet deep. They must have hit like a bullet. . . . They must have been killed instantly. They were driven into the soil head-first. Only their feet stuck out." There were two men and a woman. "I didn't want to touch them, but I wanted to make sure that the woman wasn't my mother. I grabbed a stick and turned one of her feet carefully so I could see the toenails. They were polished, and I took a deep breath. My mother never used polish on her nails."

Koepcke faced gruesome mosquitoes and stinging icy rain. She became apathetic and felt as if she was in a trance. On the eleventh day she had grown very weak; settling down on a sandbank, she saw a boat and then found a path which led to a hut, where she encountered her "angel." (He still lived there when she returned with Herzog, and they reconnected warmly.) He cleaned her and took her to a village, where people ran away because she looked so awful they thought she was a forest demon. Her rescuers brought her to a small airstrip, and she flew (!!!) to a missionary hospital, where she spent months recovering.[59]

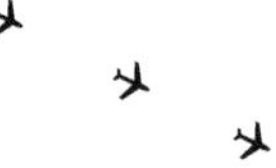

The debris is still there. Usually after a crash, the wreckage is studied, perhaps partially reconstructed, stored away somewhere or disposed of; the site is cleaned up, the debris removed. But sometimes, especially in remote locations where nobody is around to complain about the mess, it's easier just to leave it as is.

After Koepcke emerged from the jungle and told searchers where to find the debris field, they cleared a landing site for helicopters. "It was a dramatic and heart-wrenching experience when we arrived at the site of the disaster," remembers one investigator, Juan Ramirez. "We found widespread fragments of the wreckage, and we saw trees with the belongings of the travelers. Suitcases had opened in mid-air, and the presents hung in the branches as if these were Christmas trees decorated for a sad holy night, as if they were adorned for the relatives of all those who never came home."

Many corpses were recovered, brought out for analysis and burial, though uncertainty remained about identities because bodies were lacerated and decayed. Search teams were too overwhelmed by the challenges of the fifteen square-kilometer debris field, including constant heavy rain, to do much investigation beyond that, so the cause of the crash was never definitively determined,[60] though there was widespread agreement in the assumption that thunderstorms, lightning strikes, and incautious pilots were to blame.

When Herzog and Koepcke arrive at the crash site in *Wings of Hope*, the debris is scattered across the jungle just as it was in 1971, though now a thick cloak of vegetation covered it. "You can barely walk here, the fragments are so densely strewn," Herzog says. They find a coin-purse that probably belonged to a little girl: inside were coins which were no longer in circulation. Stunned by ghastly déjà vu in a scene that goes on for twenty minutes, Koepcke tramps through the jungle searching for debris. She finds several large pieces of the plane, livery still clear; an emergency exit; electronics and cables from the airplane's mechanical system; the heel of a woman's shoe; a plastic hair curler "as was the fashion in those days"; a row of three seats (mainly the frame—the fabric has disintegrated); pieces of carpet ("the color is still there, the strands have grown into the ground").[61] "I found [the debris] extremely interesting," Koepcke writes, "even the smaller finds like a piece of one of the trays from which I, too, had eaten my last breakfast before the crash" and "the metal frame of a suitcase whose clasps were incongruously still locked while the material that had originally covered it had disappeared."[62]

In terms of how meaningful the debris seems to her, she reminds me of me. The debris helps her microcosmically understand the fairly inconceivable narrative-writ-large of a plane crash. Someone locked the suitcase to keep property safe—even if it was just a few pieces of jewelry or some Christmas presents, it's something that felt valuable and that the suitcase-owners wanted to keep secure, protected, during their journey. Looking at the suitcase now in the debris field, that impulse seems perversely irrelevant. How could they have worried about their belongings when what really should have concerned them was lightning, imprudent pilots, a terrifying death plunge? "But our beginnings never know our ends!" T. S. Eliot wrote in "Portrait of a Lady"[63]—which might serve as an epigraph for every accident investigation report, or at least every humanist accident investigation report.

It's dramatic irony—we now know what they then didn't. And Koepcke is, like every crash survivor, on both ends of it: she didn't know when she boarded the flight what would happen, but she does now. Humanist investigation uncovers a blindingly vivid vein of accentuated ironies. The eroded suitcase material signifies the destruction in a small-scale way that may be more easily processed,

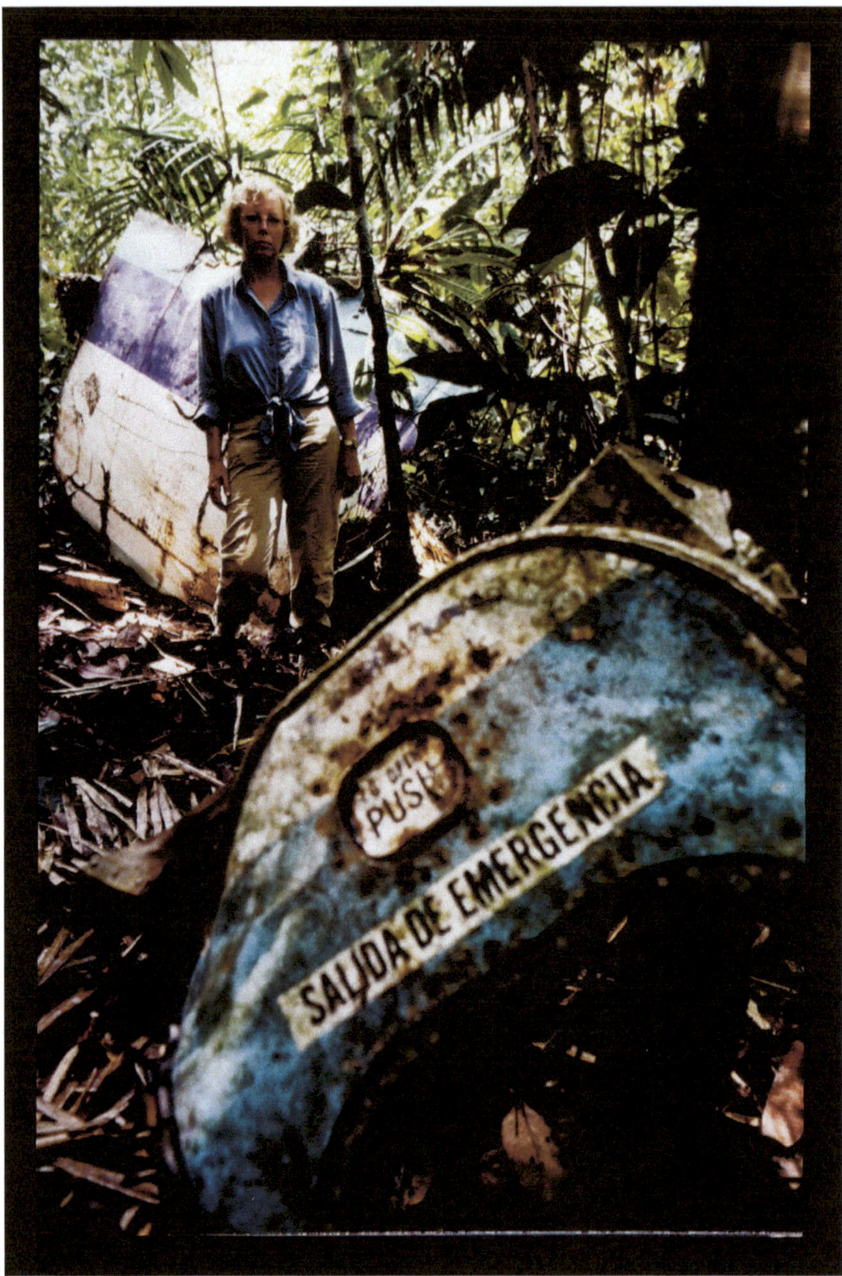

Figure 8.1 In *Wings of Hope*, Juliane Koepcke revisits and investigates the debris field she miraculously survived twenty-seven years earlier.

more concisely understood—but alongside that clarity there is also existential incoherence: paradoxically, quizzically, ironically, tauntingly, the latches have remained pointlessly locked for twenty-seven years.

The tension between the flight-as-planned compared to the flight-as-flown (the flight-as-crashed), resonates in the details Koepcke zeroes in on as she revisits the debris field. Full of little tokens of passengers' existence before the crash, she reflects on how their lives would have progressed if this plane, like most planes, had reached its destination safely. Everything was so normal (until it wasn't). *Wings of Hope* resonates with this motif that infuses so many other crash narratives as well: if only we could return to that innocent moment. Excuse a touch of the macabre, but we might think of it as a prelapsarian time—before the *fall*.

Herzog lingers on Koepcke's quiet observational process in the debris field. She picks up an instrument panel, holding it out to the camera so we can read the lettering over each switch and toggle: "Load Ctr. Fan"; "Norm. Feeder"; "Feather Pumps"; "Fuel Scavenge": such obtuse jargon for something so important, keeping the plane aloft (or not). As she studies the debris methodically, Herzog says in a voice-over: "Her nightmare, the nightmare of every one of us, had become so concrete that it was finally palpable."

She describes finding "wreckage that looked as if it had just fallen into the jungle. Since most of the pieces were made of stainless steel or aluminum, all the years in the humidity of the jungle had apparently passed them by without a trace. The rainforest had appropriated them, grown over and around them, pulled them into its ground as if they belonged to it. The airplane parts seemed so untouched."[64] Coming upon the largest piece of wreckage hidden in the undergrowth, they clear away the plant cover. It looks to be about ten meters long: the hull—the undercarriage, the wheels. "Juliane appeared deeply affected by the sight of this," Herzog says. "Only now did the catastrophe and her solitude acquire real dimension." Herzog frames Juliane's return to the debris field as cathartic, as she confronts and reenacts her trauma; her own demeanor and commentary seem to confirm that. The debris field concretizes an experience that had been, until then, incomprehensible to her. In my "Diversion: UTA 772 Memorial," Guillaume Denoix de Saint Marc expressed the same feeling, desperately needing to touch the debris in order to finally understand the crash that killed his father, and to move beyond it.

"We have an image of how a sunken Spanish galleon is supposed to look: the carcass of the hull, bronze cannons, an opal coffer filled with gold coins and pearls," Herzog observes. "But what a plane that has sunk into the jungle looks like has not taken shape in our imagination. We would probably walk right by it. We would recognize it only if we paid close attention."[65] In this cinematic epiphany, Herzog demonstrates how to appraise and process a debris field: *pay close attention!* This scene goes on and on—it's as fascinating to him, and her, as it is to me. With tenacious Teutonic stoicism, Koepcke (in league with her Germanic accomplice Herzog) inspects the debris piece by piece: holding it up, turning it around, figuring out what it is, and trying, somehow (as am I) to see in each piece of debris something—some clue, some reason, some explanation for what happened, why the plane didn't want to fly any more, and what comes next.

While most of the debris remained where it fell, some had been brought out of the jungle and had taken on a new function. It wasn't the investigators who had removed this debris, but local residents. (Oh, shame on me! I should have said: it wasn't official government investigators who removed this debris, but local residential investigators.) Koepcke describes something she encountered while reenacting her jungle trek for the documentary, a few miles away from the debris field:

> A woman from the Andes had opened a kiosk, where we stopped to get something to drink. I did not believe my eyes when I saw what she had leaned against the outside of the house: It was actually a fully intact door from the Lansa plane. On it the Indian woman had written, *Juliana's door*. This enterprising woman had apparently realized immediately what a magical appeal this relic of my past would have. Indeed, everyone I talk to about it calls this kiosk which had meanwhile grown into a small grocery store that sells drinks, "The Door." Whenever I've passed by since then, the people accompanying me say, "Juliane, stand there for a moment please," and they take a photo. That feels strange to me. I find it unpleasant, because for me it's not a tourist attraction, but a door through which ninety-one people went to their deaths, including my mother.[66]

The storekeeper's use of this door is a fascinating example of the upcycled afterlife of debris. The plane has crashed—long live the plane. What can people do with its useless, broken pieces? *Are* they completely useless? What can be made out of them? Do we think of such reclamations as scavenging, or as creativity (as exemplified by another German debris-fetishist, Anselm Kiefer)? How does debris retain its original condition, its essence? How does it change? By making her business more prominent, the kiosk-owner presumably monetized the debris: perhaps inappropriately or unethically, but it did fall into her community, so one might argue that she has some claim on it. Who "owns" it, if not her? Lansa (or its creditors)? The Peruvian aviation authorities who conducted a mediocre investigation? Juliane? Herzog's documentaries have a rapacious edge: maybe he thinks he owns it, having captured it on film.

Even as Koepcke describes the door's appropriation as strange and unpleasant, she also acknowledges it as a relic with "magical appeal." The kiosk-owner, an "enterprising woman," recognizes this appeal, keeping the door (as a memorial, in some sense?) for her customers and neighbors to interact with, and to appreciate, which is possible only because she had resituated it from the inaccessible debris field. Seeing the airplane door, re-named for the miraculous survivor, is a way for others to connect tangibly with Koepcke's experience, to share her against-all-odds refusal to die in a plane crash: to understand her story's "real dimension" (as Herzog characterized the force of the debris). I can imagine customers touching the door as they enter the kiosk—hoping that a bit of Juliane's luck, her fortitude, her level-headed determination, might rub off on them—and I find this vision very moving.

9

The Zen and Karma of Plane Crashes

Today I will go soaring
Now to fall with cherry blossoms in full bloom

Kamikaze death poem[1]

Happiness comes through pure actions;
suffering results from evil actions

Mahabharata, XIII.6.10[2]

Kamikaze strikes are unlike any other kind of plane crash, though we can still investigate the debris fields to try to understand them (and even, conceivably, leverage these investigations to prevent such crashes in future). They resemble the 9/11 attacks, and also "suicide by pilot" crashes in which mentally disturbed pilots aim for the ground, killing themselves along with everyone else on board. Because kamikaze pilots flew solo, only one person on the plane died in the crash, not—as in commercial pilot suicides and on 9/11—hundreds of innocent passengers. Kamikaze victims, like most 9/11 victims, died outside the plane, injured or killed in the crash, explosion, and fire caused by weaponized airplanes' impact—somewhat like the ground deaths discussed in Chapter 1, though those fatalities were accidental, while kamikaze crashes are deliberate.

Japanese special forces pilots, *tokkōtai*, who conducted kamikaze strikes from October, 1944, until the end of WWII, didn't consider their missions suicide, writes Emiko Ohnuki-Tierney. Rather, "they were killed in action, just as foot soldiers were killed on the battlefield. Their deaths came as a result of ramming into American vessels in their effort to save their country."[3] Westerners misread kamikazes as "inscrutable zealots," she writes, but "most of them wanted to live."[4] As Japan's war effort was collapsing, pilots reconciled themselves to these sorties because "with Japan's defeat in sight, their lives were in extreme danger no matter what course of action they took," and "if one was likely to die anyway, one might as well die a hero." Yet many pilots were still agonized, Ohnuki-Tierney writes, "so tormented by thoughts of their imminent death that they prayed that the time would come as soon as possible in order to terminate their agony."[5]

While combat is always inherently cruel, kamikaze warfare is especially appalling, beyond the pale. As a scholar (and passenger) who thinks a great deal about crashes, I find something particularly perverse about using a plane as if it were a missile or a Molotov cocktail; I'm not sure I can explain why. It's not that missiles and Molotovs are necessarily more ethically defensible—war is brutal no matter what weapons are deployed.

But: *the plane wants to fly*. Unshaken by my investigations of aviation and its copious discontents, I retain my faith in that premise. In the extremely rare case of a plane crash, the plane does stop flying, but it didn't want to. In kamikaze attacks, does the plane still want to fly? The *pilot* doesn't; presumably he assumes that the plane, lacking its own ethical framework, merely "wants" whatever he, his generals, and his Emperor, want. But I think he is wrong: I think planes did not want to do what the *tokkōtai* made them do. In addition to maiming and killing the troops they attacked, and themselves, kamikazes also committed violence against the precepts of aviation. My investigations presume that everyone everywhere—every sane person, at least—wants planes not to crash, but kamikazes undermined that ethos. Another fundamental (humanist) premise of aviation: plane crashes are ironic—they are not supposed to happen—but kamikaze attacks were premeditated, planned.

Tokkōtai operations began with combat vehicles including airplanes, gliders, and submarines. "None of these manned weapon systems was equipped with any means of returning to base," writes Michael Anderson. Most Japanese pilots "had seen their friends already die, they knew the war was lost. There was also a shared and strong sense of fatalism," inspiring the cult of a hero's death, and alluring rewards: "Imperial Japan posthumously promoted kamikaze pilots by two ranks, and families received the payments, so in death they not only provided for their families for the future but with increased salaries."[6]

"Thou shalt die like beautiful falling cherry petals for the emperor," military propaganda proclaimed.[7] The word *kamikaze* had an idealized historical/cultural resonance: it means "divine wind" or "god-wind," referring to thirteenth-century typhoons that fortuitously dispersed a Mongol invasion fleet, saving Japan from defeat by Kublai Khan's forces.

Pilots volunteered under tremendous coercion from officers and peers. "If a soldier had been courageous enough not to volunteer, he would have been consigned to a living hell." Some demurred, "but their refusal was disregarded."[8]

The Japanese state promoted the idea that everyone, especially soldiers, must sacrifice their lives for their country. Ohnuki-Tierney quotes a soldier's diary: "I will fight as much as I can, leaving my fate in your hands. I would not mind my body being ripped apart innumerable times."[9]

Manuals instructed pilots how to prepare and attack, how to be mentally ready to die, write Albert Axell and Hideaki Kase. "Attain a high level of spiritual training" and "keep your health in the very best condition." Diving for a target, "aim for a point between the bridge tower and the smokestacks," or for a horizontal attack, "aim at the middle of the vessel, slightly higher than the waterline." They were told to keep their eyes open: "Just before the collision it is essential that you do not shut your eyes for a moment so as not to miss the target. Many have crashed into the targets with wide-open eyes. They will tell you what fun they had." (How exactly would they convey their reminiscences about these pleasures, I wonder?) In the moment before impact the pilot should yell "*hissatsu*" at the top of his lungs, which means "certain kill."[10]

During attacks, pilots often got high, both atmospherically and pharmacologically. They commonly took methamphetamines by injection, or orally via *totsugeki-jo* ("assault tablets") or *genki-shu* ("energy alcohol," meth-infused), intended to augment their missions with a synthetic rush of euphoric pleasure, increased energy, focus, confidence. In schools, students wrapped chocolates bearing the Emperor's seal, a chrysanthemum emblem, to send kamikazes: "the last things the pilots ate before their suicide missions." One girl who snuck a piece "felt a strange sensation, 'as if there were a strong drug in it.' She told her father, who said, 'Maybe they're putting *hiropon* [methamphetamine] in it." A teacher who supervised preparation of these chocolates researched the practice of drugging pilots and found testimony from a confectionery company executive acknowledging: "we were supplied with large amounts of *hiropon*, which were then covered with chocolate, embossed with the chrysanthemum emblem, and periodically given over to the military." Kamikazes were drugged, Fumiyo Ooka believes, "to keep the pilots awake on their long flights, but the military probably also counted on the drug's ability to cause an abnormally excited state so the pilots would not feel fear."[11]

Kamikaze pilots were also called "human torpedoes" (*kaiten*), and their crash was a "body attack" (*taiatari*). For years before the kamikaze strategy began, Japanese pilots committed *jibaku* attacks, meaning that if planes became seriously damaged in battle and probably wouldn't make it back to safety, they might as well crash into a target if one was available. *Jibaku* attacks were more spontaneous, while kamikaze pilots "set out from their carriers with the intention of crashing into enemy warships." Japanese tactics also included "human bullet" assaults (*nikuhaku kōgeki*), comparable to what we now call suicide bombers.

Three to four thousand planes flew *tokkōtai* missions, and about that many Japanese pilots died, though only one in ten hit a warship; most crashed and died in failed attacks. Those who did hit their target were highly effective: "Being hit by a fast-diving bomb-laden aircraft was likely to be far more devastating than a conventional attack by bomb or torpedo. The physical impact of the airframe weighing a ton or more and the burning of unspent fuel in that airframe caused damage far beyond that caused by the explosion of the aircraft's payload." There was also a profound psychological impact, writes Robert Stern: "consider the effect it had on the sailor staring up at the dark specks against the sky so clearly intent on doing him harm." Some Americans "expressed a sense of admiration for the desperate courage of the pilots" while others felt "incomprehension and more than a little fear." The Japanese military meant these attacks to demonstrate "the superiority of the Japanese national spirit to what was believed to be the weak and corrupted spirit of the enemy."[12]

Even from the low percentage of missions accomplished, Allied sailors suffered 7,000 casualties, with 400 vessels sunk or damaged, though none of the more important classes (fleet carriers, cruisers, battleships).[13] Kamikazes did not ultimately change the war's course.

Kamikaze debris fields

In kamikaze attacks, the battlefield and the debris field were one and the same. Battles were fought amid and against the debris. Kamikazes exploded on impact, and the scope of danger burgeoned enormously beyond just the crash because ships carried their own large stores of fuel and ordinance. More kamikazes often followed in a second wave, a few minutes or hours behind the first. In most plane crashes, debris fields become relatively inert and controlled soon after the moment of impact: immediate dangers pass as fires burn out or are doused by safety teams, while first responders mitigate threats and attend to survivors. But kamikaze debris fields pose enormous ongoing threats. "Debris" is definitely a verb in this scenario, a pretty intense one.

During the Battle of Iwo Jima on February 21, 1945, nine kamikazes attacked the USS *Saratoga* ("Sara"), as military historian John Fry describes:

> *Saratoga* had just launched fourteen fighters and a torpedo plane, when six Japanese planes were observed coming out of the clouds to the east. Sara's gunners opened fire. The first plane, hit and on fire, struck the starboard side, penetrating to the hangar deck and causing fires. Kamikaze number two had also been hit by anti-aircraft fire and was in flames. It hit the water and bounced into the starboard side, bursting Sara's blister and causing a list of 6°. Plane number three was shot down clear of the ship. The fourth plane came up from astern and dropped a bomb, which bounced off the flight deck near the port bow. The next aircraft dove into the anchor-windlass room and exploded, creating a huge conflagration. The final bogey [unidentified aircraft] passed Sara's bridge to starboard and struck the airplane crane. A portion of the plane crashed into the #1 gun gallery, and the rest of the craft slid off over the port side, but not before its bomb exploded on the flight deck. Three more kamikaze planes attacked the ship an hour and a half later. The first two were shot down, but the third crashed into the flight deck after dropping a bomb.[14]

The attacks killed 123 and wounded 192, destroying thirty-six aircraft aboard the carrier. Jack Bytheway, a nineteen-year-old Utahan who served as lookout and gunner's mate, wrote a memoir that recounts with extraordinary and haunting detail his experience of that debris field:

> Our lookout leader advised me to proceed to my battle station as bogeys had shown up on our radar screen at 80 miles. I sprang into a dead run, as did all the other sailors, and as I arrived at my battle stations, our starboard guns began firing, while at the same time, the ship was jolted heavily as I heard loud explosions. I suddenly realized that this was the real thing—we were under attack.

Over the water he saw a plane leveling off low, heading directly for the ship.

> Thinking it was one of our F6F Hellcats, I started to say, as I pointed, "What's he doing?" All of a sudden our gun swung into position and began firing rapidly at it, as did all other guns on the port side. I then realized it was not one of ours—it was a Japanese Zeke! (also known as a Zero). I pulled my helmet down tight on my head and began to pass ammunition as fast as I could. At this time, our 20 mm began firing and then I knew that he was getting in close to us.
>
> A few moments later, the ship again was jolted heavily as a loud explosion followed. We were showered with pieces of teakwood and metal fragments. Heavy black smoke blew over us. The noise was intense and I had no cotton in my ears. I don't know if the plane I saw was the one that hit us or not. We had

> already taken several hits, and the entire forward end of the flight deck was on fire. We continued firing, but at what, I don't know. The ship would quiver every few moments and I realized we were really taking a beating.

Water was pumped aboard to douse the fires, but once again,

> the ship was jolted, as though it had been blown entirely out of the water. And almost immediately, black smoke poured through the large ventilation fans from the hangar deck and onto our gun mount. We nearly choked. A suicide plane had crashed into the starboard side of the ship and had gone through to the hangar deck. A fire followed as some of our planes began to explode and burn.

Another bomber drew near, which gunners shot down just before it hit them. Taking on more water now,

> we began to list to starboard as the ship began losing speed. A lull in the firing ensued and we were instructed to smear flash burn cream on our faces, neck and on the back of our hands to protect us from any flashes from bombs or other explosions. After that we began dumping empty shell casings, clips and ammunition cans over the side. By now we were dead in the water and we all began to put on life preservers as some began to cut life rafts loose. I began to prepare for the worst. A terrible fright came over me as I thought of abandoning ship and having to jump into that cold, gray Pacific. I knew that at this time of year, a person would only last a few minutes there, even with a life preserver.

As darkness arrived, bilge pumps cleared the ship of water and Sara began moving slowly forward. Bytheway felt relieved they weren't sinking.

> The smell of fire and burning chemicals was everywhere and the stench was more than we could stand. The fires on the flight deck were put out only after much effort. Some of our air group was still aloft, so we turned into the wind and landed them. Because we were under fire, some of our pilots couldn't land. Some probably just ran out of gas and were ditched, others were probably shot down.

Then it was time to deal with the dead, and the debris:

> The stench was worse than ever now as the smell of burned flesh was mixing with it. Corpsmen with stretchers were now moving through the passageways on their way to sickbay. Morning finally dawned. I moved about on the ship assessing the damage. It was incredible. It was sickening. Some men had been blown to bits and their flesh had to be hosed off the bulkhead and decks. The smell of burnt flesh turned my stomach and I nearly vomited. I learned that the marine detachment suffered extremely heavy losses. Some were burned to death, many went over the side never to be found.

> I was approached by someone to proceed to the bomb locker and help remove some badly burned bodies. I declined, as I'm sure the person who asked me could see my sickened condition and knew I would be of no use to him. I later learned that those bodies there were literally roasted and if you tried to pick them up, they fell apart. They finally had to shovel them up.

They cleared away debris and dumped damaged planes over the stern.

> The dead bodies were being taken to the flight deck for burial at sea. The most sickening sight of all was to see those dead bodies, row after row. They put whatever bodies they could into mattress sacks. It was terrible to see the sack tied around their ankles and their feet protruding out of the sack. Most of them still had their shoes on. We all went back to work to make the ship as clean as possible. All day long, more debris and damaged aircraft were being dumped into the sea. The thing that kept us from sinking was that most of the damage was above the water line. This was the only good thing about the whole battle. Even at that, it could have been much worse. I felt very lucky.[15]

Bytheway's memoirs douse us with the debris field's sounds, smells, and sights, along with its intangible air of terror. He describes its unimaginable horrors, alongside people's survival instincts, more extensively than any other report I've seen, which makes sense because this is a debris field unlike any other. In every other debris field, people end up there accidentally, so reports from survivors are consequently haphazard because they weren't prepared to document the event: they were surprised, bewildered. But after months of Pacific kamikaze attacks, Seaman First Class Bytheway and his shipmates knew it was quite possible something like this might happen. Perhaps that helped prepare him to capture (in military terms, and also personally emotional detail) a debris field experience that very few others would be able to convey so coherently and insightfully. Other crash sites I investigate resonate with an entropic and largely ineffable milieu. But Bytheway's memoir fills in this absurdist void of language with a startling level of logic, comprehension, sanity, and by-the-book military process as he soldiers on (literally) with the mission at hand, defying every other debris field's default mood, the foggy existential fugue.

In every other plane crash, debris fields seem (at least initially, in the moment of their incarnation) insensate, inattentive to our engagement, our agency, our response—which is why they appear so random and tragic, pointless and ineffable. Bytheway recounts how it *is* possible for a debris field to animate with action, rationality, agency—the agency deriving from the verb-energy in the roots of the word "debris" (see Chapter 1). Kamikazes are debris-ing, killing by shattering. As horrible as it must have been to be debris'd, Bytheway channels immense fight-or-flight energy to combat this incredibly-charged iteration of debris. As kamikaze pilots verb-debris the *Saratoga*, its sailors—most of whom survived—themselves "verbed" in response: resisting, fighting, clearing the noun-debris from their decks and battle stations. They emerged from the debris field intact and triumphant.

Zen death poems

Jack Bytheway's vibrant, literal account of kamikaze crashes contrasts acutely with an antithetical discourse in a strikingly gentler timbre: quick, stylized, and unexpectedly calm crash narratives that kamikaze pilots crafted as they imagined these crashes proleptically, just before they took place. It is hard to get one's head around the fact that these diametrically opposed perspectives and voices describe the same phenomenon.

Kamikazes carried out many rituals before their final mission. They shared ceremonial cups of sake and put on *senninbari* (belts of a thousand stitches) from their mothers. And they composed death poems, a tradition called *jisei* dating back to tenth-century *samurai* warriors who wrote them just before committing *seppuku*, the defeated soldiers' ritual suicide. Kamikaze pilots inscribed these ethereal poems at the end of farewell letters to their families.

Spare and aestheticized, these poems have a kind of perverse beauty, as if the poet-pilots are trying to negate, or at least soften, what they are about to do. "Death poems are typically graceful, natural, and emotionally neutral, in accordance with the teachings of Buddhism and Shinto," writes Eugene Thacker. The mood is "enigmatic, even ambivalent about death," which was usually not mentioned explicitly in older examples of the form, though kamikaze pilots are more prone than their predecessors to acknowledge their imminent demise. *Jisei* traditionally suppressed death in favor of "metaphorical references such as sunsets, autumn or falling cherry blossom" suggesting life's transience,[16] and many kamikaze death poems still used such metaphors. *Jisei* reveals what people consider most important as they abandon life, what they think about (or, at least, what they *say* they think about) before they die.

The minimalist form "invites reflection on the brevity of both the *jisei* and life itself." The poems convey "the general precepts of Buddhism: impermanence, the universality of suffering and the sense that the world is simply a dream—that one's life, one's very own body, will evaporate like dew, fade like mist, dissipate like smoke." They are not elegies, eulogies, or suicide notes, "neither the summary of a life nor the culmination of a life," Thacker explains. Instead, they are "the emptying of a life, of a body, of a self."[17] The poems are supposed to embody moments of enlightenment, clarity of mind. As last words, they strike a very different tone from "Fuck," though perhaps that too, in some sense, reflects an epiphany of lucidity.

The psychological benefits of such contemplative Zen mindfulness, quiet acceptance, seem salubrious for a young pilot on the brink of crashing his plane. I wonder, though, whether the state of consciousness induced by this poetic exercise might interact precariously with the meth: it seems like chalk and cheese.

These poems seem as unreal as Bytheway's memoir is real. Yet while literal debris fields such as his help illuminate kamikaze crashes, so too do the detached Zen death poems. Polite and formal, often somewhat similar to each other, they embody a tender touch of humanity that seems so disjunctive with the impending crash. But while the poetry may have seemed incongruous with the suicide missions, it was not: the same person was responsible for both. As a humanist, I feel compelled to try to discover some *truth* in the poems, something that helps explain the problematic phenomenon of intentional plane crashes, which I have characterized as a lie because the truth of aviation is that planes should fly, not crash.

An important distinction between these short quiet lyrics and accounts like Bytheway's: *jisei* precede the attack, composed by soldiers who will die quickly in combat (before the verb-debris, the shattering, unfolds)—so they won't see what Bytheway sees. They have a great deal of poetic license, imaginative fancy: the poets are free to aestheticize rampantly as they depict debris fields they will inhabit consciously for only an instant, if all goes according to plan.

I am wary of overreading these self-serving, self-censored poems. They required deft rhetorical legerdemain to leave behind something that would comfort loved ones despite the pilots' gruesome deaths. *Jisei* may be merely traditional conceits, and/or, they may be, at least in part, genuinely expository of how these pilots felt. I don't believe their poems mitigate imperial Japan's military brutality, but they may help us see why the pilots did what they did—or why they thought they did what they did, or were manipulated to think whatever they thought their missions meant. In some sense, I contend, these Zen death poems shed light on why these crashes happened, which is what we are investigating.

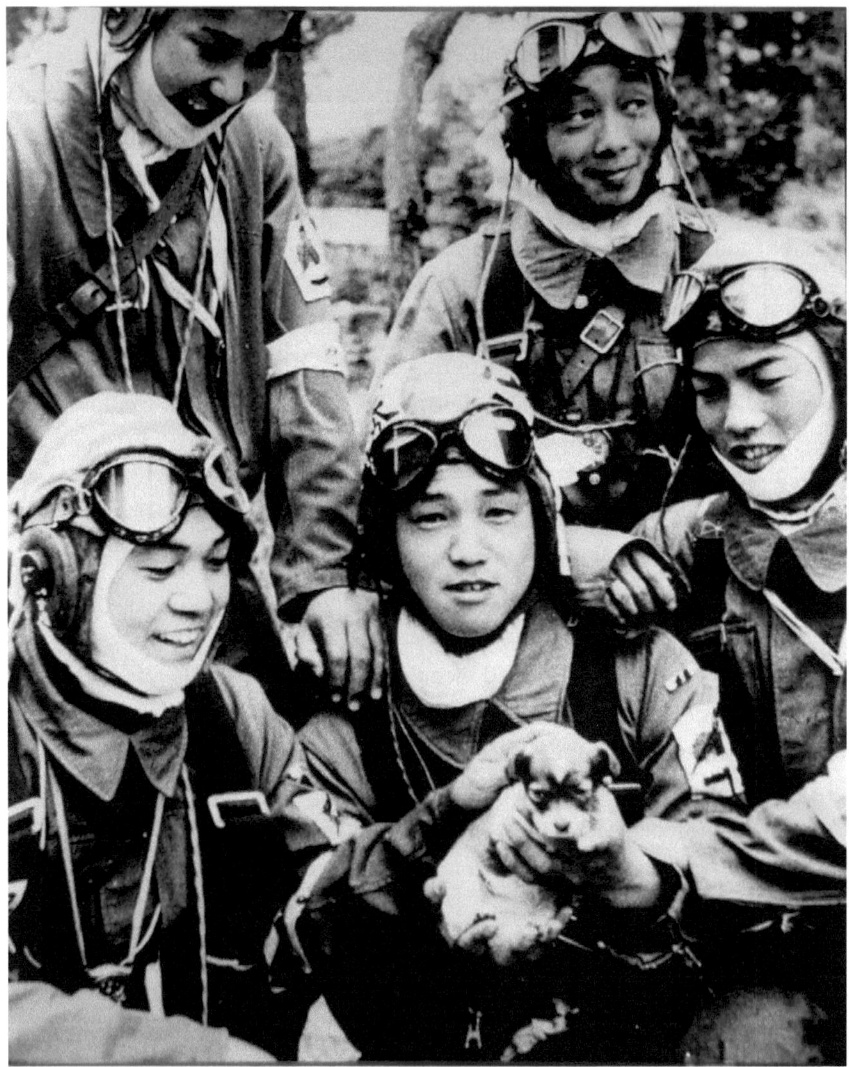

Figure 9.1 Be the person your dog thinks you are. Photograph taken May 26, 1945, the day before these 72nd Shinbu Squadron pilots died on kamikaze missions. Three were seventeen years old, the other two were eighteen and nineteen.

I've culled these poems from a superb Internet archive, kamikazeimages.net, created and curated by Bill Gordon.[18] In addition to extensive information about the history of kamikaze forces, and links to films, books, museums, and other cultural archives, Gordon includes his translations of hundreds of diaries and letters from kamikaze pilots to their families, many of which include *jisei*. Second

Lieutenant Hiroshi Maeda's is one of the most condensed death poems I've found, and one of the most powerful:

When I die
How many should cry?[19]

Maeda's poem exemplifies how Japanese artists and writers "use the fewest words or strokes of brush to express their feelings" in the Zen aesthetic of "simplicity, naturalness, directness, profundity," Lucian Stryk explains.[20]

Corporal Yasuo Fukushima's poem recalls Major Robert Gregory foreseeing his death.

Beforehand
Time that I must fall
Can be seen[21]

The fatalistic/proleptic frisson that animates W. B. Yeats's poem infuses this one as well. Reading "An Irish Airman Foresees His Death" (and "High Flight" too, with its lurking intuitions of death) alongside these *jisei* illuminates resonant similarities, or coincidences: during wartime aviation, poetry helps make peace with abnormally dangerous aeromobilities. I can't think of another example in any literary tradition where a passive construction ("can be seen") seems so effective, paradoxically powerful. That indirect predicate works well here because the point of these Zen performances is precisely to transpose activity into passivity. That shift diffuses the frenzied fugue of action—which, for Corporal Fukushima, involves killing, dying, destroying, in a loud, fast, violent attack (*hissatsu!)*—into language that facilitates a more placid, contemplative mode. Yes, grammar can do that.

Some kamikaze death poems resist conventional *jisei* lexicon by unabashedly invoking military bravado and triumphalism. Corporal Takao Adachi, seventeen years old, wrote this just before his death:

Decisive battle has come for me
Excitement also with instant enemy sinking[22]

Perhaps he feels the times demand eschewing the usual poetic niceties, given the intensity of this exceedingly violent conflict. Possibly, too, the meth could be impinging Adachi's ability to embrace Zen ideology as earnestly as he might.

Another blatantly martial death poem comes from Corporal Kōji Andō, a nineteen-year-old kamikaze who died in an attack west of Okinawa:

Imperial command received
I will go
For Empire
As shield of skies
I will fall[23]

Some violent *jisei* use the trope of *taiatari* from the martial art *kendo.* It means hitting your opponent with your body, and metaphorically describes a kamikaze attack, as in Second Lieutenant Fukujirō Nagashima's poem:

Now I go
Seeking carrier
Taiatari[24]

Flight Petty Officer Hiroshi Yabuta writes:

Against many enemies coming to Japan
Thrilled to make *taiatari* attack with plane[25]

A similar metaphor appears in the poem by Second Lieutenant Saburō Ishikura, twenty-two:

Receiving my order for a sortie on the day cherry trees bloomed
I also will follow on behalf of the Emperor
Sure death resolved to be human bullet hitting target[26]

A lurid, aggressive Imperial enthusiasm flourishes in poems like these. If they do not much tone down the impending mission's violence, the verb-debris, still even here we find a brief dulcet moment, as Ishikura balances the tragedy of his impending fate in the third line with the restorative balm of cherry blossoms emerging in the first.

Indeed, that particular floral image pervades these death poems. For a century, cherry blossoms—imagined as unique to Japan (although they are actually not)—had been "the master trope of Japan's imperial nationalism," emblematic of the Japanese soul. *Tokkōtai* pilots often "flew to their deaths with blooming cherry branches adorning their uniforms" and painted on their planes; "falling cherry petals came to signify the soldiers' sacrifice for the Emperor,"[27] writes Emiko Ohnuki-Tierney. *Tokkōtai* squadrons were all named for cherry blossoms: *Yamazakura-tai* (mountain cherry blossoms corps), *Sakon-tai* (Sakon refers to a specific cherry tree planted beside the Imperial Palace), *Yoshino-tai* (Yoshino is the mountain range best known for cherry blossoms), and so on.[28]

Flight Petty Officer Mitsuo Yoshinaga, nineteen, who died in an attack near Okinawa, conjoins his anticipated aeronautical and mortal trajectories: his rise and fall. His fall is like the fall of cherry blossoms, which is sad because the blooming is over, but it is mitigated by the fact that the flowers gave great pleasure before they dropped off the tree. Cherry blossoms fall relatively quickly after they bloom, like these kamikaze pilots: as the crème de la crème from Japan's university culture, the young men paralleled the flowers' life-cycles.

Today I will go soaring
Now to fall with cherry blossoms in full bloom[29]

What goes up must come down. Compactly balancing soaring and falling, Yoshinaga achieves something like what Yeats's "An Irish Airman" did: facing impending death and poetically tempering the horror of the inevitable crash.

Let me present a quick cherry blossom (poetry) festival to savor a literary burst of blooms. From Ensign Shunsuke Yukawa:

Time now has come when mountain cherry blossoms must fall
This the path where we will live[30]

Flight Warrant Officer Hisaoki Yoshizawa wrote:

Mountain cherry blossom
At time to go to fall
If it does not fall
The time to go to fall
Already goes away[31]

By Second Lieutenant Yoshio Usui:

Cherry blossom to fall bravely
Bloom beautifully, cherry blossoms that can stay[32]

Corporal Saburō Hasegawa's death poem is especially basic, but, paradoxically, richly and delicately entrancing. I think it's my favorite:

Falling cherry blossoms
Remaining cherry blossoms too
Falling cherry blossoms[33]

In Sergeant Tatsuo Wakao's last words, the botanical image of a flower dropping represents the termination of life in the most painless way imaginable—so profoundly unlike images from literal accounts of kamikaze attacks :

Young cherry blossom
Waits for spring
Going to fall
In midst of storm
Freed from branch[34]

Woody Guthrie's "Deportee," in a similar vein, characterizes victims of a plane-crash fireball as "scattered like dry leaves" (see Chapter 4). Figurative debris fields of leaves or flowers are so much less traumatic than every other one we have seen.

Other images besides flowers convey beauty in death poems. Ensign Tokuya Tsuda writes:

Empire's
Eternal prosperity
I am praying for
My body will fall as jewel
Shattering American fiends[35]

The plane-of-death symbolically becomes a "jewel." Tsuda employs synecdoche: "My body" stands for a larger implicit unit, "My body in a kamikaze plane," showing the complex transmogrifications these death poems enact. Tsuda's poem presents the only explicit reference I found in *jisei* to America, or any country besides Japan.

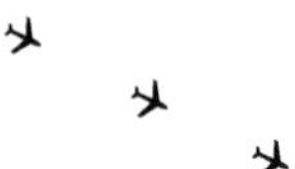

Finally, saving the best for last: a few death poems explicitly depict crashing airplanes and/or debris fields, obviously in the same compact, minimalist portrayals that the genre requires. In Corporal Teruo Usami's poem, the pilot is the plane:

Even though my wings are broken and control stick smashed to pieces
I will not stop pursuing an enemy aircraft carrier

A cherry blossom falling in a splendid dive at Okinawa
Aircraft carrier with me to the other world

Blizzard of cherry blossoms leaving to fall in special attack
Not expecting to return alive from first battle[36]

The broken wings and smashed control stick in the first line are proleptic, and conditional: *even if* my plane is destroyed and crashing, I will still pursue ... It is more militarily violent, less Zen, than these poems traditionally were; the cherry blossom tucked into the third line doesn't restore the mindful serenity that the poem is supposed to embody—on the contrary, its floral tranquility is coopted, in a "splendid dive," by the airplane imagery that dominates this poem. This crash poem is more enthusiastically excited about the actual crash than most other kamikaze *jisei*. It's almost as if Usami is writing an advance-version of his crash report. (That's a fascinating way to think of these poems: an unparalleled example of dead plane-crash victims foresightfully sketching out their own bespoke auto-investigations.)

Other cultural debris field artifacts have presented premonitions of crashes, and technically Usami's does too, though the nature of kamikaze aviation makes the premonition pretty much a foregone conclusion, as the pilot is determined to actualize it. (He might or might not "successfully" crash into a ship, but he will almost certainly crash somewhere.) Premonitions are usually fearful, but this one might be characterized as joyful. Sergeant Tatsuo Wakao, too, inscribes an airplane, and a pilot-as-plane crackup, in his death poem:

Even if I
With my plane
Shatter to pieces
My spirit eternally
Will protect country[37]

I have looked at multitudinous debris fields to discover what endures from the shattered wreckage—what survives it. Wakao's first three lines ask that same question, and his last two lines answer it—a conciseness that impresses me as I approach 130,000 words in my less-minimalist text.

Corporal Toshio Chizaki's death poem, like Usami's and Wakao's, envisions and describes the debris field before he causes it. (Should I say, "before he creates it"? Creating a debris field, *creating destruction*—that's a disturbing paradox to ponder.)

For His Majesty, not thinking about either family or parents
For my country this body will no longer be
Now I will go riding above smoke of guns and rain of bullets
Aimed at a large enemy aircraft carrier

Waiting for decisive battle at Okinawa where I will go
This body with my plane will break into pieces[38]

"This body with my plane" resembles Tsuda's body/plane synecdoche above. Chizaki describes body-and-plane as two separate entities, but for all practical purposes functioning as a single unit, which is also what happens when Usami and Wakao inscribe planes in their poems: the plane will be broken like the pilot's body, in tandem with his body. These body-planes anticipate, proleptically, the debris fields that will soon manifest, composed of mixed human and mechanical remains like Bytheway's description of the *Saratoga* debris field (and many others, *most* others, as well). The body/plane remains a unit, inseparable, after the crash as it was before. That word *will*—"will break into pieces"—recalls similar expressions of forthcoming aviation tragedies described with certitude, when a writer or singer *seems* sure that a plane crash is on the horizon. (Modest Mouse, "Shit Luck": "This plane is definitely crashing!") But Chizaki's expression has a different degree of certitude, and agency: it *will* happen because he *will* make it happen—he *wills* it.

Anticipating the debris field to come is a pretty rare point-of-view: fascinating and highly disturbing. The 9/11 terrorists could have had something similar in mind, but they didn't write poems about it (as far as I know). Let me clarify: I am not arguing that kamikaze-poets are transforming their violence into art. What they are doing is attempting, via art, to understand, or explain, or culturally/ethically engage with, their mission to kill enemy forces with plane crashes, a horrible undertaking.

I find it interesting that they tried to combine their violence with art, or even more brazenly, that they *tried* (but failed) to transform their violence into art—because I know about art, and I can investigate art, as well as investigating plane crashes; there is a great deal for me to work with here. *I* can use art to understand and perhaps even somehow help "transform" plane crashes, and in fact I have been doing this, or trying to, throughout my book. Can the kamikaze pilots do this? I am inclined to say, mostly, no. If they had written death poems and then decided to fly off to some distant hidden place instead of an aircraft carrier—and indeed some actually did this, abandoning their suicide mission—then I would say, yes, you are an artist: you understand how art works, and your creation of this Zen death poem *did* transform violence into beauty, chaos into order. If there were any *jisei* that fit these criteria, I haven't found them. But I'm not inclined to regard the poems I investigate here, by pilots who wrote their last words and then flew their last missions, as art. They are data, roughly similar to what's compiled in a black box (their brains, their psyches, being the figurative boxes here) that reveal to investigators what was going on that made the plane crash. ("*Mais qu'est-ce qui se passe*!!?" "どうしたの！！？")

Such vividly intense crashes and debris fields captured in a short line or two—whether or not it's art, it's pretty amazing material for us investigators: as readers, as humanists, as people who do not crash planes into other people and hope to figure out how to inspire other people, also, not to crash planes into people. Further investigations are warranted.

Karma

I think of plane-crash victims, generically, as innocent people, good people, who had rich lives ahead of them that were cruelly truncated. Certainly many of them are, but bad people, too, can crash. Are there people in crashes who deserved to die? Whose fates embody some measure of justice?

Colonel Alexander von Scheele, a Luftwaffe commander of the Nazi Condor Legion, which supported Franco's Nationalists in the Spanish Civil War, crashed in his German Junkers Ju 52 on the way to Madrid in 1939. It seems likely that his death prevented more deaths and violence in the years ahead, and I feel comfortable saying, though I'm aware of how dicey this sounds, that he had it coming; and it's not hard for me to extend that sentiment to any Nazi who crashed while trying to conquer the world. In war, there is a proclivity to read a fatalistic sense of glee into enemy plane crashes. When four Russian military aircraft were downed, nearly simultaneously, just before crossing into Ukraine in 2023, an advisor to Ukrainian President Volodymyr Zelenskyy described it as "instant Karma. Killers on wings were destroyed BEFORE the next crime would be committed."[39]

Dominican dictator Rafael Trujillo wanted to celebrate Columbus's "discovery" of the Americas by erecting a monument, *Faro a Colón*, in Santo Domingo. A notorious white supremacist, Trujillo embraced the European origin story specifically to obscure his country's Indigenous and African heritages.[40] To fund the project, he organized an airplane tour of Latin America in 1937, featuring four planes: the Niña, the Pinta, the Santa Maria, and one named after Columbus. (Remember Chapter 2: ships are planes, planes are ships.) Flying with excessively heavy loads in bad weather, three of them crashed (the Colón didn't), killing everyone onboard. Was the universe trying to make a point about the legacy of European imperialism? Or racism? I'd say both.

Yevgeny Prigozhin, founder of Russia's brutal Wagner mercenaries, died in a 2023 plane crash, along with several associates, when a bomb exploded onboard.

The sabotage was almost certainly ordered by President Vladimir Putin after Prigozhin's attempted putsch during the Ukraine war. Both men were murderous villains: it's hard to say who was more reviled, but everyone saw it coming; Prigozhin seemed to have gotten his just desserts. Putin leaned into the idea of karma after the crash, calling his nemesis "a man of difficult fate" who had "made serious mistakes in life."[41] The 9/11 hijackers all died, which they deserved, though it's harder to feel the satisfaction of pure karma because so many others died along with them. If I were the king of karma, it would target only evil-doers; there would be no collateral deaths.

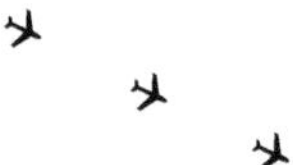

In 2022, the US Supreme Court reversed a ruling from a half-century earlier, *Roe v. Wade*, that enshrined abortion as a constitutional right. The decision was extremely controversial for many reasons: a solid majority of US citizens support abortion rights; the far-right Court's make-up had been orchestrated by a now-disgraced president (who also groped women on airplanes: see Chapter 7); and it flew in the face of stare decisis, a fundamental legal principle which means judges must follow precedent to safeguard the evenhanded, predictable, consistent development of legal principles.

The ruling did not make abortion illegal, but it removed the federal guarantee of protection. The Court handed authority back to the individual states, which immediately began a chaotic, highly politicized and polarized process of revising abortion laws individually, piecemeal: some states sought to enhance support for abortion, enshrining it as a state-constitutional right, and others restricted its accessibility, often drastically. Doctors in some states could no longer perform abortions to end nonviable pregnancies. Some states allowed exceptions for pregnancies resulting from rape or incest, others didn't.

In this scrum, the first state-level repercussion took place less than two months after *Roe* was overturned. In Kansas, whose state constitution guaranteed abortion rights, anti-choice activists, emboldened by the Court's decision, advanced a referendum for an amendment that would remove those rights—a step, many thought, toward instituting an absolute statewide ban on abortion. The referendum was called "Value them Both"—that is, both pregnant women and fetuses—a rhetorical smokescreen for its diminution of women's rights and bodily autonomy.

As Kansas is a reliably "red state," the common wisdom was that the amendment would pass. But it didn't: it lost (meaning women won) by an overwhelming 59–41 margin. The pro-choice camp was elated (and anti-choice factions stunned) to see citizens, especially from a conservative electorate, emphatically resisting the Supreme Court ruling at the state level. Women's reproductive freedom was valued more strongly than pundits had imagined, and voters turned out to protect those rights. Anti-choice forces' short-lived feelings of triumph after *Roe*'s repeal vanished as they realized there would be strong blowback. Abortion rights were not resolved by the Court's ruling—indeed, the issue became all the more unsettled, setting off advocacy movements, pro and con, that will continue fighting for their causes probably for many years, even decades, to come.

Amid one of the most highly charged ethical conflicts in modern US culture, enter Mark Gietzen—"Zealous Lieutenant in Anti-Abortion Movement," according to his obituary headline. His activism began in a 1991 campaign called Summer of Mercy, when thousands of people converged on Wichita to block access to abortion clinics. As chairman of Kansas Coalition for Life, he spent years protesting the practice of Dr. George Tiller, an abortion provider. Gietzen's followers harassed women who came to Tiller's clinic, blockaded it, tailed him with hidden cameras, sued him, and threatened him. One member of the group bombed Tiller's clinic, and another tried to kill him in 1993, shooting him five times and wounding him in both arms.[42] Finally, in 2009, Tiller was shot and killed while attending church. Celebrating the closure of Tiller's clinic after his murder, Gietzen said: "It looks like our prayer was answered."[43]

After the 2022 Kansas referendum's lopsided loss, most abortion opponents realized that they needed to regroup and reformulate their strategy, but Gietzen refused to accept defeat. He spent nearly $120,000 of his own money to finance a recount of the vote. (Governments conduct recounts at their own expense in tight contests, but when it's not a close call, private citizens have to pay for them.) In post-2020 US politics, a common right-wing strategy after electoral losses—originated by the disgraced ex-president himself—was claiming the vote was rigged; defeats reflected "deep-state conspiracies" rather than the voters' will. Recounts were conducted not so much to challenge the election results at hand, but rather to sow cynicism more generally about democracy. It was unheard of, though, to hold recounts when the margin was as large as it was in Kansas: it was an incredible case to make that *that many* ballot boxes were stuffed, or that many votes manipulated by foreign adversaries, George Soros, or vaccine microchips.

But Gietzen was nothing if not determined. Although the results were loud and clear, he did everything he could to stir the pot of anti-democratic sore-loser conspiracies. The recount obviously did not change the outcome: the referendum had lost by 165,000 votes; the recount resulted in changing fewer than 100 votes.

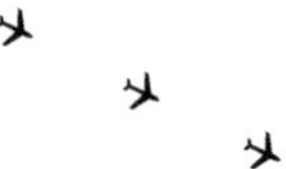

In an interview during the recount, Gietzen told *The Wichita Eagle* that "the nearly $120,000 he spent on the statewide recount would likely complicate his plans to renovate the old Cessna"—it was a 1963 model—"which he said he flew for the first time in the summer of 2022 after he put 15 years of work into it."

> "My only drawback on this Value Them Both recount is that that airplane is going to sit and collect dust for a little while," he said in August. "Well, not collect dust. I'll just go fly it in uncontrolled airspace, and we have to put 50 hours on it before you can fly with passengers anyway, which is a necessary and good rule. I've already got so much invested in that plane, I want to get finished. I'm so proud of this thing." Gietzen said the airplane was allowed only in uncontrolled airspace until he could afford to install instrumentation that would give onboard notice to other air traffic in the area.[44]

Flying his Cessna 172 Skyhawk from Newton, Kansas to Glen Ullin, North Dakota in bad weather on May 14, 2023, Gietzen crashed in Nebraska; the accident was not discovered until two days later, when a rancher came across the debris field on his property. Gietzen hadn't filed a flight plan or obtained a weather brief. The only person on board, he was pronounced dead at the scene. Gravity is a force, and karma is a force: extremely different in nature, they intersected at this Nebraska crash site.

Shakespeare often infused his drama with karma, exemplified when Polonius dies behind the arras, "hoist with his own petard." Dante too, in his poetry, appreciated what he called *contrapasso*, meaning that souls are punished in a way that relates to their sin. Contrapasso "functions not merely as a form of divine revenge," writes Peter Brand, "but rather as *the fulfillment of a destiny freely chosen* by each soul during his or her life" [emphasis mine].[45] Poetic justice is a cognate concept—"experiencing a fitting or deserved retribution for one's actions," as the *OED* defines it. As an English professor, I especially appreciate that frame of reference: poetry *does* facilitate justice, with a cherry on top.

Humanist investigators know what we're talking about here. You get what you deserve. You made your bed, now lie in it.

Karma is about consequences: cause and effect. Good intent, good deeds, make for good karma, while bad intent and deeds precipitate bad karma. A keystone of Buddhist and Hindu cosmologies, it is reprised in Abrahamic sacred texts: "They will eat the fruit of their ways and be filled with the fruit of their schemes" (Proverbs 1:31)—that is, you reap what you sow. In Qur'an: "whoever does an atom's weight of good shall see it; and whoever does an atom's weight of evil shall see it" (99.7–8). An intuitively sensible ethical proposition, it has been in the zeitgeist forever: it feels right.

If my verdict on Gietzen's crash, death by karma, seems egregious, well, in my defense, I am not the only one—far from it—with this reaction: the marketplace of ideas (Twitter) overbrimmed with macabre crash humor, heavily karma-tinged.

> Says he's pro-life. Dies anyway.
> @davenewworld_2
>
> It's a bit of a late-term abortion. But hey! Better late than never!
> @Father9
>
> He said that he spent so much money hurting women, he couldn't afford necessary maintenance on the plane. Seems like a Darwin award.
> @MarkStretch7
>
> My thoughts and prayers go out to . . . . the plane . . . .
> @1_OldGeezer1950
>
> God is a woman.
> @MeBeKristyna
>
> Guess gravity is for Abortion Rights ☹☹☹
> @SabioScientist
>
> The Lord called him home. Painfully
> @antoneta_silva
>
> He died as he lived. Not given the choice.
> @AzmodeusRedbear

God works in mysterious ways.
@nevilledog33

He aborted himself.
@LStecher2

He refused to abort.
@BGlennCreech

I guess he should have . . . aborted takeoff.
@the_b_ho_show

If he had said just ONE MORE prayer, he would've totally lived.
@IBeenFranklin

Please let him be a trend setter
@BillyDings

Did he have to take a plane with him? They arent making a lot of Cessna 172s these days.
@Public_Service1

Misogyny kills
@brooklynmarie

I guess the plane was Pro-Choice.
@jdgratz

At least he didn't take a woman with him.
@davenewworld_2

Too bad for him. Great for the rest of us.
@mornews

I guess God had a plan.
@otack58

Rest in pieces.
@irish_sprinkle

> Karma was the pilot.
> @lisaditejeda

At the risk of kicking the corpse, I'll add my own coda:

> What goes around comes around.
> @randymalamud

Karmic debris fields uniquely, astonishingly, offer insights unlike any others I've come across in terms of how we interpret and respond to crashes. "You pays your money and you takes your choice!" wrote Mark Twain in *Huckleberry Finn*.[46] Gietzen paid his money (for a preposterous recount), and made his choice (to defer maintenance on his decrepit old Cessna), while also making it his life's work to abrogate other people's choices. That's where the karma comes rushing in, guns blazing, hooting and clamoring, with might and main … bearing repercussions. If there's a god of karma (which there is—his name is Shani!), Gietzen swaggered into his crosshairs and implored him to pull the trigger. Gietzen's epitaph for Dr. Tiller became Twitter's epitaph for him: It looks like our prayer was answered.

Karma makes for extremely powerful, compelling crash narratives. I realize this is a provocative, controversial, even potentially offensive facet of my investigations, but I cannot imagine leaving it out. If conventional crash investigators eschew opinionated personal convictions, we humanists pile them on exuberantly. NTSB's dispassionate manner serves their rhetorical objectives, as our unabashedly passionate articulations enrich ours. I hope my investigations have made the case that there's a place for both, and that such polyvocality advances our shared, overarching goal of understanding plane crashes.

The end of crashes

Crashes inflected by Zen and karma are weirdly unusual and shocking—as are those animated by existentialism, sexism, racism, imperialism, capitalism, communism, terrorism, coin-flips, suicide, mansplaining, feathery plummeting, imperfect English proficiency, get-there-itis, irony, metaphor, peripeteia, prolepsis, premonition, reading beyond the ending, and all the rest of them.

All happy flights are alike; each unhappy flight is unhappy in its own way.

What can humanist crash investigations reveal about how to prevent future plane crashes by bad people (or people who do bad things)? For investigators who examine wiring and engines, pitot tubes and flight deck management, their intricate and extensive analyses are almost always able to find the precise problems and fix them. What if the problem is kamikaze pilots? If I could go back in time, I'd say to those university students who were snatched out of their classes to crash planes: Stay in school! Stamp out nationalist propaganda. Study literature (poetry is the opposite of propaganda)—*world* literature, instead of world war. Pour your youthful Sturm und Drang into minimalist art rather than maximalist military-imperial insanity. You are better students than you are warriors, better poets than pilots.

Going back in time, unfortunately, is not actually possible. (NTSB investigators can't time-travel either: they can't clear out the clogged pitot tubes that made a plane crash, but only redesign them so it doesn't happen again.) But cultural studies, historical studies, allow us to understand and apply the lessons of the past in our own time, so I'll have to settle for that: don't be a kamikaze, and don't delude yourself that delicate floral fancies can alleviate the tragic horror of plane crashes. Aviation is power and knowledge, and intentionally perverting both of those forces is profoundly wrong—ethically as well as intellectually and aesthetically.

And for Mark Gietzen: what's the object lesson here? An amateur pilot with a shoestring do-it-yourself maintenance plan should pay *really close attention* to mechanical and safety issues. If you're flying a sixty-year-old Cessna, don't skimp on parts: you get what you pay for. Also: mind your own #ing business, especially if you don't have a uterus yourself. Keep busy tinkering with your vintage airplane, and let other people worry about their own lives, their own choices.

Notes

1 Aviation and Its Discontents

(All websites accessed November 18, 2023.)

1 Virginia Madsen, "Critical Mass (an Interview with Paul Virilio)." *World Art* 1 (1995), 78–82.

2 Richard Stimson, "Wright Airplane Disaster." wrightstories.com/wright-airplane-disaster/

3 Fred Howard, *Wilbur and Orville: A Biography of the Wright Brothers*. New York: Knopf, 1987, 274.

4 *FAA Aviation News: A DOT/FAA Flight Standards Safety Publication*. Flight Standards' Accident Prevention Program Branch, Federal Aviation Administration, Department of Transportation, September/October 2009, Volumes 47–49, 28.

5 Stimson, "Wright Airplane Disaster."

6 Tara Dixon-Engel and Mike Jackson, *The Wright Brothers: First in Flight*. New York: Sterling, 2007, 108.

7 "Last Words." planecrashinfo.com/lastwords.htm

8 "Fatal Fall of Wright Airship." *New York Times*, September 18, 1908, 1.

9 Wright State University Libraries' Special Collections and Archives, "Selfridge Crash Described in New Acquisition." September 17, 2015. libraries.wright.edu/community/outofthebox/2015/09/17/selfridge-crash-described-in-new-acquisition/

10 "1LT Thomas Etholen Selfridge." militaryhallofhonor.com/honoree-record.php?id=3063

11 Wright Brothers Aeroplane Company, "Tragedy at Fort Myer." wright-brothers.org/History_Wing/Wright_Story/Showing_the_World/Tragedy_at_Fort_Myer/Tragedy_at_Fort_Myer.htm

12 "Hoxsey's Winnings For His Mother." January 2, 1911. nytimes.com/1911/01/02/archives/hoxseys-winnings-for-his-mother-the-wrights-will-also-pay-her-a.html

13 Paul Virilio, *Politics of the Very Worst*. New York: *Semiotext(e)*, 1999, 89.

14 Charles Perrow, *Normal Accidents: Living with High-Risk Technologies*. Princeton: Princeton University Press, 1999, 130.

15 Richard Hugo, "Where We Crashed." In *Making Certain it Goes On: The Collected Poems of Richard Hugo*, New York: Norton, 1983, 122–3.

16 *Oxford English Dictionary*, "black box."

17 George Bibel, *Beyond the Black Box: The Forensics of Airplane Crashes*. Baltimore: Johns Hopkins University Press, 2008, 6.

18 Perrow, *Normal Accidents*, 124.

19 Jeffrey Milstein, *Do Not Open*. Blurb, 2016, 2.

20 Nick Ross, "AIR FRANCE 447: 'Damn It! We're Going To Crash!'" May 1, 2012. businessinsider.com/air-france-447-damn-it-were-going-to-crash-2012-5

21 ANI, "Last words uttered from doomed Air France flight 447 were co-pilot's 'F**k, we're dead.'" October 14, 2014. business-standard.com/article/news-ani/last-words-uttered-from-doomed-air-france-flight-447-were-co-pilot-s-f-k-we-re-dead-114101400211_1.html. There is some controversy about the CVR transcript: Air France officials decried what they call inaccurate and/or irreverent publication of this conversation. Some versions do not include Robert's profanities, although some do. The BEA transcript lists "curses" as "(!)."

22 John Urry, *Mobilities*. Cambridge: Polity, 2007, 3, 18.

23 Maansi Kumar and Amyaz Moledina, "Mobility Studies." June 13, 2017. challengingborders.wooster.edu/blog/tag/mobility-studies/

24 F. Scott Fitzgerald, *The Crack-Up*. New York: New Directions, 1945, 69.

25 *Oxford English Dictionary*, "bought the farm."

26 snopes.com/fact-check/buy-the-farm/

27 almanac.com/fact/what-is-meant-by-the-phrase-bought

28 T. S. Eliot, "The Hollow Men." *Collected Poems 1909–1962*. New York: Harcourt, 1971, 79–80.

29 Rilo Kiley, *Take Offs and Landings*, 2001.

30 Scott McDonald, "Top 20 Quotes From Chuck Yeager." December 8, 1920, newsweek.com/top-20-quotes-chuck-yeager-first-man-break-sound-barrier-1553038.

31 Ireneusz Jozwiak, "The Probability of Dying in a Plane Crash or Having a Safe Flight." *Aviation* 19.1 (2015), 1–6.

32 National Safety Council, "Airplane Crashes." injuryfacts.nsc.org/home-and-community/safety-topics/airplane-crashes/

33 Randy Malamud, "Rising Above a Fear of Flying." *Chronicle of Higher Education*, December 9, 2011, B20.

34 Sarah Vander Schaaff, "Lots of Americans have a fear of flying." October 12, 2019. washingtonpost.com/health/lots-of-americans-have-a-fear-of-flying-there-are-way-to-overcome-the-anxiety-disorder/2019/10/11/d4746d84-d338-11e9-86ac-0f250cc91758_story.html

35 Sophie McBain, "The haunting spectre of plane crashes." *New Statesman*, March 15–21, 2019, 18.

36 genius.com/Moe-plane-crash-lyrics

37 Arjun Appadurai, "Disjuncture and Difference in the Global Cultural Economy." *Theory Culture Society* 1990 (7), 295–310.

38 Mihaly Csikszentmihalyi, *Flow: The Psychology of Optimal Experience.* New York: Harper, 1990.

39 Ole Jensen, "Blue Sky Matter: Toward an (In-flight) Understanding of the Sensuousness of Mobilities Design." *Transfers* 6.2 (Summer 2016), 23–42, 23.

40 Mary Roach, *Stiff: The Curious Lives of Human Cadavers.* New York: Norton, 2003, 116.

41 Elizabeth Shim, "North Korea military aircraft may have crashed, says Seoul." July 31, 2015. upi.com/Top_News/World-News/2015/07/31/North-Korea-military-aircraft-may-have-crashed-says-Seoul/6241438393219/

42 BBC, "North Korean plane crashes in China." August 18, 2010. bbc.com/news/world-asia-pacific-11008466

43 Albert Camus, *The Myth of Sisyphus and Other Essays.* Trans. Justin O'Brien. New York: Vintage 1955, 4.

44 "Liverpool apologise after Twitter account mocks Munich air disaster." August 30, 2013, theguardian.com/football/2013/aug/30/liverpool-twitter-munich-air-disaster

45 Eric Schatzberg, *Wings of Wood, Wings of Metal.* Princeton: Princeton University Press, 1999, 132–4.

46 Bibel, *Black Box*, 1–3.

47 Veronika Zuskáčová, "How We Understand Aeromobility." *Transfers* 10.2–3 (2020), 4–23, 15.

48 Steve Dougherty, "Sweet Dreams No More." April 1, 1991. people.com/archive/cover-story-sweet-dreams-no-more-vol-35-no-12/

49 Paul Roth, "Patsy Cline." musiclinernotes.wordpress.com/2010/06/02/patsy-cline/

50 Thomas Frank. "Celebrity plane crashes draw special scrutiny from the NTSB." December 4, 2014. usatoday.com/story/news/nation/2014/12/04/celebrity-plane-crash-victims/70053950/

51 E. L. Hamilton, "Clark Gable never recovered from the tragic death of his wife, Carole Lombard, in a plane crash." thevintagenews.com/2018/01/01/clark-gable-carole-lombard-2/?utm_source=penultimate&safari=1&A1c=1

52 Alexandra Jacobs, "Vivien Leigh and Laurence Olivier's Turbulent Relationship, Retold With Compassion." March 22, 2022. nytimes.com/2022/03/22/books/review-truly-madly-vivien-leigh-laurence-olivier-stephen-galloway.html

53 Terry Gross, "Laurie Anderson Reflects On Life And Loss In 'Heart Of A Dog.'" NPR, "Fresh Air," November 19, 2015. npr.org/2015/11/19/456655545/laurie-anderson-reflects-on-life-and-loss-in-heart-of-a-dog

54 Rich Juzwiak, "Paula Abdul Keeps Talking About Surviving a Plane Crash for Which NoRecordExists."June13,2019.jezebel.com/paula-abdul-keeps-talking-about-surviving-a-plane-crash-1835445212

55 Camus, *Myth of Sisyphus*, 20.

56 Dan Bilefsky, "Rift Over Air Crash Roils Poland's Artists." May 28, 2013. nytimes.com/2013/05/29/movies/polands-divide-over-smolensk-film-on-2010-air-crash.html

57 "10 April 2010 – Polish Air Force 101." tailstrike.com/database/10-april-2010-polish-air-force-101/
58 Bibel, *Black Box*, 10.
59 "Monument to the Victims of Smolensk Tragedy 2010." http://monuments-remembrance.eu/en/panstwa/polska-2/469-pomnik-ofiar-tragedii-smolenskiej-2010.
60 Kyle Chayka, "Anselm Kiefer Talks Religion, Politics, Ruins at 92Y." November 3, 2010. hyperallergic.com/11870/anselm-kiefer-92y/
61 David Morgan, "German Post-War Master Anselm Kiefer." February 4, 2018. cbsnews.com/pictures/german-post-war-master-anselm-kiefer/
62 Sebastian Smee, "Anselm Kiefer: Inside a black hole." September 18, 2014. prospectmagazine.co.uk/magazine/anselm-kiefer-inside-a-black-hole
63 Emily Esfahani Smith, "We Want to Travel and Party. Hold That Thought." June 24, 2021. nytimes.com/2021/06/24/opinion/covid-pandemic-grief.html
64 National Transportation Safety Board, "NTSB Aircraft Accident Report–Trans World Airlines Flight 800, Near East Moriches, NY July 17, 1996." ntsb.gov/investigations/AccidentReports/Reports/AAR0003.pdf
65 Joan Lowy, "Jet fuel-tank protection ordered." July 16, 2008. seattlepi.com/business/article/jet-fuel-tank-protection-ordered-1279529.php
66 Michael Gold, "Wreckage of T.W.A. Flight 800 to Be Destroyed Years After Explosion." February 25, 2021. nytimes.com/2021/02/25/nyregion/twa-flight-800-reconstruction.html
67 Randall Jarrell, *Selected Poems*. New York: Farrar, Straus & Giroux, 1990, 145.
68 "Randall Jarrell, Poet, Killed by Car in Carolina." October 15, 1965. nytimes.com/books/99/08/01/specials/jarrell-obit.html
69 Federal Aviation Agency, "Wildlife Hazard Mitigation: FAQ." faa.gov/airports/airport_safety/wildlife/faq/
70 Ed Brotak, "When Birds Strike." historynet.com/when-birds-strike.htm
71 Craig Greenlee, *November Ever After*. Bloomington: iUniverse, 2011, xvi.
72 "Red Arrows crash: Souvenir hunter in eBay sale claim." August 31, 2011. bbc.com/news/uk-england-dorset-14731599
73 Tom Demerly, "B-70 Valkyrie Wing Section on eBay: An Aviation History Mystery Continues." July 13, 2017. theaviationist.com/2017/07/13/xb-70-valkyrie-wing-section-on-ebay-an-aviation-history-mystery-continues/
74 T. S. Eliot, *The Waste Land*. poetryfoundation.org/poems/47311/the-waste-land
75 Leo Mellor, "Words from the bombsites: debris, modernism and literary salvage." *Critical Quarterly* 46.4 (December 2004), 77–90, 77.
76 Jonathan Glancey, "The crashes that changed plane designs forever." April 14, 2014. bbc.com/future/article/20140414-crashes-that-changed-plane-design

77 Richard Sandomir, "Don Bateman, Trailblazer in Airline Safety, Dies at 91." June 2, 2023. nytimes.com/2023/06/02/technology/don-bateman-dead.html
78 Mikita Brottman, ed., *Car Crash Culture*. New York: Palgrave, 2001, xv, xxiv–v, xxxviii.
79 Don DeLillo, *White Noise*. New York: Viking, 1985, 218–19.
80 Tom Judd, "Deconstructed." 2017. tomjuddart.com/artwork/deconstructed/
81 Ibid.
82 Roach, *Stiff*, 120.
83 Camus, *Myth of Sisyphus*, 22, 51.
84 Robert Browning, "Andrea del Sarto." poetryfoundation.org/poems/43745/andrea-del-sarto
85 Ibid., 62.
86 Jack Reynolds, *Understanding Existentialism*. New York: Routledge, 2014, 16.
87 Libby Nelson, "The Boy Who Survived a 1960 Midair Crash." June 30, 2009. archive.nytimes.com/cityroom.blogs.nytimes.com/2009/06/30/the-boy-who-survived-a-1960-midair-crash/
88 Gary Buiso, "The day death came from the sky." December 6, 2010. brooklynpaper.com/the-day-death-came-from-the-sky/
89 Michelle Young, "Remnants of a 1960 Park Slope Plane Crash Hidden in Plain Sight in Brooklyn." December 16, 2022. untappedcities.com/2022/12/16/park-slope-plane-crash-brooklyn/
90 US Civil Aeronautics Board, Aircraft Accident Report, June 12, 1962. ia800707.us.archive.org/27/items/Cab-aar1960-12-16-united-826-twa-266/Cab-aar1960-12-16-united-826-twa-266.pdf.
91 BBC News, "DR Congo: Is it one of the most dangerous places to fly?" November 30, 2019. bbc.com/news/world-africa-50562593
92 "Here is a List of All Blue Angels Accidents." June 23, 2018, fighterjetsworld.com/air/blue-angels-crash-videos-list-of-blue-angels-accidents/4911/
93 Damien Jurado, "Air Show Disaster." genius.com/Damien-jurado-air-show-disaster-lyrics
94 "James Jackson, "West Germany Hellfire from The Heavens." September 12, 1988. time.com/time/magazine/article/0,9171,968416,00.html
95 National Transportation Safety Board, Accident Report NTSB/AAR-10/01 PB2010-910401. 2010. https://www.ntsb.gov/investigations/accidentreports/reports/aar1001.pdf.
96 Karen Wielinski, *One on the Ground*, xi.
97 Ibid., 288, 333.
98 Ibid., 91, 129, 214, 219.

2 Plane Crashes Before Planes

1 William Moran, *Offaly History*. offalyhistory.com/wp-content/uploads/2018/02/Early-History-of-Tullamore-Dr-Moran.pdf, 8–9.

2 Tim Sharp, "The First Hot-Air Balloon Flight." April 9, 2019. space.com/16595-montgolfiers-first-balloon-flight.html.

3 Sarah Murden, "Two Tragically Die in Balloon Accident –15th June 1785." *All Things Georgian*, 15 June 2014, georgianera.wordpress.com/2014/06/15/two-die-in-balloon-accident/

4 Sam Howe Verhovek, "Before condemning the Titan's pilot, consider his side of the story." June 24, 2023. washingtonpost.com/opinions/2023/06/24/titan-submersible-pilot-stockton-rush-explorer/

5 Murden, "Balloon Accident."

6 David Mondey, "Parachutes." *Guinness Book of Aircraft.* Bath: Bath Press, 1992, 65.

7 Douglas Adams, *The Hitchhiker's Guide to the Galaxy*. New York: Ballantine, 2009, 270.

8 Whitney Hopler, "Meaning and Symbolism of Angel Wings in Bible, Torah, Quran." *Learn Religions*, April 27, 2019, learnreligions.com/why-do-angels-have-wings-123809

9 Geoffrey of Monmouth, *History of the Kings of Britain*. Trans. Aaron Thompson. Cambridge, Ontario: Medieval Latin Series, 1999, 28.

10 This story's main source is the 1878 book by imperial marauder Sir Henry Morton Stanley, *Through the Dark Continent* (London: Sampson Low, Marston, Searle, Rivington).

11 Sophia Nahli Allison, "Revisiting the Legend of Flying Africans." March 7, 2019. newyorker.com/culture/culture-desk/revisiting-the-legend-of-flying-africans

12 Ibid.

13 John Fuller, "Top 10 Bungled Attempts at One-person Flight." science.howstuffworks.com/transport/flight/classic/ten-bungled-flight-attempt.htm

14 Alice Oswald, *Falling Awake.* New York: Norton, 2016, 2.

15 Catherine Graham, "'The Whole Art of Everything is about Forgetting Yourself'–A Conversation with Alice Oswald." October 10, 2017. torontoreviewofbooks.com/2017/10/whole-art-everything-forgetting-conversation-alice-oswald/

16 "The 16th-Century Flight Of John Damian of Falcuis." thehistorianshut.com/2017/10/08/the-16th-century-flight-of-john-damian-of-falcuis/

17 William Dunbar, "A Ballad of the Friar of Tungland." allpoetry.com/poem/15427664-A-Ballad-of-the-Friar-of-Tungland-by-William-Dunbar

18 Fuller, "Top 10 Bungled Attempts."

19 Francesco Milizia, *The lives of celebrated architects, ancient and modern*, vol. 2. Trans. Mrs. Edward Cresy. Architectural Library, High Holborn, London, 1826, 150–2.

20 Fuller, "Top 10 Bungled Attempts."

21 Thomas Van Hare, "João de Almeida Torto Flies." fly.historicwings.com/2012/06/joao-de-almeida-torto-flies/

22 "Base Fatality List." bfl.baseaddict.com/list

23 Pranjal Pande, "The Story Behind Pan Am's Clipper Name Changes." December 24, 2020. simpleflying.com/pan-am-clipper-name-changes/

24 Clive Hart, *The Prehistory of Flight*. Berkeley: University of California Press, 1985, 188–90.

25 *Oxford English Dictionary*, "craft," "aircraft," "airship."

26 BBC News, "Hovercraft capsize disaster off Hampshire coast recalled 50 years ago." March 4, 2022. bbc.com/news/uk-england-hampshire-60236843

27 Howard, *Wilbur and Orville*, 274.

28 Juliane Koepcke, *When I Fell From the Sky: The True Story of One Woman's Miraculous Survival*. Trans. Ross Benjamin. Munich: Piper Verlag, 2011, 13.

29 Elizabeth Howell, "Chelyabinsk Meteor: A Wake-Up Call for Earth." January 9, 2019. space.com/33623-chelyabinsk-meteor-wake-up-call-for-earth.html

30 National Safety Council, "NSC Injury Facts." injuryfacts.nsc.org/home-and-community/safety-topics/bicycle-deaths/

31 Emily Sohn, "Why the Great Molasses Flood Was So Deadly." January 16, 2020. history.com/news/great-molasses-flood-science

32 *Breaking Bad*, season 3, episode 1. https://en.wikiquote.org/wiki/Breaking_Bad_(season_3)

33 National Transportation Safety Board, "NTSB Go-Team." ntsb.gov/investigations/process/Pages/goteam.aspx

34 National Transportation Safety Board, Aircraft Accident Report: Continental Airlines, Inc, Flight 1713." ntsb.gov/investigations/AccidentReports/Reports/AAR8809.pdf

35 Ibid., v.

36 Ibid., 2–3.

37 Ibid., 5, 37.

38 Ibid., 12–13.

39 Ibid., 90.

3 Existential Aviation and Poetic Premonitions of Death

1 George Carlin, *Napalm & Silly Putty*. New York: Hachette, 2001, 27.

2 Hervé Le Tellier, *The Anomaly* (trans. Adriana Hunter). New York: Other, 2022, 195–6, 53–4.

3 Ibid., 391.
4 Don DeLillo, *White Noise*. New York: Viking, 1985, 90–2.
5 James Pethica, "Yeats's 'perfect man.'" *Dublin Review* (Summer 2009). thedublinreview.com/article/yeatss-perfect-man/
6 W. B. Yeats, "An Irish Airman Foresees His Death." poets.org/poem/irish-airman-foresees-his-death
7 W. B. Yeats, "Reprisals." war-poetry.livejournal.com/788178.html
8 Joe Gleeson, *Irish Aces of the RFC and the RAF in the First World War*. Stroud, Gloucestershire: Fonthill: 2015. N.p.
9 Pethica, op cit.
10 Ray Burke, "Challenge to official accounts of Gregory death in WWI." January 2, 2018. rte.ie/news/analysis-and-comment/2018/0101/930446-robert-gregory/
11 Pethica, op cit.
12 See Rachel Blau DuPlessis, *Writing Beyond the Ending*. Bloomington: Indiana University Press, 1985.
13 Howard Nemerov, "The War in the Air." poetryfoundation.org/poems/47698/the-war-in-the-air
14 John Gillespie Magee Jr., "High Flight." poetryfoundation.org/poems/157986/high-flight-627d3cfb1e9b7
15 Lee Bailey, *The Enchantments of Technology*. Urbana: University of Illinois Press, 2005, 133.
16 Anne Morrow Lindbergh, *Hour of Gold, Hour of Lead*. New York: Harcourt, 1973, introduction.
17 Richard Bach, *Nothing By Chance*. New York: Simon & Schuster, 2012, 96.
18 Van Meter Ames, "America, Existentialism, and Zen." *Philosophy East and West* 1.1 (April 1951), 35–47, 45.
19 Søren Kierkegaard, *The Concept of Dread*. 1844. Trans. Walter Lowrie. Princeton: Princeton University Press, 1944, xii.
20 Søren Kierkegaard, *The Sickness Unto Death*. 1849. Trans. Alastair Hannay. New York: Penguin, 1989, 65.
21 Mark Vernon, "When did people stop thinking God lives on a cloud?" May 16, 2013. bbc.com/news/magazine-22480793
22 R. C. Lahoti, "Report of Court of Inquiry on Mid-Air Collision between Saudi Arabian Boeing 747 and Kazakhstan IL-76." November 12, 1996, 5. baaa-acro.com/sites/default/files/2020-12/HZ-AIH.pdf
23 planecrashinfo.com/cvr970927.htm
24 planecrashinfo.com/cvr980216.htm
25 Karen Wielinski, *One on the Ground*. Buffalo: Librastream, 2017, x.
26 Mark Hosenball, "'I Put my Trust in God': The Mystery of Flight 990." November 28, 1999. newsweek.com/i-put-my-trust-god-mystery-flight-990-164288

27 Yaron Steinbuch, "Texas pilot's last words before cargo plane crash: 'Lord, you have my soul.'" December 20, 2019. nypost.com/2019/12/20/texas-plane-pilots-last-words-before-crash-lord-you-have-my-soul/
28 Ames "America, Existentialism, and Zen," 46.
29 Christina Anders, "John Gillespie Magee's 'High Flight' (1941)." In *Discourses of Mobility–Mobility of Discourse*. Ed. Peter Wenzel. Trier, Germany: WVT Trier, 2010, 135–41, 138.
30 Thomas Devlin, "Jargon Watch: Pilot Lingo And The Language Of The Sky." May 15, 2018. babbel.com/en/magazine/jargon-watch-pilot-lingo-and-the-language-of-the-sky
31 Lahoti, op cit., 7.
32 Ames, "America, Existentialism, and Zen," 37.
33 A. Martin-Saint-Laurent, et al. "Clinical aspects of inflight incapacitations in commercial aviation." *Aviation, Space, and Environmental Medicine* 61.3 (1990), 256–60.
34 Antoine de Saint-Exupéry, *Saint-Exupéry: Art, Writings, and Musings*. Ed. Nathalie des Vallieres, trans. Anthony Zielonka. New York: Rizzoli, 2003, 71.
35 Winged Sandals, "Radio Communications." wingedsandalssquadron.wordpress.com/radio-communications/
36 Marconi Heritage, "The Wireless War in the Air." marconiheritage.org/ww1-air.html
37 Pethica, op cit.
38 Magee, "High Flight."
39 Peter Armenti, "John Gillespie Magee's 'High Flight.'" September 3, 2013. blogs.loc.gov/catbird/2013/09/john-gillespie-magees-high-flight/
40 Mike Jennam, "The Last High Flight." *Flying* 120.1 (1993), 36–8.
41 Tom Walsh, warbirdinformationexchange.org/phpBB3/viewtopic.php?f=3&t=11024
42 Armenti, "Magee's 'High Flight.'"
43 Anders, "Magee's 'High Flight' (1941)," 135.
44 Bomber Command Museum of Canada. bombercommandmuseum.ca/chronicles/john-gillespie-magee/
45 Charles Garton, "Slipping the Surly Bonds." *ANQ* 7.7 (1994), 154–62. 161
46 John Denver, "Flight (The Higher We Fly)." youtube.com/watch?v=2gUvmB3Bg2I
47 Command Performance, Program 99, December 21, 1943. oldtimeradiodownloads.com/variety/command-performance/command-performance-43-12-21-099-fred-waring-kate-smith-orson-welles
48 Garton, "Surly Bonds," 154.
49 Anders, "Magee's 'High Flight' (1941)," 135.
50 Ben Lerner, *10:04: A Novel*. New York: Farrar, Straus & Giroux, 2014, 114.
51 Ronald Reagan, Speech on the Challenger Disaster, January 28, 1986. teachingamericanhistory.org/library/document/speech-on-the-challenger-disaster/

52 Justin Moyer, "Exactly the right words, exactly the right way." January 28, 2016. washingtonpost.com/news/morning-mix/wp/2016/01/28/how-ronald-reagan-explained-the-challenger-disaster-to-the-world-its-all-part-of-taking-a-chance/
53 Lerner, *10:04: A Novel*, 114–15.
54 Carey Morewedge, "When Dreaming Is Believing: The (Motivated) Interpretation of Dreams." *Journal of Personality & Social Psychology* 96.2 (February 2009). 249–64, 249.
55 Virginia Woolf, *A Room of One's Own*. New York: Harvest, 1957, 31–2.
56 Gabrielle Moss, "What Do Plane Crash Dreams Mean? Experts Explain." July 13, 2021. bustle.com/life/what-do-plane-crashing-dreams-mean-7330697
57 "What Do Dreams of a Plane Crash Mean?" dreams.co.uk/sleep-matters-club/what-do-dreams-of-a-plane-crash-mean
58 "16 Spiritual Meanings When You Dream About A Plane Crash." basaltnapa.com/dream-about-a-plane-crash/
59 Don Kuiken, "The Contrasting Effects of Nightmares, Existential Dreams, and Transcendent Dreams." In *Dream research: Contributions to clinical practice*, ed. M. Kramer, 174-87. New York: Routledge, 2015, 178–9.

4 The Day the Music Died

1 Cure For Sanity, "Nightmare at 20000 Feet." 1990. genius.com/Pop-will-eat-itself-nightmare-at-20000-feet-lyrics
2 Modest Mouse, "Shit Luck." 1997. genius.com/Modest-mouse-shit-luck-lyrics
3 The Rolling Stones, "Flight 505." 1966. genius.com/The-rolling-stones-flight-505-lyrics
4 Philippe Margotin, *The Rolling Stones: All the Songs*. New York: Black Dog & Leventhal, 2016.
5 Richie Unterberger, "The Rolling Stones." N.d. allmusic.com/song/flight-505-mt0010710833
6 Søren Kierkegaard, *The Sickness Unto Death*, 1849.
7 Veronika Zuskáčová, "Aeromobility," 13.
8 moe., "Plane Crash." 1998. songmeanings.com/songs/view/107415/
9 The History Channel, "'American Pie' hits #1 on the pop charts." history.com/this-day-in-history/american-pie-hits-1-on-the-pop-charts
10 Madeline McMahon, "McLean's American Pie Manuscript sells for $1.2 million." April 7, 2015. bostonglobe.com/business/2015/04/07/mclean-american-pie-manuscript-sells-for-million/R9y3oYyjnOfNTt2E4DhPrK/story.html

11 Rich Everitt, *Falling Stars*. Augusta: Harbor, 2004, 14–15.
12 Tom Ott, "Waylon Jennings' Close Call on 'The Day the Music Died.'" December 15, 2020. biography.com/news/waylon-jennings-plane-crash-day-the-music-died
13 *Rolling Stone*, "500 Greatest Songs of All Time." rollingstone.com/music/music-lists/500-greatest-songs-of-all-time-151127/the-byrds-eight-miles-high-63040/
14 McMahon, op cit.
15 Rob Crilly, "Don McLean explains enigmatic lyrics to American Pie." April 8, 2015. smh.com.au/entertainment/music/don-mclean-explains-enigmatic-lyrics-to-american-pie-20150408-1mgbso.html
16 Rob Walker, "Don McLean on the tragedy behind American Pie." October 22, 2020. theguardian.com/music/2020/oct/22/don-mclean-american-pie-its-meaning-family-deaths-tragedy-60s
17 Gina Martinez, "Mother weeps over open coffin of Brazilian pop star daughter Marilia Mendonca, 26." dailymail.co.uk/news/article-10172815/Thousands-line-outside-STADIUM-pay-respects-Brazilian-singer-Marilia-Mendonca.html
18 Katherine Ellison, "The Curious Return of Infante." May 26, 1990. washingtonpost.com/archive/lifestyle/1990/05/26/the-curious-return-of-infante/111797e5-9539-4b3e-8233-132854adbd2b/
19 Mark Yakich, *The Dangerous Book of Poetry for Planes* (London: Eyewear, 2017), 50.
20 Nick Keppler, "The Strange Case of Buddy Holly's Final Pair of Glasses." February 27, 2016. mentalfloss.com/article/76207/strange-case-buddy-hollys-final-pair-glasses
21 Civil Aeronautics Board, "Aircraft Accident Report 2-0001." September 23, 1959. wikisource.org/wiki/Aircraft_Accident_Report_for_Buddy_Holly%27s_crash
22 Drive-By Truckers, "Angels and Fuselage." 2001. genius.com/Drive-by-truckers-angels-and-fuselage-lyrics
23 Justin Vicory, "The night Lynyrd Skynyrd fell from the sky." October 21, 2017. clarionledger.com/story/news/local/2017/10/21/lynyrd-skynyrd-plane-crash-survivors/761163001/
24 drivebytruckers.com/records-southernrockopera.html
25 "Lynyrd Skynyrd Crash Site Monument." roadsideamerica.com/tip/67255
26 NOFX, "Falling in Love." 1997. genius.com/Nofx-falling-in-love-lyrics
27 La Dispute, "Such Small Hands." genius.com/La-dispute-such-small-hands-lyrics
28 "Your Son is Dead." horntip.com/mp3/1980s/1989--2002_a_night_at_the_bar_with_the_boys_(CD)/20_dear_mom_your_son_is_dead.htm
29 *Virginia Argus* (Richmond, Va.), June 5, 1805, 2. chroniclingamerica.loc.gov/lccn/sn84024710/1805-06-05/ed-1/seq-2/
30 gknauth, Aviation Stack Exchange. March 30, 2014. aviation.stackexchange.com/a/2896

31 Adrian Vargas, "Premiere: Le Couleur Embrace Macabre Sensuality On Latest Single 'Concorde.'" February 6, 2020. atwoodmagazine.com/lecc-le-couleur-concorde-premiere-2020/
32 Jordan Currie, "Le Couleur Explore Death Through Dance on 'Concorde.'" September 8, 2020. exclaim.ca/music/article/le_couleur_concorde_album_review
33 Elizabeth Maxham, "The Story Behind James Taylor's 'Fire and Rain.'" January 13, 2022. grunge.com/733123/the-story-behind-james-taylors-fire-and-rain/
34 Rammstein, "Dalai Lama." Affenknecht, affenknecht.com/lyrics/rammstein-dalai-lama-lyric-with-english-translation/
35 Jimmy McHugh and Harold Adamson, "Comin' In On A Wing and a Prayer." 1943. genius.com/Four-vagabonds-comin-in-on-a-wing-and-prayer-lyrics
36 "The meaning and origin of the expression: On a wing and a prayer." phrases.org.uk/meanings/on-a-wing-and-a-.prayer.html
37 Dario Leone, "How an Israeli F-15 Eagle managed to land with one wing." September 15, 2014. heaviationist.com/2014/09/15/f-15-lands-with-one-wing/
38 "Plane crash changes meaning of a joyful song." November 18, 2001. baltimoresun.com/news/bs-xpm-2001-11-18-0111180400-story.html
39 Admiral Cloudberg (Kyra Dempsey), "Days of Our Discontent: The crash of American Airlines flight 587." admiralcloudberg.medium.com/days-of-our-discontent-the-crash-of-american-airlines-flight-587-9913f66814e8
40 Gary Younge, "Flight to the Death." November 11, 2006. theguardian.com/lifeandstyle/2006/nov/11/weekend.garyyounge
41 Anne Barnard, "Hit Hard by 9/11, a Piece of Queens Struggles to Let Go." September 11, 2011. nytimes.com/2011/09/11/us/sept-11-reckoning/queens.html
42 "Plane crash changes meaning," op cit.
43 Evan Serpick, "Kinito Mendez's Tragic Note." November 23, 2001. ew.com/article/2001/11/23/kinito-mendezs-tragic-note/
44 Lyrics, Kinito Méndez. lyrics.com/artist/Kinito-Méndez/141726
45 Bruce Springsteen, "Deportee." youtube.com/watch?v=7mO4Um2a7lk
46 Tim Hernandez, *All They Will Call You: The Telling of the Plane Wreck at Los Gatos Canyon.* Tucson: University of Arizona Press, 2017, 18–19.
47 Woody Guthrie, "Deportees," 1948. woodyguthrie.org/Lyrics/Deportee.htm
48 Hernandez, *All They Will Call You,* 18–19.
49 "The Plane Wreck at Los Gatos Canyon." check-six.com/Crash_Sites/Deportee_1948_crash.htm
50 Hernandez, op cit., 5, 10.
51 Diana Marcum, "Naming the shadows; 28 Mexican citizens returning home perished in a fireball over Central California. Who were they?" *Los Angeles Times,* July 10, 2013: A 1.

52 Pierre Köchel, "What If You Fell out of an Airplane at 30,000 Feet." August 5, 2019. insh.world/science/what-if-you-fell-out-of-an-airplane-at-30000-feet/
53 "Bill Barilko, the Tragically Hip & the Most Famous Goal in Maple Leafs History." April 21, 2022. thehockeywriters.com/maple-leafs-barilko-tragically-hip-mission-cap/
54 Kevin McGran, "Leafs mourn 'huge inspiration' Downie." thestar.com/sports/leafs/2017/10/18/leafs-mourn-inspiration-downie.html
55 Bright Eyes, "At the Bottom of Everything." 2005. genius.com/Bright-eyes-at-the-bottom-of-everything-lyrics
56 "31 January 2000, Alaska Airlines 261." tailstrike.com/database/31-january-2000-alaska-airlines-261/

5 Crashes in Art

1 Deborah Solomon, *American Mirror*. New York: Farrar, Straus & Giroux, 2013, 113–14.
2 "ASCII." outpost9.com/reference/jargon/jargon_16.html
3 Megan Garber, "'Screamer,' 'Slammer,' 'Bang.' . . . and 15 Other Ways to Say 'Exclamation Point.'" April 4, 2013. theatlantic.com/technology/archive/2013/04/screamer-slammer-bang-and-15-other-ways-to-say-exclamation-point/274687/
4 DC Comics, "The Battle Hawk," in *All-American Men of War*, 92 (July/August 1962), 3–15.
5 Tate Museum, "*Whaam!*" tate.org.uk/art/artworks/lichtenstein-whaam-t00897
6 Richard Cork, "A Bitter Truth." *Apollo* 179.616 (January 2014), 36–42, 37.
7 Charles Hall, "Aerial Creatures: Paul Nash." London: Imperial War Museums, 1996, 8.
8 Robert Hemmings, "Modernity's Object: The Airplane, Masculinity, and Empire." *Criticism* 57.2, (Spring 2015), 283–308, 298.
9 Imperial War Museums, "Battle of Britain." iwm.org.uk/collections/item/object/20102
10 Hemmings, "Modernity's Object," 297.
11 Hall, "Aerial Creatures," 9.
12 Imperial War Museums, "Battle of Britain."
13 Hall, "Aerial Creatures," 7, 15.
14 "English Surrealism versus the Luftwaffe: Paul Nash's *Bomber in the Corn*." goshandgolly.wordpress.com/2012/05/25/english-surrealism-versus-the-luftwaffe-paul-nashs-bomber-in-the-corn/
15 The Battle of Britain London Monument, "The War Artists–Paul Nash." bbm.org.uk/airmen/PaulNashindex.htm

16 Robert Hemmings, "Beautiful objects, dutiful things: waste, ruins and the stuff of war." *Word & Image* 32.4 (2016), 360–74, 368.

17 Hall, "Aerial Creatures," 31–3.

18 Paul Nash, "The Personality of Planes." *Vogue* March 1942, 43–4, 76.

19 Hall, "Aerial Creatures," 32.

20 Michael Prodger, "Paul Nash: the modernity of ancient landscapes." October 28, 2016. newstatesman.com/culture/2016/10/paul-nash-modernity-ancient-landscapes

21 Tate Museum, "Paul Nash, Totes Meer." tate.org.uk/art/artworks/nash-totes-meer-dead-sea-n05717

22 Richard Cork, "The Killing Fields," *New Statesman.* August 4, 2003, 27–9, 29.

23 The Art Story, "Paul Nash." theartstory.org/artist/nash-paul/

24 Hall, "Aerial Creatures," 32–3.

25 Prodger, "Paul Nash."

26 Museum of Oxford: "Repair, reuse, redeploy: Morris Motors during WW2." museumofoxford.org/repair-reuse-redeploy-morris-motors-during-ww2

27 Tate Museum, "Paul Nash."

28 Ibid.

29 "Totes Meer (Dead Sea) postcard." commons.wikimedia.org/wiki/File:Totes_Meer_(Dead_Sea)_postcard_-_Paul_Nash.jpg

30 Hemmings, "Beautiful Objects," 369–70.

6 Art in Crashes

1 "Newark Airport Administration Building Murals At Newark Museum." livingnewdeal.org/projects/newark-museum-aerial-map-mural-newark-nj/

2 Personal correspondence, Parker Field, June 21, 2022.

3 Civil Aeronautics Board, "Investigation of Aircraft Accident. American Airlines: Jamaica Bay, Long Island, NY." rosap.ntl.bts.gov/view/dot/33668

4 *Mad Men*, "Flight 1," season 2, episode 2, August 3, 2008.

5 AP, "Picasso Painting Lost in Crash." web.archive.org/web/20080423221854/http://www.cbsnews.com/stories/1998/09/14/world/main17411.shtml

6 Aly Thompson, "'Treasure, it just makes people crazy': Diamonds and jewels from Swissair Flight 111 still missing, 20 years on." August 30, 2018. nationalpost.com/news/canada/the-enduring-mystery-of-the-lost-diamonds-from-the-crash-of-swissair-flight-111

7 Anthony Depalma, "Swissair Jet's Cargo Had Painting By Picasso and Other Valuables." September 15, 1998. nytimes.com/1998/09/15/nyregion/swissair-jet-s-cargo-had-painting-by-picasso-and-other-valuables.html

8 "Pablo Picasso, *Le Peintre* (*The Painter*), 1963." MFA Masterworks. masterworksfineart.com/artists/pablo-picasso/collotype/le-peintre-the-painter-1963/id/W-5891
9 "The Painter." sartle.com/artwork/the-painter-pablo-picasso
10 Mychael Schnell, "$500M compensation fund opens for Boeing 737 Max victims' families." June 22, 2021. thehill.com/policy/transportation/aviation/559608-500m-compensation-fund-opens-for-boeing-max-737-victims/
11 AP, "Korean Airline To Pay Victim's Kin $10 Million." May 29, 1996. deseret.com/1996/5/29/19245323/korean-airline-to-pay-victim-s-kin-10-million.
12 Saundra Torrey, "Payments to Crash Survivors Called Inadequate." October 28, 1988. washingtonpost.com/archive/politics/1988/10/28/payments-to-crash-survivors-called-inadequate/84b0eb4c-803e-4bcd-aff4-91dfff17fd75/
13 Nicholas Parco, "Swissair Flight 111 cargo included Picasso painting, valuable jewels." September 2, 2015. nydailynews.com/news/world/swissair-flight-111-cargo-included-picasso-painting-jewels-article-1.2346330
14 BBC, "'Up to' $100m art lost in attacks." October 5, 2001. news.bbc.co.uk/2/hi/entertainment/1581737.stm
15 Whitney Museum, "Order and Ornament: Roy Lichtenstein's Entablatures." whitney.org/exhibitions/roy-lichtenstein-entablatures
16 Smithsonian Museum, "Modern Head." americanart.si.edu/artwork/modern-head-77128
17 Biblioklept, "List of Artworks Destroyed in the 9/11 World Trade Center Attack." biblioklept.org/2012/09/11/list-of-artworks-destroyed-in-the-911-world-trade-center-attack/
18 Eden Gordon, "The Top 10 Secrets of NYC's Zuccotti Park." untappedcities.com/2017/06/12/the-top-10-secrets-of-nycs-zuccotti-park/7/
19 Tom Miller, "John Seward Johnson II's 'Double Check'–Zuccotti Park." March 27, 2012. daytoninmanhattan.blogspot.com/2012/03/john-seward-johnson-iis-double-check.html
20 *New York Times*, "Louise Nevelson Dedicates Her Sculpture at Trade Center." December 13, 1978. nytimes.com/1978/12/13/archives/louise-nevelson-dedicates-her-sculpture-at-trade-center.html
21 István Hargittai. *New York Scientific: A Culture of Inquiry, Knowledge, and Learning.* Oxford: Oxford University Press, 2017, 264.
22 Donna Urschel, "Lives and Treasures Taken: 9/11 Attacks Destroy Cultural and Historical Artifacts." *Library of Congress Information Bulletin*, November 2002. loc.gov/loc/lcib/0211/911-treasures.html
23 Noah Adams, "Found Art: Parts of Calder Sculpture Retrieved from Trade Center." October 22, 2001. legacy.npr.org/news/specials/response/home_front/features/2001/oct/foundart/011022.foundart.html

24 "Alexander Calder's Bent Propeller–A Lost Work Of Art." notestothemilkman.wordpress.com/2013/07/05/alexander-calders-bent-propeller-a-lost-work-of-art/
25 Ibid.
26 Heritage Preservation, "Cataclysm and Challenge." 2002. cool.culturalheritage.org/byorg/hp/PDFS/Cataclysm.pdf
27 Holland Cotter, "The Studios Were Lost, But the Artists Get Their Day." December 3, 2001. nytimes.com/2001/12/03/arts/art-review-the-studios-were-lost-but-the-artists-get-their-day.html
28 Victoria Valentine, "Retrospective of Michael Richards Showcases Rigor, Promise of Artist who Died in Sept. 11 Terrorist Attack on World Trade Center." September 11, 2021. culturetype.com/2021/09/11/retrospective-of-michael-richards-showcases-rigor-promise-of-artist-who-died-in-sept-11-terrorist-attack-on-world-trade-center/
29 Karen Rosenberg, "The Ascendant Legacy of Michael Richards." July 1, 2021. artfuljaunts.com/magazine/the-ascendant-legacy-of-michael-richards
30 Heritage Preservation, "Cataclysm and Challenge."
31 "Are you down?" by Michael Richards. cafriseabove.org/artifact/are-you-down-by-michael-richards/
32 Theopolis Johnson, "Tuskegee Experience." tuskegee.edu/Content/Uploads/Tuskegee/files/TuskegeeExperience(1).pdf
33 Cotter, "The Studios Were Lost."
34 Heritage Preservation, "Cataclysm and Challenge."
35 Dale Gyure, "Minoru Yamasaki (1912–1986)." February 21, 2019. architectural-review.com/essays/reputations/minoru-yamasaki-1912-1986
36 Ibid.
37 Moby, "eulogy for the twin towers." October 6, 2001. moby.com/journal/eulogy-for-twin-towers/
38 Cora Sowa, "Epilogue to 'Holy Places': the World Trade Center as a Mythic Place." minervaclassics.com/wtcholy.htm
39 Hannah Kinney, "John Bachmann's New York." visualizingnyc.org/essays/john-bachmanns-new-york/
40 Bart Jansen, "As this (intentional) 727 crash shows, you can survive." October 1, 2012. usatoday.com/story/travel/flights/2012/10/01/inside-a-doomed-jetliner-tv-show-stages-727-crash/1606749/
41 *The Economist*, "A museum in the sky." October 11, 2001. economist.com/node/814452
42 Adrian Wilson, "Piecing Together the Stories of Art Lost During 9/11." cultbytes.com/author/adrianwilson/
43 Dan Barry and William Rashbaum, "Born of Hell, Lost After Inferno; Rodin Work From Trade Center Survived, and Vanished." May 20, 2002. nytimes.

com/2002/05/20/nyregion/born-hell-lost-after-inferno-rodin-work-trade-center-survived-vanished.html

44 Ibid.

45 Ibid.

46 Ann Uhry Abrams, *Explosion at Orly*. Atlanta: Avion, 2002, 5.

47 Ibid., 64, 141–3, ix–xiii.

48 See warhol.org/timecapsule/andy-warhols-time-capsule-21/time-capsule-21-artwork/

49 David Pascoe, *Airspaces*. London: Reaktion, 2001, 60–1.

50 AP, "Death of All 17 on Airliner in Maryland Laid to Swans." March 22, 1963. timesmachine.nytimes.com/timesmachine/1963/03/23/96968662.pdf

51 ABC, "Passengers were mostly businessmen plus one bomber," May 23, 2010. abc7.com/archive/7457547/

52 Paul Boshears, "Reading Warhol's *129 Die in Jet!*" paulboshears.com/2018/11/11/reading-warhols-129-die-in-jet/

7 Race, Crash, and Gender

1 Mary Roach, *Stiff*, 125.

2 Milena Evtimova, "Forever and Always Wright." September 15, 2006. oberlin.edu/stupub/ocreview/2006/09/15/features/Forever_and_Always_Wright.html

3 David McCullough, *The Wright Brothers*. New York: Simon & Schuster, 2015, 195–200.

4 Evtimova, "Forever and Always Wright."

5 Cicero, *De natura deorum* (*On the Nature of the Gods*), II.xxvi. Trans. H. Rackham. Cambridge: Harvard University Press, 1933, 187.

6 Seneca, *Naturales quaestiones*, III.14.2. Trans. John Clarke. London: Macmillan, 1910. naturalesquaestiones.blogspot.com

7 Clive Hart, *The Prehistory of Flight* (Berkeley: University of California Press, 1985), 1–4, 10–11.

8 Gilbert King, "Sophie Blanchard—The High Flying Frenchwoman Who Revealed the Thrill and Danger of Ballooning." October 18, 2012. smithsonianmag.com/history/sophie-blanchard-the-high-flying-frenchwoman-who-revealed-the-thrill-and-danger-of-ballooning-89106237/

9 Grenville Mellen, *Sad Tales and Glad Tales*. Boston: Goodrich, 1828, 185.

10 Charles Dickens, "Over the Water." *Household Words* 1853 (7), 488.

11 Erin McComb, Review, *Weekend Pilots* by Alan Meyer. *Technology and Culture* 58.1, 2017, 288–90.

12 Harriet Baskas, "Note left for female pilot: Cockpit 'no place for a woman.'" March 5, 2014 today.com/news/note-left-female-pilot-cockpit-no-place-woman-2D79324042
13 "Cockswain," *Oxford English Dictionary*. Now commonly "coxswain."
14 William Dubois, "Why is the cockpit called the cockpit?" September 21, 2020. generalaviationnews.com/2020/09/21/why-is-the-cockpit-called-the-cockpit/
15 "Cockpit," *Oxford English Dictionary*.
16 Ann Pfau, *Miss Yourlovin: GIs, Gender and Domesticity During World War II*. New York: Columbia University Press, 2013, 9.
17 "What do you call a cockpit when the pilots are female?" reddit.com/r/Jokes/comments/xm4j47/what_do_you_call_a_cockpit_when_the_pilots_are/
18 US Bureau of Labor Statistics, "Labor Force Statistics from the Current Population Survey." 2021. bls.gov/cps/cpsaat11.htm
19 Niraj Chokshi, "The End of the All-Male, All-White Cockpit." April 23, 2022. nytimes.com/2022/04/23/business/pilots-diversity.html
20 Amanda Laughead, "Fighting for the Right to Fly: Marlon D. Green." February 22, 2023. airandspace.si.edu/stories/editorial/marlon-green
21 Lisa Tyler, "Marlon Green's Legal Battle to Break Aviation Barriers." September 29, 2020. medium.com/faa/marlon-greens-legal-battle-to-break-aviation-barriers-600b2c12898f
22 Elizabeth Blair, "'Segregated Skies' tells the story of the first Black pilot for a commercial airline." February 18, 2022. npr.org/2022/02/18/1080731249/segregated-skies-tells-the-story-of-the-first-black-pilot-for-a-commercial-airli
23 Chokshi, "The End."
24 Mitchell Jackson, "Flying First Class: Luxurious Treat or Insidious Bastion of Racism?" February 10, 2022, esquire.com/lifestyle/a39008063/first-class-travel-racism-essay/
25 Michael Goldstein, "The Bumping And Beating Of Dr. David Dao." December 20, 2017. forbes.com/sites/michaelgoldstein/2017/12/20/biggest-travel-story-of-2017-the-bumping-and-beating-of-doctor-david-dao/?sh=2ce525cff61f
26 "NY-Israel flight delayed by ultra-Orthodox men's refusal to sit next to women," July 18, 2018. timesofisrael.com/flight-delayed-over-ultra-orthodox-mens-refusal-to-sit-next-to-women/
27 Selena Hill, "Black Doctor Removed From American Airlines Flight Due to 'Inappropriate' Outfit." July 10, 2019. blackenterprise.com/black-doctor-plane-inappropriate-outfit/
28 Larry Neumeister, "Woman testifies that she too was sexually attacked by Trump." May 2, 2023. apnews.com/article/trump-rape-trial-carroll-columnist-315e42c5190b086c84dd0708c41490fe

29 Jose DelReal, "Trump mocks sexual assault accuser: 'She would not be my first choice.'" October 14, 2016. washingtonpost.com/news/post-politics/wp/2016/10/14/trump-mocks-sexual-assault-accuser-she-would-not-be-my-first-choice/
30 Melanie Cox, "Fight and Flight." September 2, 2020. marieclaire.com/politics/a33252517/sexual-misconduct-on-airplanes/
31 Rett Nelson, "Pilot killed in plane crash was 'adventurous, beautiful' woman who 'brightened the room with her smile.'" April 14, 2022. eastidahonews.com/2022/04/pilot-killed-in-plane-crash-was-adventurous-beautiful-woman-who-brightened-the-room-with-her-smile/
32 K. L. McFadden, "Comparing pilot-error accident rates of male and female airline pilots." *Omega* 24.4 (1996), 443–50. sciencedirect.com/science/article/abs/pii/0305048396000126
33 G. J. Vail et al., "Pilot-error accidents: male vs female." *Applied Ergonomics* 17.2 (December 1986), 297–303.
34 Susan Baker, "Gender Differences In General Aviation Crashes." publichealth.jhu.edu/2001/gender-aviation-crashes
35 Eileen Lebow, *Before Amelia: Women Pilots in the Early Days of Aviation.* Washington, DC: Potomac, 2002. 137, 250.
36 Kerri Alexander, "Bessie Coleman." December 2022, womenshistory.org/education-resources/biographies/bessie-coleman#
37 Michael Graham, "First Licensed Woman Pilot in Germany." earlyaviators.com/ebeese2.htm
38 Lebow, *Before Amelia*, 50–1.
39 "Mrs Stocks, A pioneer British pilot." *Times* (London), May 7, 1971. 18.
40 Lebow, *Before Amelia*, 137.
41 Hannah Chan, "Blanche Stuart Scott." faa.gov/sites/faa.gov/files/about/history/pioneers/Blanche_Stuart_Scott.pdf
42 Lebow, *Before Amelia*, 13–14, 21.
43 Kerri Alexander, "Bessie Coleman. National Women's History Museum. womenshistory.org/education-resources/biographies/bessie-coleman
44 Daniel Slotnik, "Overlooked No More: Bessie Coleman, Pioneering African-American Aviatrix." December 11, 2019. nytimes.com/2019/12/11/obituaries/bessie-coleman-overlooked.html
45 Federal Aviation Administration, "Top 5 Lessons from Bessie Coleman's Legacy." January 25, 2021. medium.com/faa/top-5-lessons-from-bessie-colemans-legacy-f12e0576e2f3
46 Barbie, Inspiring Women, Bessie Coleman doll. Promotional copy on packaging.
47 Samuel Beckett, *Worstword Ho*. New York: Grove, 1983. samuel-beckett.net/w_ho.html
48 Lebow, *Before Amelia*, 250–1.

49 "Beese Biography." earlyaviators.com/ebeese1.htm
50 Wendy Boase, *The Sky's the Limit: Women Pioneers in Aviation.* New York: Macmillan, 1979, 12.
51 Lebow, *Before Amelia*, 251.
52 Leslie Kerr, *Harriet Quimby: Flying Fair Lady.* Atglen, PA: Schiffer, 2016, 70.
53 Don Dahler, *Fearless: Harriet Quimby, A Life Without Limit.* New York: Princeton Architectural Press, 2022, 291–3, 297.
54 Carly Courtney, "Lincoln J. Beachey: The Tragic Rise and Fall of the Master Birdman." disciplesofflight.com/aviation-pioneer-lincoln-j-beachey/
55 Dahler, *Fearless,* 298.
56 Ibid., 300
57 Leo Stevens, "On the Death of Miss Quimby." *Aeronautics* (August 1912), 67.
58 Kerr, *Harriet Quimby*, 134.
59 Dahler, *Fearless*, 295.
60 Kerr, *Harriet Quimby*, 87.
61 Ibid., 88–9.
62 Judith Thurman, "Amelia Earhart's Last Flight." *The New Yorker*, September 7, 2009. newyorker.com/magazine/2009/09/14/amelia-earhart-last-flight?
63 9/11 Memorial and Museum, "The Collection." 911memorial.org/visit/museum/collection
64 Hannah Smith, "No truth to claims no plane parts were found at 9/11 crash sites." September 16, 2022. fullfact.org/online/9-11-plane-debris/
65 James Lindsay, "Seven Resources Debunking 9/11 Conspiracy Theories." September 1, 2021. cfr.org/blog/seven-resources-debunking-911-conspiracy-theories
66 Jake Heller, "8 Crazy Conspiracy Theories About Aviator Amelia Earhart's Demise." July 13, 2017. thedailybeast.com/8-crazy-conspiracy-theories-about-aviator-amelia-earharts-demise
67 Zahid Mahmood, "Bones from Pacific island likely those of Amelia Earhart, researchers say." March 8, 2018. cnn.com/2018/03/08/health/amelia-earhart-bones-island-intl/index.html
68 Thurman, "Last Flight."
69 Joe Sharkey, "Drinking and Flying: Nothing New Under the Sun." July 7, 2002. nytimes.com/2002/07/07/weekinreview/word-for-word-wild-blue-yonder-drinking-and-flying-nothing-new-under-the-sun.html
70 Mara Gay, "Why Amelia Earhart Just Isn't All She's Cracked Up To Be." October 23, 2009. theatlantic.com/national/archive/2009/10/why-amelia-earhart-just-isn-t-all-she-s-cracked-up-to-be/347778/
71 Thurman, "Last Flight."
72 Samuel Broadnax, *Blue Skies, Black Wings.* Westport, CT: Praeger, 2007, xi–xii.

73 Wounded Warrior Project, "Legends in Flight." newsroom.woundedwarriorproject.org/Legends-in-Flight-Tuskegee-Airmen-Paved-History-as-First-African-American-Military-Pilots
74 Lloyd Richardson, "Tuskegee Red Tails were a force to be reckoned with." August 26, 2016. sj-r.com/story/opinion/columns/2016/08/27/tuskegee-red-tails-were-force/25576287007/
75 Broadnax, *Blue Skies*, 140–1.
76 Jack Lang, "Tragedy strikes Chapecoense, serial overachievers dubbed a 'Brazilian Leicester.'" November 29, 2016. theguardian.com/football/2016/nov/29/chapecoense-brazilian-football-team-plane-crash-colombia
77 Dan Bilefsky, "A History of Air Disasters Involving Sports Teams." November 29, 2016. nytimes.com/2016/11/29/world/americas/plane-crashes-sports-teams.html
78 Kevin Soong, "The terrible plane crash that devastated US figure skating—and still shapes it today." February 20, 2018. washingtonpost.com/news/retropolis/wp/2018/02/20/the-terrible-plane-crash-that-devastated-u-s-figure-skating-and-still-shapes-it-today/
79 Maura Hohman, "The entire US figure skating team died in a plane crash 60 years ago. The impact lives on." February 15, 2021. today.com/news/remembering-1961-us-figure-skating-world-team-plane-crash-t208568
80 National Transportation Safety Board, "Aircraft Accident Report, Southern Airways Inc. DC-9, N97S." ntsb.gov/investigations/AccidentReports/Reports/AAR7211.pdf
81 Greenlee, *November*, 124–37, 2, 24–34, xv–xvi, 53.
82 Corydon Ireland, "Radcliffe Fellow, poet Elizabeth Alexander reads." May 8, 2008. news.harvard.edu/gazette/story/2008/05/radcliffe-fellow-poet-elizabeth-alexander-reads/
83 Elizabeth Alexander, "Crash," 2001. poetryfoundation.org/poems/52119/crash
84 David Font-Navarrete, "'Import': Musical Distortion, Exoticism, and Authenticité in Congotronics." *Ethnomusicology Review* 16 (2011). ethnomusicologyreview.ucla.edu/journal/volume/16/piece/460
85 Douglas Wolk, Review, "*Assume Crash Position*," June 10, 2010. pitchfork.com/reviews/albums/14314-assume-crash-position/
86 Spencer Bailey, "Elizabeth Alexander on Moving Forward in the Face of Adversity." timesensitive.fm/episode/elizabeth-alexander-on-moving-forward-in-the-face-of-adversity/
87 Mina Kaji et al. "Diversifying the flight deck: Less than 1% of US pilots are Black women." September 30, 2020. abcnews.go.com/Politics/diversifying-flight-deck-us-pilots-black-women/story?id=72880810
88 "Our Story," sistersoftheskies.org/
89 Dani Shapiro, "Plane Crash Theory." *Ploughshares* 27.1 (Spring, 2001), 162–76, 163.

90 Eiléan Ní Chuilleanáin, *Acts and Monuments* (Dublin: Gallery Press, 1972), 40.
91 Vibeka Venema, "The Sahara memorial seen from space." January 22, 2014. bbc.com/news/magazine-25643103
92 Institute for Public Art, "Case Studies." instituteforpublicart.org/case-studies/
93 Venema, "Sahara memorial."
94 Matthew Bannister, "Memorial in the Sahara Desert." September 18, 2013. bbc.co.uk/programmes/p01ggtc0
95 William Kremer, "Germanwings: Why visit the site of a relative's death?" March 15, 2015. bbc.com/news/world-europe-32071094
96 "Our Goals," International Federation of Associations of Victims of Terrorism. ifavt.org/
97 Louis Colvert, "Les passagers du DC-10 d'UTA mort deux fois." *Le Canard Enchaîné*, December 13, 2023, 5.
98 "Niger: le mémorial des victimes de l'attentat contre le vol DC10 d'UTA vandalisé." December13,2023.www.rfi.fr/fr/afrique/20231213-niger-le-m%C3%A9morial-des-victimes-de-l-attentat-contre-le-vol-dc10-d-uta-vandalis%C3%A9?fbclid=IwAR0-rrwxKYPsyoiOMuZpBwrbXxlmKMuyfreoQDAigYAMuYqqT9bacqT-Z1o

8 I Will Survive

1 European Transport Safety Council, "Increasing the Survival Rate in Aircraft Accidents." December 1, 1996. etsc.eu/increasing-the-survival-rate-in-aircraft-accidents-impact-protection-fire-survivability-and-evacuation/
2 National Transportation Safety Board, "Survivability of Accidents Involving Part 121 US Air Carrier Operations, 1983 Through 2000." ntsb.gov/safety/safety-studies/Documents/SR0101.pdf
3 National Transportation Safety Board, "Survivability of Accidents Involving Part 121 US Air Carrier Operations: 2020 Update." ntsb.gov/safety/data/Pages/Part121AccidentSurvivability.aspx
4 Alexandra Jacobs, "Vivien Leigh and Laurence Olivier's Turbulent Relationship, Retold With Compassion." March 22, 2022. nytimes.com/2022/03/22/books/review-truly-madly-vivien-leigh-laurence-olivier-stephen-galloway.html
5 Patricia Green, "Aurelia Grigore: The Flight Attendant Who Cheated Death Twice." May 4, 2023. simpleflying.com/aurelia-grigore-flight-attendant-who-cheated-death-twice/
6 Alexander Elliott, "The survivor of two air crashes in one day." November 17, 2019. ruv.is/english/interview-the-survivor-of-two-air-crashes-in-one-day

7 Vala Hafstað, "Survived Two Plane Crashes in a Single Day." November 10, 2019. icelandmonitor.mbl.is/news/news/2019/11/10/survived_two_plane_crashes_in_a_single_day/
8 National WWII museum, "The Little Prince's Last Flight." September 19, 2020. nationalww2museum.org/war/articles/the-little-prince-antoine-de-saint-exupery
9 Anthony Burgess, *Ernest Hemingway and His World*. London, Thames & Hudson, 1978, 104.
10 Ernest Hemingway, "The Christmas Gift," 2. *Look* 18.9 (May 4, 1954), 83.
11 Selma Karayalçin, "Hemingway's Fishing Rod: A Study of the First African Plane Crash and Rescue." *Hemingway Review* 36.1 (Fall 2016), 49–64, 52–3.
12 Ernest Hemingway, "The Christmas Gift," 1. *Look* 18.8 (April 20, 1954), 29–37, 31.
13 Ibid., 32.
14 Karayalçin, "Fishing Rod," 56.
15 Hemingway, "Gift," 1, 37.
16 Hemingway, "Gift," 2, 79–89, 80, 86, 83–4.
17 Hemingway, "Gift," 1, 37; 2, 83.
18 Donald Sturrock, "The Plane Crash that Gave Birth to a Writer." *Daily Telegraph*, August 9, 2010, 21.
19 Ibid.
20 Roald Dahl, *James and the Giant Peach*. New York: Puffin, 1961, 98–9.
21 Sturrock, "Plane Crash."
22 Roald Dahl, "Lucky Break," in *The Wonderful Story of Henry Sugar and Six More*. London: Jonathan Cape, 1977, 118–19.
23 Roald Dahl, "Shot Down Over Libya." *Saturday Evening Post*, August 1, 1942, 29.
24 Ibid., 38.
25 Ibid.
26 Roald Dahl, "A Piece of Cake," in *The Wonderful Story of Henry Sugar and Six More*. London: Jonathan Cape, 1977, 124–5.
27 Roald Dahl, *The Gremlins*. Milwaukie, OR: Dark Horse, 2006. N.p.
28 Roald Dahl, "Beware of the Dog." *Harper's Magazine* 189 (October 1944), 436.
29 Ibid., 437.
30 Sturrock, "Plane Crash," 21.
31 Antoine de Saint-Exupéry, *The Little Prince* (trans. Richard Howard). New York: Houghton Mifflin, 1943, 3.
32 Ibid., 66.
33 Ibid., 74.
34 *Oxford English Dictionary*, "robinsonade."
35 Faber, "The Story Behind the Publication of William Golding's *Lord of the Flies*." faber.co.uk/journal/new-bbc-programme-sheds-light-on-the-story-behind-the-publication-of-lord-of-the-flies/

36 William Golding, *Lord of the Flies*. New York: Penguin, 1954, 6–7, 33.
37 Ibid., 5–6, 8, 39.
38 "The Scar in Lord of the Flies: Symbolism and Analysis." study.com/learn/lesson/scar-lord-of-the-flies-symbol-analysis.html#:~:text=What%2C%20exactly%2C%20does%20the%20scar,island%2C%20and%20on%20each%20other
39 "The Scar in Lord of the Flies." study.com/academy/lesson/the-scar-in-lord-of-the-flies.html
40 "The Scar: Symbol Analysis." litcharts.com/lit/lord-of-the-flies/symbols/the-scar
41 "Scar In Lord Of The Flies Quote Analysis." ipl.org/essay/Scar-In-Lord-Of-The-Flies-Quote-FCFJ8L7UZT
42 "What is the Scar in *Lord of the Flies*?" gradesfixer.com/q/what-is-the-scar-in-lord-of-the-flies/
43 "*Lord of the Flies*: What is the 'scar' in chapter one?" gradesaver.com/lord-of-the-flies/q-and-a/what-is-the-scar-in-chapter-one-86675
44 Tim Lambert, "Part of Flight 93 crashed on my land. I went back to the sacred ground 20 years later." September 3, 2021. npr.org/2021/08/31/1033059826/9-11-flight-93-crashed-on-my-land-i-went-back-to-the-sacred-ground-20-years-l
45 Ibid.
46 Werner Herzog, *Wings of Hope*, 1998. 5:30
47 Koepcke, *When I Fell*, 106–07, 118.
48 Herzog, *Wings of Hope*, 9:45.
49 Ibid., 11:00.
50 Koepcke, *When I Fell*, 11, 13.
51 Ibid., 10.
52 Herzog, *Wings of Hope*, 2:30.
53 Koepcke, *When I Fell*, 21.
54 Ibid., 18.
55 Franz Lidz, "She Fell Nearly 2 Miles, and Walked Away." June 18, 2021. nytimes.com/2021/06/18/science/koepcke-diller-panguana-amazon-crash.html
56 Koepcke, *When I Fell*, 19, 118–20.
57 Lidz, "She Fell."
58 Koepcke, *When I Fell*, 193, 199ff.
59 Herzog, *Wings of Hope*, 40:00
60 Koepcke, *When I Fell*, 109 ff.
61 Herzog, *Wings of Hope*, 4:30, 21:45.
62 Koepcke, *When I Fell*, 184.
63 T. S. Eliot, "Portrait of a Lady." poetryfoundation.org/poems/44213/portrait-of-a-lady-56d22338932de
64 Koepcke, *When I Fell*, 184–5.

65 Herzog, *Wings of Hope*, 35:45, 20:00.
66 Koepcke, *When I Fell*, 180.

9 The Zen and Karma of Plane Crashes

1 "Last Letter of Flight Petty Officer 2nd Class Mitsuo Yoshinaga to His Parents." kamikazeimages.net/writings/yoshinaga/index.htm
2 Christopher Chapple, *Karma and Creativity*. Albany: State University of New York Press, 1986, 96.
3 Emiko Ohnuki-Tierney, *Kamikaze, Cherry Blossoms, and Nationalisms: The Militarization of Aesthetics in Japanese History.* Chicago: University of Chicago Press, 2002, 20.
4 Ibid.
5 Emiko Ohnuki-Tierney, *Kamikaze Diaries: Reflections of Japanese student soldiers.* Chicago: University of Chicago Press, 2006, 8–9.
6 Michael Anderson, "Kamikazes: Understanding the Men behind the Myths." December 30, 2020. ijnhonline.org/kamikazes-understanding-the-men-behind-the-myths/
7 Ibid., 28.
8 Ohnuki-Tierney, *Diaries*, 8–9.
9 Ibid., xiii.
10 Albert Axell and Hideaki Kase, "Advice to Japanese kamikaze pilots during the second world war." September 7, 2009. theguardian.com/world/2009/sep/07/japanese-kamikaze-pilots-second-world-war
11 Sanae Kameda, "Booklet details history of meth chocolates wrapped by students for Japanese suicide pilots." January 10, 2022. mainichi.jp/english/articles/20220107/p2a/00m/0na/018000c
12 Robert Stern, *Fire from the Sky*. Barnsley, UK: Seaforth, 2010, 28, 17–18.
13 Steve Zaloga, *Kamikaze: Japanese Special Attack Weapons 1944–45*. Oxford: Osprey, 2016, 12.
14 John Fry, *USS Saratoga CV-3: An Illustrated History of the Legendary Aircraft Carrier 1927–1946*. Atglen, PA: Schiffer, 1996, 148. kamikazeimages.net/books/ships/saratoga/index.htm
15 Jack Bytheway, "The Kamikaze Attack." February 21, 2016. web.archive.org/web/20230610103232/https://johnbytheway.com/the-kamikaze-attack/
16 Eugene Thacker, "Black Illumination: Zen and the Poetry of Death." July 2, 2016. japantimes.co.jp/culture/2016/07/02/books/black-illumination-zen-poetry-death/
17 Ibid.

18 Bill Nelson, webmaster, kamikazeimages.net.

19 "Last Letter of Second Lieutenant Hiroshi Maeda to His Parents." kamikazeimages.net/writings/maeda/index.htm

20 Lucien Stryk, *The Penguin Book of Zen Poetry*. New York: Penguin, 1981, 21.

21 "Last Letter of Corporal Yasuo Fukushima to His Parents." kamikazeimages.net/writings/fukushima-yasuo/index.htm

22 "Last Letter of Corporal Takao Adachi to His Grandmother and Father." kamikazeimages.net/writings/adachi/index.htm

23 "Last Letter of Corporal Kōji Andō." kamikazeimages.net/writings/ando/index.htm

24 "Last Writings of Second Lieutenant Fukujirō Nagashima." kamikazeimages.net/writings/nagashima/index.htm

25 "Last Letter of Flight Petty Officer 2nd Class Hiroshi Yabuta to His Parents." kamikazeimages.net/writings/yabuta/index.htm

26 "Last Letter of Second Lieutenant Saburō Ishikura." kamikazeimages.net/writings/ishikura/index.htm

27 Ohnuki-Tierney, *Kamikaze*, 3, 106.

28 Ibid., 164.

29 "Last Letter of Flight Petty Officer 2nd Class Mitsuo Yoshinaga to His Parents." kamikazeimages.net/writings/yoshinaga/index.htm

30 "Last Letter of Ensign Shunsuke Yukawa." kamikazeimages.net/writings/yukawa/index.htm

31 "Last Letter of Flight Warrant Officer Hisaoki Yoshizawa to His Parents." kamikazeimages.net/writings/yoshizawa/index.htm

32 "Last Letters of Second Lieutenant Yoshio Usui to His Parents." kamikazeimages.net/writings/usui/index.htm

33 "Last Letters of Corporal Saburō Hasegawa to His Mother." kamikazeimages.net/writings/hasegawa-saburo/index.htm

34 "Last Letters of Sergeant Tatsuo Wakao to His Parents." kamikazeimages.net/writings/wakao/index.htm

35 "Last Letter of Ensign Tokuya Tsuda to His Mother." kamikazeimages.net/writings/tsuda/index.htm

36 "Last Letters of Corporal Teruo Usami to His Mother." kamikazeimages.net/writings/usami/

37 "Last Letters of Sergeant Tatsuo Wakao to His Parents." kamikazeimages.net/writings/wakao/index.htm

38 "Last Letter from Corporal Toshio Chizaki to His Mother." kamikazeimages.net/writings/chizaki/index.htm

39 "Reports of 4 Russian military aircraft downed near Ukraine border." May 14, 2023. aljazeera.com/news/2023/5/14/reports-of-4-russian-military-aircraft-downed-near-ukraine-border

40 Dixa Ramírez, *Colonial Phantoms: Belonging and Refusal in the Dominican Americas, from the 19th Century to the Present*. New York: NYU Press, 2018, 111–52.
41 Associated Press, "Grenade fragments were found in bodies in Prigozhin's plane crash, Putin claims." October 5, 2023. npr.org/2023/10/05/1203948340/russia-putin-grenade-prigozhin-wager-plane-crash
42 Alex Traub, "Mark Gietzen, 69, Dies; Zealous Lieutenant in Anti-Abortion Movement." May 18, 2023. nytimes.com/2023/05/18/us/politics/mark-gietzen-dead.html
43 Monica Davey, "Kansas Abortion Clinic Operated by Doctor Who Was Killed Closes Permanently." June 9, 2009. nytimes.com/2009/06/10/us/10abortion.html
44 Matthew Kelley and Chance Swaim, "Wichita anti-abortion activist Mark Gietzen dies in Nebraska plane crash." May 18, 2023. kansas.com/news/local/news-local-obituaries/article275501041.html
45 Peter Brand, *The Cambridge History of Italian Literature*. Cambridge: Cambridge University Press, 1999, 63–4.
46 Mark Twain, *Adventures of Huckleberry Finn*. 1895. gutenberg.org/files/76/76-h/76-h.htm#chap28

Select Bibliography

Abrams, Ann Uhry. *Explosion at Orly*. Atlanta: Avion, 2002.

Ames, Van Meter. "America, Existentialism, and Zen." *Philosophy East and West* 1.1 (April 1951).

Appadurai, Arjun. "Disjuncture and Difference in the Global Cultural Economy." *Theory Culture Society* 1990 (7), 295–310.

Bibel, George. *Beyond the Black Box: The Forensics of Airplane Crashes*. Baltimore: Johns Hopkins University Press, 2008.

Broadnax, Samuel. *Blue Skies, Black Wings*. Westport, CT: Praeger, 2007.

Brottman, Mikita, ed. *Car Crash Culture*. New York: Palgrave, 2001.

Bytheway, Jack. "The Kamikaze Attack (All Hell Breaks Loose)." February 21, 2016. https://web.archive.org/web/20230610103232/https://johnbytheway.com/the-kamikaze-attack/

Camus, Albert. *The Myth of Sisyphus and Other Essays*. Trans. Justin O'Brien. New York: Vintage 1955.

Carlin, George. *Napalm & Silly Putty*. New York: Hachette, 2001.

Csikszentmihalyi, Mihaly. *Flow: The Psychology of Optimal Experience*. New York: Harper, 1990.

Dahl, Roald. *The Gremlins*. Milwaukie, OR: Dark Horse, 2006.

Dahl, Roald. "A Piece of Cake," in *The Wonderful Story of Henry Sugar and Six More*. London: Cape, 1977.

Dahl, Roald. "Beware of the Dog." *Harper's Magazine* 189 (October 1944).

Dahl, Roald. "Lucky Break," in *The Wonderful Story of Henry Sugar and Six More*. London: Cape, 1977.

Dahl, Roald. "Shot Down Over Libya." *Saturday Evening Post*, August 1, 1942.

Dahler, Don. *Fearless: Harriet Quimby, A Life Without Limit*. New York: Princeton Architectural Press, 2022.

DeLillo, Don. *White Noise*. New York: Viking, 1985.

Golding, William. *Lord of the Flies*. New York: Penguin, 1954.

Greenlee, Craig. *November Ever After*. Bloomington: iUniverse, 2011.

Hart, Clive. *The Prehistory of Flight*. Berkeley: University of California Press, 1985.

Hemingway, Ernest. "The Christmas Gift," part 1. *Look* 18.8 (April 20, 1954), 29–37, 31. Part 2. *Look* 18.9 (May 4, 1954), 83.

Hernandez, Tim. *All They Will Call You: The Telling of the Plane Wreck at Los Gatos Canyon*. Tucson: University of Arizona Press, 2017.

Herzog, Werner. *Wings of Hope*, Zweites Deutsches Fernsehen, 1998.

Howard, Fred. *Wilbur and Orville: A Biography of the Wright Brothers*. New York: Knopf, 1987.

Karayalçin, Selma. "Hemingway's Fishing Rod: A Study of the First African Plane Crash and Rescue." *Hemingway Review* 36.1 (Fall 2016).

Kerr, Leslie. *Harriet Quimby: Flying Fair Lady*. Atglen, PA: Schiffer, 2016.

Kierkegaard, Søren. *The Concept of Dread*. 1844. Trans. Walter Lowrie. Princeton: Princeton University Press, 1944.

Kierkegaard, Søren. *The Sickness Unto Death*. 1849. Trans. Alastair Hannay. New York: Penguin, 1989.

Koepcke, Juliane. *When I Fell From the Sky: The True Story of One Woman's Miraculous Survival*. Trans. Ross Benjamin. Munich: Piper Verlag, 2011.

Le Tellier, Hervé. *The Anomaly*. Trans. Adriana Hunter. New York: Other, 2022.

Lebow, Eileen. *Before Amelia: Women Pilots in the Early Days of Aviation*. Washington, DC: Potomac, 2002.

Lerner, Ben. *10:04: A Novel*. New York: Farrar, Straus & Giroux, 2014.

Ohnuki-Tierney, Emiko. *Kamikaze, Cherry Blossoms, and Nationalisms: The Militarization of Aesthetics in Japanese History*. Chicago: University of Chicago Press, 2002.

Ohnuki-Tierney, Emiko. *Kamikaze Diaries: Reflections of Japanese student soldiers*. Chicago: University of Chicago Press, 2006.

Pascoe, David. *Airspaces*. London: Reaktion, 2001.

Perrow, Charles. *Normal Accidents: Living with High-Risk Technologies*. Princeton: Princeton University Press, 1999.

Roach, Mary. *Stiff: The Curious Lives of Human Cadavers*. New York: Norton, 2003.

de Saint-Exupéry, Antoine. *The Little Prince*. Trans. Richard Howard. New York: Houghton Mifflin, 1943.

Stryk, Lucien. *The Penguin Book of Zen Poetry*. New York: Penguin, 1981.

Urry, John. *Mobilities*. Cambridge: Polity, 2007.

Wielinski, Karen. *One on the Ground*. Buffalo: Librastream, 2017.

Yakich, Mark. *The Dangerous Book of Poetry for Planes*. London: Eyewear, 2017.

Zuskáčová, Veronika. "How We Understand Aeromobility." *Transfers* 10.2–3 (2020).

Acknowledgments

The author thanks Virginia Madsen for permission to reprint excerpts from her publication “Critical Mass (an Interview with Paul Virilio).” “Where We Crashed,” from *MAKING CERTAIN IT GOES ON: COLLECTED POEMS OF RICHARD HUGO* by Richard Hugo. Copyright © 1984 by The Estate of Richard Hugo. Used by permission of W. W. Norton & Company, Inc. Excerpt from “The Hollow Men,” from *Collected Poems, 1909–1962* by T. S. Eliot, Copyright © 1963 by T.S. Eliot, used by permission of HarperCollins Publishers and Faber and Faber Ltd.

“Plane Crash,” Words and Music by Rob Derhak, Al Schnier and Chuck Garvey. Copyright © 1997 Spaz Medicine Music. All Rights Administered by BMG Rights Management (US) LLC. All Rights Reserved Used by Permission. *Reprinted by permission of Hal Leonard LLC.* “Swan,” from *FALLING AWAKE: POEMS* by Alice Oswald. Copyright © 2016 by Alice Oswald. Used by permission of W. W. Norton & Company, Inc. Excerpt from George Carlin’s comedy is from *Napalm & Silly Putty* by George Carlin, copyright © 2002. Reprinted by permission of Hachette Books, an imprint of Hachette Book Group, Inc.

Excerpt from Howard Nemerov’s “The War in the Air” is reprinted courtesy of Alexander Nemerov, Executor, Howard Nemerov Estate. “COMIN IN ON A WING AND A PRAYER,” Music by JIMMY MCHUGH, Words by HAROLD ADAMSON © 1943 (Renewed) EMI ROBBINS CATALOG INC. and JIMMY MCHUGH MUSIC. Rights for the Extended Term of Copyright in the U.S. Assigned to COTTON CLUB PUBLISHING (Administered by UNIVERSAL-MCA MUSIC PUBLISHING, a Division of UNIVERSAL STUDIOS INC.) and HAROLD ADAMSON MUSIC (Administered by the SONGWRITERS GUILD OF AMERICA). All Rights Reserved. Used by Permission of ALFRED MUSIC.

“ANGELS AND FUSELAGE” written by Patterson Hood. ©2001 Soul Dump Music (BMI), administered by Hipgnosis Songs Group, LLC. All Rights Reserved. Used by Permission. International Copyright Secured. “Nightmare At 20,000 Feet” by Clint Mansell. Copyright © 1990 DECCA MUSIC GROUP LTD. All Rights Administered by UNIVERSAL - SONGS OF POLYGRAM

INTERNATIONAL, INC. All Rights Reserved Used by Permission. *Reprinted by permission of Hal Leonard LLC.* "Shit Luck," Words and Music by Isaac Brock, Eric Judy and Jeremiah Green. Copyright © 1997 Ugly Cassanova, Tschudi Music and Crazy Gnome. All Rights Administered by Sony Music Publishing (US) LLC, 424 Church Street, Suite 1200, Nashville, TN 37219. International Copyright Secured All Rights Reserved.

"Flight 505," Words and Music by Mick Jagger and Keith Richards. Copyright © 1966 BMG Rights Management (UK) Limited and Promopub B.V. Copyright Renewed. All Rights Administered by BMG Rights Management (US) LLC. All Rights Reserved Used by Permission. *Reprinted by permission of Hal Leonard LLC.* "American Pie," Words and Music by Don McLean. Copyright © 1971, 1972 BENNY BIRD CO., INC. Copyright Renewed. All Rights Controlled and Administered by SONGS OF UNIVERSAL, INC. All Rights Reserved. Used by Permission. *Reprinted by permission of Hal Leonard LLC.*

"Falling in Love," Words and Music by Mike Burkett. Copyright © 1997 SONGS OF UNIVERSAL, INC. All Rights Reserved Used by Permission. *Reprinted by permission of Hal Leonard LLC.* "Concorde" Copyright © Éditions Lisbon Lux. Laurence Giroux-Do (Composer & Author), Patrick Gosselin (Composer & Author), Steeven Chouinard (Composer & Author).

"Dalai Lama," Words and Music by Oliver Riedel, Doktor Christian Lorenz, Christopher Doom Schneider, Richard Kruspe, Paul Landers and Till Lindemann. Copyright © 2004 TamTam Fialik Musikverlag, Discoton Musik Ed. GmbH and Unknown Publisher(s). All Rights for TamTam Fialik Musikverlag Administered by Kobalt Music Publishing Worldwide Ltd. All Rights for Discoton Musik Ed. GmbH Administered by Universal Music - MGB Songs. All Rights Reserved. Used by Permission. *Reprinted by permission of Hal Leonard LLC.*

"PLANE WRECK AT LOS GATOS (Deportee)," words by Woody Guthrie; music by Martin Hoffman. WGP/TRO-© Copyright 1961 (Renewed), 1963 (Renewed) Woody Guthrie Publications, Inc., & Ludlow Music, Inc., New York, NY, administered by Ludlow Music, Inc. International Copyright Secured. Made in U.S.A. All Rights Reserved Including Public Performance For Profit. Used by Permission. "Death," Words and Music by Harry McVeigh, Charles Cave and Jack Brown. Copyright © 2008 BMG Rights Management (UK) Limited. All Rights Administered by BMG Rights Management (US) LLC. All Rights Reserved Used by Permission. *Reprinted by permission of Hal Leonard LLC.*

"30kft," Words and Music by Thomas Shear. Copyright © 2004 FUTUREPOP MUSIC. All Rights. Administered by SONGS OF INGROOVES. All Rights

Reserved Used by Permission. *Reprinted by permission of Hal Leonard LLC.* "At the Bottom of Everything," Words and Music by Conor Oberst. Copyright © 2005 Sony/ATV Songs LLC and Bedrooms Bedrooms And Spiders. All Rights Administered by Sony Music Publishing (US) LLC, 424 Church Street, Suite 1200, Nashville, TN 37219. International Copyright Secured. All Rights Reserved. *Reprinted by permission of Hal Leonard LLC.*

Thanks to Mary Roach and Norton for permission to reprint an extract from *Stiff: The Curious Lives of Human Cadavers*, © 2003 by Mary Roach. Elizabeth Alexander, "Crash" from *Crave Radiance: New and Selected Poems 1990- 2010.* Copyright © 2001 by Elizabeth Alexander. Reprinted with the permission of The Permissions Company, LLC on behalf of Graywolf Press, graywolfpress.org, and Faith Childs Literary Agency, Inc. "Death and Engines" by Eiléan Ní Chuilleanáin from *Collected Poems* (2020) is reproduced by kind permission of the author and The Gallery Press. www.gallerypress.com, as well as Wake Forest University Press.

"September 1, 1939," copyright 1940 and © renewed 1968 by W. H. Auden; from *COLLECTED POEMS* by W. H. Auden, edited by Edward Mendelson. Used by permission of Random House, an imprint and division of Penguin Random House LLC. All rights reserved. Reprinted also by permission of Curtis Brown, Ltd. All rights reserved. © 1940 by W.H. Auden, renewed. Thanks to Werner Herzog Film GmbH for permission to quote dialogue from *Wings of Hope.*

Index

Numbers in italics indicate figures.